C. VANN
WOODWARD

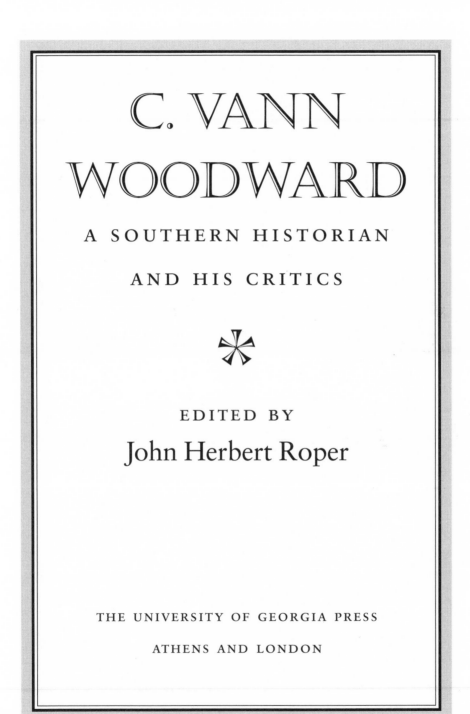

C. VANN WOODWARD

A SOUTHERN HISTORIAN
AND HIS CRITICS

EDITED BY

John Herbert Roper

THE UNIVERSITY OF GEORGIA PRESS

ATHENS AND LONDON

© 1997 by the University of Georgia Press
Athens, Georgia 30602
All rights reserved
Designed by Betty Palmer McDaniel
Set in 10 on 13 Sabon with Castellar
by G & S Typesetters, Inc.
Printed and bound by McNaughton and Gunn, Inc.
The paper in this book meets the guidelines for
permanence and durability of the Committee on
Production Guidelines for Book Longevity of the
Council on Library Resources.

Printed in the United States of America

01 00 99 98 97   C   5 4 3 2 1

01 00 99 98 97   P   5 4 3 2 1

Library of Congress Cataloging in Publication Data
C. Vann Woodward : a southern historian and his critics /
edited by John Herbert Roper.
p.   cm.
Includes bibliographical references (p.   ) and index.
ISBN 0-8203-1876-0 (alk. paper).—ISBN 0-8203-1877-9 (pbk. :
alk. paper)
1. Woodward, C. Vann (Comer Vann), 1908– . 2. Southern
States—Historiography. I. Roper, John Herbert, 1948– .
E175.5.W66C2   1997
975'.007202—dc20   96-21759

British Library Cataloging in Publication Data available

Frontispiece: C. Vann Woodward.
Courtesy of Pach Brothers, New York

for Edmund and Connie

Contents

✳

Preface

✳

To know the history, Edward Hallett Carr says, you must know the historian.[1]

He says this because history is not only events that happened but also our understanding of those events. More, history is the interaction among events, historians, and the readers. Only by knowing more about the historian and the history that he or she has lived through can we really know the history as recorded by that historian. The uniqueness of those interactions will define the choices made about what to include, what to exclude, what to emphasize, and what to deemphasize. History, as a serious study then, is historiography.

Such an insight explains much of the history as written, and as lived, by C. Vann Woodward, southern historian of small-town Arkansas—but also of Atlanta, Chapel Hill, Baltimore, and New Haven. Such an approach, too, infuriates those who cry out against *presentism,* defined as a perspective that looks at the past purely in terms of present interests, thereby losing the context of the contemporaneous stories and thus committing the logical fallacy of *nunc pro tunc.* Woodward himself was far more sympathetic in his early scholarship than he has been in his later years to the concept of the usable past. Even so, he has always considered the past *problematically,* that is, as a series of questions that must be addressed, even if wrongly answered, in order to move toward solutions through dialogue among scholars and the general reading public. For instance, in 1986 when he had become the acknowledged dean of American historians, Woodward wrote:

> Questions have to be asked before they can be even wrongly answered. Answers have to be ventured before we are sure they are addressed to the right questions. Errors have to be made before they can be corrected and contrary answers provoked. All of which leads to controversy to be sure; but controversy is one of the ways we have of arriving at what we assign the dignity of truth.[2]

Because of this approach, Woodward has always employed irony as a device, a tool, a way to get at the truth by exposing the gap between someone's stated intention and his or her eventual actions. As Voltaire put it, irony strips away delusion; and certainly Woodward has used irony—usually gently, but occasionally with a rough-scrubbing edge—to strip away the delusions not only of actors on the stages of the southern past but also of the readers in today's world who must interact with historians then and now. Above all, Woodward has emphasized a cleansing dialogue among historians, critics, and readers. He has been quick to acknowledge his own factual errors and equally quick to credit the observations of others. Moreover, he has incorporated the insights of others into his own evolving work, although that characteristic has, on occasion, frustrated more than one critic. As noted by Paul Gaston in these pages, Woodward has been fond of quoting William Faulkner's character, Gavin Stevens, who says that the past is not dead, it is not even past. In the same vein, and borrowing again from Carr, Woodward has assumed that history itself is in motion and that the historians who record and interpret it are themselves no less in motion.[3]

With such a perspective, and by bringing such a perspective to bear on his South during a time of profound regional change, Woodward has, of course, attracted critics. In fact, he has intended to attract critics and then to engage them in continuing discussions and debates that sharpen the focus of his own thoughts. Thus he has often sought out critics who have pointed out flaws in his works. He has directed forty-two doctoral theses, and the writers of those dissertations at The Johns Hopkins University and at Yale University have become important members of the profession. But, even more so, he has produced, or at least provoked, a host of interacting critics, most of them the friendliest of antagonists, who have joined with him in the ongoing dialogue about the region of the United States most noted for its distinctive way of life, whether in speech, politics, manners, diet, music, economy, novels, or memory.

Besides Woodward's scholarly monographs are his many essays aimed at a reading public of generalists. He has taken such essay-crafting seriously, he is very good at it, and, to some degree, he has served as our era's Montaigne, if our era could have such a thing. It is Woodward who compelled both generalist and specialist audiences to take seriously the decade of the 1880s. It is he who focused attention on such historiographical questions as the origins and evolution of segregation, the continuity and discontinuity of southern history, the nature of the Southern Literary Renaissance, the symbolic relationships of the South with the nation as a whole, and the myriad but connected questions of irony and identity in the region's interactions with the rest of the United States and the world.

So influential has he been and so important have been the responses to him that it is appropriate to gather the significant criticism into one volume. Such dialogue between Woodward and his critics encompasses the major issues of southern history and historiography, and readers may use the essays as lightly or as intensively as fits their needs. Specialists already familiar with debates in one particular area can work their way carefully and critically through the essays, including the revised and updated endnotes, in order to rethink their own research and writing. However, generalists who seek a broad overview will find that these critics, following Woodward's own lead, write accessibly for a nonspecialist audience.

In assembling these essays, I was struck by the high quality as well as the sheer volume of Woodward criticism, despite the fact that nothing in here is in any sense new to me. Taken collectively, the scholarly literature concerned with Woodward is itself quite impressive. Only a great historian could inspire such criticism. Above all, this volume is offered to keep alive the dialogue and so to keep alive concerns about larger questions in southern history. As Woodward once dedicated a set of reminiscences to his critics, so these critics present our essays in honor of a historian who has made us think.

NOTES

1. Edward Hallett Carr, *What Is History?* (1961. Reprint, New York: Alfred A. Knopf, 1996), 26. Carr is actually quoting Robin George Collingwood but significantly amending the latter's concept. Cf. Collingwood, *The Idea of History* (London: Oxford University Press, 1948), passim.

2. Comer Vann Woodward, 1986, Roper Papers.

3. Lester G. Crocker, introduction to *Candide and Zadig,* by Voltaire, ed. idem (New York: Simon & Schuster Pocket Books paper ed., 1962), xvi–xxii; Carr, *What Is History?* 35, 69, 143, 203–9.

Acknowledgments

*

Thanks to all those who contributed articles, with special acknowledgments to some whose contributions may not be readily obvious to the reader:

Willie Bordwine; Malcolm Call; Kelly Caudle; L. James Cumbo; Michael Donathan; Nancy Griffin; John Inscoe; John Lang; John Morgan; Michael O'Brien; Rita Perry; Eugene L. Rasor; Jennifer Manley Rogers; Craig Skeens; Dian Thompson; and Lisa Williams.

The staff of Kelly Library at Emory & Henry College, particularly Jane Caldwell, Claudine Daniel, Patty Greany, and director Thelma Hutchins.

The staff of the Southern Historical Collection of the University of North Carolina at Chapel Hill, particularly Richard Shrader, John White, and director David Moltke-Hansen.

Grateful acknowledgments to C. Vann Woodward for his remarkable life and career.

While these named, and some not named, deserve credit, any errors in facts or judgment are not their blame, but are entirely my responsibility.

The editor and publisher gratefully acknowledge permission to use the following:

Edward L. Ayers, "Narrating the New South," *Journal of Southern History* 61 (August 1995), 555–66, © 1995 by the Southern Historical Association. Reprinted by permission of the Managing Editor.

M. E. Bradford, "The Strange Career of C. Vann Woodward," *The World & I*, Nov. 1987, 651–62 is reprinted with permission from *The World & I*, a publication of *The Washington Times Corporation*, © 1987.

Excerpt reprinted from *Place over Time: The Continuity of Southern Distinctiveness* by Carl N. Degler (Baton Rouge: Louisiana State University Press, 1977), with permission of Carl N. Degler.

Gaines Foster, "Woodward and Southern Identity," *Southern Review* 21 (1985), 351–60, is reprinted with permission of *Southern Review*.

Paul M. Gaston, "C. Vann Woodward, Southern Historian," review of *Race, Region, and Reconstruction: Essays in Honor of C. Vann Woodward*, ed. J. Morgan Kousser and James M. McPherson (New York: Oxford University Press, 1982), *Virginia Quarterly Review* 59 (1983), 327–34, is reprinted with permission of Paul M. Gaston and *Virginia Quarterly Review*.

Sheldon Hackney, "*Origins of the New South* in Retrospect," *Journal of Southern History* 38 (May 1972), 191–216, © 1972 by the Southern Historical Association. Reprinted by permission of the Managing Editor.

August Meier, "An Epitaph for the Writing of Reconstruction History?" *Reviews in American History* 9 (1981), 82–87, is reprinted with permission of The Johns Hopkins University Press.

James Tice Moore, "Redeemers Reconsidered: Change and Continuity in the Democratic South, 1870–1900," *Journal of Southern History* 44 (Aug. 1978), 357–78, © 1978 by the Southern Historical Association. Reprinted by permission of the Managing Editor.

Excerpt from Albert Murray, *South to a Very Old Place* (New York: McGraw-Hill, 1971), 16–26, is reprinted with permission of Wylie, Aitken & Stone, Inc.

Michael O'Brien, "C. Vann Woodward and the Burden of Southern Liberalism," *American Historical Review* 78 (1973), 589–604, is reprinted with permission of Michael O'Brien and American Historical Association, © 1973.

Allan Peskin, "Was There a Compromise of 1877?" *Journal of American History* 60 (June 1973), 63–75, is reprinted with permission of Allan Peskin and the *Journal of American History*.

David Morris Potter, "C. Vann Woodward," in *Pastmasters*, ed. Marcus Cunliffe and Robin Winks (New York: Harper & Row, 1969), 375–407, is reprinted with permission of HarperCollins.

Excerpts from John Herbert Roper, *C. Vann Woodward, Southerner* (Athens: University of Georgia Press, 1987), are reprinted with permission of the University of Georgia Press, © 1987.

Howard Rabinowitz, "More Than the Woodward Thesis: Assessing the *Strange Career of Jim Crow*," *Journal of American History* 75 (Dec. 1988), 842–56, is reprinted with permission of Howard Rabinowitz and the *Journal of American History*.

Joel Randolph Williamson, "C. Vann Woodward and the Origins of a New Wisdom" is printed with permission of Joel Williamson, © Joel Williamson.

Bertram Wyatt-Brown, "The Sound and the Fury," review of C. Vann Woodward, *Thinking Back* (Baton Rouge: Louisiana State University Press, 1986), *New York Review of Books*, 13 Feb. 1986, 12–15, is reprinted with permission from the *New York Review of Books*, © 1986 Nyrev, Inc.

Introduction: The Historian

✳

"Vann's a controversialist," said longtime colleague and coworker, Yale historian John Morton Blum.[1]

Like the man described, the description itself was at once an understatement and wildly off the mark. Comer Vann Woodward, born 13 November 1908 to an aristocratic southern family, has been the academic's academic. By the 1990s he had become the undisputed dean of the country's historians: past president of the three national professional organizations, he could not display in one place all his honors, from a lectureship named for him at a small college to the Pulitzer Prize. Yet he has borne the accolades lightly, remaining soft-spoken and prone to self-deprecation, while generous with praise for some of his most severe critics. With the ingrained manners of one who grew up in an academic family, he has spoken with nuances so subtle that they escape most hearers; and with the practiced art of the landed aristocrat, he could skillfully shift the attention of conversation and discussions away from his own person and onto others. This Ivy League don a controversialist?

Controversialist he has been. In the 1920s, he was a college kid on a small Arkansas Methodist campus, where he caused trouble for a reactionary administration, in the process of which the disgraced and harried president resigned. As the Great Depression came on, he shifted his own scene of controversializing to Atlanta, hanging out with avant-garde poets and literary theorists and traveling the routes of the day's dissidents. He made his way across Weimar Germany, staying in the home of a Jewish family as Adolf Hitler was coming to prominence. He traveled the Soviet Union of Josef Stalin's early days, riding the freight trains and talking with peasants and laborers and onetime Cossacks and party officials. On his return to the Georgia capital, he formed his "first equal friendship with a Negro." This latter, J. Saunders Redding, eventually would become prominent as a Christian existentialist and major civil rights leader, but in the early years of the Depression, he was an actor, bold and experimental in the roles that he chose on an African American Atlanta stage that was at once off-off-Broadway and avant-garde. The playwright of greatest interest for Redding, and for his admiring white friend, was Eugene O'Neill, with his self-consciously psychological characters.[2]

There followed a student's sojourn in New York City, Thomas Wolfe's "million footed city" and the place that all southern boys and girls of all ages then loved to hate and could not resist. The City was for him: Manhattan, with its "colonial" sovereignty over regional farm finance and its universities and publishing houses and newspapers, all of them together able and willing to exercise no less cultural and intellectual power over Woodward's South, then styled "Sahara of the Bozarts." Morningside Heights, where he studied political science in the graduate program at Columbia University after a "miscarriage of majors." Broadway, which he drank in lustily. Harlem, where he performed in an African American review, the one white face—though hardly the only southerner—represented on the stage, despite the fact that the big onetime football center was not then or later known for singing, dancing, acting, or otherwise performing the arts of the muses. Woodward was everywhere in New York, but not as often in the classroom as in the streets and on the scenes; his political science master's thesis, about Alabama's racist but populistic politician "Tom-Tom" Thomas Heflin, he did not consider especially good scholarship.[3]

Good scholar or not, in 1932 he cadged a teaching job, in English, at Georgia Tech, largely because of his reformist friend Glenn Weddington Rainey. Woodward again joined up with "the wrong crowd" of dissidents in Atlanta. There, he and Rainey marked among other friends leaders of the Atlanta Interracial Commission, the white Will Alexander and the black John Hope. But there were also experimental poets and theorists, including African American scholars in the Atlanta University system, and there were the brave antilynching newspaper people Julia and John Harris, the socialist leader Mary Raoul Millis, members of the area Communist party (CP), and even visiting leaders from the national CP and editors of the CP organ, *The Daily Worker*. When the young black CP speaker Angelo Herndon gave a speech condemning industrial capitalism for its abuse of displaced workers, he was arrested and charged with inciting to riot, and Woodward, in complicated and ironic processes, wound up as chairman of the legal defense team of civil libertarians, liberals, socialists, labor leaders, civil rights people, crusading journalists, and the CP. He handled things more bravely than wisely and alienated national CP officials and area liberals, while the defense team predictably lost the case.[4]

Banished from Georgia Tech in 1934 (probably more for economic than ideological reasons, but his high-profile dissidence did make him easily disposable in a financial crunch), he spent a season in south central Georgia, serving as fieldworker and reporter for the Works Progress Administration's investigations of rural poverty. Then an avid reader of the contemporaneous novelist Erskine Caldwell, Woodward saw at first hand the white and black tenants and croppers who were housed and fed in conditions almost medieval in nature. Shaken so deeply that he could barely communicate what he saw to his confidant Rainey, Woodward was frustrated by his inability to do anything for these sufferers. With guilt, but relief too, he accepted a Rockefeller Foundation fellowship for graduate studies. This award, likely arranged through his once aggrieved but forgiving liberal friend Will Alexander and his family friend Regionalist sociologist Howard W. Odum, he applied to study history at the University of North Carolina in the era before that school had to be designated *at Chapel Hill.*[5]

This Chapel Hill community was actually a small place, but people who claimed citizenship there lived as far east as Raleigh and as far west as Greensboro. It was the 1934 season, effervescent with experimentation, political protests, schemes of regional economic planning, questioning of all things that were, and answering with visions of what might be, such visions unbounded by the economic constraints of the Depression. The reformist Edwin Mims a few seasons earlier featured this community and its impoverished but then bold state university as one of his major "stories of progress . . . in the advancing South." Frederick Henry "Proff" Koch offered innovative folk drama by the Carolina Playmakers, and the greatest Playmaker, Paul Eliot Green, who also taught philosophy, was a recent recipient of the Pulitzer Prize for *In Abraham's Bosom,* a play limning the tragedy of a mulatto African American who tried to educate his people in eastern Carolina. Frank Porter "Doc" Graham was UNC president, and he protected his faculty from the racists and reactionaries among the university trustees and in the state general assembly. Then, most of the best scholars were also activists who spoke up on behalf of labor rights, rural education, amelioration of racism with at least some integration, and an aggressive assault on regional poverty. Gathering places included the campus Young Men's Christian Association (YMCA, or just "the Y"), a center of activists seeking international peace and local justice, and Ab's Bookstore, run by Milton Abernethy, who with his protégé Anthony Buttitto offered avant-garde books, his own locally produced and visionary small magazine, *Contempo,* readings and performances by local artists, and personal visits by F. Scott Fitzgerald, Thomas Wolfe, Gertrude Stein, and William Faulkner. Ab himself told wild tales of CP intrigue and radical derring-do, a few stories of which may have been something more than showing off to impress the Left Bank. The expression for all this committed energy was the University of North Carolina Press, managed with pluck and luck by William Terry Couch, an editor unafraid to produce, among other things, a set of essays by a minister supporting Darwin's theory of evolution, a monograph featuring a Marxist interpretation of slavery and capitalism, and a series of sociological studies of racism and poverty in the farmland. These Couch sponsored in an era of regional fundamentalist outrage over Darwin's theory, of textile-owner and landowner paranoia about anything Marxist, and of a generalized refusal to talk about slavery or its successor, caste tenantry.[6]

In fact, the family friend and hometown sponsor Odum was especially anxious about Woodward's recent dissidence back in Atlanta, and the mentor warned him against fooling around with the same kind of "wrong crowd"— Chapel Hill version. This Odum inoculation did not "take" at all, however, and Woodward was soon hanging out at the Y and at Ab's, reading *Contempo,* and involving himself in a legal controversy concerning a textile strike and its attendant violence. As before, he was not quite putting in the expected tithe of hours in reading and discussion seminars with his professors. The thing was, he had already written a draft of his dissertation, a study of Populist-gone-sour Thomas E. Watson, of his adoptive Georgia. He did do research, working the already magnificent primary sources being gathered by Joseph Gregoire de Roulhac Hamilton at the new Southern Historical Collection on campus. Hamilton, the aggressive pioneer collector known to other archivists in the region as "Ransack" Hamilton, gave Woodward much personal attention, and the graduate student learned the scholarly thing that good historians have always learned at Carolina, namely, how to use the bountiful primary sources there.[7]

More controversial stories abound, including a half-truth that he nearly flunked his doctoral comprehensive oral examinations. Actually, he did confess to his confidant Rainey that he bollixed the Hanoverian dynasty in an answer, a mistake that raised doubts concerning his understanding of the context of colonial and Revolutionary America; and in general he performed as in the graduate classroom, that is, with a certain indifference. For decades thereafter, graduate students at Carolina regaled themselves with the "knowledge" that Vann Woodward nearly flunked these things, something decidedly not the case but certainly a useful myth for the local professoriat trying to get the charges to study hard. What did happen at that examination was that the newly arrived Howard Kennedy Beale was deeply impressed by answers Woodward offered to questions concerning the region during Reconstruction and during the 1880s.[8]

This Beale was an eccentric of the top drawer, and there have been richly woven legends about his odd behavior and his occasional mistreatment of graduate students and colleagues. But he was also a superb scholar, especially so between 1935 and 1940. Beale only marginally improved the already well written dissertation draft, but he showed Woodward how to be a historian who could write for a discerning profession whose members have sharp eyes and often sharper tongues. Too, Beale encouraged Woodward's research into and writing about the Reconstruction era and the 1880s, both periods then inadequately studied; and he encouraged an attention to class analysis, economic development, race relations, and conflict of all kinds, each theme a hallmark of Woodward's long scholarly career. Of Beale's many eccentricities and his dissident politics Woodward said that the man in the late 1930s was mostly misunderstood: "[Beale is] not *left* of Frank Graham at all; he is *north* of Graham" and the other Chapel Hill reformists. Beale, by this view (one corroborated in his extensive correspondence), supported the same causes championed locally by the fully accepted Graham, Green, Koch, Couch, et al., but his manners, combined with local prejudices, kept him on the outside. It was characteristic of Woodward that he not only celebrated Beale when the Yankee outsider was a book-a-year man but also continued to defend him and to arrange appointments and paid engagements for him when his writing machine slowed down. At any rate, Woodward credited Beale with teaching him "the rigors" of scholarship, the hard self-denial and the painstaking attention to detail that it required; and such teaching-by-example seemed exactly what the feisty graduate student needed at that phase of his life in order to make it in the profession.[9]

Beale, and more conventional Carolina historians for whom Woodward had much less regard, plus a graduate-school friend, the late J. Carlyle Sitterson, helped him get a job at the University of Florida in 1937. There too he was involved in everything, making friends with still other dissidents, namely, William G. Carleton and Manning J. Dauer. These two political scientists were actually "mounted humanists," in novelist John Ehle's fine phrase for southern liberals of the 1930s. For their part, they called themselves "The Three Musketeers." Carleton, Dauer, and Woodward were inseparable, even after Woodward married Glenn Macleod, an elegant Carolina woman whom he began seeing in Chapel Hill during graduate school there. The two delayed their wedding until 1938, when he had a secure job and she had some savings accumulated from her secretarial work. Then the threesome became a foursome comprised of a couple and two bachelors, but they still called themselves The Three Musketeers. This team did the "juke joints" of north Florida and south Georgia, in search of soulful music, strong liquid spirits, and good stories; and, in the same high spirits, the team worked together on behalf of civil rights until Woodward was left alone in the 1980s by their successive deaths.[10]

In his Gainesville troublemaking, however, Woodward had at least two paid-up insurance policies: One was that the administration, in the wry words of Carleton, thought him "a prize"; and the other was that his virtually unrevised dissertation was published by Macmillan in trade edition under the title *Tom Watson: Agrarian Rebel*. Reviewer response was glowing, most notably the high praise on the front page of the Sunday *New York Times Book Review* by Columbia University's Allan Nevins, then the dean of American historians. *Tom Watson* not only secured Woodward's position in Gainesville and offered him opportunities elsewhere, but also laid down three historiographic lines of debate, all of which would continue in Woodward's long career and among his many students and his many critics. These three lines of debate concerned the economic rationalism or irrationalism of Watson himself and of all the Populists; the racial liberalism or illiberalism of the man and his fellow Populists in the 1890s; and the characterization of William Jennings Bryan's free-silver campaign of 1896 as the "cowbird" that dislodged the "real" Populist program items.

Woodward's biography argues forcefully that the man Watson and the broader movement Populism developed fully rational economic plans; in fact he said that they proffered blueprints for some Progressive Era reform and for most New Deal era reform. He argued that Watson and the Populists were liberal, at least in political terms if not in social relations, and that the man and his party effectively helped African Americans to vote and to hold office, all the while fighting against the *classes,* that is, the armed establishment of landowners who were violently negrophobic, and also against the *masses,* that is, a powerful grassroots Ku Klux Klan paramilitary force of poor whites. Finally, Woodward insisted that Watson's program of economic reform was a carefully considered one, involving elements of "restraining" organizational capitalism at a moment when that political economy was fraught with abuses of working-class people and also recklessly courting its own self-destruction.[11]

As much as Woodward's foursome enjoyed activism and recreation together in north Florida, Woodward, in the period 1937 to 1946, was a man on the make, and thus half of the foursome was a couple on the move. There were chances to move on—and up; and Woodward took these opportunities as they came. In fact, during this period, the Woodwards became three, for Peter Vincent Woodward was born in 1943 with a future as bright and golden as the family's new home in southern California. The little family engaged in two kinds of travel as World War II broke out and then broke in on their lives. The first travel involved a succession of temporary jobs, each a fortuitously placed rung on a career ladder. Never much of a classroom teacher, Woodward used each appointment as a place to earn a stipend while doing primary search work in nearby archives: the University of Virginia, with its own large manuscript collection and the nearby National Archives; Scripps College, accessible to the Huntington Library; and U.S. Naval Intelligence in Washington, D.C., with the National Archives and the Library of Congress close to hand. Too, a Rosenwald Fellowship and Scripps's generous policy of official leave allowed Woodward to spend much research time in the east while employed in the west. The other kind of travel was an intellectual one, for Woodward absorbed a more sophisticated social-science analysis of regional economic development and also came to understand literary modernism, largely by meeting some of its master practitioners, including Robert Penn Warren, Allen Tate, Cleanth Brooks, and Donald Davidson. These meetings were not invariably pleasant, but Woodward learned from each exposure. As the Southern Literary Renaissance matured during the years of the Depression and World War II, two major groups of thinkers emerged. One was the Chapel Hill Regionalists, who focused on neopopulist economic planning with an on-again, off-again assault on extreme racism. The other was the Nashville Agrarians, who emphasized a southern distinctiveness of "historical consciousness" about shared experiences (slavery, the Civil War, Reconstruction, enduring commitments to agricultural economy and rural life, with big extended families and pietistic churches—what Donald Davidson called the "long road" to community cohesiveness through parochialism and poetry) that made a uniquely modernist and humanist counterpoint to the national patterns of urbanization, industrialization, commercialization, secularization, and hedonistic individualism. To a remarkable degree, Woodward was a polymath of an old sort, one given to simultaneous study of economics, sociology, comparative history, philosophy, and literary arts of all kinds. What resulted from this second kind of travel was that Woodward, for a time acting almost alone, could be at once a Chapel Hill Regionalist and a Nashville Agrarian without putting up a permanent residence, physical or figurative, in either the University of North Carolina or Vanderbilt University.

He commanded the economic data and the sociologic models, and he used them on behalf of liberal reform, but he also commanded many of the techniques of the modernist literati, with their plural perspectives, shifting narrative voices, immanent values rather than the transcendence of eternal verities, and ironies of all kinds. When he completed the tricky processes of putting all these disparate things together, he restored a sense of tragedy to all of American history by making readers really feel the distance between the national rhetoric of promise and the actual performance. He did so by focusing on the southern failure to meet the national expectations; and his telescopic lens was ground by an ironic, subjective, personalistic, and deeply humane consciousness of race and class in our regions.

All the traveling in both spheres did not slow the writing machine. For his government employers, Woodward produced two official battle studies; and for trade publication, he wrote the popular *The Battle for Leyte Gulf*, which is dedicated to his son, Peter. That study, ostensibly in the genre of military history, itself reflected the wisdom he developed as he traveled, since it was a shrewdly analytical and detached social-science formula; it exhibited a systematic search of official records, but it also was based on some hard questions posed to officers otherwise inclined to celebrate themselves and their own roles in a great victory that irrevocably broke the power of the Japanese great-ships. At the same time, *The Battle for Leyte Gulf* was in the modernist genre, for Woodward emphasized the irony that the Japanese gambled the main force of their navy in so brilliant a way that major victory could have been theirs; but American misunderstanding—even tactical errors—along with luck, saved the U.S. naval forces from themselves. And the narrative was poetically rounded and thematically doubled, since Woodward closed by saying that Cape Engano, "the obscure point of land from which the battle took its name," referred to "a Spanish word translated variously as 'mistake, deception, lure, hoax, misunderstanding, misapprehension, misconception'— in about that order of preference." [12]

Neither the traveling nor the writing slowed the controversializing. Not only his interpretations were bold and dissident, but so too were his words and acts of protest. Overly zealous francophile colleagues at Scripps tried to prosecute, if not persecute, those on the faculty and staff who were German-Americans or otherwise rumored to be in some sort of sympathy with Germany during World War II. The maltreatment, likely unconstitutional and certainly uncollegial, occurred before the United States declared war on the Axis powers. Moreover, the abuses and the academic restrictions were broadly anti-German, finally not very different from the very fascist ethnic-repression and damnation-by-association that the francophiles rightly complained about in Hitler's empire. Despite, or perhaps because of, his own firsthand experience of the German brownshirts and their tactics, Woodward defended his beleaguered colleagues, in actions at once courageous and lonely, on the principles of free speech, academic prerogative, and ethnic tolerance. By the same signs, he defended and assisted his old mentor, Beale, who came to California to try to help Japanese-Americans whose property was impounded and all but stolen while they themselves were imprisoned by the tens of thousands in detention camps because of their racial identity.

Whether he thus stored up treasures in liberal heaven, he was in any case coincidentally rewarded in the earthly sphere, for in 1946 The Johns Hopkins University hired him, thereby giving him the chance to start training the many fine graduate students who would become leaders in the history profession (see Appendix A for a list of fifteen doctoral students from Baltimore, including two Pulitzer Prize recipients). During the next five years, the artful combination of more search work in the National Archives, more thoughtful mulling over of modernism, and more application of social science produced two volumes of significance, *Reunion and Reaction: The Compromise of 1877 and the End of Reconstruction* and *Origins of the New South, 1877–1913*, the latter described in these pages by a critic as "the pyramid [that] still stands." [13]

Both books have something old, something new, something borrowed, and something blue. Old, especially in the era of 1950s consensus history writing, with its emphasis on American social harmony, were: the class analysis insisted on by Karl Marx (and Woodward has called himself, among other things, *Marxoid,* that is, shaped by Marx); the New Dealer's passion for examination of the rural economic structure; and the economic interpretation of Charles Austin Beard, as well as the Beardian preference for negotiated settlement of intersectional and interregional conflicts, even if the peace attained was somewhat morally compromised. Something new was the modernist irony and the shifting voices and visions featured in the narrative of both volumes. The borrowed something was the angle of the detective story, with the author and the reader puzzling out a plot and together finding the guilty party, in a context of extremely fragmentary and certainly centrifugal pieces of evidence where no one seemed truly innocent and no one told the whole story. Something blue was the palpable sadness and melancholy, though subtly nuanced and not fey, because a reformist energy set a vigorous pace and there was some considerable hope. For all that, however, something blue was the tone of regret, as well as responsibility, for "the fools these mortals be."

Woodward slammed the aristocracy of the New South, its railroad-building, real-estate-developing, and industrial-managing elite; and he was hard on their apologists in press, pulpit, and academy, that is, exactly the places and stations where the men in the Woodward family, especially father Hugh and uncle Comer, lived and moved and had their being. Like Faulkner, he insisted that the new elite's claims to legitimacy through tradition were bogus on two counts. The first was that all the talk about Old Virginia and the Old North State and the Lost Cause and so forth was conscious and devious manipulation of symbols on behalf of structural changes so profound that the real revolutionaries were not at all the northerners who freed the slaves (especially since that "freedom" was so limited with racist restrictions and so economically tethered with class confinements) but rather the deep-drawling yet fast-talking new bourgeoisie who asked to be called Redeemers as they themselves were kicking over the old agrarian order in favor of a brand-new political economy that was consumption-driven, hedonistic, atomistically competitive, profit-motivated, and withal interested in poetry and music only to hide and misinform and delude about its own works. The second count of the indictment, not pressed as hard but still registered, claimed that the ancien régime was itself more parvenu than truly ancient, having arrived on the stage barely in time to strut and fret in cavalier costume during the sound and the fury of the Civil War. Finally, as it was for Faulkner, this blue quality was self-analysis and self-criticism through study of one's own class. Both intellectuals found that self-identifying group to be willfully destructive and deceitful in their own youth and pretentious, bumptious, and effectively (if accidentally) destructive in their grandparents' days of the not truly *old* Old South.

All of these points, even and especially the reading of Faulkner, were fully debatable, and Woodward at once sparked discussion in his profession. Much of the subsequent debate took place on his terms and even in his language, one of the things accounting for the dominance of his ideas until very recently when an entirely new generation of scholars, especially feminists and those attracted to postmodernist theories about time, value, and language, began to ask utterly different questions instead of reanswering Woodward's, or Faulkner's, original questions. Some of these new kinds of questions have been apparent in essays in this volume by critics Howard Rabinowitz, Joel Williamson, August Meier, and Edward L. Ayers. For a long spell, however, it was Woodward, especially before the 1990s, who set the agenda for the discourse.

With *Reunion and Reaction,* the railroad-economics story in detective motif, Woodward raised an important question: *How did Reconstruction come to an end?* And behind that question was another: *Why did Reconstruction come to an end?* By and large, historians had agreed before 1951 that a combination of lagging northern commitments to racial justice, intransigence (really, paramilitary counterrevolution) at the South, and opportunities for plunder on a grand scale if only the unpopular experiment in democracy would cease, produced true Gilded Age maneuvering among politicos and business tycoons in Wormley hotel rooms where the ceilings were high, the cigars expensive, the whiskey cheap, and the dealings low. In this study, Woodward did not so much disprove that story of tawdry thievery as transform it, setting it on a higher plane befitting a tragedy of competing dreams, in which the dream of racial justice did not die but was gradually overwhelmed by other, less noble, dreams. By pushing hard on the question *why,* and pushing from a different angle, Woodward changed the historiography of Reconstruction and the Gilded Age. It was not really a case of flagging commitments to justice and progress, because those commitments were never robust. Rather, it was a reconciliation between the victorious northern capitalists and a new group of southern bourgeoisie who supplanted the landed gentry, defeated in battle by those same Yankee entrepreneurs.

The negotiations were larger and much more complex than once told. True enough, there was the infamous horse trade in which the Republicans got the White House and the Conservative Democrats got the governors' mansions in South Carolina, Florida, and Louisiana, even though it was unlikely that any of these four candidates for executive office actually won the popular majority. More important than that horse trade of executives, and closely related to it, were interregional dealings that were quite far-flung and more in the character of diplomatic relations among nation-states. This complicated package of deals Woodward called the Compromise of 1877, and he considered it to be on a par with the Missouri Compromise or the Compromise of 1850. Again, the horrors of large-scale war compelled such negotiations, even if entailing some damage to principles, in preference to another civil war, something that Woodward thought a possibility in the final phases of the First Reconstruction. Moreover, the needs of the new political economy of this postbellum age necessitated a reconciliation between northern and southern sections: Fully integrated nationwide systems of credit, transportation, and communication were the sine qua non of the macroeconomic development in this era that Walt Whitman Rostow styled the "take-off" into sustained growth.

Against the panoramic backdrop of the dawning of the American Century, after the long night of Civil War, Woodward necessarily painted with broad strokes. However, there were many subtleties on the oversized canvas, and even the subtle gestures changed thinking, if only by compelling criticism. As noted by everyone, the Compromise of 1877 sounded the death knell for federal oversight of (and much more so for any active assistance *to*) black voting, office holding, and other aspects of citizenship. Yet 1877 did not usher in the death of African American suffrage, or of African American office holding; in fact, compared to what went before and to what was to come, the 1880s were a relatively "cool" temperature for race relations and not a period of carnage. This often neglected phenomenon Woodward traced in part to the binding nature of the Compromise: those Conservative Democrats for a decade did protect fundamental rights in their interregnum of home rule; and they did it not because Wade Hampton and Lucius Quintus Cincinnatus Lamar were naturally compassionate paternalists but because they took seriously the debt owing the other side in the negotiations.

Others before him discussed these negotiations with the assumption that there was much to gain and much to lose and that complete failure at the negotiations could result in political catastrophe and perhaps even war. But in *Reunion and Reaction,* the interesting things were in that unique blending of messages: The Beardian economic suggestions (it was not statecraft so much as protecting one's material intrests in economic development, especially by, with, and for railroads, the single enterprise with enough capital resources to contemplate truly grand-scale development); Marxian class analysis (the new bourgeoisie of the northeastern corridor created an intersectional alliance with a new elite of the South, and that new southern elite was self-consciously an understudy to the masters of this bourgeois-capitalist universe that had won the Civil War); and race relations (the abolitionist heritage was not strong enough within the Republican Party to continue to impose moral obligations on the national administration, but yet the New South leaders were still unsure what to do with "the freedmen," and thus the questions about black rights, especially voting, were left unanswered for the nonce); and the richly ironic, questioning, self-doubting, and cynical tone, adapted from his literary circle of modernist friends (not only "Red" Warren, but before him the Chapel Hill *Contempo* crowd, and before them the Harlem Renaissance experimenters, and before them the short-lived Georgia pathbreaker-poet Ernest Hartsock).

Woodward made *Reunion and Reaction* with its Compromise of 1877 story a major part of his *Origins of the New South,* a book that won even more accolades. Widely employed in classrooms, it came to be styled the Old Testament by the not always admiring students who read it at the command of the admiring professors. Indeed, as critic Allan Peskin has noted in his essay herein, Woodward's version of the 1877 negotiations dominated classroom lectures and college textbooks, especially since Woodward was responsible for the post-Reconstruction chapter in one of the most widely distributed college textbooks, *The National Experience,* edited by a group headed by John Morton Blum. It was some two decades before Peskin himself asked the question a different way: Not *what kind of Compromise was there in 1877?* but *was there a Compromise at all?* Even after Peskin's broadside assault, which did some considerable damage, Woodward's version remained the preferred one in the textbooks. In any case, the *Reunion and Reaction* book and the *Origins* textbook in combination likely ended any more celebration of the southern Redeemer figures as larger-than-life saviors. As Sheldon Hackney has said in these pages, "[h]enceforth the contending parties would be considerably more corporeal."

Yet there was a powerful reformist energy in Woodward's books of the era, and neither *Reunion and Reaction* nor *Origins* was purely cynical. There are different levels of irony, and there are different types of irony, and Woodward used them all; but in 1951 it was always to show the way to a better world and to direct attention to the least-favored people, the middling farmers and the small-scale landowners of both races and the mill workers and the miners who were the victims of the capitalist shenanigans. Following the suggestions laid out by his literary friends (and later colleagues) the late Red Warren and Cleanth Brooks, Woodward became a modernist author confident of his ability to command the structure of language to make it do what he must: In their images, opposition, as from critics or other reversals, was like the wind that let a kite, "fully loaded," rise up and fly; and the result was not something open to interpretation by readers or audiences, but rather a "well wrought urn" brought off by the artist-creator.[14] These neglected and abused peoples did have their day in the pages of *Origins,* as the author showed the Populist party offering rational and carefully considered programs for modern farming, well-organized by and for both sexes and both races in the emerging new economic order. In other words, the part-time New Dealer and full-time reformist discovered and here displayed an early version of the Second New Deal. From this perspective, the more traditionally celebrated reformists, the Progressives, especially in North Carolina and Virginia, emerged as, at best, pale copies of the Populists and, at worst, flaming hypocrites and enemies of fundamental reform. Whatever else, and there were significant portents of future interpretations in the observation, it was the Progressives who declared that reform was "for whites only," and it was they who took away voting and other rights, though in this work Woodward focused more on disfranchisement than on segregation and elimination of public accommodations.

Having rubbed off much of the Progressives' historiographical glow, however, Woodward yet made no bones about the fact that it was a good thing that the 1912 elections brought into national office not only Woodrow Wilson, Virginia-born and Carolina-Georgia-bred, but five southern cabinet members, fifteen House committee chairpersons, and a monopoly of Senate committee chairs. Whatever he might say in criticism of behavior down home, Woodward was ever the Arkansan-Georgian who disliked the idea of his South, despite its collective sins, being absent from national office between 1860 and 1912. Too, in *Origins,* Woodward both scored regional literature and celebrated it: Impatient with "the romantic haze" of Thomas Nelson Page and his school of writers, and bored with empty "local color" as from "Charles Craddock" (actually Mary Noailles Murphree), he was at pains to show how bad was the regional artistry against which his own modernist friends and colleagues strove to produce the literary renaissance in the 1920s. Even so, he gave full credit to important precursors James Branch Cabell and Ellen Glasgow, especially the latter, whose novels sought to "penetrate the romantic haze" and inject some realism into regional artistry. Best of all, Glasgow attacked the injustices done to the poor of both races and both genders, and only occasionally fell into romanticization of those subjects.

Critic Hackney has also noted herein that *Origins* was a cynic's book and that it has endured despite rather than because of its tone, which Hackney marked as neither "ennobling" nor "uplifting" in message. On the other hand, critic Bertram Wyatt-Brown in this volume has claimed that Woodward's real achievement, even in *Origins*, was to find something encouraging, something worthy of positive note, something of a "usable past" that included at least a few moments in which real people did some good things and did so in an inspiriting, exemplary way. Both men are correct: It was Woodward's modernism that made things cohere, and it was also his modernism that made the result hard to describe. Ellen Glasgow and jazz musicians, Populist leaders, big-city philanthropists, besieged and underpaid college professors of both races, these were heroes worthy of emulation and celebration, and their partial successes were an inspiration as well as a warning that the best-laid plans of the best people can go astray. Significantly, it was not the Civil War with its manic infantry charges and beau geste cavalry sorties that Woodward celebrated, for he judged that catastrophe overdone as a cause; instead it was harder, steadier, slower-paced, and more realistic work—living a life after the disaster of The War—that Woodward offered as a model for the best life.

Woodward's accomplishment in *Origins* was thus to meld the elements of modernism that he learned from literary figures with the Beardian economic determinism and the Marxian class analysis that was in the air of his graduate-school days. The blending made him a major player both for the unfolding literary criticism that had to come to grips with an ongoing and self-conscious literary renaissance and for social scientists caught up in a related but separate scholarly renaissance in their fields. Because of his accomplishment, professors in departments of English and departments of history began taking note of him—and criticizing him. As he noted often, it was better to be criticized than to be forgotten, and no one was forgetting him in the 1950s. But *Origins*, fittingly named, was actually only a starting point for Woodward's career: He soon produced two more works, *The Strange Career of Jim Crow* and *The Burden of Southern History*, that made him the subject of notice—and praise and criticism—not only from the professors in the academy but even among the student body and, even more incredibly,

among the "middle-brow" educated laity interested in southern developments in the 1950s and 1960s.[15] That latter group, a modern middle class of
professionals and service-sector people, was well educated, had some leisure
time, and had some money to buy books in the halcyon days of the "paperback revolution," when pocket change could purchase a two-hundred-page
book. It was this group in this era that found Woodward the ideal bridge into
issues that concerned them—race relations, regional identity, war, peace,
and guilt—and, unlike most of his colleagues in English or in history departments, he wrote for them in prose that was accessible and, more than
that, downright fun to read. That group found in Woodward their own ci-
ceronian guide to the great social transformations of his region between 1954
and 1968.

The essays collected in *The Burden of Southern History* were for the most
part written years before the book's publication in 1960, and some of the
signal essays were even written before publication of *The Strange Career of
Jim Crow*. Indeed, the flagship essay, "The Irony of Southern History," was
closely related to the personal and regional histories that combined to produce the insights of Woodward's famed civil rights essay. As I note in some
detail in these pages, Woodward wrote the "Irony" essay for the occasion of
his presidential dinner address at the Southern Historical Association (SHA)
meeting in Knoxville in 1952. Already active in efforts to integrate the SHA,
Woodward chose this moment to take a firm stand on behalf of integration
of the organization, which was the one that then had the most African American members, because of research interests and because their employing institutions, the historically black colleges and universities, were preponder-
antly in the South. Woodward insisted that the dinner be integrated and,
in order to accommodate his command, the program director LeRoy Graf
transferred the first night's session from his own University of Tennessee,
with its state-mandated segregated dining facilities, to a club restaurant in
Whittle Springs, now a suburb of Knoxville but in that day a place some
distance removed from the city. This phase of the long campaign to integrate
the history profession was successful, although full accessibility of Clio's
ranks still remained decades away and seemed unlikely to be accomplished
in the final moments of the twentieth century.

The activist dimensions of the phenomenology of Woodward's "Irony"
speech prevented much serious attention to his particular message on that
fall evening. Officers of the SHA and committed activists were exhausted by
the logistical problems of getting everyone to Whittle Springs (for instance,
program director Graf had to transport several late-arriving African American historians in his own car, since Knoxville's white taxicab drivers, at least

on that evening, refused to serve blacks); and, because the little details so wore out officers and activists, they did not really pay full attention to the complex speech. As for others, less emotionally involved in all the brouhaha, they were unable to hear clearly, because Woodward gave his address in his trademark single-toned mumble.

When it was printed, the speech impressed historians, and also English professors and theologians, the latter a self-referential irony of no little size for the ironist himself, since Woodward had consciously abandoned the Methodist Church of his family and proclaimed agnosticism for himself. Yet the essay was deeply in debt to theologian Reinhold Niebuhr, as Woodward did acknowledge. Niebuhr used his own concept of irony to describe democratic societies in an imperfect—and perhaps imperfectible—world. Woodward borrowed from Niebuhr the concept that people by their nature face great limits on what they can achieve: But there remains a duty to choose, especially when the choices are unattractive and even repellent; and there remains a responsibility to learn from the past, from the record of the evils that can transpire if citizens avoid hard decisions. For Niebuhr, the concept of *original sin* was crucial to the argument, since the enveloping irony was that the nature of people created by the fall from Edenic grace prevented their attaining perfection or true good: But the continued willingness of a forgiving God to accept repentance further implies committed efforts by these forgiven sinners to make a better world. That special tension, as manifest in the public pietism of his own family, Woodward rejected; but there remained in him some secular equivalent of an overarching, almost supernatural, and certainly romantic call to seek justice despite the unlikelihood of attaining it.

Turning to the specific case in point, Woodward in "Irony" was much affected by the contemporaneous Cold War attacks on the academics, particularly the pressures brought to bear on his JHU colleague and friend Owen Lattimore, a political scientist and also a sometime State Department officer who was unfairly accused of Communist sympathies. Woodward began the essay by marking the anti-Communist hysteria of the search for the *un-American*. Thus launching a defense that was actually an attack, he then slipped in the observation that southerners were in some senses un-American, particularly since public opinion polls during 1950 and 1952 registered the lowest temperatures for anti-Communism in that region, in contrast with much higher measurements in the Northeast, Midwest, and West.

In asking about other un-American characteristics of southerners, then, Woodward was establishing a high moral ground for an otherwise benighted place: To be un-American was often to be wrongly accused in the era of Senator Joseph McCarthy and Vice President Richard Milhous Nixon, and perhaps some of the un-American traits were worth more careful examination before condemnation. What in particular was un-American? He answered that the historical experiences of undeniable guilt, military failure and indeed defeat in a war, and widespread poverty were the elements of southern identity peculiarly un-American in a country that, at least in the early 1950s, found itself wealthy, militarily undefeated, and culturally self-conscious as the moral example to the world. According to Niebuhr, Americans made two related assumptions: First, among nations, we claimed to be innocent; and second, because of this innocence, we claimed to be invincible. To the concept of military invincibility was added a dimension of economic invincibility, for, as Woodward's friend the late David Morris Potter marked it in *People of Plenty*, a folk so accustomed to such abundance in all resources came to identify themselves by this national bounty and later came to accept, even demand as a right, the material plenty vouchsafed by innocence and invincibility.[16] Surely, however, those who maintained the evil institution of slavery during three different centuries, who then lost the largest military campaign in world history to that date, and who subsequently persisted as "the nation's number one economic problem," as FDR put it, surely such a people were plainly un-American.

Yet, the ironist implied that parallels in world history could exist for our self-examination. Did not the British once consider themselves invincible? In fact, did not metahistorian Arnold J. Toynbee recall that, as a boy watching a parade in honor of Queen Victoria's empire, he had the inescapable impression that history was something that happened to other people and not to the British, who had lifted themselves up and out of the limitations of the past? Woodward then implied still other questions: Were there any dangers in making these assumptions of wealth as a national birthright, of moral superiority as the starting point for diplomatic relations and international negotiations, of military invincibility on the field of battle, when those battles were now fought with a stockpile of A-bombs in reserve for each combatant? Without answering, in fact without even specifically stating each of those implied questions, Woodward then asked, *who really was unusual and atypical?* The people in the suffering world outside the United States could not avoid their historical records of undeniable past sins writ in blood and guilt, could not deny the fact of military and other defeats, and certainly had to acknowledge poverty and scarcity of resources in their ranks. The South, then, the ironist recorded, was more *like* than unlike the rest of the world, and it was the United States, exclusive of the region, that stood out as the exception, while southerners constituted the norm, in world history.

But none of that exceptionalism troubled Americans until new events gave one pause: frustrating military campaigns, including stalemate and even defeat, riots because of poverty and racism in our largest cities, the acknowledgment of intractable poverty in places outside the South, the Third World pointing an accusing collective finger at the United States as the economic imperialist and oppressor. These things lay ahead for the Americans first reading Woodward's "Irony" essay, but he even then sounded warnings by indirect and subtle gestures toward a future that troubled him, even as he first wrote in 1952 and as he rewrote in 1959. For the moment, he asked if the study of southern history, the exception that was actually the norm, might not have some redemptive qualities, if nothing else by restoring some common sense and some humility. The implication was that the evil region could redeem, if studied carefully.

The essay, which set the tone for all of the pieces in *The Burden of Southern History,* was more gently suggestive than clearly descriptive. One aspect of the speech was noted by Richard King in his study of the humanists of the Southern Renaissance: "The Irony of Southern History" could be both descriptive and prescriptive. As description, it could be all wrong, since in fact southerners, from Lyndon Johnson and Dean Rusk to Jimmy Carter and Bill Clinton, have been notoriously uninterested in dealing with limitations and have quickly fallen into the same moral excesses as all other Americans when they have had the chance to share in leadership. As prescription, however, the "Irony" essay still had much to commend it and, in fact, may have been unequaled as a moral wake-up call for the self-satisfied and historically unconscious Americans of all regions.[17]

Woodward's irony, then, was to be *usable,* and the bitterness of southern exceptionalism was said to have its sweet compensations: It prevented delusions of innocence, it prevented delusions of invincibility, it disconnected wealth from virtue. Most of all, it disengaged intent and act from a morality play of simplistic cause and effect: as Potter has noted in this volume, Woodward restored a sense of the tragic to the historians' depictions of human developments, thereby forcibly reminding readers that the good sometimes made an evil result despite the opposite intention, and that evil sometimes made a good result. Not only could southerners ask to be listened to by other Americans, but also southerners had something of a duty to prophesy from experiences that were either unknown for nonsoutherners or known to such slight degree that they were forgotten. Collecting a number of related essays, Woodward provided the title *The Burden of Southern History* (wording that did not appear in the essays proper, and a phrase that showed again the obvious influence of his friend Robert Penn Warren, who even used the image in naming the character of erstwhile graduate student Jack Burden in *All the*

King's Men).[18] The burden appeared to be not so much guilt as the weight of responsibility to teach about limitations and possibilities, to use lessons from the southern past to chart the Scylla of overweening ambitions borne by arrogant innocence and the Charybdis borne by the resigned surrender of fey irresponsibility. The ship of people simply had to go forward, avoiding both perils, and the irony, while nuanced and carefully measured by an urbane artist, was yet an optimist's, and certainly an activist's, irony. Above all else, this ironist's essay of the usable southern past, written as it was for the occasion of integrating the SHA banquet in Knoxville/Whittle Springs, also prepared the way for the little book that the Reverend Martin Luther King Jr. called the bible of the civil rights movement.

During this same period, between 1952 and 1954, Woodward, his friend John Hope Franklin, and other academics were all hard at work on behalf of Thurgood Marshall, plaintiff attorney in school desegregation and other accommodation cases for the National Association for the Advancement of Colored People (NAACP). Woodward prepared a paper for Marshall concerning Reconstruction-era law and civil rights, and those researches were a part of the attorney's successful presentation before the U.S. Supreme Court in the 1954 case *Oliver Brown, et al. v. Board of Education of Topeka, et al.* Too, the preliminary judicial proceedings involved a very Woodwardian character—South Carolina's Judge Waites Waring, whose strong opinion in dissent from the segregation norm, while unsuccessful, was still a worthy example and one that gave civil rights litigants and activist scholars "heart to fight," in the fine phrase of social psychologist Thomas F. Pettigrew. Finally, such work put Woodward shoulder to shoulder with a trend in the era, that is, the use of social sciences, especially social psychology and the then New History, in service to Brandeisian New Law that considered environmental concerns and the human context of the political economy in the search for legal equity in disputes. A voracious reader and "quick study" of ideas, Woodward in that period showed clear signs of important influence from Konrad Lorenz's studies of the relationship between societal frustrations and aggressions against a weaker minority. In those days, he also was in some intellectual debt to existentialist psychologist Gordon Allport's studies of societal *scapegoating* of "outside" groups, as well as social psychologist Kenneth Clark's memorable demonstrations of the impact on African American children wrought by the powerful signs and symbols of damnable Jim Crow.[19]

With such things roiling and moiling in the context of his ironic activism, and with his fervent desires to make his South a more humane place, Woodward received the most portentous invitation to speak, in a career marked by many such fortunes. He was asked to deliver the Richard Lectures at the University of Virginia, and of course he chose to address these questions: Where did Jim Crow come from? How long was he with us? What was the nature of his growth and development over time? And especially, what was his significance for southern identity? All questions were asked within this context: Where can we go from here, after the *Brown* decision? Above all, there was this dreaded question: Were some southern segregationists actually ready to fight a second Civil War, or more probably, a second resistance campaign as in the first Reconstruction? His audience was a university community, academic, professional, and civic-minded. As Paul Gaston has reminded us, the politics of the campus in 1954 were certainly conservative, but its mood was also tolerant and curious. The audience included African Americans, who were seated in a separate section, itself an ironic arrangement, since Howard Rabinowitz has demonstrated that Woodward (and most of his critics) often focused so intensely on integration and segregation that he missed the more basic questions of *access* and *opportunity* as against pure exclusion.

Woodward spoke no more distinctly than was his wont, but this audience listened hard and heard a message of great hope: Woodward revealed Jim Crow to be a virtual interloper, albeit a big and rough one, who arrived after Reconstruction, indeed after the Populist campaigns of the mid-1890s. He came more as a product of political expediency during economic hard times than as an expression of some *longue durée* of deep cultural patterns or as long-held *folkways* and *mores*. Always his career was *strange,* marked by quirky exceptions and complex and fast-moving patterns, rather than by the deep furrows of a soil worn by ages-old plowing. Perhaps most important for this most self-consciously and studiedly southern audience of latter-day Jeffersonians, Woodward told them about three forgotten alternatives in their regional history: Conservative, Liberal, and Radical. Each of these ideological traditions was said to have a strong integrationist impulse in its past experiences and expressions. Likely, some carefully qualified nuances escaped hearers, as no less carefully qualified nuances have subsequently escaped readers. But just as likely, judging from memories of contemporaneous conversations with John Hope Franklin, William Carleton, Manning Dauer, and David Potter, the speaker himself laid emphasis on the hope of the forgotten alternatives, speaking with a tone of optimism and faith, however poorly inflected, rather than with a tone of genuine ambivalence. The history and the irony were usable. The tragedy was real, but even the tragedy itself was available as a warning that the alternatives to barbarity were there, if only people, like Plato's cave dweller, could remember the light of the true sun and their own best moments and then act in the memory of those ideals, instead of concentrating on the murky shadows and indistinct sounds of their present time of troubles.

Right away, Oxford University Press, nonpareil in such pursuits, arranged to publish in 1955 a revised manuscript, *The Strange Career of Jim Crow*, and the publisher offered a version in paperback as well. As Rabinowitz has shown, there were distinct stages in the subsequent developments of the three revised editions that appeared during the next twenty publishing seasons (with the final revision itself persisting and enduring in its compleat form still another twenty publishing seasons—and counting). Rabinowitz was surely right to chide historians for neglecting what was nothing less than historical and phenomenological development over time, and all of us have found our knuckles smarting from the schoolmaster's deftly wielded yardstick of reprimand. Yet even Rabinowitz must concede that a distinct continuity stretched from speech to final revised and expanded edition; that continuity was the insistence that once it was different, that there have been alternative beliefs and behaviors in the region. Too, there was a slower-moving, less obvious because more deeply running, current in these waters: This author was a fully committed and principled integrationist who had no truck with the segregationism of white supremacists and very little empathy (albeit some sympathy for Malcolm X) for the strategies of the many African Americans who have sought separatism as a means to cultural (and perhaps even physical) survival in a world of murderous racism. As Joel Williamson has said often, few historians provided colleagues more employment than did Woodward with *The Strange Career of Jim Crow* in its different versions and with its different debates and conflicts. It was because of this work more than any other that Woodward became most shrewdly aware of life's bittersweet character and began to remark that it was better to be criticized than to be forgotten.

However, the scholarly attention from critics was of a character wholly different from the largely uncritical acceptance of the nonspecialists in the lay population. In a scholarly world, where a professional hoped to sell several thousand copies of a publication, where ten or twenty thousand copies meant a roaring success, Oxford University Press was selling Woodward's long essay by the hundreds of thousands. Further, *Strange Career* has been a book that people carry around in their heads and actually talk about. It said that one did not have to abandon southern identity in order to integrate and otherwise seek equity for African Americans, and such a message was a vital one for southern reformists, probably not least for Vann Woodward. To be liberal in the 1950s and 1960s in the South was no easy thing, and Woodward provided desperately needed help. The Reverend Martin Luther King Jr. understood this perfectly, and that master of the art of "crossing over" to reach the mainstream of the white bourgeoisie read passages from *Strange Career* on the steps of Alabama's state capitol building prior to leading the march to Selma in 1963. King surely knew that the black people among his marchers needed other sorts of assurances, but the native whites needed to be told that they were not about to "denature themselves," as David Potter once put it. Californians may have achieved a willful autonomy from the past, New Englanders may be secure in a righteous tradition, New Yorkers may know of their long-running leadership and power, and midwesterners may have the security of their own hard and practical goodness on the advancing frontier. But Virginians and Carolinians and Mississippians have had their own *Aeneid* to live out, have carried their ancestors on their backs, and have not "cottoned" to the suggestion that the people of the past hold no claim over their souls, even and especially when they know that their fathers have sinned.

During the 1960s *Strange Career* proved no less popular as Woodward revised it to take account of new findings and some significant criticisms, and he otherwise stayed before the reading public with essays in Willie Morris's *Harper's Magazine,* Max Ascoli's *Reporter,* and Gilbert Harrison's *New Republic.* When he collected other essays for publication in *The Burden of Southern History* along with "The Irony," he thus provided bookend paperbacks for widespread distribution among both undergraduates and the "middle-brow" laity. A favorable review of a work in southern history, if written by David Potter or David Herbert Donald, could certainly improve a young scholar's standing among peers in the profession; but such favorable notice from Woodward could help *sell the book.*

Winning such an audience in the yeasty 1960s, Woodward took other prizes. Yale University hired him, with a generous grant of an initial year's leave of absence to do research. At Yale, the graduate students were just as good as those at JHU (see appendix B for a full list, which, like the Baltimore group, includes a Pulitzer Prize recipient), and he thus became colleagues with old friends Warren and Brooks as well as new friends historians John Morton Blum and Robin Winks, conservative jurist Alexander Bickel, economist James Tobin (later winner of the Nobel Prize), and reformist administrator Kingman Brewster. In New Haven he could also play a reversed and doubled role, a southern King Arthur in Connecticut's Court, tweaking the Yankees on the nose with what the canny and inventive literary observer Albert Murray has called "downhome truths" that have "feedstore/seedstore" practicalities as well as "barnyard fiddles" in foreground. To this Yale he attracted African American scholars John W. Blassingame—whose father once swept out the building for Woodward's father—Thomas Holt, and Barbara Jeanne Fields, all of whom have become well recognized in their own time and on their own terms.

Woodward closed out the decade with twin addresses that demonstrated at once his power and authority within the profession and his sharp sense for the coming trend. Elected president of the Organization of American Historians (OAH) for 1968–69 and president of the American Historical Association (AHA) for 1969–70, Woodward, as for the SHA, used the bully pulpit to full advantage. In "Clio with Soul," he demanded that his colleagues take up African American history with more serious attention. Some were already doing so, but the Woodward imprimatur on the subject helped, and some particularly thoughtful social history examining black issues, and from a black point of view, ensued during the 1970s. Most of that work would have happened anyway, but Woodward's dramatic call created a more receptive audience among professionals, who paid attention to that good work as it came.

At the same time, Woodward, in "The Future of the Past," reminded any still complacent colleagues that the fat days for historians would not survive the decade; an American people always willfully innocent of history, whose demographics were changing so that fewer college-age people would be around and whose curriculum tinkerers and fiddlers were hard at work, were about to dramatically reduce demand for professional historians in the nation's colleges and universities. In his wry way, he forced the audience to recall that it was the 1960s, with its plentiful jobs and rising salaries, that constituted the exception. Historians have always known that exceptions, by their nature, do not last forever, and thus leaner times were an inescapable eventuality in the 1970s. The fatness of the 1960s would make the unavoidable leanness of the incoming decade seem worse by contrast. Even so, Woodward forcefully told his colleagues, there remained the pursuit of what he called *the subject* (usually to mean a committed understanding of southern history but here more generally to mean history itself). That pursuit must needs continue, no matter how age demographics, curriculum disasters, and other factors of demand devolved. Further, he gently chided the audience for harboring any tendencies to develop inaccessible language or to dwell too long in the text on complex methodologies that might drive away the readership of nonprofessionals. This second speech was thus a mirror of the first: Where the former suggested a healthy trend and sent colleagues in that direction, the latter spotted an unhealthy trend, only part of which a historian could control, and suggested a kind of stoic's first aid for the maladies to come. When he offered these warnings in "The Future of the Past," he sounded almost alarmist, but within five years his warnings were hopelessly understated. Too, his own comfortable position, the amply endowed Sterling Chair at Yale, inevitably reduced his legitimacy as he scolded junior colleagues who faced underemployment.[20]

Nevertheless, his popularity and influence grew as he opposed the Vietnam War, as he continued the fight for civil rights, and as he campaigned for a truly free academy that included places for Marxist voices. As the 1960s closed out, the gentle warnings of David Potter and of Richard Hofstadter, the sharper warnings of Alexander Bickel and William Carleton, plus his own knowledge of *the subject,* in combination suggested to Woodward that all the popularity, all the respect, and all the successes could not possibly go on. In particular, his celebration of the Populists as *the* forgotten alternative (both for race relations and for economic policies) for the entire nation became an independent phenomenon that grew wildly beyond his ability to control. As former "Musketeer" William Carleton had warned, *Populism* and *Populists* could and did become terms to describe all manner of leftist reform, very nearly the single "good" term for the left-leaning era, even as it was very nearly the single "bad" term for the right-leaning 1950s. George Brown Tindall reminded all that there was a "semantic identity crisis" developing for *Populists* and *Populism,* with the terms being applied willy-nilly to groups utterly unrelated to the farmers' movement of the 1890s. While Tindall took pains not to blame Woodward for these strange and ironic results,[21] it was apparent that the ironist was done in by his own words and that Woodward must share the responsibility and certainly the discomfiture when the era of the 1990s—the centennial of the agrarian revolt—witnessed the term *Populism* seized by none other than congressperson Newt Gingrich, Republican of Georgia, who used the word to describe a program of cutting taxes, removing government oversight of corporate business, reducing commitments to the welfare state, and reestablishing right-wing social values. Not exactly the Ocala platform! Indeed, Gingrich even proclaimed the election of 1896 to be a *Populist victory* because sound-money policies triumphed over unsound-money practices, although the written record showed that the people who registered themselves contemporaneously as Populists (and the people who supported "unsound-money" of bimetallic currency) went down to flaming defeat in that year.

Partly because of such strange effects, Woodward, in the early 1970s, sounded a tocsin about presentism, not to exclude any of his own indulgences. After previously urging scholars to cross disciplinary lines in the humanist and social-scientist traditions he shared with Potter, Hofstadter, Aaron, Degler, Gaston, and other friends and colleagues, Woodward began telling seminar students at Yale to study history proper, and historians to use proper methods and perspectives. Some of this new emphasis was likely inevitable due to the process of aging; some of it was his reaction as a modernist to the new and more radical claims about language and communication made by postmodernists, as noted for us by Edward Ayers; some of it was in response to undeniable scholarly excesses in the so-styled New Left; and some of it was in response to equally undeniable excesses on academic campuses, especially at his own Yale, where he filed with President Brewster an angry report about lack of freedom of expression (these cases enraged him particularly because the source of the threats came not from outside, that is, from corrupt politicians and badly informed businessman-trustees, but rather from inside, from the academy's own self-appointed agents of *political correctness*).[22] But some of this new tone, occasionally chalky and bitter, was related to what he has called a personal "time of troubles": the death from cancer of his son, Peter Vincent Woodward, inveterate sportsman and an aspiring political scientist of some promise; and the deaths from the same disease (described by Woodward as "my enemy"), in the same period, of Alexander Bickel, David Potter, and Richard Hofstadter, plus the onset of debilitating and finally fatal illnesses for his wife, Glenn Woodward. Results for scholarship were not unrelated to the "time of troubles," although it was a story of some complexities. Above all, he never completed a long-planned, and long-expected, major reinterpretation of Reconstruction, thereby disappointing himself and the profession, which fumbled along with no significant useful overview of that "dark and bloody ground" until Eric Foner at last accomplished the task in 1988.[23] In fact, Woodward went through the entire 1970s with no research monograph, though his deeply reflective, often poignant essays were collected in a lovely volume, dedicated in memoriam to son Peter, *American Counterpoint*.[24]

There were also repercussions in the academy, especially—and with an irony approaching bathos—over the issue of an attempted special visiting-teaching appointment for the Communist Herbert Aptheker. Despite Woodward's self-described "Marxoid" tendencies, despite his youthful enthusiasms for the early experiments in the Soviet Union, despite friendship with and sponsorship of Marxist scholars (most prominently Eugene Dominick Genovese), the mature Woodward has had no truck with the American Communist party, and especially none with Aptheker. This scholar-activist held a Ph.D. from Columbia University and had written a study, *American Negro Slave Revolts*, that was praised by Woodward's students John W. Blassingame, Barbara Jeanne Fields, and Otto Olsen because of its emphasis on agency and activism among the southern slaves.[25] He was also the legal executor for William Edward Burghardt Du Bois, and there were few people anywhere, certainly no scholars, who had known Du Bois better than had Aptheker. Still Woodward disliked the tactics of the American CP, and he regarded Aptheker as strictly a partisan and as no scholar at all. As he said often, Aptheker's books on the shelves (which Woodward judged to be essentially polemical, not to exclude *American Negro Slave Revolts*) proved his unfitness for a professorial appointment.

In fact, Woodward, along with a number of other prominent scholars, including John Hope Franklin and Louis Harlan, removed himself from sponsorship of Aptheker's ambitious project to edit and publish the papers of Du Bois for the University of Massachusetts Press because of the ironist's concern that Aptheker was producing "a partisan job."[26] And when Aptheker was nominated in 1975 by students at the Davenport College of Yale to serve as resident scholar for a special, reduced-credit, elective course concerning Du Bois, Woodward led a campaign in his department to refuse the necessary disciplinary sanction for the course as a history offering or for Aptheker as visiting historian on special appointment. In 1976, when Yale's political science department nominated Aptheker for such a special course, Woodward attempted, this time unsuccessfully, to block that appointment. He offered scholarly reasons that could be supported, although the judgment here is that Davenport's visiting appointments really have not been the same thing as tenure at Yale University. For instance, sports commentator the late Howard Cossell once held such a Davenport appointment, and Woodward had done nothing to block that invitation. After these well-publicized struggles, Woodward found himself scorned by leftist scholars, with the interesting exceptions of Eric Foner and Eugene Genovese; he also found himself celebrated by the right wing, by none other than the editors of the *National Review* and the *Wall Street Journal*. And, while cleared of any wrongdoing by the official investigative committee for the OAH and the AHA, he did not emerge from these disputes without losing affection and sometimes even respect among many professional historians.[27]

In 1974 Woodward returned to the good graces of liberals and at least most other left-wingers because of his leadership of a professional team's study of presidential misconduct during discussions about Richard Nixon and the Watergate affair. His carefully edited and brilliantly orchestrated *Responses of the Presidents to Charges of Misconduct* gave the academy's full weight to the then politically popular movement to compel Nixon's resignation. This *Responses* volume, while laying out plenty of evidence of misbehavior by all presidents, presented the case that there was no equal to the Nixon administration's sheer abuse of power at a time of overwhelming popularity. For Woodward, as for his mentor Beard long ago, such abuse of power constituted a far greater threat to the citizenry than the more commonly occurring presidential thieving, lying, drinking, sexual indulging, and cronyism among Nixon's predecessors. For the record, Woodward took care to point out that the political dynamics leading to Nixon's resignation were in successful motion long before *Responses* was published; nevertheless, the volume certainly gave a scholar's resounding punctuation to the dismissal of a powerful and popular president; and in the 1980s and 1990s, as historians have looked back at these events during a time of revising Nixon's career, the weighty evidence in *Responses* has given reason to pause and reconsider some of the more enthusiastic reevaluations of the Nixon administration.[28]

In the late 1970s, Woodward returned to the scholar's archival task, after some years of virtual easy-chair essay-crafting. He accepted, after initial de-murrals, the overwhelming challenge of editing Mary Boykin Chesnut's diaries, attempted novels, and other papers. Some of these materials, in much bowdlerized fashion, had been preserved in 1949 as *Diary from Dixie*, edited and prepared by novelist Ben Ames Williams. There was also another version developed in 1929, essentially as neo-Confederate apologia.[29] Yet Woodward and every other scholar of "the subject" knew that the sharp-eyed and tart-tongued Chesnut was no cheerleader for the Lost Cause, and that her manuscripts in the South Caroliniana Library of the University of South Carolina were rich and complex and deserved to be shared with an audience larger than that constituted by scholars with the time and money to go to Columbia to search the documents there. Although he went into this research task with a formidable team of assistants, Woodward was yet again the mole, the scholar up to his tweed elbows in the original papers in Columbia and in other points south of the Connecticut "court." By 1981 he had produced two handsome volumes, one an edition that disentangled Chesnut's diaries, properly considered as on-the-spot observations, from her retrospective recollections that were neither fiction ("she didn't make anybody up") nor exactly history, but rather her own artistry, sui generis. This volume, *Mary Chesnut's Civil War,* he produced as a celebration of one woman's uniquely ironic feminism, a verdict that in the later 1980s and 1990s came under considerable disputation from feminists, and from conservatives; but at the time of presentation it was so brilliant an argument, and the volume so wonderfully useful in the classroom, that he was awarded the Pulitzer Prize for it in 1982. Two years later, he, with his able "collaborator" Elisabeth Muhlenfeld, produced the second volume, *The Private Mary Chesnut,* an edition that captured her more acerbic contemporaneous judgments of the conduct of a war in which madmen and incompetents seemed to be in charge.[30]

Woodward was again the scholar-activist with a vengeance, no longer the optimist of the 1950s and 1960s, or again the bitter cynic of the early 1970s, but a more complex auctorial activist, almost in the style of the eighteenth-century *public man* as limned by Richard Sennett: "connecting with strangers in an emotionally satisfying way and yet remaining aloof from them . . . [using the scholar's signs and symbols and rituals of the professional practitioner to enter] the forum in which it becomes meaningful to join with other persons without the compulsion to know them as persons."[31]

Moreover, in 1982 Woodward enjoyed a return to the most meaningful of his fields of combat, that of civil rights. With the election of Ronald Reagan, there was considerable discussion about not extending the Voting Rights Act of 1965, although Woodward and other scholars were convinced of the continuing need for such protections as preclearance by federal agents before voting procedures could be changed in southern states with a history of racist abuses. There were hints that Reagan would veto any voting-rights extension, and even fears that Congress could not pass such a measure. Woodward went into action, testifying memorably before the House of Representatives, in tandem with his former student J. Morgan Kousser. Representatives Peter Rodino and Don Edwards and congressional staff members have insisted subsequently that his recorded testimony, with its scholarly evidence and documentation, was instrumental in the successful campaign to extend the Voting Rights Act. In any case, by the time Congress passed the legislation, the public mood was very favorable, and Reagan did not veto it.[32]

In this refined role of the elder essayist with a purpose, in 1986 Woodward offered his memoirs, *Thinking Back,* a kind of celebration of his relationships with his critics.[33] *Thinking Back* was so little self-revelatory that some, such as Bertram Wyatt-Brown in this volume, have been puzzled by its character. However, it was consistent with the "public man" traditions, since Woodward eschewed "self-referentiality" or other such postmodernist devices and designs. Instead, he used modernist signs and symbols to compel discourse on issues rather than on personalities. This graceful essay was deftly, even cleverly, argued so that Woodward still got the best of most disputes, at least as cast in this essay done for the Walter Lynwood Fleming Lectures of 1985. (Thirty years earlier, Woodward had delivered Fleming Lectures, but that set of addresses was never published, a sad result since the series has aimed at collecting the seminal thoughts of the best scholars of the South, and Woodward was arguably the best of the best; all of which made this 1985 set a gratifying kind of Fleming II.)

Still more essays were collected and published in 1989 as *The Future of the Past,* a volume in which Woodward very self-consciously assumes two roles, not only *public man* but also dean of American historians and even, to some degree, dean of American humanists. He also, in 1992, produced *The Old World's New World,* a complex discussion of European travelers to the United States and a consideration of how America was transformed in slow stages of transcontinental dialogue. Beginning as the metaphorically innocent land filled with promises to solve European maladies, America the symbol gradually was transformed into *the* problem bedeviling Europeans.[34] In all of these essays, Woodward was the ironist and the modernist, and in all he experimented with language but always with the assumption that a rational man or woman could control the words he or she was using. The style of such structuralism thus put him considerably at odds with the postmodernists and led him into disputes with the dominant literary theorists of the 1990s. Indeed, by the era of the 1990s, these postmodernist trends were attracting some historians, including his onetime seminar student Edward Ayers, who in this volume has argued with Woodward about how language works, how to "open up"—or close down—a narrative, and how much to expect readers to interpose themselves in the processes of such written communication.

Nor did Woodward step down from his dais in the political forum, since he joined in the 1994 controversies involved in the attempt by Walt Disney Corporation to build a theme park in the Virginia Piedmont on the site of Civil War battlefields, a suggestion that Woodward derided as "a Mickey Mouse idea" attempting to displace real history with fantasyland. In these campaigns, Woodward at last showed some of the effects of great age, for he served as elder statesman and advisor, while his former student James M. McPherson actually led the battle. Yet McPherson was careful to credit his elder with sage advice and with the most useful effects on other historians just by lending his name to the cause.[35]

A controversialist Woodward certainly remained, in a scholarly career that has encompassed seven very full decades of activity. Obviously, he changed over the long years, and much of what he wrote or said no longer speaks effectively to his very junior colleagues pursuing "the subject." By the most generous judgments, he offered women's history little more than half a loaf; his hard work on behalf of integration in civil rights excluded serious consideration of black separatism; his modernist assumptions have become quite dated in a world of postmodernists, without being useful to those who reject both modernism and postmodernism; his most famous work on Jim Crow has come to seem most fatally flawed; and his most substantial research work has been largely supplanted. Still, he remains significant if only for first asking vital and provocative questions, regardless of what answers eventually emerge. Above all, the remarkable thing has been the sustained leadership in a man who has been both wonderfully impertinent and unremittingly dignified: C. Vann Woodward, Southerner.

NOTES

Unless otherwise noted, the facts of this essay come from research documented in the editor's biography *C. Vann Woodward, Southerner* (Athens: University of Georgia Press, 1987).

1. Interview with John Morton Blum (13 Dec. 1984), John Herbert Roper Papers, Southern Historical Collection, Library of the University of North Carolina at Chapel Hill, hereinafter cited as Roper Papers.

2. Interview with Woodward (18 July 1978), Roper Papers.

3. Interviews with Woodward (18 July 1978, 20 June 1983), Roper Papers.

4. Interviews: Glenn Weddington Rainey (25 and 27 Mar. 1980); LeRoy Loemker (11 Aug. 1979), Roper Papers; correspondence, Woodward and Rainey, 1933–66, Glenn Weddington Rainey Papers, Manuscript Division, Emory University Library, Atlanta, hereinafter cited as Rainey Papers.

5. Correspondence, Woodward and Rainey, 1933–66, especially Woodward to Rainey, 13 June 1934, Rainey Papers; interview with Woodward (13 Apr. 1979), Roper Papers.

6. Edwin Mims, *The Advancing South: Stories of Progress and Reaction* (Garden City, N.Y.: Doubleday, Page, 1926); Woodward to Rainey, 20 Aug. 1939, Rainey Papers; Interviews: Woodward (18 and 19 July 1978, 12 Oct. 1980); William Terry Couch (10–11 Jan. 1980), Roper Papers.

7. Interviews with Woodward (18 and 19 July 1978, 12 Oct. 1980), Roper Papers.

8. Ibid.; George Brown Tindall in 1988 showed the editor a student circular that offered an especially melodramatic account of Woodward persecuted and nearly perishing in the comprehensive examinations.

9. Ibid.; see also Beale correspondence, 1936–38, History Department Papers, University Archives, University of North Carolina, Chapel Hill. Personal correspondence of Beale's was also kindly shared by J. Merton England through Joseph A. Herzenberg, correspondence in possession of England.

10. Interviews: William G. Carleton (21 July 1979); Manning J. Dauer (21 July 1989), Roper Papers.

11. Ibid.; Dauer was speaking after he had made a careful search in the University Archives of the Library of the University of Florida, Gainesville; *Tom Watson: Agrarian Rebel* (New York: Macmillan, 1938); Allan Nevins, "Tom Watson and the New South," review of *Tom Watson, New York Times Book Review,* 3 Apr. 1938, 1, 26.

12. C. Vann Woodward, *Kolombangara and Vella Lavella, 6 August — 7 October 1943* (restricted distribution; Washington: U.S. Government Printing Office, n.d. [ca. 1947]); idem, *The Bougainville Landing and the Battle of Empress Augusta Bay,*

27 October—2 November 1943 (restricted distribution; Washington: U.S. Government Printing Office, n.d. [ca. 1947]); idem, *The Battle for Leyte Gulf* (New York: Macmillan, 1947), quote, 162.

13. C. Vann Woodward, *Reunion and Reaction: The Compromise of 1877 and the End of Reconstruction* (Boston: Little, Brown, 1951); idem, *Origins of the New South, 1877–1913*, vol. 9, The History of the South, series ed. Ellis Merton Coulter and Wendell Holmes Stephenson (Baton Rouge: Louisiana State University Press, 1951); quote is from Sheldon Hackney.

14. Cleanth Brooks, *The Well Wrought Urn: Studies in the Structure of Poetry* (New York: Reynal and Hitchcock, 1947); Brooks and Robert Penn Warren, *Understanding Fiction* (New York: F. S. Crofts, 1943); and Brooks and Warren, *Understanding Poetry*, 3d rev. ed. (New York: Holt, Rinehart and Winston, 1960).

15. C. Vann Woodward, *The Strange Career of Jim Crow* (New York: Oxford University Press, 1955); idem, *The Burden of Southern History* (Baton Rouge: Louisiana State University Press, 1960).

16. Reinhold Niebuhr, *The Irony of American History* (New York: Scribner, 1952); David Morris Potter, *People of Plenty: Economic Abundance and the American Character* (Chicago: University of Chicago Press, 1954). During 1950 Potter also gave a series of speeches on this theme, available to and cited by Woodward.

17. Richard King, *A Southern Renaissance: The Cultural Awakening of the American South, 1930–1955* (New York: Oxford University Press, 1980).

18. Gaines M. Foster has pointed out this influence of Robert Penn Warren and his character Jack Burden, in Foster, "Woodward and Southern Identity," *Southern Review* 21 (1985): 351–60. See also Robert Penn Warren, *All the King's Men* (New York: Harcourt, Brace, 1946).

19. Woodward, "Monograph on the History of Reconstruction in the South to Brief for *Oliver Brown, et al. v. Board of Education of Topeka, et al.,* filed in U.S. Supreme Court, 16 November 1953; Thomas F. Pettigrew, *A Profile of the Negro American* (Princeton: Van Nostrand, 1964); Konrad Lorenz, *On Aggression*, trans. Marjorie Kerr Wilson (New York: Harcourt, Brace and World, 1966); Gordon W. Allport, *ABCs of Scapegoating*, 6th rev. ed. (New York: Anti-Defamation League of B'nai B'rith, 1969); and idem, *The Nature of Prejudice* (Reading, Mass.: Addison-Wesley, 1954).

20. C. Vann Woodward, "Clio with Soul," *Journal of American History* 56 (1969): 5–20; idem, "The Future of the Past," *American Historical Review* 75 (1970): 711–26.

21. George Brown Tindall, "Populism: A Semantic Identity Crisis," *Virginia Quarterly Review* 48 (1972): 501–18; in a telephone conversation of 31 July 1995, Tindall emphatically reminded the editor, a former student of his, that Woodward has not been the culprit in this semantic crisis. Robert C. McMath Jr., in his presidential address for the Agricultural History Society, noted similar problems about the terminology, although he reaffirmed Woodward's conception that a broadly reformist and essentially noble element of the common person's thought could be located:

"Populism in Two Countries—Agrarian Protest in the Great Plains and the Prairie Provinces," *Agricultural History* 69 (1995): 517–46.

22. C. Vann Woodward, "The Erosion of Academic Privileges and Immunities," *Daedalus* 103 (1974): 33–37; interview with Woodward (14 Dec. 1984), Roper Papers; C. Vann Woodward, "Report on Freedom of Expression at Yale University," 1975, revised and published for all undergraduates in *Undergraduate Regulations* (New Haven: Yale University, 1986–87), 9–11.

23. Eric Foner, *Reconstruction: America's Unfinished Revolution* (New York: Harper & Row, 1988).

24. C. Vann Woodward, *American Counterpoint: Slavery and Racism in the North-South Dialogue,* 2d ed. (Boston: Little, Brown, 1983).

25. Herbert Aptheker, *American Negro Slave Revolts* (New York: International Publishers, 1963).

26. Herbert Aptheker, ed., *The Correspondence of W. E. B. Du Bois,* vols. 1–2 (Amherst: University of Massachusetts Press, 1973–78).

27. Interviews: Woodward (4–5 Nov. 1982, 13 Apr. 1979); John Morton Blum (13 Dec. 1984); William Samuel McFeely (4–5 Dec. 1984); Herbert Aptheker (23 Mar. 1985). Aptheker to Roper, 1 and 16 July 1985, Roper Papers. Henry A. Turner to Roper, 2 Mar. 1983, with enclosure from *Yale Alumni Magazine,* Feb. 1984, 10, 52–53. Herbert Gstalder to Roper, 28 June 1985 (Gstalder also made available Kraus-Thompson Organization, Ltd. official correspondence concerning a legal controversy involving Paul G. Partington and Aptheker, summary of notes in Roper Papers). Malcolm Call, in charge of the University of Massachusetts Press project for Du Bois Papers, made available copies of correspondence (summary of notes in Roper Papers). "Report of the Joint AHA–OAH Committee for the Defense of Historians under the First Amendment in the Yale–Aptheker Controversy," 1978. Aptheker, "Comment on the Report of the Joint AHA–OAH Committee . . . ," *AHA Newsletter* 16 (1978): 3–4. See also correspondence from Woodward, Aptheker, and Paul Partington, Roper Papers. Cf. Eugene Genovese, "Herbert Aptheker," in Genovese, *The Southern Front* (Columbia: University of Missouri Press, 1995), in which the great Marxist scholar reassesses Aptheker and expresses regret for his own role in the series of incidents.

28. C. Vann Woodward, ed., *Responses of the Presidents to Charges of Misconduct* (New York: Delacorte, 1974).

29. Mary Boykin Chesnut, *A Diary from Dixie,* ed. Ben Ames Williams (Boston: Houghton Mifflin, 1949); idem, *A Diary from Dixie,* ed. Isabella D. Martin and Myrta Lockett Avary (New York: Peter Smith, 1929).

30. Mary Boykin Chesnut, *Mary Chesnut's Civil War,* ed. C. Vann Woodward (New Haven: Yale University Press, 1981); idem, *The Private Mary Chesnut: The Unpublished Civil War Diaries,* ed. Woodward and Elisabeth Muhlenfeld (New York: Oxford University Press, 1984).

31. Richard Sennett, *The Fall of Public Man* (New York: Knopf, 1976), 340.

32. U.S. Congress, House Committee on the Judiciary, *Extension of the Voting*

Rights Act: Hearing, 1999–2028; Woodward to Roper, 25 June 1981; interviews: staffers of House Committee on the Judiciary (22 Mar. 1983); Don Edwards (22 Mar. 1983), Roper Papers. Roper, "Essay on the Voting Rights Extension Act," *Phylon* 45 (1984): 188–96.

33. C. Vann Woodward, *Thinking Back* (Baton Rouge: Louisiana State University Press, 1986).

34. C. Vann Woodward, *The Future of the Past* (New York: Oxford University Press, 1989); idem, *The Old World's New World* (New York: Oxford University Press, 1992).

35. C. Vann Woodward, "A Mickey Mouse Idea," *New Republic* 20 June 1994, 15–16; James M. McPherson to Roper, 23 March 1995, Roper Papers.

I

Style and History

Narrative Form in
Origins of the New South

EDWARD L. AYERS

✳

This essay, a version of which appeared in the *Journal of Southern History,*
considers the nature and characteristics of narrative form. Ayers proposes a
poststructuralist narrative form that is more "open" than traditional forms.
However, Ayers does not argue a case for so-styled deconstruction. Rather,
by "open," Ayers means to say, among other things, open to more than one
interpretation because offered in more than one voice, in more than one tone,
and from more than one perspective. While deeply appreciative of Woodward's own experimentation, and often inspired by Woodward's playful use
of language, Ayers is the postmodernist experimenting far more radically
with narrative form and subject than did Woodward, the modernist of a previous era for whom structure and authorial command are both much more
crucial.

✳   ✳   ✳

In the spring of 1977 I found myself a member of the last graduate seminar
taught by C. Vann Woodward. All of us in the class felt the significance of
the event, but only one fellow student had the presence of mind and sense of
symbolism to do something special for the final class meeting. He read a
letter of recommendation from the 1930s, found in some southern archive,
attesting to the abilities and promise of one C. Vann Woodward. We all
chuckled appreciatively at the letter; though the description of the young
Woodward was suitably fulsome, any prediction the recommendation could
have offered was bound to prove inadequate to the accomplishments that
lay in the young scholar's future. After a characteristically wry response by
Woodward, we went on with our discussion of the assigned reading. At the
end of the class, we all fell silent and remained in our seats as the new professor emeritus smiled at us, slowly rose, and left the room.

At the time, I was embarrassed that we had not done more, that we had
not presented him with some commemorative object of esteem. But I have

assuaged myself in the years since with the feeling that that last class meeting symbolized more to us than it did to Woodward. His edition of Mary Chestnut's writings won him the Pulitzer Prize four years later, after all, and the number of books, essays, reviews, and lectures he has written since that seminar would constitute an impressive career-long record for most of us. Woodward's work was as challenging and exciting in 1977 as it had been when it was first written. The noticeable lack of closure to that last class may have been the most appropriate symbolism we could have offered, however unwitting and awkward it seemed at the time.

Because I came to southern history late and somewhat reluctantly, that class with Woodward was the only class I ever took on the subject. But that seminar and a book I read for the first time that semester—*Origins of the New South*—made me an aspiring southernist. A seminar paper I wrote for another class that term directly applied Woodward's colonial economy argument to my hometown; that argument seemed, in a sudden flash, to explain the entire history of the place. Although I handled the argument clumsily, it did provide my first publication. My dissertation, too, grew directly from *Origins*—in this case, its brief but powerful portrayal of the convict lease system. As that dissertation eventually spread into a book, covering crime and punishment in general before and after the Civil War, it no longer depended quite so heavily on *Origins,* even though the New South component fit comfortably within Woodward's interpretation.

The research I did on lynching in the New South slowly pushed me in a direction I had not anticipated. As I sat in front of the microfilm reader day after day, looking (somewhat ghoulishly, it seemed) for stories of crime and retribution in the newspapers of the late nineteenth-century South, I came to feel that I was seeing a New South I had not seen before. Right beside the articles on lynching, murder, and moonshining appeared articles on football games, modern revivals, and technological innovations. Such things did not fit with what I thought I knew of the South. That sense of surprise, even discomfort, eventually grew into a book covering the same period and topics as *Origins*.

I came to realize that Woodward's perspective would not be mine. We were of different generations, different backgrounds, different temperaments; I had questions and passions that were not his. People indeed assumed that any new history of the New South would necessarily be a revisionist attack on *Origins of the New South*. But, despite our differences and despite my hope for an original vision, my approach to Woodward's book could not be straightforward repudiation. The more I read Woodward's book, the more I came to see *Origins* as a model of the historian's craft. The book I was writing, so different from his in many ways, emulated that book's style and structure.

Origins' chapters interlock at several levels, including those of language, metaphor, and mood, making Woodward's narrative powerful and resistant to scholarly displacement. It has no introduction and no conclusion; it does not define itself against any one historian but against an ingrained way of seeing the South; it often seems to work by indirection, aside, and allusion. William B. Hesseltine, reviewing Woodward's book in the *American Historical Review* in 1952, praised *Origins* for "wisely" refraining "from attempting to impose a nonexistent unity" upon the New South. An overview of the New South, Hesseltine argued, would not, could not, supply a "clearly defined synthesis" because the New South was simply not "a coherent, unified period of southern history."

I found this aspect of Woodward's book extraordinarily appealing. More overt and obvious ways of writing history seemed to foreclose opportunities that Woodward's style did not, seemed to age in ways that Woodward's did not. Even as the notecards piled up and more specific kinds of arguments began to form, I continually looked for theories and examples that would let me capture some of the flexibility of Woodward's narrative. Slowly, I developed a way I wanted to tell the story. That style was designed to embrace as many people and kinds of activity as possible, to convey a sense of contingency and possibility even within powerful structures. I did not have a name for what I was trying to do until after I had published the book, *The Promise of the New South,* and was pressed to explain its intentions more fully, but I had a clear agenda all along. The remainder of this essay is intended to describe that agenda and compare it with Woodward's.

One way to describe the idea behind *Promise* is to suggest a distinction between "fixed narratives" and "open narratives." Most works of professional history mix, in various proportions, nineteenth-century styles of storytelling with twentieth-century forms of social science. These fixed narratives tend to be organized in a linear way, either chronologically or in the form of an argument, seeking balance and authority. Though history writing is not as formalized as, say, sociology or political science, historians do rely on introductions, chapter summaries, and conclusions, do expect arguments to be clearly labeled as such, and do ask that works be positioned in relation to other studies. Most works of history are implicitly and explicitly measured against this standard of the fixed narrative, tailored to an audience of students and professors, effectively designed for historiographical utility.

Open narratives challenge various parts of that formula. In some open histories the authors let the reader in on the way the argument is being constructed; rather than presenting history as a self-contained and authoritative argument, these historians openly grapple with problematic sources and presentation. Their narratives suggest that the appearance of coherence and a commanding argument may ultimately be less useful than a reckoning with the limits of our knowledge or understanding. Other open histories ask storytelling and language to do more work. Instead of using the narrative as a means to an analytical end outside the story, these histories attempt to fold the analysis into the story itself. They do not simply relate facts or lay out a chronicle—they analyze their topics and make arguments—but not in ways that obviously segregate judgment from storytelling. These open histories may intentionally leave ambiguities unresolved or seek tension and resolution less in professional debate than in evidence, characters, and situations.

Most of our books, of course, range along a continuum somewhere between fixed and open narratives. There is no need to force books into one camp or another. It is impossible to write a perfectly fixed narrative; slippery language and evidence see to that. It is equally impossible to write a perfectly open narrative, for we write and read books precisely to find coherence of some kind. Different tasks call for different kinds of narratives. Anyone who opens an encyclopedia or dictionary does not want to find contingency and uncertainty; by contrast, someone who wants a broadly inclusive portrayal of a time or place may expect to find pieces that do not fit together snugly.

I tried to combine open and fixed narratives in *Promise* precisely because each kind of writing does things the other does not do as well. The book's broad introductory chapter, "Junction," is relatively open, for example, because it tries to create a sense of diverse but interconnected activity. The detailed and chronological story of Populism, on the other hand, follows a relatively fixed form because a political movement unfolds specifically in time, with clear events and contingencies creating its shape. Other chapters of *Promise* follow intermediate strategies, though open-ended chapters and a sort of anti-epilogue have made some readers feel as if the whole book rejects closure.

It was not sheer perversity or a quest for novelty that impelled me to experiment with narrative, but rather an attempt to balance two competing goals. I hoped, on the one hand, that my book would appeal to people who knew little and perhaps cared less about the New South; on the other hand, I wanted to synthesize the large professional literature on the period. Toward the first end, I tried to make my narrative—like *Origins'*—self-contained, dependent on no previous academic knowledge, its historiographic ropes and pulleys hidden. I tried to make the various parts of the story connect with one another in ways that were not announced. I tried to embody thoughts, emotions, and behaviors in individuals, and to dramatize them in action. I tried to use resonance and dissonance, things implied and suggested, to make the story more interesting and supple. These strategies reflected my admiration for the open styles of John Dos Passos and James Agee, the fine texture of histories such as Emmanuel Le Roy Ladurie's *Montaillou*.

Toward the second goal, of dealing with the historiography, I refused to build the story around the familiar and rather tired debates that had grown up over the decades around Woodward's work, debates over continuity and discontinuity, the timing of segregation, or the colonial economy. Instead, I tried to portray the New South in a way that embraced rather than suppressed complexity and contradiction, that gave us some new material to think about, and that arranged the story in a way that challenged our usual perceptions.

Promise's overarching theme is that the currents of industrial capitalism, the national state, and new cultural styles ran deeply throughout the New South—far more deeply than Woodward had suggested. Those currents created, directly and indirectly, a complex series of backlashes, countercurrents, unexpected outcomes, and archaisms. As a result, there were things going on simultaneously in the New South that appeared to have little to do with one another but that in fact sprang from a common source: the conflict between the economic, ideological, and cultural legacies of the slave South, and those conveyed by the human and material carriers of late-nineteenth-century modernity. The personal and public struggles involved in that multifarious conflict were more complicated than any of the categories historians have devised to explain them.

Because it tells this morally complicated story, the narrative of *Promise* is built around contained tension, a tension signaled by the ambiguous and ironic title of the book itself. I might, it is true, have been able to boil the tensions down to a series of generalizations, but generalizations numb us to the very things the book is after: the emotional shadings of historical experience, the subtle and shifting contexts in which people had to make choices, the contradictory effects of the decisions people did make, the instability of even the most apparently permanent structures. *Promise* tried to evoke the New South by evoking the hard choices its people had to make, every day and in every facet of life, whether they wanted to or not. I intended a consonance between subject and style.

Promise differs from its predecessors, including Woodward's *Origins*, not only about the overt content of their arguments but also about the assumptions behind their work. It is a gentle quarrel with some of my favorite books and historians. I try to undercut the notion of southerners as being ideologically resistant to the market and pulled into it against their will; my southerners, black and white, want things and work mightily for them, even though they understand the high costs exacted by buying and selling. I challenge a view of the Populists as a new democratic culture; my Populists draw on the considerable strengths they already possess and do not need evangels from outside to tell them how to save themselves. I see southern industrialization as a glass a quarter full, stressing that our habitual comparisons with the North obscure real change in the South and real opportunities for black men and white women. I cut against the picture of communal mill workers and coal miners; mine appear restless and open to the outside world. I admit the divisions within the black "community" and give Booker T. Washington the benefit of the doubt. I take New South religion seriously, on its own terms, not simply as a hegemonic force of cultural captivity. I portray southern music as more commercial than folk, southern literature as more modernist than reactionary, southern culture, in general, as innovative rather than as conservative.

As I have suggested, *Origins* was both a model for my book and, necessarily, its object of revision. Woodward's book was "open" to the extent that it refused to follow a straightforward argument and to the extent that it was remarkably subtle and complex. But it was fixed in other important ways. Woodward—and the reader—watches over the New South from the viewpoint of omniscient observer. We are able to see through the guises and ruses of the New South leaders, able to see that the Populists should have stayed in the middle of the road, able to see that Booker T. Washington's compromise gave away far too much, able to see that philanthropists' gifts came with strings attached, able to see that religion and Prohibition left the real problems unaddressed. We enjoy the sense of perspective, and a certain superiority, that comes from hindsight and from seeing things with Woodward's shrewd and ironic vision.

As Woodward recalls, his "interest was in discovering the character, identification, motives, and alliances of the leaders of the new order in the South." He wrote as an admirer of Charles Beard, seeing economic self-interest, reflected directly in political behavior, driving everything else. He advocated Beard's economic interpretation all the more fervently and self-consciously, Woodward tells us, to define himself against the emerging consensus history of the late 1940s and early 1950s. Given the assumptions of Beardianism, the historian's job is to peel away the layers of illusion—of legend, myth, deception, self-deception, bombast, wishful thinking, stereotype, and foolishness—to get at the reality underneath. For Woodward, that reality was the social, racial, and economic privilege created in the sordid Gilded Age and perpetuated in the decades afterward.

Such a view is very much from the top down, despite the obvious sympathy Woodward showed for the oppressed, black and white. The key protagonists for *Origins* are the Redeemers and their heirs, the Democrats who succeeded the Republicans of Reconstruction. They won power unfairly; they wielded it in their own narrow interests and against those of the South as a whole; their blindness gave rise to a Populism which they then destroyed; they conspired with the former Populists to disfranchise and segregate black people and poorer whites. The Democrats are the active agents in every part of Woodward's story. The first 106 pages of *Origins*—nearly a fourth of those in the book—are devoted to getting the Redeemers on stage; many of the remaining pages are devoted to the Democrats' struggles with the Populists, their business dealings, and their co-optation of the Progressives. The Democrats are central to *Origins,* because Woodward's is essentially a story about political economy.

Woodward's focus on political leaders gives his story of the New South a narrative arc of status quo, challenge, and resolution that fits our expectations of a good story. The writing is beautiful, the arguments subtle, the qualifications carefully placed, but the basic explanation is that certain identifiable people called the shots, directed the society where they wanted it to go. The haves and have-nots were in struggle, with the rich white men who, as Woodward put it, "pretty much ran things" on the one hand and those "who were run, who were managed, and maneuvered and pushed around" on the other. It is, in part, the clarity of that struggle that makes the book so appealing, that gives the reader the sense of seeing through the Redeemers, of identifying with the oppressed.

Promise does not seek to redeem the Redeemers or to argue that the New South was better than Woodward believed. Where, then, do we differ? The basic issue seems to be this: I think that when the central drama of the society is located so firmly in Beardian political economy, the other kinds of drama in the society are made to seem falsely peripheral by comparison. Many kinds of power operated in the New South, and they were not seamless and congruent. The planters ran their plantations but were neglected by the town-based politicians; politicians ran the statehouse but were sneered at by the railroad companies; preachers guided large congregations but were detested by many profane people; women supervised their households but could always be overruled by their husbands; rural merchants held their customers' futures in their hands but saw their own futures controlled by town-based wholesalers; white people assumed themselves superior to the blacks among whom they lived, but blacks laughed at white pretension. *Promise* is about all these various kinds of power—some that operated by coercion, some that operated by persuasion. It does not ignore power but multiplies it, puts various kinds of power in competition with others. It is clear from the proportions of space I devote to public life—to voting, segregation, disfranchisement, and Populism, for example—that I do not consider all forms of power commensurable or interchangeable. But I do consider all of them important.

Even on Woodward's own political turf, we differ. *Promise* pays as much attention to the attitudes and actions of the rank and file as to officeholders, as much attention to the anomalies and weaknesses of the political system as to its apparent successes. It tries to see why people would vote in ways that seem to us antithetical to their own interests, why they were so wedded to issues—such as Prohibition—that seem to have little to do with the struggles over economy or race that we now see as central. In Woodward's account, the major changes in public life, segregation and disfranchisement, were largely partisan phenomena, the products of political manipulation imposed by well-placed leaders; in *Promise* they appear as social phenomena, systemic and deeply rooted, that politicians tried to harness and contain. For Woodward, segregation was mainly the result of displaced white frustration, a backlash. For *Promise*, statewide segregation was not that at all, but rather a halting and uncoordinated reaction to a series of deep changes in transportation, gender roles, and black class structure. I argue that disfranchisement had far less to do with the overt Populist challenge to the Redeemers than it did with black population movement, generational conflict, the growth of towns and cities, and the winner-take-all politics of the American Gilded Age. *Promise*'s explanations branch out more than those of *Origins* because they try to describe social change that reverberated throughout the entire society.

In *Origins*, Populist leaders such as Tom Watson stand as testimony to the possibility that lived even in the New South; *Promise* takes this argument even further, trying to show how social progress or human kindness did not depend on the decisions of the undependable men at the top. People of every walk of life in the South had their own struggles with poverty, injustice, and prejudice that had nothing to do with the Redeemers. A society has many pressure points, many domains where people can make a difference. I do not think that the New South would have been a fundamentally different society if only the Populists had won—the promise that drives Woodward's narrative—because the challenges rural southerners confronted went much deeper than the political or even the credit system.

Some of my most insightful reviewers, such as Robert J. Norrell, have wondered whether the open and empathetic approach of *Promise* can help those who are concerned with "the continuing reality of poverty, racial hatred, and profound ignorance" of our region. In the eyes of such readers Woodward offers something I do not, an explanation that seems to be politically useful in a way mine is not. I understand why people say this: I do not offer clear blame or alternatives. *Promise* is not a focused, crusading book in the way that *Origins* or *The Strange Career of Jim Crow* were—though I often wished it could be. There are still plenty of southern politicians who deserve all the ridicule and anger that can be directed against them, still plenty of irresponsible corporations, still plenty of shallow boosters ready to give away their communities to anyone willing to put up a factory or chain store. Bitter histories of such people have been written, and written well, and we still need to put those people in perspective.

But there are other stories that need telling, too, stories with their own political meaning. It is dangerous to let southern poverty and oppression be the entire story of the South. Told often enough, exclusively enough, such stories unintentionally flatten southerners, black and white, into stock figures, into simple victims and villains. Such stories have become common fare on television and in movies; they crowd out other possible stories, choking our understanding of the human richness created in southern history. A history book may tell horrendous stories of race and class domination, but jaded readers, young readers, will nod and turn the page. They have heard it all before.

The South has become a formula. The South and its people get to play only limited roles in the story of America; they are dragged into the textbooks and movie houses to demonstrate slavery, to cause the Civil War, to suffer in poverty, to inflict and partially overcome injustice. The result is a South that is easily pegged, easily caricatured, easily explained. That is an injustice, I came to believe, that a history book might actually do something, however small, to counter. *Promise,* in that sense, was meant to be politically engaged, even if I saw little use in discovering once more that southern planters, mill owners, and politicians were often unjust. Woodward made that point powerfully forty years ago when he felt it needed to be impressed upon a readership lulled by Southern boosterism and self-congratulation. What we needed when I wrote my book, I thought, were new ways, perhaps less familiar and direct ways, to let people reading about the South for the first time feel the shock and surprise of how deep the injustice ran—and how many people struggled in so many ways with and against that injustice.

Innovative social histories of the South have expanded the cast of characters in our stories. Mill workers, sharecroppers, dispossessed farmers, mountaineers, criminals, and apparently marginal people of all sorts now populate our histories. *Promise* attempted to carry this effort forward by including not only categories of people who had been neglected but individuals who did not fit within the categories we have constructed. Moreover, the book pursues the democratizing and inclusive efforts of social history at the same time it recognizes self-defeating behavior or miscalculations within oppressed groups. I came to believe that romanticization was patronizing, that to hold only elites accountable for the course of southern history belied our efforts to write a truly democratic history. It is this insistence, I think, that makes *Promise* look apolitical to some readers, though my intention was to make the book more fully political.

Promise was written in what I take to be the spirit of Reinhold Niebuhr, the inspiration for the "irony" in Woodward's famous series of essays that came after *Origins*. Niebuhr argued that all people are capable of both self-awareness and self-deception, are "children of light" and "children of darkness"; moral struggles are located within individuals as well as between them. I tried to evoke the way people of every sort wrestled with those forces within themselves, not only on the political stage, but in their families, in their churches, in their relations with neighbors of another skin color. Rather than merely denouncing long-dead politicians and planters, I tried to make readers feel by analogy our own complicity in social processes that are still going on, to strike notes that might resonate with our own lives. We might see ourselves reflected in those middle-class southerners and northerners who patronized the poor of both races so easily, who so easily explained injustice as the fault of rednecks and robber barons, who sneered at the music and religion loved by millions, who saw the South as a sort of alternately amusing and terrifying place, removed a convenient distance from their own lives.

Narratives such as the one I have tried to write, to be sure, are not the only kind of history we need. A southern history devoted entirely to open and ironic narratives would be no more satisfying than one tolerant only of thesis-driven, problem-addressing analyses. Fixed narratives have served us well for generations, creating powerful and stirring books; experiments with other kinds of history writing must build on and honor that literature. But, all that said, there may still be a role for histories that try to make us a bit less certain about the South we think we know so well, a place for other kinds of southern stories.

The Sound and the Fury: Woodward Thinking Back

BERTRAM WYATT-BROWN

✳

This essay, from *New York Review of Books* (1986), considers issues of style, especially as style relates to subject and political stance in all of Woodward's works. The essay is by a student who has very much gone his own way in working with modernist and postmodernist literary theory, anthropology, folklore, and post-Freudian psychology to develop a southern history of a complexity and richness inspired by his mentor, Woodward. A generational gap is obvious here, in addition to the student declaration of independence from the teacher, for Woodward stops *Thinking Back* (1986), his essay on sources and influences, exactly where Wyatt-Brown wants him to explain much more.

✳   ✳   ✳

Few other American historians living today command the respect of their colleagues that C. Vann Woodward rightfully enjoys. The Sterling Professor of History Emeritus at Yale has received all the honors that the academy can offer. He won them fairly, has taken them seriously, wears them lightly. The admiration rests not upon the substance of his work alone but also upon the manner of the man. Although *Thinking Back* is not an autobiography, it provides insight into the life of the working scholar and illuminates his approach and contribution to southern history.

With a special but also very southern gift for language, Woodward reflects in this book upon each of his major works, its origin and changing fortunes, directing his remarks to three themes, all interrelated: the ephemeral nature of historical truth; the criticism that has been made of his own work; and, most important, the discontinuity of the southern past. With the first theme, Woodward's concern is personal as well as intellectual. As the opening chapter suggests, he grew up where the rocklike verities of southern life were supposedly changeless. In Vanndale, Arkansas, his birthplace in 1908, and later in Oxford, Georgia, where his father was a college dean, few doubted the glories of the Lost Cause, the villainies of "black republicanism," or the sanctities of white superiority. Woodward does not say how he came to question local pieties. We would like to know more about those early years.

In any event, he soon lost conventional faiths and replaced them with others that were radical by southern standards. A summer visit to the Soviet Union during college at Emory, a postbaccalaureate year's study of political science at Columbia in 1932, an involvement in the defense of a persecuted Atlanta black communist, an association with the wrong crowd at Chapel Hill (so defined by Woodward's academic sponsor Howard Odum, the sociologist), and a growing involvement in his study of Tom Watson and Georgia Populism for his Ph.D. dissertation—all these formative experiences encouraged a drastic reappraisal of his homeland and its assumptions.

Today it is hard to imagine the difficulties facing the rebel against southern conformities during the years of Woodward's youth. Some failed utterly, turning to alcohol as a lonely or boisterous defiance against local hypocrisies. Other gifted thinkers, like Woodward's friend Robert Penn Warren, could turn to poetry or fiction, but few of similar talents found in the writing of history the means to deal with a region they both loved and lamented. W. J. Cash also felt the pressures of provincialism and discovered a creative voice in meeting the tensions that southern intellectuals have always had to confront, but in one work, *The Mind of the South* (1941), he may have exhausted his ideas; in any event, suicide cut short further promise.

Not yet the ironist and skeptic that he would later become, Woodward conceived his first book, *Tom Watson: Agrarian Rebel* (1938), around heresies. Research for the biography plunged him, he recalls, "into all the dark, neglected, and forbidden corners of Southern life shunned by the New South school." His scholarly contemporaries of that school pursued the theme of "progress, prosperity, peace, consensus, white solidarity, black contentment, sectional reconciliation and the overarching themes of unity, continuity, and nationalism." The young scholar dwelled almost entirely upon their opposites.

Like Woodward, Tom Watson had a solitary temperament, a sense of cause, a love of history, and unusual literary skill. He first devoted his talents to dramatic performances as a lawyer in the circuit courts, then to political insurgency. Elected in 1890 as an independent-minded north Georgia Democrat in the midst of economic depression, Watson bolted the congressional party caucus and joined the small Populist circle. The crusade of the new Populist party was then stirring beleaguered farmers in a wide arc from the northern grain belt through the Texas plains to the eastern Cotton South. Proclaiming himself a true disciple of Thomas Jefferson and of the credo of agrarian virtue, Watson united white farmers, sharecropping blacks, and industrial workers in brief, idealistic coalition against Bourbon capitalism and oligarchy. On one dramatic occasion, Woodward tells us, Watson helped to arm and organize white members of his cause to protect a black Populist campaigner threatened with lynching. The opposition was outraged at the violation of racial rules, and the incident helped to defeat Watson in the next election. Gradually, the Populist enterprise, Woodward explained, fell victim to internal squabbling, to changed economic conditions, and, chiefly, to countercampaigns by Democrats in which racism, reaction, fraud, and intimidation all had a large part.

The story was a grand one, especially for a young historian of the thirties. Woodward recalls: "It was a book *for* the 1930s and *of* the 1930s, a book for hard times and hard scrabble, when rebellion was rife and the going was rough." At a time when anti-Semitism and dictatorship dominated the news from Europe, Watson's story had other, even grimmer parallels. After 1908 or so, Woodward records, the editor of the *Jeffersonian* tragically changed from crusading Jekyll into hate-mongering Hyde, inciting the South's worst passions against Jews, socialists, Catholics, and blacks. But the nadir of Watson's moral decline was his part in the killing of Leo Frank. For two years his filthy editorials stirred fury against an Atlanta Jew falsely accused, convicted, and sentenced for the rape and murder of a white girl in his employ. With Watson's gleeful approval, a mob broke into the state prison, kidnapped Frank, hanged and mutilated him. Meantime, the governor of Georgia, in Watson's eyes a traitor for commuting Frank's death sentence, had to flee the state. With Klan support, Watson won a senate seat in 1920 and served until his death two years later. The transition from reformer to racist owed much, the biographer surmised, to Watson's twisted reaction to the defeat of Populism. The young author's interpretation would later prompt objections, but, Faulknerian in theme, the work is Faulknerian also in its quality of observation, the most brilliant American biography I have ever read.

After World War II, during which Woodward experimented with writing military history, he resumed his scholarly assault on the region's self-delusions. In *Reunion and Reaction* (1951) he explored the "Bargain of 1877," which resolved the electoral confusion of the 1876 presidential contest. The Republican, Rutherford Hayes, obtained the White House over Samuel Tilden, but only, Woodward claimed, with the surreptitious help of southern politicians who were promised home rule, nonintervention by the federal government, and assistance in channeling pork-barrel dollars southward, most especially into the floundering, largely unbuilt, transcontinental Texas and Pacific Railroad. Woodward stressed economic motives in the concealed transactions, an emphasis that critics would later claim was over-drawn. In 1951, however, the work was hailed as a masterful "detective story," and it blasted a favored southern conceit: that the counterrevolution-aries who recaptured the region from carpetbaggers, scalawags, and "nigger" rule were high-minded heroes.

In the monumental *Origins of the New South, 1877–1913* (1951), Wood-ward pursued essentially the same mission on a broader but similarly relent-less front. Powerful in its conceptions, and based on deep research, *Origins* has a subtlety of texture hard to recapture in a brief review. In a memorable section, the historian demonstrated that the Bourbons who ruled the South under Hayes, Arthur, and Cleveland were not, as long thought, paladins of clean government and economic prudence. Instead, they improved on scala-wag chicanery when they plundered state treasuries and sold the South's raw materials and convict labor to industrialist cronies for a pittance. The New South Progressives, from the largely urban and middle class, were shown to deserve credit for some civic reforms, but Woodward could not overlook their indifference to black aspiration and their smug complicity in creating and prolonging the all-white suffrage system.

Woodward's analysis projected an iconoclasm that recalled the radical economic history of Charles A. Beard, whose point of view had not often been applied to matters below the Mason-Dixon line. Woodward did so, moreover, in contradiction to prevailing trends in history writing. In the early Cold War years, some scholars, including Woodward's close friend Richard Hofstadter, had abandoned not only the economic interpretation associated with Charles Beard but also their earlier zeal for political reform. Aware of the social injustices that persisted during postwar prosperity, Woodward re-mained true to principles shaped in the New Deal decade. Most especially, he sustained an intense regard for underdogs, black and white, though within a democratic rather than a collectivist or utopian perspective. Southern to the core, Woodward was no dreamer. He had Watson's experience to remind him of human frailties and backsliding.

Thinking Back is most effective when Woodward conveys the unremitting urgency with which he learned his craft and found his mission. Yet New South conservatism was the order of the day in historical circles. In 1938, for in-stance, the editors of the prestigious *History of the South* series unenthusiast-ically selected him to write the volume on the period following Reconstruc-tion. One remarked confidentially to another, "Woodward can't write." The judgment says much about his chosen profession, one in which then—and sometimes now—dullness seemed requisite to good scholarship and good prose aroused mistrust. In these recollections, however, Woodward seldom strays from the main point: his growing recognition of the time-bound character of the search for historical truth, a factor not easily squared with the idea of mission.

Woodward's particularly absorbing and thoughtful chapter on *The Strange Career of Jim Crow* (1955) reveals his growing recognition of the historical perils of "presentism," the distorting of past events to meet current political or ideological objectives. Woodward had been invited to present a lecture series at the University of Virginia in the fall of 1954. On the previous May 17, Warren's Supreme Court ruled segregation in public education unconstitutional, but the justices had not yet mandated procedures for implementing their decision. In the "phony war" atmosphere that the interval occasioned, southerners, Woodward reasoned, might be receptive to direct assaults upon cherished convictions. He explained that black segregation and disfranchisement were relatively new mechanisms that arose early in this century in the aftermath of Populism, out of fear of its resurrection. Mouthing pieties about cleaning up rampant campaign frauds in which they themselves had participated, racist politicians had legislated grandfather clauses, eight-ballot-box laws, direct primaries, poll taxes, and literacy tests by which to strip from election rolls blacks and, by hidden or overt design, poor whites, too. With the abolitionist and carpetbag generation long since vanished, few Yankees, from federal justices to Republican ward bosses, objected. At long last, Woodward concluded, Woodrow Wilson's South really was solid and white, but the road there had been stony and rutted.

Unlike his other interpretations in New Southern history, the propositions about Jim Crow earned the author an unanticipated following that could be reckoned in the hundreds of thousands. Americans were seeking some rationale for desegregation as angry whites screamed "Never!" at frightened black schoolchildren. Each court order provoked yet another outbreak of defiance from southern governors. *Jim Crow* appealed as a tract for cooling passions, healing wounds. It offered laymen testimony that between the post-Reconstruction period and *Plessy v. Ferguson* (1896) southern whites obeyed (reluctantly) federal race statutes, accepted (ungracefully) mixing schooling at least in some experimental locations, lived (grumblingly) in close proximity to freedmen, and even appealed (gingerly) for their votes in ordinary political give-and-take. The historian seemed to predict that what had happened before could occur again with more lasting and harmonious results.

It was exhilarating for Woodward to become a national figure, to march with King at Selma and hear him pronounce *Jim Crow* the civil rights movement's "historical Bible." But he was conscious, he recalls, that he was miscast as the counselor of militants. By this point, he had tempered his earlier idealism with a mature appreciation for Niebuhrian irony. From this perspective, Woodward pointed, for instance, to the dangers arising from the arrogance of power; he urged that a true reading of the southern past with its miseries and defeats should have a sobering effect upon Cold War passions. But, while he advocated such cautionary, rational uses of history, he realized that pursuit of the subject had the disconcerting habit of becoming like Alice's nightmarish game of croquet. Independent of the writer's intention, *Jim Crow*'s readers marched off in unpredictable directions. The oversized audience, including "the truly uninformed," he observes, "often sought for the cheering and hopeful message," then shamelessly "used it as they wished." He sympathized with the aims of most who seized a phrase or quotable term from the book, but he was appalled at their disregard for context. Subsequent revisions of the work corrected overstatements, ambiguous passages, and issues of fact as later scholarship revealed them. By then, though, public interest had faded. Nonetheless, the book conceived as a "mythbuster" had produced its own myths—an ironic outcome, particularly for an ironist.

The second subject of *Thinking Back,* criticism of Woodward's own work, closely follows the first, the transiency of established historical opinion. Each of his books, as the author points out, has aroused extended disputes among scholars. With much wit and agility, Woodward overcomes the perils of pomposity, bitterness, or truculence that await the reviewer of his critics. Woodward can avoid such snares because his sense of self-deprecation never becomes self-effacement and because he has always been genuinely curious about shifts in historiography, quite apart from their bearing on his own work.

He considers the charges of his critics, using the form of a fictional trial. Courtesy and consideration for others are virtues associated with southern gentility, a much abused style whose adherents grow fewer each year, but the spirit is as much alive in these pages as in Woodward's professional and literary transactions.

Among the charges are these: he overromanticized Populism, most especially Watson's earlier sympathies for blacks and the Populists' own political virtue and racial tolerance; he underestimated southern intransigence and oppressiveness in the post-Reconstruction period; and he misconceived New South leadership in which, critics say, old planter families like Faulkner's rough-hewn Compsons, McCaslins, and Benbows figured more largely than the "new men" that Woodward likened to Snopeses. Others objected to essays or published lectures such as "The Irony of Southern History," on the grounds that they supposedly twisted the past in order to make a moral comment on a current problem. Yet, one suspects, *The Burden of Southern History* (1960) and other collections will be read for many years not only as historical documents but also as literary ones, regardless of the circumstances in which they were written. In any case the critics, some of whom were Woodward's students, raise useful questions. The wheel of historical fashion is perhaps tipping somewhat toward Woodward's emphasis on conflict and away from the historians who searched for a "consensus" among conflicting social groups, a change exemplified by the work on Populism and race by Lawrence Goodwyn, Joel Williamson, J. Morgan Kousser, and Steve Hahn.

The third theme of *Thinking Back*, the specific character of southern history, is by far the most revealing. Seeking a thread through all his work, Woodward finds a persistent stress upon what he calls regional "discontinuity." Like other memorable terms in Woodward's work, this one bears much intellectual weight. For him it means that the history of the South is a long, dismaying record of conflicts over class and color, and of deep fissures in southern experience: secession, defeat, and emancipation; Reconstruction and Bourbon Restoration; Populist revolt and a second white redemption of Jim Crowism; the "bulldozer revolution" of World War II and a second reconstruction during the 1960s. It means, too, a southern past drearier than its northern counterpart; it signifies as well a region more dissonant and diverse in character than reputation and homegrown myth would allow. Woodward's insight here is the most important contribution to southern history that he has made. The revelation of a fractured past provided a means for rescuing a dissenter tradition from the obscurity to which it had been consigned. In effect Woodward asked: Why should southerners glorify only men like Lee, Jackson, or the New South promoter Henry Grady, all of whom upheld a class and an order of traditions in need of shaking down? There were braver, more deserving figures—the young Tom Watson, for example, or the novelist George Washington Cable and the businessman Lewis Harvie Blair, both of whom spoke out for racial justice in the 1880s. Towering above all, in Woodward's judgment, was the genius Thomas Jefferson, appropriated though he was by southerners of every political persuasion.

By no means was Woodward engaged in mythologizing, a common southern habit, but rather in providing a history for the South that had a freedom from myth and a dignity forever denied it by the old parochial history. When he began, the historiography of the New South suffered from "prose so pedestrian, pages so dull, chapters so devoid of ideas, whole volumes so wrongheaded or lacking in point," Woodward recalls, that fresh blood and new aims had to reinvigorate the discipline if the South were ever to achieve a self-respect commensurate with its real meaning. Although other scholars like David Potter and David Donald were engaged in the same enterprise, Woodward's careful, complex studies were especially important in raising professional standards to new heights even as they overturned received wisdom about race, governance, and class. Given the disaster of the Depression and the new money, ideas, and growth of federal power of the postwar era, the idea of "discontinuity" made historical sense. Moreover, it provided those southerners sensitive to the urgency of change a tradition of their own. It was a remarkable achievement, a congruence of historical validity and current intellectual need.

At last, because of Woodward, the South had a genuinely tragic history. There could be no tragedy without nobility. That quality of heart, in Woodward's argument, was not to be found at Chancellorsville alone, and certainly not in the politically manipulated legends of "the Glorious Dead." The appeal of the idea of chivalry in the postwar South had obscured a different heroism, a courage found in the lonely voices of protest, speaking out in such unlikely places as the convict labor camp, the black sharecropper's church, and the Populist hall where grizzled freeholders met to air grievances. In some ways Woodward anticipated the concept of history written from the bottom up that has been popular in more recent times. But most important, he showed that an unglamorous postwar South exemplified the human condition in ways the rich and glamorous North could not. Like Faulkner's novels of Yoknapatawpha County, Woodward's history transcended regional limits and united southern history with the careworn past that has been the heritage of most of mankind.

To accent the singularity of Woodward's insight, one need only draw a contrast with the themes in Cash's *The Mind of the South*, which appeared in 1941, a contrast Woodward himself makes in the pages in which he continues his long-standing dispute with the North Carolinian's ghost. Cash, he claims, has been holding séances lately with an odd assortment of leftists and conservatives, each with a political point to make. Woodward's disagreement with Cash is rooted in philosophical and temperamental differences even though both writers aimed at the same target: the falsity of the South's self-image. The "continuatarian" Cash, as Woodward calls him, accepted the traditional concept of an unchanging South. He did so, though, to expose the region's wastefulness and essential savagery. Cash proposed that, from the landing at Jamestown to the building of Atlanta's skyscrapers, the southern pretension to aristocracy had been hollow, the intellectual culture second-rate, the tradition of dissent weak, all of which, in his unabashed dismissal of exceptions, ironies, or ambiguities, violated the spirit and sense of Woodward's approach.

In Cash's South, there were no heroes, not even Jefferson living on the famous hill; there was no golden age of the founding fathers from a liberal, almost antislavery Virginia. In Cash's judgment the nonconformist had no chance. Community opinion drove out recusants like Cash or pressed them into ugly reaction or silence—the actual outcomes, for instance, of Tom Watson and Lewis Blair. Instead, Cash peopled his world with archetypal "Josh Venables" and other rustic mediocrities of indeterminate energy, lineage, and rank. Raw and uncouth, the South lived by a wilderness code that slavery and later color prejudice helped to perpetuate. He called it the "Savage Ideal," a complicated tangle of masculine and racist impulses.

Cash's structural approach to southern ethics was no less damning of "New South" complacency than Woodward's theme. Much of what he wrote was painfully valid and memorably presented, but it had a deep flaw. Without heroes, without a sense of future possibility, without appreciation of change, Cash had fashioned a vision of a social ethic so monolithic in character that it seemed to allow only for estrangement or cynicism. It explained the southern suspicion of intellectuality, apathy about education, fear of outsiders and labor unions, reliance on family, mistrust of government and taxation, chest-thumping masculinity, and traditions of personal and mob violence, including such matters as the ritual killing of Leo Frank. But Cash's vision could not lead to action. Nor could he confer upon southern history the dignity that Woodward gave it. Those who favor him, Woodward says in effect, run that risk as well. Just as Cash ignored the dissent and dissonance that Woodward revealed, he also failed to create a usable past, just when the South was about to depart from well-trodden paths. Woodward's account of W. J. Cash here is partly a meditation on the temptations of historical despair.

Thinking Back seems to me Woodward's most felicitous book. It matches the vitality, grace, and wisdom he has brought to the rest of his writing. It should be widely read not only because the journey through the sequence of the author's works is so rewarding but also because it is, itself, a new genre with a lightness and profundity all its own. Yet it is altogether too brief. One would welcome a sequel in the form of a genuine autobiography, a detached yet personal commentary on the intellectual movements of his time. Woodward, however, closes *Thinking Back* with the common-law phrase: "Further, deponent sayeth not." Perhaps that dismissal applies only to the work at hand and is not a statement of finality. One hopes so. He has yet much to tell Americans about their past and present.

Woodward and Southern Identity

GAINES M. FOSTER

✳

Gaines M. Foster grew up in the Pee Dee region of low-country South Carolina, earned the Ph.D. from the University of North Carolina, and since 1982
has taught with distinction at Louisiana State University. Always deeply concerned with the nature of southern identity, Foster has written an important
study, *Ghosts of the Confederacy: Defeat, the Lost Cause, and the Emergence of the New South, 1865–1913* (1981), which explains the relationship
of southern identity to the loss of the Civil War. In particular, Foster has been
concerned with the effect of such an overwhelming military loss on a people
so intensely religious, especially given the prevailing Protestant assumptions
that a just God would not let a just people lose such a war. Such concerns
by their very nature have brought Foster to read Woodward early, often,
and always with great discernment. While deeply respectful of Woodward
and his works, this critic has functioned as a gently ironic critic of the gentle
ironist. In the following essay, Foster plays with old civil rights language
and with folk-religious gospel lyrics to suggest that it may well be time for
the master to lay down his own burden—in this case, that of southern
identity.

✳ ✳ ✳

They yelled for the old, crippled, age-ridden soldiers; for the flags riddled with
shot, powder-burnt, moth-eaten, but grand in the sublimity of defeat, and it must
be borne in mind that every shout was for the living and the dead of a cause long
since buried. . . . I well remember a lad not six years old who stood near me on
that memorable occasion and whose absolute abandon of enthusiasm attracted
the attention of all around. An old gentleman approached him and began to question him, but the boy found time to reply only between yells. The dialogue was
something like this: "What is your name?" "———, Ya-hoo!" "What are you?"
"A Confederate, ya-hoo!" "Who was the greatest man on earth?" "General Lee,
ya-hoo!" The old gentleman smiled, saying, "The boy has learned his lessons
well," but the boy was still yelling.

— *From a northerner's account of a Confederate
veterans' parade in 1896.*

Rarely had defeat and guilt proved so appealing. In 1960 historian C. Vann Woodward published a collection of essays, *The Burden of Southern History,* which examined certain aspects of the South's "distinctive heritage." Woodward quoted historian Arnold Toynbee on how as a young boy at the Diamond Jubilee procession in England he had believed that he and his country were "on top of the world" and had "arrived at the peak to stay there—forever! There is, of course, a thing called history, but history is something unpleasant that happens to other people." If he "had been a small boy in New York in 1897," Toynbee added, he would have "felt the same." But if he had been "a small boy in 1897 in the Southern part of the United States," he said, "I should not have felt the same; I should then have known from my parents that history has happened to my people in my part of the world." Woodward, who had also used Toynbee's observations as an epigraph for his earlier *Origins of the New South, 1877–1913,* concurred. This peculiar sense of the past, Woodward explained, emerged from the region's experience of defeat, poverty, frustration, and guilt. The rest of the United States, on the other hand, seemed blinded by what Reinhold Niebuhr, in *The Irony of American History,* described as illusions of innocence and virtue. More readily than other Americans, Woodward argued, southerners therefore should have developed "a special awareness of the ironic incongruities between moral purpose and pragmatic result, of the way in which laudable aims of idealists could be perverted to sordid purposes, and of the readiness with which high-minded ideals can be forgotten." [1]

In the 1960s the Vietnam War, for many a tragic example of the dangers of American innocence, led Woodward to doubt if southerners had developed such an awareness. The South had offered no warning about the perils of Vietnam. In fact, during much of the war a Texan served as president, a Georgian as secretary of state, and a South Carolinian as commander of American forces in Vietnam. The white South supported United States intervention in the conflict with at least as much enthusiasm as, and possibly more than, the rest of the nation. In Spartanburg, South Carolina, in 1971, an audience at an all-night gospel sing even stood for the singing of "The Battle Hymn of the Republic," the hated war hymn of the Yankee armies and virtual anthem of American innocence, because it had been dedicated to "our boys in Vietnam." Four years later, when the United States made what some considered a dishonorable peace, one veteran wanted to return to Vietnam to continue the fight under a Confederate flag.

Southern response to Vietnam, in sum, had revealed no special regional perspective on American innocence. Southerners appeared no more cognizant of the possibility of failure, no more aware that good intentions could have bad results, than were northerners or westerners. In a second edition of *The Burden,* published in 1968, Woodward speculated that one should not have expected the South to learn from its history or southern politicians not to adopt American myths when in the national arena. Roughly a decade later, Woodward reiterated his conclusion that the South had not embraced his vision of its past. The heritage of defeat, frustration, and guilt, he admitted in an essay on "The Aging of America," found expression in only a "few" of the South's "brilliant writers." Most southerners accepted national myths and therefore failed to serve the nation and themselves. "It is doubtful," Woodward concluded, with a hint that he still did not want to abandon his vision of a southern identity, "that the defeated South was ever able to make its heritage of adversity contribute substantially to its maturity and wisdom save among a few individuals." [2]

Within a few years, however, the notion of a distinctive southern view of the past crept back into Woodward's writings. In 1980 he asserted that Jimmy Carter's role in the post-Watergate era "seemed to confirm rather than expose the old American (but not Southern) heresies of exceptionalism. These included the dream of a special destiny, a faith in collective innocence, and immunity from the evils of history and from the guilt of wielding power." That same year, in a review of a book on Lyndon Johnson, Woodward argued that the notion that America "could police the world and offer it a moral example at the same time" was not something "that Johnson picked up on the banks of the Pedernales or Rusk along the Chattahoochee." [3] Other historians in the 1980s, too, still clung to the vision of a South ennobled and educated by its historical experience. Woodward's observations on southern identity had an obvious appeal for southerners. Yet long before Vietnam the Spanish-American War demonstrated that the south had not been "able to make its heritage of adversity contribute substantially to its maturity and wisdom." [4]

The lack of maturity and wisdom, or, in other words, the failure of the South to perceive the ironies of its past so clearly or interpret its experience so wisely as its brilliant writers did and Woodward wanted it to, rested in the South's interpretation of its defeat in the Civil War. If ever came a moment when the South should have appreciated Woodward's observation that nothing about its history "was conducive to the theory that the South was the darling of divine providence," it came at Appomattox. Having fought a war that their ministers assured them had been God's cause, the Confederates suffered overwhelming defeat. Southerners had to wonder why God had deserted them. A very few offered the obvious answer: God had punished them for the sin of slavery or—in a variation offered more often—for abuse of the godly institution of slavery. Others agreed that the South had displeased God but argued that it had done so through sins of dance, drink, or various other failings of personal holiness. Their accounts of these sins, however, sounded less like the fiery jeremiads of Cotton Mather than the casual comment of Claude Rains at the end of *Casablanca:* "Round up the usual suspects."

Most white southerners, even some who lamented the South's sins, turned to their faith not for judgment but for solace. They read in their Bibles and heard from their preachers the promise of God's consolation. They reminded themselves that "all things work together for good to them that love God," and this scriptural promise came to underlie the South's interpretation of history. God, most southerners believed, allowed their defeat only to ensure a greater triumph in the future. The loss of the war, in other words, did not shatter southerners' faith that the South was the darling of divine Providence. They considered defeat only a detour on the way to the South's fulfillment of God's will, not a denial of divine mission.

Even if bolstered by faith in their continued status among God's chosen, white southerners still had to face the accusations of the conquering North. Northern churches demanded a confession of the sin of slaveholding, and northern congressmen demanded an admission of the evils of secession. Although rendered defensive by the onslaught, the former Confederates admitted neither moral nor political sins. Queried by a visiting Yankee about his fears of divine judgment, one feisty southerner looked perplexed and replied that the South expected God to punish the North for its abuse of southerners. He spoke for many. Southerners, most of whom were Protestants who believed in the necessity of the admission of sin, confessed little. More important, they did not publicly enunciate any feelings of guilt over the South's role in the war. In the decades after Appomattox, in fact, individual Confederates and southern periodicals reviewed the alleged sins of morality and politics and proclaimed the South guiltless. Slavery southerners considered a moral and humane institution. Secession they believed a reasonable and legal response to northern violations of the Constitution.

While southerners easily banished any feelings of guilt, they still faced the frustration of defeat—the failure to achieve independence and preserve slavery. Yet even the sense of frustration and failure rapidly diminished. By the late 1880s the issues of the war no longer seemed terribly important. Most southerners had accepted reunion, and almost no one harbored a desire for independence. The South had replaced slavery with a system of racial separation and exploitation that proved almost as effective, though not so romantic, as slavery. Many southerners still idealized the old ways or bewailed lost wealth, of course, but most had adapted to the new order. As a result, southerners as a group no longer felt so acutely frustrated by the results of defeat, even though former Confederates still carried painful memories.

The disgrace of corporate and personal failure on the field of battle proved one of the more painful memories. In the first years after Appomattox, some of the former Confederates claimed that a reliance on such and such a strategy or a failure by some leader or another brought on defeat. A few even blamed the southern people as a whole for not supporting the cause with sufficient dedication. Before too long, however, a consensus emerged that the Confederates had not failed at all: they had only succumbed to the overpowering numbers and resources of the North. Southern soldiers, therefore, had no reason to be ashamed. They needed to feel no personal sense of failure, but rather should proudly remember their contribution to one of the world's greatest armies.

By the end of the 1880s, white southerners had created a public memory of the war that incorporated little sense of guilt, defeat, or frustration. They believed that God had not abandoned the South in defeat but had only prepared it for a higher purpose. They considered the South blameless in pressing the war and heroic in fighting it. In the decades that followed, southerners conducted a public celebration of the war, a cultural ritual of vindication, based in this interpretation of the conflict. They erected monuments in public squares to the memory of the heroism of the soldiers, joined in joyous veterans' reunions, and cheered parades of the former Confederates. At these parades a young southern boy would not have felt the painfulness or the reality of the past. Rather, he would have learned the lessons of heroism inherent in his society's interpretation of the war and would have shouted for joy. He would have developed little appreciation for the ironies of history, and, amid the revelry, he would not have paused to contemplate the way grand causes have of ending in failure.

When during the 1890s the United States began to discuss increased activism in the world, most southerners, therefore, expressed little more awareness of the possible incongruence between moral purpose and results than the boy at the parade would have. In 1891, when an incident in New Orleans generated talk of war with Italy, one Georgia Confederate veteran wired the War Department for permission, in the event of war, "to raise a company of unterrified Georgia rebels to invade Rome [sic] disperse the mafia and plant the stars and stripes on the dome of St. Peters." He hardly sounded chastened by defeat. Four years later, the South's premier expansionist, John T. Morgan, extrapolated a defense of involvement abroad from the southern interpretation of God's will for a defeated South. "If, in the history of men," the Alabama senator wrote, "a nation had been 'set apart' and qualified by long suffering for the vicarious work of bettering the conditions of the world, that nation is the people of our Southern States. We have not suffered in vain, and

we will not have to wait long for the revelation of the fact that we have supposed to redeem."[5]

In 1898 the United States did undertake a crusade to better the conditions
of part of the world, as Morgan had expected. Yet the Spanish-American
War, in which Americans sought to be active agents for good in the world,
resulted, in places, in tragic consequences. Southerners issued few warnings
and most enthusiastically joined the crusade. Before a group of Confederate
veterans, John B. Gordon, one of the region's preeminent spokesmen, celebrated the sense of American mission. He claimed that our "boys are to bear,
wrapped in the folds of the American flag, the light of American civilization
and the boon of Republican liberty to the oppressed islands of both oceans;
they are to place on a higher plane than ever before the influence of America in the councils of the nations, and are to command for their country a
broader and more enduring respect for its prowess on land and sea throughout the world." His speech revealed no appreciation of the fact that great
causes had tragic results and no awareness of any incongruities between
moral purpose and result. At a memorial service in Boston the following
year, Gordon's fellow Confederate general Joseph Wheeler joined Julia Ward
Howe in singing "The Battle Hymn of the Republic" in honor of the ongoing
crusade abroad. Christian soldiers had once more marched off in innocence
to trample out evil, and they came as readily from the South as the North.[6]

When the aftermath of the crusade for Cuban freedom brought hard
choices about imperialism, some southerners did question national policy.
Few critics, however, based their opposition on the wisdom gleaned from the
South's history, unless it was the lesson that trying to govern dark-skinned
people was unwise. No "southern position" emerged, and many southerners
supported the taking of colonies. Young southerners enthusiastically participated in the most tragic consequence of this grand crusade, a nasty guerrilla
war to suppress a nationalistic revolution in the Philippines. They helped
quell the rebels with a rebel yell and displayed no apparent appreciation of
the irony. In a letter, one even thanked a Confederate general for the example
of the soldiers of the 1860s and expressed his hope that southern troops in
the Philippines had lived up to it. Like the boy at the parade, he had learned
his lessons well. The white South's interpretation of the Civil War had not
encouraged him to question his nation's purpose but rather had led him,
like his counterpart from the North, to consider it part of a divine plan. The
celebration of the Confederacy during the decade before he went off to war
had not communicated an appreciation of tragedy or irony but instead had
glorified loyalty and martial skills.

The South's involvement in the Spanish-American War and its aftermath should have rendered its reaction to Vietnam less surprising. In both instances, white southerners responded to the nation's foreign crusades much like other Americans and not as Woodward's vision would have suggested. They did so, in part, because the South's interpretation of the Civil War contained less sense of the tragic, less acknowledgment of guilt, and less awareness of defeat and frustration than did Woodward's. His hope that southerners would challenge American innocence rested on the assumption of a special southern sense of history; yet the South's interpretation of the Civil War had helped make its view of the past less special than Woodward believed. As Richard H. King has proposed, Woodward's argument owed more to the critical consciousness of the 1930s, the work of Faulkner, Warren, and other intellectuals, than to the traditional southern interpretation of the past.[7] Not just their influence guided Woodward, though, and the forces shaping his vision may suggest something about the burden of southern historians.

Woodward's frequent and insightful use of an ironical approach has obscured the fact that *The Burden of Southern History* incorporated two different visions of what the past is and how it can speak to the present. "The Irony of Southern History," originally presented in 1952 and therefore the first of the major essays in which Woodward developed his interpretation, raised the idea of a special southern sense of the past, but the argument did not depend upon it. In the heart of the piece, Woodward held up the South's intolerant reaction to criticism of slavery in the 1830s to expose the dangers of the hysteria of the McCarthy era. Woodward then suggested that, because of the peculiar nature of the southern experience, historians might find other instances in which the history of the region would protect against the nation's obliviousness of problems or evils. He expressed the hope that southern historians would be especially active in the task of exposing American innocence but pointedly admitted that any historian could use the South's past to do so. In this essay Woodward in effect acted, and asked other historians to act, as a "moral critic," in John Higham's later phrase.[8] Woodward had created a dialogue between the reality of the past and the needs of the present. The "lessons" of history emerged out of this dialogue, out of the process of studying history.

Five years later, Woodward developed what had been a minor theme in the first piece, the South's special experience of the past, into a major interpretation of southern identity. The South's experience with defeat, poverty, frustration, and guilt, Woodward argued in "The Search for Southern Identity," constituted a special heritage "that should prove of enduring worth" to the South and the nation. When Woodward published both essays in *The Burden of Southern History,* its introduction and title expanded the idea of the special heritage's worth, which was only touched upon in "The Search." The introduction referred to the collection as a study of a distinctive southern "character," a term that implied that Woodward described not just a possible identity but an existing perception. By explicitly labeling both "The Search" and "Irony" explorations of that character, he encouraged the reader to assume that all southerners shared an appreciation for the ironies of the southern past and the dangers of American innocence. Putting *burden,* a word that did not appear anywhere in the text, in the title strongly reinforced the idea. Especially because of the dedication of the book to Robert Penn Warren, the word unintentionally evoked Warren's character, Jack Burden, and thereby suggested southerners were not only troubled by their past but called by it to act in history.[9]

The emphasis on "identity," "character," and "burden" overpowered Woodward's usual cautious understatement and his specific emphasis on the conditional. Therefore in 1960, when the book was published, Woodward offered a slightly different vision of the past than in the first of its essays published nine years before. The South's experience had become less an external reality to be studied and more an internal perception to be exercised. The wisdom from the southern past did not emerge when the historian—be he southern or not—studied the history of the South as a moral critic, but rather existed within the southern heritage—if only southerners would exercise it.[10]

The change probably had several sources. Surely the rising popularity of studies of national character and the increasing use of the term *identity* among historians during the 1950s influenced Woodward. Yet the subtle shift in emphasis may also have reflected Woodward's reaction to the civil rights struggle in the South. He responded both as a liberal reformer and as a loyal southerner—two seemingly contradictory attitudes that had always characterized his work, as David Potter has shown.[11] In the essay on southern identity, Woodward the liberal reformer continued the crusade to ease racial change that he had begun shortly before in *The Strange Career of Jim Crow.* That book attempted to remind southerners that segregation had not existed forever, so that they would be encouraged to accept an alternative. Similarly, "The Search" offered a basis for southern identity other than white supremacy, so that southerners could more easily accept its end.

At the same time that Woodward wrote as a liberal reformer, he also wrote as a southern loyalist. "The Search" explicitly worried that in the midst of economic development and racial change all sense of southern identity might disappear. Woodward feared that the "Southern heritage [had] become an old hunting jacket that one slips on comfortably at home but discards when he ventures abroad in favor of some more conventional or modish garb." Woodward's reformulation of southern identity in terms of the South's past offered a means to preserve a regional heritage no matter how much contemporary developments altered the region.

But Woodward also offered an identity that could be worn proudly in the North. He seemed as worried by the increasing northern attacks on a benighted, racist South as he was by the economic transformation of the region. The year before he published "The Search," Woodward had commented in "The Disturbed Southerner," an article not republished in *Burden,* on the tendency of southerners, as a minority, to become defensive when attacked by northerners for the mistreatment of blacks.[12] At about the same time, Woodward himself displayed a certain defensiveness in a review of Carl Rowan's description of southern race relations, *Go South to Sorrow.* "Mr. Rowan is not the first who has gone South to sorrow, nor is this his first lamentation," Woodward remarked with uncharacteristic bite. "The South has long served as the wailing wall of the national conscience."[13] Woodward's vision in *The Burden of Southern History* simply transformed the South from the wailing wall to the foundation of the national conscience. The South's moral failings and evil past became in Woodward's analysis a possible source of wisdom. Its character, forged in its special experience and understanding of the past, could offer an escape from American innocence.

In this positive identity, Woodward had unconsciously constructed a secular version of the postwar South's interpretation of the Civil War. Defensive under northern attack, white southerners had maintained that God had allowed defeat in order to prepare them for some greater purpose. Woodward's version of history also made defeat a source of mission. The experience of poverty, frustration, and defeat, Woodward argued, should have chastened and ennobled southerners. It had placed the South in a position to save, or better, had forged a southern character capable of saving, the nation from itself.

In offering such a vision, and in wanting to hold to it even after events in the 1960s made that difficult, Woodward demonstrated his loyalty to the South and his defensiveness when the region came under northern attack in the 1950s and 1960s. That so acute and severe a southern dissenter as Woodward wanted or needed to defend the South suggests that defensiveness had deeper roots in the southern heritage than an appreciation of irony or an absence of innocence. It certainly had been a greater burden for the southern historian.

The 1960s should have encouraged Woodward to lay down this burden. As the decade progressed, racial problems seemingly moved North; the South appeared less specially cursed. Americans should have come to realize that the guilt of slavery rested on both North and South, as Abraham Lincoln had pointed out in his second inaugural address, and that racism was truly an American, not just a southern, dilemma. In the wake of the moral confusion over the Vietnam War, Americans discovered guilt in the nation's history. Wallowing in guilt has its dangers, as Woodward has pointed out, but this rethinking of the past after Vietnam does suggest that, in a nation that dispossessed the Indians, fought the Philippine War, and dropped the atomic bomb, the South has no monopoly on tragedy, irony, or evil.

If the South has no monopoly on evil, then its historians have no reason to be especially defensive. They should, instead, turn their attention to serving not as defenders but as moral critics of both the South and the nation. When they do, they can find no finer examples of the approach than Woodward's *Origins of the New South* or "The Irony of Southern History." Woodward has been a most astute observer of the South's history and a most able practitioner of the art of addressing the past to the needs of the present. In letting the South's past speak to the nation's present, as Woodward admitted in "Irony," the historian need not have a drawl. And, perhaps for the historian at least, southern identity should become simply an old hunting jacket, worn at home or among strangers.

NOTES

1. Reinhold Niebuhr, *The Irony of American History* (New York: Scribner, 1952); see also idem, *The Children of Light and the Children of Darkness: A Vindication of Democracy and a Critique of Its Traditional Defence* (New York: Scribner, 1944); quoted, Woodward, *The Burden of Southern History* (Baton Rouge: Louisiana State University Press, 1960), 189. Unless otherwise noted, quotations from *Burden* are from the 1960 edition.

2. Woodward, *Burden* (1968 rev. ed.), 230–31.

3. Idem, "*Lyndon*," review of Merle Miller, *Lyndon* (New York: Putnam, 1980), *New Republic*, 1 Nov. 1980, 29–30.

4. Quoted, idem, *Burden*, 168–70.

5. Quoted, Gaines M. Foster, *Ghosts of the Confederacy: Defeat, the Lost Cause, and the Emergence of the New South, 1865–1913* (New York: Oxford University Press, 1987), 149; see also *Congressional Record*, 54th Cong., 1st sess., 6 May 1896, 5346.

6. Quoted, Foster, ibid. See also "John Tyler Morgan to Mrs. Clopton," 31 March 1895, C. C. Clay Papers, Manuscript Department, Perkins Library of Duke University; and William J. Cooper and Thomas E. Terrill, *The American South: A History* (New York: McGraw-Hill, 1991), 446–49.

7. Richard H. King, *A Southern Renaissance: The Cultural Awakening of the American South, 1930–1955* (New York: Oxford University Press, 1980). Specifically, King makes a distinction between *descriptive* irony in Woodward and *prescriptive* irony in Woodward. King observes that Woodward's complex syntax makes interpretation difficult, but that, much of the time, especially in the later essays, Woodward seems to be *prescribing* an ironic interpretation for southerners rather than claiming that most southerners so interpret their past.

8. John Higham, *Writing American History: Essays on Modern Scholarship* (Bloomington: Indiana University Press, 1970). See also idem, *History: Professional Scholarship in America* (Englewood Cliffs, N.J.: Prentice-Hall, 1965).

9. The Jack Burden character is in Robert Penn Warren, *All the King's Men* (New York: Harcourt, Brace, 1946).

10. Cf. the related formulation in King, *A Southern Renaissance.*

11. See Potter in this volume.

12. Woodward, "The Disturbed Southerners," *Current History* 32 (1957): 278–82.

13. Idem, review of Carl Thomas Rowan, *Go South to Sorrow* (New York: Random House, 1957), *Commentary* 24 (1957): 271–72.

II

One South or Many?
Places and Passages

Origins of the New South
in Retrospect

F. SHELDON HACKNEY

✳

Hackney has provided proof that student can criticize mentor, even on the issues involving Woodward's favorite people, the Populists, and even on the issues involving those for whom Woodward has professed the most sympathy, that is, the struggling farmers of both races in the backwoods countryside. Hackney, in turn president of Tulane University and later the University of Pennsylvania, eventually became head of the National Endowment for the Humanities. However, he began academic life in the teaching ranks, and his primary research there concerned the Populists and other agrarian politics at the turn of the century, especially in Alabama. His *Populism to Progressivism in Alabama* is no celebration of his mentor's party (Woodward sometimes introduces himself as "the last living Populist"), for Hackney finds that, at least in Alabama, that group, like the other politicians in the state, was more interested in gaining and holding office than in implementing reform—or even in talking much about issues. He says that they are "power-oriented," rather than "issue-oriented." The essay below he wrote in 1972, at a time when the term *Populist* was being appropriated by various left-wingers, even as it would be appropriated by various right-wingers in the 1990s.

✳   ✳   ✳

One of the facts of intellectual life that makes publishers happy and students sad is that every generation writes its own history. The elapse of more than the traditional span of two decades since the publication of *Origins of the New South* by C. Vann Woodward[1] makes it an appropriate time to wonder whether a new generation has begun to alter Woodward's masterful portrait of the South between 1877 and 1913. Of the three general sources of revisionist impulses—new information, new questions, new worldviews—all have had ample time and sufficient cause to wash away Woodward's version of the origins of the New South. Yet, given the amazing frequency with which the generational waves are now rolling over our cultural breakwaters, the remarkable thing is that there has been so little fundamental challenge to the outlines of the story established by Woodward twenty years ago.

Of one thing we may be certain at the outset. The durability of *Origins of the New South* is not a result of its ennobling and uplifting message. It is the story of the decay and decline of the aristocracy, the suffering and betrayal of the poor whites, and the rise and transformation of a middle class. It is not a happy story. The Redeemers are revealed to be as venal as the carpetbaggers. The declining aristocracy are ineffectual and money-hungry, and in the last analysis they subordinated the values of their political and social heritage in order to maintain control over the black population. The poor whites suffered from strange malignancies of racism and conspiracy-mindedness, and the rising middle class was timid and self-interested even in its reform movement. The most sympathetic characters in the whole sordid affair are those who are too powerless to be blamed for their actions.

Such a somber view differs sharply from the confident optimism exuded by the New South school of historians such as Philip Alexander Bruce, Broadus Mitchell, Paul H. Buck, and Holland Thompson.[2] Embellished by various degrees of hyperbole, their principal themes were those of sectional reconciliation and the casting off of the dead hand of the past. "Most of the real Southern colonels are dead," Holland Thompson wrote in 1919, "and the others are too busy running plantations or cotton mills to spend much time discussing genealogy, making pretty speeches, or talking about their honor. Not so many colonels are made as formerly, and one may travel far before he meets an individual who fits the popular idea of the type. He is likely to meet more men who are cold, hard, and astute, for the New South has developed some perfect specimens of the type whose natural habitat has been supposed to be Ulster or the British Midlands—religious, narrow, stubborn, and very shrewd."[3] "New South," for Thompson, meant not only this new spirit of enterprise but a desire to accept the results of the Civil War as the best thing that could have happened, to face the future without rejecting the past, and the determination to play a part in national life. "Economically," Thompson maintained, "the South has prospered in proportion as the new spirit has ruled."[4]

Thompson himself was very cautious about his claims as regards the real economic changes in the South, but he was typical of the New South historians in many other things. In accord with the interpretation of Reconstruction then dominant, that associated with the name and work of William Archibald Dunning, Thompson viewed Reconstruction as a fiasco of disorder and dishonesty. Consequently, the men who returned the South to (conservative white) home rule, the Redeemers, appeared in a favorable light.

Even though Thompson indulged in no cult of the Redeemers, he presented them as honest men, justifiably concerned about white supremacy. Their only fault, according to Thompson, was perhaps an unhealthy fixation upon maintaining low taxes to the detriment of progressive services such as good schools and good roads. Toward the irrational and ill-informed rebellion of the Populists against their natural and traditional leaders, Thompson was condescendingly tolerant. Similarly, he pictured cotton-mill operatives as content with their lot except when stirred up by malcontents and agitators, and the political conflict of the Progressive movement is largely swallowed up in Thompson's account by the general swell of a developing social consciousness that resulted in humanitarian reforms and more schools, roads, and hospitals. The South looked to the future with a sense of well-being and optimism.

Though the Black Reconstruction myth already had been subjected to effective criticism by the time Woodward wrote, the buoyant picture of the succeeding era created by the New South historians still stood. It had been deflated neither by the attacks from the right by the Agrarians nor from the left by regionalists such as Howard W. Odum and Rupert B. Vance. Thus the themes that wound their way through *Origins of the New South,* camouflaged though they were by a gently seductive prose style and by subtle qualifications, were nonetheless a radical departure, one that not only veered to the left in response to Depression-era outlooks but that recast the story of the late-nineteenth-century South. No longer could historians write as if the central conflict of the period pitted disembodied forces representing the agrarian past and the industrial future against each other. Henceforth the contending parties would be considerably more corporeal.

Phrased baldly, the thesis of *Origins of the New South* builds from the perception that, though the Civil War deflected the course of southern history and altered the nature of southern society, there was considerable continuity between the policies of the Radical Republican governments of Reconstruction and the Conservative Democratic regimes established by the Redeemers. Regardless of who was in power, railroads and other special interests continued to enjoy privileges granted by government. The final act of Redemption itself took place as part of the electoral crisis of 1876–77 when a Whiggish alliance between southern Democrats and national Republicans arranged to swap the presidency for home rule, political patronage, and internal improvements, an arrangement made possible through the good offices of that selfless public servant, Thomas A. Scott of the Pennsylvania Railroad. Railroads were the only national force strong enough to bring the warring sections and parties together.

So, Redemption was not a restoration. The old planter aristocracy was not returned to power with the Democratic party, because the party had received a large admixture of Hamiltonian-Whig-industrial elements, dynamic components that quickly rose to the top of the party. Conservative in most matters, the mésalliance that was the Democratic party was liberal in its use of fraud and violence to achieve Redemption, in its creation of a corrupt political system to maintain itself in power, and in the frequency with which its officeholders absconded with public funds. Frightening the poor whites into line with the specter of black domination, and holding planter opposition within bounds by playing upon their fear of poor-white insurgency, the Redeemers captured the slogans of white supremacy and home rule and used these banners to cloak the pursuit of their own political and economic purposes. The history of the New South period, according to this view, is largely the story of how the Redeemers ruled in a manner that was against the interests of the mass of common people.

Debunking the Redeemers was one of the most important contributions of *Origins of the New South*. In their previous incarnation, they had been seen often as heroic statesmen and, at worst, as a trifle shortsighted because of their policies of minimum government and maximum financial stringency. It is now clear that Redemption was no moral demarcation.

Nor was it an economic demarcation dividing a glorious agrarian past and a glorious industrial future, as the New South ideologues would have it. Despite their glowing rhetoric, the South had to run hard just to keep from losing ground. Over the period from 1877 to 1913, the South's percentage of the nation's manufacturing establishments and its share of capital engaged in manufacturing remained constant. Never, in fact, had the South been more distinct from the North in every measure of wealth and social well-being and never more similar in the values espoused by the leaders of the two sections. Contrary to what some previous historians had believed, according to *Origins of the New South*, high profits as well as moral fervor accounted for the growth of cotton mills in the South, a growth that began long before the 1880s date emphasized by New South historians. Contrary also to the romantic notions of Wilbur J. Cash and Broadus Mitchell, members of the new middle class were not the sons of the old planter aristocracy. More often than not they derived from families of urban merchants or men of the professions. Wherever they came from, economic history does not explain why the captains of industry were in control, because the industrial revolution simply did not happen.

The reasons for the slow rate of industrial development are not far to seek. The South's was a colonial economy. It remained overwhelmingly a region of

staple-crop agriculture and extractive industries. This meant that southerners bought almost all their manufactured goods, and not a little of their
food, from outside the region. Not only that, but southern railroads and
other establishments in the modern sector were increasingly controlled by
outside capital. Profits that might have been reinvested in southern enterprise
or might have helped to stimulate the local economy were drained off to the
North. More important, decisions affecting the economic health of the region
were made by men in northern boardrooms who had a vested interest in
maintaining it in its colonial status. Industrialization under the New South
formula hurt the South, for the Redeemers were not simply advocating industrialization, they were arguing for laissez-faire capitalism and a changed
way of life. This cultural reason could not be hidden by the nostalgic view of
the Old South created in the 1880s to dissolve the Great Recantation in the
syrup of romanticism.

Political conflict during the New South period consisted of sporadic in-
surgencies by the "wool-hat boys," frequently supported by the obsolescing
planter aristocracy, against the Redeemer coalition and its alliance with the
capitalist East. After twenty years of falling farm prices, the agrarian uprising
finally coalesced in the Populist movement and burst the bonds of the Democratic party in 1892, only to be decisively defeated in 1896 after a fatal decision to attempt fusion with the Democrats under the pennant of free silver,
held aloft by William Jennings Bryan. *Origins of the New South* presents the
Populist movement in the tradition of *The Populist Revolt* of John D. Hicks
as a rational, economic-interest political movement.[5] Contrary to Hicks, who
slighted the southern branch of Populism and the issue of race relations
within Populism, Woodward argued that Populism was stronger and more
radical in the South than in the West, and that southern Populists made a
sincere, though doomed, effort to effect a political alliance with blacks on
the basis of economic self-interest. The ingrained racist feelings of the white
Populist constituency contributed to the downfall of Populism.

As if determined not to be handicapped by the same problem, the Progressives, who inherited the mantle of reform from the Populists, aided or acqui-
esced in disfranchisement and fashioned a brand of Progressivism for whites
only. Like Progressivism outside the South, southern Progressivism was urban and middle class. Though indigenous, with tinges of picturesque leadership and sectional rhetoric, it contained all the varieties of reform thought
and action that were present on the national scene, and its leaders attacked
business and finance as vigorously as did those anywhere. The problem with
Progressivism was that it did not go far enough: "it no more fulfilled the
political aspirations and deeper needs of the mass of people than did the first

New Deal administration."[6] The Progressives carried over a strain of humanitarianism adapted from the tradition of patrician paternalism of the old ruling class. Nevertheless, the South that returned to national political power with Woodrow Wilson in 1913, after an absence of two generations, was a region very different from the South that had attempted to establish its independence in the 1860s. A new middle-class leadership had guided it back into the mainstream of American life.

If one may apply labels without implying value judgments, *Origins of the New South* is a Beardian analysis. It is concerned throughout with the cynic's question: Who is in control and what are they after? It seems to accept, at times, the dualistic worldview of the Populists and Progressives themselves, a view in which the world is an arena of conflict between two contending forces: the classes versus the masses, or business versus the people.[7] Similar views of the nature of conflict in the era of the Constitution, the early Republic, Jacksonian America, the secession crisis, Reconstruction, Progressivism, and the New Deal have been destroyed or superseded during the last twenty years of historiography. To the extent that *Origins of the New South* is a Beardian analysis—and its deviations from the Beardian analysis will concern us later—one must wonder how much of it has survived the chippings and scrapings of scholars in the 1950s and 1960s.

There has been a gratifyingly large volume of monographic literature in the field since 1951, making this appear to be a case of the general preceding the particular. This is not unusual. As David H. Fischer reminds us, "The monographs do not commonly come first and the general interpretations second. Instead some master architect—not master builder—draws a rough sketch of a pyramid in the sand, and many laborers begin to hew their stones to it. Before many are made ready, the fashion suddenly changes—pyramids are out; obelisks are in."[8] The real surprise, in this case, is that the pyramid still stands. There has been no major challenge to *Origins of the New South,* except for the demurrers registered against its interpretation of trends in race relations, which are outside the concern of this essay, and certainly there has been no new master architect to offer a different design. The excellent essays by T. Harry Williams and Dewey W. Grantham Jr., the only essays attempting a broad overview of southern politics between 1877 and 1913 to appear since the publication of *Origins of the New South,* follow the main furrows plowed by Woodward,[9] as do the most recent texts, *The South since 1865* by John S. Ezell, *The South since Appomattox* by Thomas D. Clark and Albert D. Kirwan, and *The American South* by Monroe Billington.[10] This is not to argue that the contributions to the field in the last twenty years have not been significant, for they have been. It is merely to say that they have been, for the most part, complementary and supplementary, rather than contradictory.

The contradictions within *Origins of the New South* are nevertheless heightening in several important places. One of the most striking and original contributions of Professor Woodward in this book has been his revision of the story of the Compromise of 1877, the deal by which Rutherford B. Hayes was awarded the contested presidential election of 1876 by southern forbearance in exchange for his promise to withdraw the last of the federal troops from South Carolina, Louisiana, and Florida and to appoint David M. Key to the postmaster generalship, thus bringing Reconstruction to a formal close. In a brilliant piece of detective work reported first in *Reunion and Reaction*,[11] and then more briefly in *Origins of the New South,* Woodward uncovered an economic aspect of the deal and argued that the famous Wormley House bargain was a charade masking political and economic arrangements made in more discreet ways by representatives of Hayes and Whiggish southern politicians. Among the most active of the "honest brokers" was Tom Scott, who stood to gain a federal subsidy for his faltering Texas and Pacific Railroad, a project in which southern congressmen were interested for a variety of reasons.

One of the problems with this marvelous conspiracy—which captures in microcosm the Woodward view of the economically motivated Whiggish alliance of southern Redeemers and the capitalist East behind a movie-set facade of loyalty to the Old South, white supremacy, and home rule—is that, though one can be sure the conspiracy existed and that Hayes gave his assurances through intermediaries that he would honor his end of the bargain, including "internal improvements of a national character," we do not know how committed Hayes was to specific economic aspects of the deal. Similarly, the link between the performance of the southern congressmen during the electoral crisis and the efforts of the Texas and Pacific lobby are inferential and circumstantial. After compiling a mass of evidence lending weight to the theme of persistent Whiggery, Thomas B. Alexander has expressed surprise that so few items in the Hayes papers refer to economic matters, and he suggests that, given their backgrounds, perhaps the southern congressmen would have behaved as they did in 1877 even without a conspiratorial bargain.[12] A recent biography of David M. Key by David M. Abshire, using Key papers not available to Woodward, reinforces Woodward's reconstruction of events, though Abshire understandably places more importance than does Woodward on the necessity of Key's role.[13] Despite the new evidence, however, there are still gaps filled only by inference and doubt. The problem is cast into an even murkier state by the fact that Key had not been a Whig, though his political associates had, and by Professor Alexander's researches into the identity of antebellum Whigs, which lead to the conclusion that there was little to differentiate Whig from Democratic voters except ideology.[14]

Whatever the social status of Whigs before the war, there have been some doubts expressed about Woodward's view of their role after the war. Lillian A. Pereyra's biography of James Lusk Alcorn describes a Whig who persisted by joining the Republican party, a path taken by some other Whigs in Mississippi, particularly in the early days of Reconstruction.[15] Allen W. Moger, in his thorough reexamination of Virginia political history from the Bourbons to Byrd, denies the validity of the persistent-Whiggery theme in Virginia and argues that attitudes rather than old party affiliations motivated the men in control of the Virginia Democracy. This highlights the ambiguity in Woodward's account between Whiggery as an institutional loyalty and Whiggery as an aristocratic ideology, but Professor Moger's impression is sharply contradicted in the more detailed account of Virginia politics during the Reconstruction era by Jack P. Maddex Jr.[16] According to Maddex, former Whigs accounted for approximately half of the Conservative party's leadership and, more important, the Conservative party adapted itself to postwar realities by adopting the values that had characterized the Union Whigs before the war. Even though Maddex portrays the Conservatives as forward-looking modernizers rather than as agents of the colonial power as in the Woodward account, and though he departs from Woodward in other small ways, he provides impressive confirmation of the major lines of interpretation in *Origins of the New South*.

A more substantial contradiction comes in the case of South Carolina, where the Woodward thesis does not fit. According to William J. Cooper Jr., the South Carolina Bourbons were neither former Whigs nor the agents of northern capital. Far from being new men, they were the offspring of planters. Political conflict in the Bourbon period, writes Cooper, did not take the form of class antagonism but was the outgrowth of other alignments, chiefly intrastate sectionalism.[17]

The import of Cooper's findings for the thesis of *Origins of the New South* is less clear, because South Carolina may be a special case. As Cooper himself points out, the major reason for Whiggery not to persist in postwar South Carolina politics is that there was no significant Whig party before the war. In addition, Cooper's portrait of Tillmanism as something other than a class movement supports Woodward's view of Tillman as a charlatan in his role as a radical agrarian leader.

This leaves the question of whether South Carolina Bourbonism was in fact a restoration of the antebellum planter aristocracy or whether even in

South Carolina the Civil War marked a significant interruption and redirection of the political structure. One statistical fact that historians should become aware of and attempt to explain is the dramatic shift in the occupational base of the political elite in the South between the 1850s and the 1880s. Ralph A. Wooster's painstaking quantitative studies of the power structure in the 1850s reveal that South Carolina was the most elitist of the southern states in terms of the economic status of its state officeholders.[18] Almost two-thirds of the South Carolina legislators in 1850 and in 1860 were planters or farmers, yet two-thirds of Cooper's sample of forty-three members of the postbellum elite were composed of lawyers, though the fathers of most of them had been planters. This implies a shift in the social basis of politics that is consistent with the views expressed in *Origins of the New South*. Future analyses should disclose whether Cooper is justified in taking the South Carolina Bourbons so much at their own evaluation in attributing their actions to a system of values deriving from a firm loyalty to the Old South, in attributing their defeat to rhetorical obsolescence rather than to clashes of class and economic interests, and in cleansing them of the charge of industrial quislingism by imputing innocence to the observation that "[t]he Conservatives welcomed industry to South Carolina and worked to create a favorable atmosphere for its growth."[19]

The crucial question of continuity or discontinuity across the Civil War involves more than simply the antebellum political identity of the dominant element of the postbellum Democratic party. Wilbur J. Cash, the South's foremost mythmaker, incorporated into his spellbinding evocation of the Piedmont mentality the New South propaganda's image of the planter's son becoming first a captain of cavalry and, then after the war, a captain of industry as the civilization of the Old South blended into the New South with scarcely a ripple in the social structure.[20] Woodward has dissented from this picture by implication in *Origins of the New South* and more explicitly in a recent publication.[21] William B. Hesseltine's study entitled *Confederate Leaders in the New South* takes some beginning steps toward a rigorous analysis of this problem by tracing the postwar careers of 656 Confederate officers.[22] His finding that they overwhelmingly held influential positions in society in the late nineteenth century is a welcome piece of evidence for the continuity school, but it is not a definitive answer for several reasons. We do not know much about the antebellum backgrounds of the Confederate officer corps as a group, or about the degree of political dominance of Hesseltine's sample in the postbellum years, or about the extent to which the postbellum careers of Hesseltine's leaders are a fair sample of the postbellum careers of the surviving members of the antebellum elite. One of the next steps toward an answer

to the continuity question should be a prosopographical study of the southern political elite in the 1880s. A comparison of the social origins and affiliations of the elites of the 1880s and the 1850s should tell us something about
the transformation of the South in the era of the Civil War and lead us on to
fruitful refinements of the question of continuity.

Woodward's mosaic of discontinuity includes an explication of the divided
mind of the New South in which the dual loyalties of the Redeemer appear
to be a more or less conscious exercise in Catoism. Recent histories, such
as those by Cooper and Moger, tend to take the Redeemer's professions of
loyalty to the values of the Old South civilization more seriously than does
Woodward. This is also true of Paul M. Gaston's beautiful and authoritative
intellectual analysis entitled *The New South Creed*.[23] Economic regenera-
tion, national reconciliation, and racial adjustment were the major motifs of
New South propaganda, in and around which played the idea of sectional
self-determination and even dominance. Emulating the conquerors, the New
South theorists thought, was the best way of getting rid of them. Though it is
a major contribution to our understanding of the proponents of southern
industrialization, Gaston's study is not primarily revisionist. He agrees with
the judgment that the New South theorists served the region poorly by ratio-
nalizing industrialization on the disadvantageous terms set by northern capitalists, and he reinforces the perception of discontinuity by demonstrating
how a revolutionary regime mobilizes the symbols of tradition in the service
of change.

Those who resist change generally attract much less attention from historians than those who advocate it, particularly when the advocates win, and
the South in the late nineteenth century is no exception to this rule. Clement
Eaton takes a small step toward rectifying this oversight in his Lamar lectures, published as *The Waning of the Old South Civilization, 1860–1880s*,
in which he places great emphasis upon "the tenacity of old forces and ideas
rooted in the soil of the ante-bellum South."[24] A biography of Charles Colcock Jones that is now in progress should also add to our appreciation of the
backward-looking elements in the New South.[25] That the plantation as a system of agriculture was not destroyed by the Civil War and emancipation is a
well-known fact, documented by Roger W. Shugg's study of Louisiana, reiterated by J. Carlyle Sitterson's study of the cane sugar industry, and incorporated by Woodward in *Origins of the New South*.[26] We are still in need of
detailed studies of landownership, rural mobility patterns, and local econo-
mies and politics before we can be certain as to the effects of the Civil War
upon southern social structures.

Robert L. Brandfon, in his study of the development of a rich plantation agriculture in the Yazoo-Mississippi Delta after the Civil War, contends that the postbellum planter, of whose origins we are still uncertain, differed from the antebellum planter in being conscious of the need for efficiency: "Underneath the romantic 'moonlight and magnolia' was the businesslike quest for profits."[27] Whether profit orientation was less a part of the planter's consciousness before the Civil War than after is an important topic for future scholarship,[28] but, for the present, Brandfon reminds us that the modernizers of the New South had an agricultural as well as an industrial policy. Brandfon thinks that both policies rested upon an unjustified and ultimately detrimental faith in the beneficence of outside capital, thus reinforcing the interpretive scheme of *Origins of the New South*.

In this regard Brandfon is in good company. Most of the state monographs done since 1951 reinforce much more than they revise about *Origins of the New South*. This is true of Albert D. Kirwan's narrative of Mississippi politics from 1876 to 1925 and of Allen J. Going's treatment of Alabama public life in the Bourbon period, both of which appeared soon after the publication of *Origins of the New South*.[29] Other than the deviations already discussed, Moger's account of Virginia throughout the late nineteenth century conforms to Woodward's patterns, as do those of Raymond H. Pulley on Virginia, Joseph F. Steelman on North Carolina, James S. Ferguson on Mississippi, William W. Rogers on Alabama, and William I. Hair on Louisiana.[30] Aside from the present author, who tends to see the Populists in Alabama as much more opportunistic than does Woodward,[31] the only person to directly attempt to revise a part of the story of the southern uprising has been Robert F. Durden, in *The Climax of Populism*, in which he argues, from a close examination of the evidence, that the Populists at the national convention in 1896 were not duped by a conspiratorial leadership into fusion with the Democrats.[32] Agreeing with Norman Pollack on at least this point, Durden suggests that fusion was not a desertion of principles but was logically seen by many Populists as the best next step toward general political reform. Despite the divergent results of their textual analyses, Durden and Woodward share a basic sympathy with Populism being understood as an economic interest group composed of rational but oppressed farmers. That this interpretation has probably survived the brilliant revisionist rendering of Populism fashioned by Richard Hofstadter in *The Age of Reform* can be seen in the work of Theodore Saloutos.[33]

The neglect-of-the-losers rule has also applied to the other minority party, the Republicans. Allen W. Trelease's quantitative assessment of the identity of the scalawags lends credence to the assumption of continuity among poor whites in the upland South from Unionist sentiment in 1860 to scalawag

Republicanism during Reconstruction, to Independentism during the Gilded Age, to Populism during the 1890s.[34] This progression may be traced in the various monographs covering state politics in the late nineteenth century, and particularly in Moger and Rogers of the post-1951 books. Vincent P. De Santis and Stanley P. Hirshson overlap considerably in charting the ebb and flow of national Republican policy on the Southern Question.[35] Olive Hall Shadgett's study of Republicanism in Georgia underlines the fact that national Republicans did not drop their efforts to build a southern base in 1877.[36] Successive attempts to persuade white allies from various sectors of society to join with captive black Republican votes were all wrecked on the rocks of white supremacy. Mistreated, defrauded, manipulated, and abandoned though they were, black Republicans managed to play a significant role in southern politics well into the 1890s before disfranchisement and cynical apathy ushered in the era of "post office Republicanism." We need, somehow, to gain access to the political life within the black community during the last third of the century.

With blacks relegated to unthreatening political roles, the whites were free to divide, or so the theory went. One of the unsolved, even unposed, riddles of twentieth-century southern politics is why a two-party system did not develop after disfranchisement. The absence of an opposition party, of course, did not mean the absence of conflict, because fierce conflict did occur between personal followings or through intrastate sectionalism. The question really is why there was not enough strength or persistence in the factional alignments for one or more opposition parties to emerge. State parties have usually been organized from above in response to the needs of national politics, and the Republican party certainly tried to create client organizations in the southern states in the late nineteenth century. The frequent shifts in tactics and the taboo attaching to the party of Lincoln and Grant certainly encouraged Democratic loyalty among whites, and then Solid South allegiances were frozen into place by habit and by the fact that white Republicans soon quit trying to build a strong party when they discovered the benefits of rotten-borough politics. That much of the answer is already in the literature. But when one considers that all these barriers, including an increasingly powerful black electorate, were overcome after World War II when the southern Republican party began to grow in response to the development of a heterogeneous urban culture, then one begins to suspect that there was something more than racism and habit underlying the one-party system. It may be that a homogeneity of economic interests and culture among whites was the real perpetuator of the Solid South. The argument that Democratic hegemony was supported by the voters because of the disproportionate power in national affairs accruing to long tenure rests, in fact, on the assumption that the electorate is not in conflict with the interests which such power is to serve, an assumption that has been less and less valid since the New Deal.

Woodward's intuition that the Populist period resembled the era of the New Deal was not a distorted view. Both were dominated by economic depressions and experienced a reorientation of politics in which class had an increased influence on voter decisions. Since the publication of *Origins of the New South,* however, we have been made increasingly aware of the cultural component of Populist voting. Populists derived not only from inferior economic strata but from a rural segment of society that was being left behind by advancing technology and an increasingly urban society. They were defending a rural way of life, a culture, as well as a way of earning a living. Recent scholarship on politics in nineteenth-century America emphasizes the extent to which cultural divisions, and particularly ethnic identity, rather than class, served as the basis of political divisions.[37] The implications of this are at least two: that the success of Populism was inhibited to the extent that it was a departure from the more normal cultural bases of political divisions at the time; and second, that, with the defeat of Populism and the success of disfranchisement, there were few bases of political division left in the predominantly agricultural South except personal popularity, family loyalties, intrastate sectionalism, moral questions such as Prohibition, and similar ephemeral alignments.

The result was that Progressivism in the South took place within the Democratic party. Since the publication of *Origins of the New South,* and since the path-marking essay by Arthur S. Link in 1946,[38] historians have been elaborating the idea that there was such an animal as southern Progressivism.[39] State studies, such as those by this author, Pulley, Kirwan, and Moger, have added much, and there is an extensive journal literature,[40] but biographies have played the central role in developing our knowledge of southern Progressivism. The list is long and includes: Hoke Smith by Dewey Grantham, James Stephen Hogg by Robert C. Cotner, George Washington Cable by Arlin Turner, Napoleon B. Broward by Samuel Proctor, Charles Brantley Aycock by Oliver H. Orr, Andrew Jackson Montague by William E. Larsen, Edward H. Crump of Memphis by William D. Miller, Josephus Daniels by Joseph L. Morrison, Josiah William Bailey by John R. Moore, James K. Vardaman by William F. Holmes, and Edgar Gardner Murphy by Hugh C. Bailey.[41] Together, with some perceptive comments about southern Progressivism in Robert H. Wiebe's stimulating interpretation, *The Search for Order,*[42] these works confirm the fact that the South experienced the full variety of reform, ranging from the businessman's drive for efficiency to proper middle-class concern for good government to hostility toward special economic interests, particularly toward those that were large and Yankee, to humanitarian concern for the wards of society and its weaker members. Through all of this, no one has solved the paradox of how a region so different from the rest of the nation in its history, its economic condition, and its social structure could produce a Progressive movement differing in no special sense from the national movement.

Other than a tendency to produce colorful and extravagant leaders, one of the few distinguishing traits of southern Progressivism was its sponsorship of modernization with a proviso for economic home rule. The Progressive politician's charge that there was a Yankee conspiracy to keep the South in colonial bondage, which peeks shyly from between the lines of *Origins of the New South,* has been downgraded, but not banished, during the past two decades.[43] John F. Stover's book *The Railroads of the South, 1865–1900* traces the unrelenting extension of control of northern financial interests over the southern railroad system,[44] and George W. Stocking explains the inability of Birmingham to benefit from her natural advantages in making steel by reference to the discriminatory basing-point system used by United States Steel.[45]

On the other hand, David M. Potter, in an overlooked investigation, argues that railroad rate differentials between sections existed from the earliest time, but that competition among railroads prevented appreciable territorial discrimination until after 1920, when connecting lines began to lose their independence and the Interstate Commerce Commission formalized the regional freight-rate structure of the private associations.[46]

A study by Calvin B. Hoover and Benjamin U. Ratchford, *Economic Resources and Policies of the South,* flatly states that high freight-rates were never a major barrier to the economic development of the South.[47] Much controversy surrounds the role of railroads in economic growth in the nineteenth century,[48] and, as the most powerful economic and political institutions of the period, they will continue to interest historians. Recent studies, however, have tended to focus on issues other than colonialism or to emphasize the contributions made by railroads to the development of the South.[49]

The matter on which there is the widest agreement at the present is that, contrary to the utopian visions of the New South spokesmen, no great leap or qualitative change occurred in the economy of the South until after 1940.[50] The South remained an economy of low incomes, labor-intensive enterprises, and primary industry. The question has been, why so little change in that pattern?

In addition to the possibility of a colonialist conspiracy, several answers are available. William H. Nicholls has pinned the blame on the attitudes and values of southerners themselves, in his book *Southern Traditions and Regional Progress,* a position disputed by William E. Laird and James R. Rinehart, who argue that capital stringency was the chief culprit in tying farmers to inefficient forms of agriculture and thus inhibiting industrialization.[51] Nicholls's colleague Anthony M. Tang, in an empirical investigation of development in twenty contiguous counties in the Georgia–South Carolina piedmont, avoids that particular chicken-and-egg argument by raising another one. Applying an industrial-urban matrix approach to farm income-differentials, Tang argues persuasively that the productivity of southern farmers did not keep pace with the national average because of the lack of nearby industrial developments offering markets and part-time employment. Without the flexibility that such opportunities provide, farm families are eventually unable to adapt successfully to changes in the agricultural market.[52]

The implication of this argument is that one-crop agriculture, the crop-lien system, and other malevolent institutions of the South would have collapsed as urban-industrial demands increased. Another implication is that insufficient out-migration hurt farm areas, and it may be as a hindrance to out-migration that the "passive" factor of values enters the picture, rather than, as in the Nicholls formulation, as a negative factor in entrepreneurial decisions. For instance, lacking local markets or employment opportunities in the late nineteenth century, southern farmers had the option to stay with the increasingly inadequate subsistence level of farming or migrate to the city. It is difficult to explain their unwillingness to go to cities, as European immigrants by the millions were doing, unless the standard of living on the farm was actually better or farmers preferred a lower standard of living in the country to opportunity in a strange and alien city. As to the reasons for the scarcity of urban-industrial matrices in the South, one may trace the causes back to slavery, the plantation system, the topography of the South with its excellent interior river systems, or the commercial orientations of the original settlers. That is still an open question.[53] Meanwhile, we must find out more about the history of those urban centers that did exist.

Much more work is also needed on the problem of economic development, or the lack of it, and the process of economic growth in the period from the Civil War to World War II. Given all the barriers to growth—capital destruction in the Civil War, investment opportunities elsewhere, the absence of urban centers and of a large urban middle class, low levels of education and public services, the scarcity of skilled labor, and all of the special problems faced by latecomers to the process of industrialization—it may be that historians have been asking the wrong question about growth. Nothing in the theory of regional economics would predict equilibrating capital flows, so perhaps we should not be seeking explanations for the slow rate of growth in the economy of the post–Civil War South, but rather for the fact that it kept pace at all.[54] There has been, in fact, a general convergence of per capita incomes between the South and the nation, even though it has converged by fits and starts, with a major reversal in the 1920s.[55] Furthermore, this has been accomplished despite the slow and late capital inflows from the North and despite the high rate of population growth. Any explanation must accommodate all these facts, and that is a great challenge.

Another great challenge stems from wondering about the causes for the instability of the Redeemer regimes, which were defied by independent movements and torn by factional feuds even before they suffered the Populist revolt. Barrington Moore's analysis of sporadic rural political activity in England is very suggestive, whether it is correct, in tracing the source of unrest to the destruction of communal values by the enclosure movement. For Moore, in general, the evolution from noncommercial to commercial agriculture is the underlying cause of agrarian revolution.[56] Even though this concept is not at all foreign to American historians, it points to an unexplored source of tensions in the relationship between yeoman farmer and planter, a relationship about which we do not yet know enough either before or after the Civil War, nor do we know how it was changed by the war and its associated disruptions.

The outcome of any analysis of change across the Civil War very much depends upon one's conception of antebellum society. *Origins of the New South* employs a class and sectional analysis of the postbellum period that could comfortably interlock with the model of the Old South being developed by Eugene D. Genovese. Using concepts derived from Gramsci and Marx, Genovese posits a noncapitalistic, cohesive, and self-conscious planter aristocracy whose values infuse the entire society.[57] In the sequel Woodward might have argued that the Redeemer regimes were unstable precisely because they were not based upon a popularly accepted system of values. The notables had made a much more rapid transition to capitalistic values, represented by the eastern alliance, than could the commoners, whose allegiance to old values is expressed in the desire to unite with the West. Without the controls provided by shared values, the Redeemers depended on fraud, emotional appeals to racial solidarity, and a low profile that would not excite voter opposition. But the economic crisis of the late 1880s shook loose the planter support from the Redeemer regimes and set the agrarian revolt on its course. As it gained momentum and drew more of the wool-hat set into its vortex, it spun leftward, leaving disaffected planters in its wake.

Other starting points would lead to different outcomes. Morton Rothstein has suggested the utility of considering the Old South as a dual economy, typical of developing nations.[58] Capitalistic planters, pursuing commercial profits through their links to distant markets, compose the modern sector; slaves and nonslaveholding whites who were only marginally concerned with production for the market make up the traditional sector. The linkage between the plantation, as both store and market, and the yeoman farmer completes a picture of a communal agriculture being practiced under the umbrella of an extensive commercial plantation system.[59] If this view is tenable, and there is much to recommend it, then one of the most far-reaching effects of the Civil War was to force both white and black farmers from the traditional sector into commercial agriculture, where they were unable to survive. At the same time, planters were shedding paternalistic roles to concentrate on their commercial functions. Whether one takes the cool, long view that this amounted to modernization and therefore was ultimately good, or whether one sees it as a devastating human ordeal, one result is the same: agrarian protest. Populism may have been the cry of the rural masses for the re-creation of a noncommercial community.

If historians are to place significance on the transition of poor whites from communal to commercial agriculture, we need to know a great deal more about southern agricultural communities before and after the Civil War, and we particularly need social histories of black and white tenant farmers. In the sophisticated local studies that will produce the needed knowledge, there must be a careful distinction made between "refuge farmers" and "venturing farmers," and this distinction should rest not upon the technology employed but upon the motive for farming.[60]

But until research produces new insights, the reality is that the pyramid still stands. *Origins of the New South* has survived relatively untarnished through twenty years of productive scholarship, including the eras of consensus and of the new radicalism, and remains the last of the Beardian syntheses. How can we explain this phenomenon? One possible answer is that Woodward is right about his period. Such an explanation has a certain elegance, and in this case even a plausibility, despite the notorious elusiveness of historical truth. The impeccable research that is evident in this volume has earned the respect of historians who have covered the same ground later, proving again that there is no substitute for knowing the primary sources. Nevertheless, correctness may be summarily dismissed as sufficient cause of longevity on the ground that revisionists have never been noticeably deterred by the absence of serious flaws in the body of knowledge that they wished to revise.

There is also the matter of literary grace, present in full measure in *Origins of the New South*. Frederick Jackson Turner's famous essay is a pertinent example of the lasting power of an appealing prose style. Furthermore, Woodward is adept at synthesis and an absolute genius with the carefully qualified observation, a quality that has caused some difficulty when readers have not been as careful as the writer. Having granted all these, one still feels by instinct that some additional factor is at work and that it must be linked to Woodward's essential gift, which is a gift for irony.

The most arresting irony detected by Woodward is that America's most peculiar section, set apart from the rest of the nation by the very un-American experiences of guilt, defeat, and poverty, is not at all peculiar in the context of world history. For historians who characteristically ask how a people's experience helps to explain its behavior, there is an even more profound irony to be found in the high concentration of spread-eagle patriotism in the former rebel states. It is another testimonial that suffering is not always ennobling, and another demonstration of the fierceness with which outsiders adopt the myths and pretensions of the group to which they wish to belong. The touching intensity with which Johnny Cash simultaneously celebrates Indians, convicts, God, and the American flag is but a dramatic instance of the real irony of southern history, the dual identity that is the result of a double history.

The national and the southern identities are acquiring ever more common ground. Sensitive Americans today are learning what southerners learned a hundred years ago: that defeat is possible, that suffering is real, that failure to honor moral commitments brings retribution, that the past exacts its tribute from the present, that society is a complex and not very tractable set of human relationships and needs. The world of *Origins of the New South* is, therefore, at the same time familiar and instructive. It is a world of grandiose and pious pronouncements and tawdry performances in which big people fail and little people suffer. The message that emerges from *Origins of the New South* and from the whole body of Woodward's work is that history is a burden that weighs upon the present, structuring and restricting it. This is also a major theme of William Faulkner's work, particularly of *Absalom, Absalom!, The Unvanquished,* and *The Sound and the Fury.* Though not as happy a message as the faith of the Progressive historians or as certain as that of the new radicals, it nevertheless harmonizes with some pervasive contemporary moods.

This is an age in which people attempt to find meaning in the meaninglessness of things. Historians, of course, are barred by the nature of their craft from dealing in the Absurd, or at least in the literary brand of it. Practitioners of the Absurd are engaged in dismantling appearance, eliding the boundary between illusion and reality, demonstrating the essential lack of pattern and predictability beneath our commonsense understanding of the world. Historians, on the other hand, begin with the assumption that the past is a patternless jumble of phenomena on which the historian must impose his or her own order—or one that may be found lying about. The models currently available for borrowing are not very reassuring. When one turns to our literature he finds McMurphy, Yossarian, Herzog, Portnoy, the graduate, Norwood, and a long stream of nonheroes. As Charles A. Reich contends in *The Greening of America,* the modern American feels so powerless that he is unable to conceive of a hero who can alter fate by taking action. Thus, Humphrey Bogart in *Casablanca* may be the last American hero.[61]

As the whimsical popularity of cartoon heroes implies, we have turned Carlyle upside down. When Charles Portis wrote a story of real gumption and guts, he called it *True Grit,* set it in the nineteenth century, and made it a parody of a true-life reminiscence. David Douglas Duncan's portfolio of photographs of frontline soldiers in Vietnam, for another example, is entitled *War without Heroes.*[62] The young, the mobile, and the metropolitan, having lost their sense of original sin and their belief in transcendent values, evidently find it difficult to imagine a hero. How ironic, in such a time, that we should still find compatibility in literature that documents original sin and assumes transcendent values. This springs in part from the South's old role as foil and counterpoint for national moods, but it comes in part also from the link between the nonheroic sensibility of the present and the theme in Woodward and Faulkner of the individual being bullied by fate, crushed by outside forces over which one has no control, or victimized by conspiracies of the strong. Populists and modern nonheroes have in common the fact that they are victims, yet they frequently enlist our sympathies and enlarge our vision of humanity by their willingness to struggle.

There are few heroes in *Origins of the New South,* and the few who do appear are of the tragic variety. Tom Watson is such a faulted hero, if one has compassion and empathy enough to understand him and those for whom he spoke. A hero while losing, he was transformed by defeat into a successful villain, only to be consumed by his own hatred. It is a theme worthy of William Faulkner's tragic vision of the South, a vision shared by Woodward to an extent stopping somewhat short of fatalism. *Origins of the New South* would provide a familiar context for Faulkner's characters: the decaying Sartoris family suffering for the sin of slavery, the opportunistic Compsons doomed for their materialistic rejection of the land, patrician Coldfields with enlightened racial views, poor whites like Hope Hampton who behave with honor despite racial prejudice, blacks who achieve dignity and respect like Lucas Beauchamp and Dilsey, and, of course, the Snopes tribe, filtering into the growing towns from the backcountry, taking control and losing out, transforming the South for better and worse, but always struggling.

Woodward's sensibility is both Beardian and Faulknerian, and the combination of the two is the source of the continuing appeal of *Origins of the New South*. Richard Hofstadter observed that, "[a]s practiced by mature minds, history forces us to be aware not only of complexity but of defeat and failure: it tends to deny that high sense of expectation, that hope of ultimate and glorious triumph, that sustains good combatants. There may be comfort in it still. In an age when so much of our literature is infused with nihilism, and other social disciplines are driven toward narrow positivistic inquiry, history may remain the most humanizing among the arts."[63] Woodward is certainly a humanizing historian, one who recognizes both the likelihood of failure and the necessity of struggle. It is this profound ambiguity that makes his work so interesting. Like the myth of Sisyphus, *Origins of the New South* still speaks to our condition. And who knows? Perhaps one day we will get that rock to the top of the hill. But having learned my skepticism at the master's knee, I doubt it.

NOTES

1. C. Vann Woodward, *Origins of the New South, 1877–1913*, vol. 9 of A History of the South, series eds. Wendell Holmes Stephenson and Ellis Merton Coulter (Baton Rouge: Louisiana State University Press, 1951).

2. For an intelligent brief discussion of the New South school, see Paul M. Gaston, "The New South," in *Writing Southern History: Essays in Historiography in Honor of Fletcher M. Green*, ed. Arthur Stanley Link and Rembert Wallace Patrick (Baton Rouge: Louisiana State University Press, 1965), 321–26.

3. Holland Thompson, *The New South: A Chronicle of Social and Industrial Evolution* (New Haven: Yale University Press, 1919), 203–4.

4. Ibid., 192.

5. John D. Hicks, *The Populist Revolt: A History of the Farmers' Alliance and the People's Party* (Minneapolis: University of Minnesota Press, 1931).

6. Woodward, *Origins*, 395.

7. That Charles Austin Beard's interpretation of the motivations of the makers of the Constitution was actually pluralistic is one of the points of Lee Benson's excellent analysis in his book *Turner and Beard: American Historical Writing Reconsidered* (Glencoe, Ill.: Free Press, 1960), but there are senses in which Marx was not a Marxist either. There is a rich literature on the historiography of Beardianism: Cushing Strout, *The Pragmatic Revolt in American History: Carl Becker and*

Charles Beard, Wallace Notestein essays, no. 3 (New Haven: Yale University Press, 1958); Robert A. Skotheim, *American Intellectual Histories and Historians* (Princeton: Princeton University Press, 1966); David W. Noble, *Historians against History: The Frontier Thesis and the National Covenant in American Historical Writing since 1830* (Minneapolis: University of Minnesota Press, 1965); Richard Hofstadter, *The Progressive Historians: Turner, Beard, Parrington* (New York: Knopf, 1968); Charles Crowe, "The Emergence of Progressive History," *Journal of the History of Ideas* 27 (1966): 109–24.

8. David Hackett Fischer, *Historians' Fallacies: Toward a Logic of Historical Thought* (New York: Harper & Row, 1970), 5.

9. Dewey Grantham Jr., *The Democratic South* (Athens: University of Georgia Press, 1963); and Thomas Harry Williams, *Romance and Realism in Southern Politics* (Athens: University of Georgia Press, 1961).

10. John S. Ezell, *The South since 1865* (New York: Macmillan, 1963); Thomas Dionysius Clark and Albert Dennis Kirwan, *The South since Appomattox: A Century of Regional Change* (New York: Oxford University Press, 1967); and Monroe Billington, *The American South* (New York: Scribner, 1971).

11. C. Vann Woodward, *Reunion and Reaction: The Compromise of 1877 and the End of Reconstruction* (Boston: Little, Brown, 1951).

12. Thomas B. Alexander, "Persistent Whiggery in the Confederate South, 1860–1877," *Journal of Southern History* 27 (1961): 305–29.

13. David M. Abshire, *The South Rejects a Prophet: The Life of Senator D. M. Key, 1824–1900* (foreword by Ralph McGill; New York: Praeger, 1967).

14. Thomas B. Alexander et al., "The Basis of Alabama's Ante-Bellum Two-Party System," *Alabama Review* 19 (1966): 243–76; Alexander et al., "Who Were the Alabama Whigs?" ibid., 16 (1963): 5–19; Grady McWhiney, "Were the Whigs a Class Party in Alabama?" *Journal of Southern History* 23 (1957): 510–22.

15. Lillian A. Pereyra, *James Lusk Alcorn: Persistent Whig* (Baton Rouge: Louisiana State University Press, 1966); David Herbert Donald, "The Scalawag in Mississippi Reconstruction," *Journal of Southern History* 10 (1944): 447–60; Allen W. Trelease, "Who Were the Scalawags?" ibid. 29 (1963): 445–68; William C. Harris, "A Reconsideration of the Mississippi Scalawag," *Journal of Mississippi History* 32 (1970): 3–42.

16. Allen W. Moger, *Virginia: Bourbonism to Byrd, 1870–1925* (Charlottesville: University Press of Virginia, 1968); Jack P. Maddex Jr., *The Virginia Conservatives, 1867–1879: A Study in Reconstruction Politics* (Chapel Hill: University of North Carolina Press, 1970).

17. William J. Cooper Jr., *The Conservative Regime: South Carolina, 1877–1890* (Baltimore: Johns Hopkins Press, 1968).

18. Ralph A. Wooster, *The People in Power: Courthouse and Statehouse in the Lower South, 1850–1860* (Knoxville: University of Tennessee Press, 1969).

19. Cooper, *The Conservative Regime,* 120.

20. Wilbur J. Cash, *The Mind of the South* (New York: Knopf, 1941).

21. C. Vann Woodward, "W. J. Cash Reconsidered," *New York Review of Books,* 4 Dec. 1969, 28–34.

22. William B. Hesseltine, *Confederate Leaders in the New South* (Baton Rouge: Louisiana State University Press, 1950).

23. Paul M. Gaston, *The New South Creed: A Study in Southern Mythmaking* (New York: Knopf, 1970).

24. Clement Eaton, *The Waning of the Old South Civilization, 1860–1880s,* Lamar Lecture Series (Athens: University of Georgia Press, 1968).

25. James William Berry of Princeton University studied Jones for his Ph.D. dissertation under the direction of Arthur S. Link; he covered the early years of this life story in Berry, *Growing up in the Old South: The Childhood of Charles Colcock Jones, Jr.* (Ph.D. diss., Princeton University, 1981), available University of Michigan Microfilm. See also Hugh C. Davis, "An Analysis of the Rationale of Representative Conservative Alabamians, 1874–1914" (Ph.D. diss., Vanderbilt University, 1964).

26. Roger W. Shugg, "Survival of the Plantation System in Louisiana," *Journal of Southern History* 3 (1937): 311–25; J. Carlyle Sitterson, *Sugar Country: The Cane Sugar Industry in the South, 1753–1950* (Lexington: University of Kentucky Press, 1953).

27. Robert L. Brandfon, *Cotton Kingdom of the New South: A History of the Yazoo Mississippi Delta from Reconstruction to the Twentieth Century* (Cambridge: Harvard University Press, 1967).

28. See Robert E. Gallman, "Self-Sufficiency in the Cotton Economy of the Antebellum South," *Agricultural History* 44 (1970): 5–23. This entire issue, edited by William Nelson Parker, is devoted to papers on "The Structure of the Cotton Economy of the Antebellum South" and is available in book form from the Agricultural History Society.

29. Albert Dennis Kirwan, *Revolt of the Rednecks: Mississippi Politics, 1876–1925* (Lexington: University of Kentucky Press, 1951); Allen J. Going, *Bourbon Democracy in Alabama, 1874–1890* (University: University of Alabama Press, 1951).

30. Raymond H. Pulley, *Old Virginia Restored: An Interpretation of the Progressive Impulse, 1870–1930* (Charlottesville: University Press of Virginia, 1968); Joseph F. Steelman, "The Progressive Era in North Carolina, 1884–1917" (Ph.D. diss., University of North Carolina, 1955); idem, "Vicissitudes of Republican Party Politics: The Campaign of 1892 in North Carolina," *North Carolina Historical Review* 43 (1966): 430–41; idem, "Republican Party Strategists and the Issue of Fusion with Populists in North Carolina, 1893–1894," ibid. 47 (1970): 244–69; idem, "Progressivism and Agitation for Legal Reform in North Carolina, 1897–1917," *Essays in American History* [East Carolina University] 1 (1964): 77–93; William W. Rogers, *The One-Gallused Rebellion: Agrarianism in Alabama, 1865–1896* (Baton Rouge: Louisiana State University Press, 1970); William Ivy Hair, *Bourbonism and Agrarian Protest: Louisiana Politics, 1877–1900* (Baton Rouge: Louisiana State University Press, 1969).

31. Hackney, *Populism to Progressivism.* Helen G. Edmonds, in *The Negro and*

Fusion Politics in North Carolina, 1894–1901 (Chapel Hill: University of North Carolina Press, 1951), also exposes the opportunism of the Populist racial policies, but otherwise the fusion forces appear progressive in her pages.

32. Robert F. Durden, *The Climax of Populism: The Election of 1896* (Lexington: University of Kentucky Press, 1965).

33. Richard Hofstadter, *The Age of Reform: From Bryan to F.D.R.* (1955; reprint, New York: Vintage, 1960); Theodore Saloutos, "The Professors and the Populists," *Agricultural History* 40 (1966): 235–54; and idem, *Farmer Movements in the South, 1865–1933* (Berkeley: University of California Press, 1960). For an extensive bibliography on Populism, with an introduction discussing the state of the field, see Sheldon Hackney, ed., *Populism: The Critical Issues* (Boston: Little, Brown, 1971).

34. Trelease, "Who Were the Scalawags?"

35. Vincent P. De Santis, *Republicans Face the Southern Question: The New Departure Years, 1877–1897* (Baltimore: Johns Hopkins Press, 1959); Stanley P. Hirshson, *Farewell to the Bloody Shirt: Northern Republicans and the Southern Negro, 1877–1893* (Bloomington: Indiana University Press, 1962).

36. Olive Hall Shadgett, *The Republican Party in Georgia, from Reconstruction through 1900* (Athens: University of Georgia Press, 1964).

37. Paul Kleppner, *The Cross of Culture: A Social Analysis of Midwestern Politics, 1850–1900* (New York: Free Press, 1970); Lee Benson, *The Concept of Jacksonian Democracy: New York as a Test Case* (Princeton: Princeton University Press, 1961).

38. Arthur S. Link, "The Progressive Movement in the South, 1870–1914," *North Carolina Historical Review* 23 (1946): 172–95.

39. See, for instance, Anne Firor Scott, "A Progressive Wind from the South, 1906–1913," *Journal of Southern History* 29 (1963): 53–70; Herbert J. Doherty Jr., "Voices of Protest from the New South, 1875–1910," *Mississippi Valley Historical Review* 42 (1955): 45–66; William D. Miller, *Memphis during the Progressive Era, 1900–1917* (Memphis: Memphis State University Press, 1957); and Pulley, *Old Virginia Restored.*

40. See the bibliographical essay by Dewey W. Grantham Jr., in *Writing Southern History,* ed. Link and Patrick, 410–44.

41. Dewey W. Grantham Jr., *Hoke Smith and the Politics of the New South* (Baton Rouge: Louisiana State University Press, 1958); Robert C. Cotner, *James Stephen Hogg: A Biography* (Austin: University of Texas Press, 1959); Arlin Turner, *George W. Cable: A Biography* (Durham: Duke University Press, 1956); Samuel Proctor, *Napoleon Bonaparte Broward, Florida's Fighting Democrat* (Gainesville: University of Florida Press, 1950); Oliver Hamilton Orr, *Charles Brantley Aycock* (Chapel Hill: University of North Carolina Press, 1961); William E. Larsen, *Montague of Virginia: The Making of a Southern Progressive* (Baton Rouge: Louisiana State University Press, 1965); William D. Miller, *Mr. Crump of Memphis* (Baton Rouge: Louisiana State University Press, 1964); Joseph L. Morrison, *Josephus Daniels Says . . . : An Editor's Political Odyssey from Bryan to Wilson and F.D.R., 1894–1913* (Chapel Hill: University of North Carolina Press, 1962); idem, *Josephus Daniels: The Small-d*

Democrat (Chapel Hill: University of North Carolina Press, 1966); John R. Moore, *Senator Josiah William Bailey of North Carolina: A Political Biography* (Durham: Duke University Press, 1968); William F. Holmes, *The White Chief: James Kimble Vardaman* (Baton Rouge: Louisiana State University Press, 1970); Hugh C. Bailey, *Edgar Gardner Murphy: Gentle Progressive* (Coral Gables: University of Miami Press, 1968). See also Bailey, *Liberalism in the New South: Southern Social Reformers and the Progressive Movement* (Coral Gables: University of Miami Press, 1969).

42. Robert H. Wiebe, *The Search for Order, 1877–1920* (New York: Hill & Wang, 1968).

43. Clarence H. Danhof, "Four Decades of Thought on the South's Economic Problems," in *Essays in Southern Economic Development,* ed. Melvin L. Greenhut and W. Tate Whitman (Chapel Hill: University of North Carolina Press, 1964), 7–68.

44. John F. Stover, *The Railroads of the South, 1865–1900* (Chapel Hill: University of North Carolina Press, 1955). The best monograph documenting the impact of railroads on politics is James F. Doster, *Railroads in Alabama Politics, 1875–1914* (University: University of Alabama Press, 1957).

45. George W. Stocking, *Basing Point Pricing and Regional Development: A Case Study of the Iron and Steel Industry* (Chapel Hill: University of North Carolina Press, 1954). See also Justin Fuller, "History of the Tennessee Coal, Iron, and Railroad Company, 1852–1907" (Ph.D. diss., University of North Carolina, 1966).

46. David Morris Potter, "The Historical Development of Eastern-Southern Freight Rate Relationships," *Law and Contemporary Problems* 12 (1947): 416–48.

47. Calvin B. Hoover and Benjamin U. Ratchford, *Economic Resources and Policies of the South* (New York: Macmillan, 1951).

48. See Robert William Fogel, *Railroads and American Economic Growth: Essays in Econometric History* (Baltimore: Johns Hopkins University Press, 1964); Albert Fishlow, *American Railroads and the Transformation of the Antebellum Economy* (Cambridge: Harvard University Press, 1965); and Peter D. McClelland, "Railroads, American Growth, and the New Economic History: A Critique," *Journal of Economic History* 28 (1968): 102–23.

49. Leonard P. Curry, *Rail Routes South: Louisville's Fight for the Southern Market, 1865–1872* (Lexington: University of Kentucky Press, 1969); Maury Klein, *The Great Richmond Terminal: A Study in Businessmen and Business Strategy* (Charlottesville: University Press of Virginia, 1970); and idem, "The L & N Railroad and the South, 1865–1893: A Case Study in Regional Development," address, Southern Historical Association, Louisville, 11–14 November 1970.

50. Thomas Dionysius Clark, in *The Emerging South* (New York: Oxford University Press, 1961), suggests that the crucial changes began with the failure of the cotton crop in 1921 but agrees, in his *Three Paths to the Modern South: Education, Agriculture, and Conservation* (Athens: University of Georgia Press, 1965), that no economic revolution had yet occurred in 1940. This question can be most authoritatively followed in George Brown Tindall, *The Emergence of the New South, 1913–1945,* vol. 10 of A History of the South, series ed. Wendell Holmes Stephenson and Ellis

Merton Coulter (Baton Rouge: Louisiana State University Press, 1967). Gerald D. Nash provides an informed guide to existing literature and future possibilities in "Research Opportunities in the Economic History of the South after 1880," *Journal of Southern History* 32 (1966): 308–24.

51. William H. Nicholls, *Southern Tradition and Regional Progress* (Chapel Hill: University of North Carolina Press, 1960); William E. Laird and James R. Rinehart, "Deflation, Agriculture, and Southern Development," *Agricultural History* 42 (1968): 115–24.

52. Anthony M. Tang, *Economic Development in the Southern Piedmont, 1860–1950: Its Impact on Agriculture* (Chapel Hill: University of North Carolina Press, 1958).

53. A suggestive essay on antebellum urbanization in the South is provided by Julius Rubin, "Urban Growth and Regional Development," in *The Growth of the Seaport Cities, 1790–1825*, ed. David T. Gilchrist (Charlottesville: University Press of Virginia, 1967), 3–21.

54. See, for instance, Harry W. Richardson, *Regional Economics: Location, Theory, Urban Structure and Regional Change* (London: Weidenfeld & Nicolson, 1969), 330.

55. Richard A. Easterlin, "Interregional Differences in Per Capita Income, Population, and Total Income, 1840–1950," in National Bureau of Economic Research, *Trends in the American Economy in the Nineteenth Century*, Studies in Income and Wealth, vol. 24 (Princeton: Princeton University Press, 1960), 73–140.

56. Barrington Moore Jr., *Social Origins of Dictatorship and Democracy: Lord and Peasant in the Making of the Modern World* (Boston: Beacon Press, 1966).

57. Eugene Dominick Genovese, *The Political Economy of Slavery: Studies in the Economy & Society of the Slave South* (New York: Pantheon, 1965); idem, *The World the Slaveholders Made: Two Essays in Interpretation* (New York: Pantheon, 1969).

58. Morton Rothstein, "The Antebellum South as a Dual Economy: A Tentative Hypothesis," *Agricultural History* 41 (1967): 373–82.

59. There is an extensive and illuminating literature on this unresolved set of issues. The best beginning point now is William Nelson Parker, ed., "The Structure of the Cotton Economy of the Antebellum South," *Agricultural History* 44 (1970): 1–165. See also Lewis E. Atherton, *The Southern Country Store, 1800–1860* (Baton Rouge: Louisiana State University Press, 1949); Frank Lawrence Owsley, *Plain Folk of the Old South* (Baton Rouge: Louisiana State University Press, 1949); and Fabian Linden, "Economic Democracy in the Slave South: An Appraisal of Some Recent Views," *Journal of Negro History* 31 (1946): 140–89.

60. Wayne C. Rohrer and Louis H. Douglas, *The Agrarian Transition in America: Dualism and Change* (Indianapolis: Bobbs-Merrill, 1967); Douglas C. North, "Location Theory and Regional Economic Growth," *Journal of Political Economy* 63 (1955): 243–58; John Friedmann and William Alonso, eds., *Regional Development and Planning: A Reader* (Cambridge: Massachusetts Institute of Technology Press, 1964). A step forward in the increasing sophistication of local studies is made by

George C. Rogers Jr., *The History of Georgetown County, South Carolina* (Columbia: University of South Carolina Press, 1970).

61. Charles A. Reich, *The Greening of America* (New York: Random House, 1970), 146. Reich himself is a prophetic hero of the universal variety described by Joseph Campbell in *The Hero with a Thousand Faces* (New York: Pantheon, 1949), who suffers separation, travels in the land of death overcoming obstacles, and returns to give to mankind a redemptive message providing new sources of power. But that is a different kind of hero.

62. David Douglas Duncan, *War without Heroes* (New York: Harper & Row, 1970).

63. Hofstadter, *Progressive Historians*, 466.

Redeemers Reconsidered: Change and Continuity in the Democratic South

JAMES TICE MOORE

✳

Moore, with his signal studies of Virginia published since 1974, is one of the scholars who has done most damage to Woodward's thesis of a radically New South (that is, one marked by new leaders with new ideas and, specifically, by leaders more bourgeois, with ideas more materialist, acquisitive, and aggressively industrialist-capitalist than in the days of the Old South). Moore's meticulous research in Virginia, plus his shrewd survey of monographs concerning other states, finds instead a New South elite still committed to wealth in land, still remarkably prebourgeois and occasionally even antientrepreneurial in important practices and laws, and, perhaps most interesting, still hailing from the same families of landed wealth that had dominated the Old South. Although Woodward made partial reply to Moore, subsequent studies for other southern states, especially those by Jonathan Wiener (*Social Origins of the New South: Alabama, 1860–1880*), have done much to alter the nature of the debates and discussions. Woodward changed position and thereafter maintained that the families may be the same, but their mentality is radically changed, a point that Moore disputes in the following essay.

✳   ✳   ✳

The political leaders of the post-Reconstruction South have experienced a curious fate at the hands of historians. Variously known as "Bourbons," "Redeemers," or "New Departure Democrats" (*Redeemers* is used in this essay), these men were lionized by scholars well into the twentieth century— only to suffer a sharp decline in their reputations from the 1920s to the 1950s.[1] The sources of their initial popularity are readily apparent, for they had expelled the hated carpetbag governments from the South, reestablished white supremacy on the wreckage of a defunct Radicalism, and put an end to the humiliating military occupation of the region. Reflecting this favorable climate, historians in the first four or five decades after Reconstruction rarely questioned the motives or personal integrity of the Democratic leaders. Instead, scholars generally contented themselves with eulogies on the Redeemers' Confederate war records, their heroism and sagacity in the struggles against "Negro rule," and their ties in blood and sentiment to the chivalric aristocracy of antebellum days.[2]

Occasional criticisms crept into these early analyses, to be sure; students of the period sometimes suggested that the region's Gilded Age Democrats had been too parsimonious in their spending policies and too conservative in their political outlook, too resistant to new men and new ideas.[3] Even so, historians excused these shortcomings because of the politicians' service on the battlefields and in the legislative halls. Repeatedly hailed as the heirs and equals of the patriots of 1776, the Redeemers' place in history seemed assured.[4] They were—in the eyes of scholars and public alike—the patrician saviors of their homeland, the natural leaders of the South.

This exalted image has not survived. Attacks on the post-Reconstruction leadership began to appear in the 1920s and became increasingly vitriolic for a generation. Inspired by Charles Austin Beard and other reformist historians of the Progressive Era, scholars tended to reinterpret the southern past from the perspective of the lower classes of the backwoods and farms and referred often to the region's Gilded Age dissidents—the Greenbackers, Republicans, Readjusters, and Populists who had attempted to overthrow the Democratic hegemony.[5] These historians emphasized the negative aspects of the Redeemer establishment, and an image of the Democratic elite took shape that was far different from the heroic vision of previous years.

Where an earlier generation had perceived courage, self-sacrifice, and a sincere devotion to good government, the revisionist historians of the 1930s and 1940s by and large saw only intolerance, avarice, and a shocking indifference to popular needs. Many historians examined long-forgotten Democratic financial scandals and conflicts of interest, and they attacked the Redeemers' inadequate funding for schools, asylums, and prisons.[6] Most important of all, students of the period questioned the social and economic origins of the post-Reconstruction leadership. Rejecting the previous emphasis on the Redeemers' "good blood" and patrician heritage, hostile scholars described the Democratic politicians of the 1870s and 1880s as an essentially new class of money-hungry townsmen, as upstart capitalists who had muscled their way to prominence in the turbulent post–Civil War era.[7] This revisionist trend culminated in the 1951 publication of C. Vann Woodward's *Origins of the New South,* a work that brilliantly synthesized the findings of the preceding decades.

According to Woodward, the collapse of the carpetbaggers neither restored the South's prewar leaders to office nor revitalized the region's traditional values and beliefs. The secessionist firebrands of the planter class never regained their old preeminence, and the powers of government gravitated inexorably into the hands of urban-oriented parvenus, men who had enjoyed little influence in the antebellum years. Railroad executives, corporation lawyers, and speculators of various kinds set the political tone in Professor Woodward's New South. Revisionist historians also emphasized the importance of erstwhile Whigs in the Democratic hierarchy, and Woodward exploited this theme with particular effectiveness. He insisted that probusiness Whigs monopolized public offices in the Redeemer period, displacing the old-line adherents of Jefferson and Jackson. He described a Democratic elite that allegedly ignored the farmers' demands, lavished favors on the corporate interests, and aligned itself with the northeastern capital on the great economic issues of the Gilded Age. In Woodward's opinion, therefore, the Redeemer hegemony represented fundamental, irreversible change. Parvenus presumably gained power over traditionalists, Whigs over Jacksonians, capitalists over agrarians. New men with new ideas clearly held sway in the revisionist South.[8]

Iconoclastic, even cynical in tone, this revisionist interpretation rapidly supplanted the earlier pro-Redeemer assessments. Graphic proof of this change is apparent in textbooks on southern history published from the 1950s to the 1970s. Analyses of the post-Reconstruction era in these works are often little more than paraphrases of Woodward's conclusions. Such surveys generally stress negative characteristics of the Redeemer hegemony, and their pages offer few, if any, favorable comments on the Democratic leadership.[9] In spite of its wide acceptance by historians, the revisionist appraisal, dominant for at least three decades, is now itself in need of revision. This claim is supported by the marked increase in historical research and writing on the Redeemer years since the publication of *Origins of the New South*. When Woodward and others constructed their interpretations in the 1930s and 1940s, the actual performance of the Gilded Age Democratic regimes had received little attention. Instead, scholars had been attracted to the dramatic political clashes of Reconstruction or (as in the case of the revisionists themselves) to the Populist upheavals of the 1890s. The Democratic leaders of the 1870s and 1880s were either idolized or vilified—but rarely studied—during the first half of the twentieth century. Since 1950 the Redeemer interlude has attracted considerable scholarly interest. Inspired by Woodward's provocative findings, historians have produced an array of detailed monographs about the period. Book-length studies of post-Reconstruction politics in Alabama, Louisiana, South Carolina, Tennessee, Texas, and Virginia have appeared, along with incisive articles on the other states and biographies of such prominent Redeemers as John Brown Gordon, David McKendree Key, John Henninger Reagan, and Zebulon Baird Vance.[10] This abundant new information should make possible a reassessment of the revisionist argument. Were the Democratic leaders in fact townsmen instead of farmers? Did parvenus take the place of aristocrats? Were old-line Jacksonians overshadowed by erstwhile Whigs? Did the Redeemers actually abandon antebellum traditions and favor industry and commerce at the expense of agriculture? The extent of change in the South's Gilded Age ruling class is obviously at issue, and this essay will attempt to gauge the strength of the contending forces of continuity and discontinuity, tradition and innovation.

As noted previously, revisionist scholars have concluded that the Redeemers were much more urban in occupation and attitude than were the prewar elite. Analysis of this claim suggests, however, that the evidence supporting it is too narrowly based to be conclusive. In 1922 Alex Mathews Arnett demonstrated that townsmen controlled the Georgia legislature and held almost all of the state's congressional seats in the 1870s and 1880s,[11] but subsequent investigations have offered only the most tenuous proof of similar developments elsewhere. Revisionist arguments on this point have by and large been founded more on untested assumptions and sweeping generalizations than on substantive research.[12]

C. Vann Woodward attempted to bolster the case for Redeemer urbanism, but his evidence was insufficient. Although Woodward cited examples of urban Democratic spokesmen throughout the region, including a number of governors and senators, he offered no systematic proof that these men were representative of the Redeemer leadership.[13] On the contrary, many of the pertinent statistical data support the concept of a continuing and potent agricultural influence. Publishing his findings in 1926, Francis Butler Simkins noted that farmers occupied most of the seats in South Carolina's legislature in the mid-1880s (several years before the upsurge of Tillmanite "agrarianism"), and Willie D. Halsell's 1945 analysis of Mississippi's "Bourbon" regime documented the predominance of rural lawmakers in that state as well.[14] William Best Hesseltine, in his 1950 survey of the post–Civil War careers of 656 former Confederate soldiers—men whose activities shaped the economic and political life of the Gilded Age South—acknowledged that many of these prestigious individuals pursued new opportunities in the business world, but he also showed that the percentage of agriculturalists among them increased from 20 percent in the antebellum era to almost 30 percent after the war. The number of lawyers in the group, by contrast, actually declined, further indicating that the urban ascendancy over the countryside may have been less pronounced than historians have assumed.[15] The argument that rural interests were eclipsed should be modified.

Approaching Redeemer urbanism from another direction, it is inaccurate to argue (as revisionists typically do) that the presence of a sizable group of lawyers or businessmen in a postwar southern legislature or congressional delegation constitutes prima facie evidence of a sharp break with antebellum or agrarian ideals, attitudes, or even personnel. Definitive statistical evidence on this point is lacking, but some of the "urban-oriented" Redeemer leaders may have emerged from the old plantation elite and borne its impress on their personal values and intellectual heritage. A planter or his son could move to the city and begin a new career with relative ease, but abandoning the ideological trappings of a lifetime was undoubtedly more difficult. Perhaps an even larger number of the postwar Democratic leaders lived in crossroads hamlets or courthouse towns. Although they were no longer planters, these Redeemer "urbanites" depended on rural constituencies for their livelihood and political preferment and were only little more independent of agricultural interests than the antebellum leadership had been. Such circumstances offer as great, if not greater, support for notions of continuity as for change in Gilded Age political patterns. To complicate the issue further, Ralph Ancil Wooster has demonstrated that nonfarm occupational groups, especially lawyers, were already assuming dominant governmental roles in the upper South before the Civil War and held a smaller (though sizable) number of positions in the antebellum cotton states also.[16] Developments in the 1870s and 1880s consequently represented, to some extent at least, a continuation of long-established trends. In other words, evidence concerning Redeemers' occupations does not appear adequate in and of itself to sustain the concept of a sharp break with the prewar regime.

The revisionist case for discontinuity, of course, went beyond this occupational analysis to incorporate other arguments, notably the oft-recurring theme that the Redeemer leadership comprised too many new and unfamiliar faces to constitute a "Bourbon" restoration of the antebellum ruling class. Here Professor Woodward and his compatriots touched upon an obvious truth: no full-fledged restoration of the old elite was possible in the Gilded Age. The period of war and Radical rule, lasting as long as sixteen years in some of the states, had inevitably winnowed the ranks of the traditional elite through death, old age, and disillusionment. The passage of time created vacancies in the South's power structure, naturally enough, and the Redeemers compensated for some of these losses by elevating outsiders, parvenus, and adventurers of various stripes to public office. Democrats in Florida and Virginia elected immigrants from the North (George F. Drew and Gilbert Carlton Walker, respectively) to gubernatorial terms in the 1870s, while unsettled conditions in Louisiana allowed the unscrupulous Edward A. Burke, a man of uncertain antecedents at best, a free field for his manipulations.[17] Similar accessions occurred elsewhere, weakening the aristocratic pretensions of the Democratic regimes. Even so, it is possible to carry this emphasis on the parvenu aspects of the Redeemer elite too far. Restorations of traditional ruling classes in the aftermath of wars and revolutions are rarely complete or undiluted; deaths and sociopolitical dislocations undoubtedly created opportunities for new men in the England of Charles II or the France of Louis XVIII, yet there can be no denying that restorations of a sort took place in those countries. The same is true of the Redeemer South.

In spite of the impact of the newcomers, a large number of prewar leaders successfully reasserted their influence, in many instances gaining greater power after the conflict than they had enjoyed before it. Antebellum congressman Lucius Q. C. Lamar, the author of Mississippi's ordinance of secession, won a seat in the 1870s, and Tennessee's secession governor Isham Green Harris captured a Senate post during the same decade. George S. Houston, a nine-term prewar congressman from Alabama, accomplished a similar comeback. Heading the Democratic state ticket in a bitter campaign, Houston wrested the Alabama governorship from the Republicans in 1874. Wade Hampton, one of the wealthiest planters in the United States during the slavery era, dominated South Carolina politics for more than a decade after Redemption, and erstwhile Confederate postmaster general John H. Reagan achieved national prominence as a senator from Texas in the Gilded Age. Texans manifested their loyalty to the old elite by choosing Oran Milo Roberts, the president of their state secession convention, for consecutive gubernatorial terms in 1878 and 1880. Further exemplifying this trend, former Confederate vice president Alexander Hamilton Stephens gradually rebuilt his political fortunes and won elections to the United States House of Representatives and the Georgia governorship before his death in 1883. North Carolina's Confederate governor Zebulon B. Vance captured a Senate seat in 1879, moreover, and Georgia's controversial wartime executive Joseph Emerson Brown did the same in 1880. The continuing influence of these men, and of many others like them, did not constitute anything approaching a complete restoration of the old order, but it did set a tone that lent credence to the concept of a "Bourbon" triumph in the post-Reconstruction era.[18] Once again, the case for continuity with the antebellum period is perhaps as strong as that for change.

The revisionists' stress on the emergence of new men in the Redeemer leadership appears at first glance to contradict another, more vital tenet of their interpretation—their emphasis on the continuing importance of Old Whigs in the southern Democratic regimes of the 1870s and 1880s. The Whigs had been a vigorous political force in the antebellum South, battling the Democrats on relatively even terms for a generation before the Civil War. The presence of many erstwhile Whigs in the Gilded Age Democratic ranks (their own party having collapsed in the 1850s) would seem, therefore, to provide yet another link between antebellum and postbellum days, another evidence of continuity with the past. Accentuating change, however, Woodward and like-minded scholars have contended that former Whigs not only survived into the New South era but actually achieved a dominant role in the politics of the period—successfully imposing their nationalistic, capitalistic views on their old-line Democratic rivals. This dramatic upsurge of Whigs and Whiggery, according to the Woodward appraisal, thus further differentiated the New South from the Old.

This "Old Whig" thesis, like other aspects of the revisionist interpretation, is not altogether convincing. The impact of Whig views on Redeemer economic policies will be considered later, but at this point some assessment of the extent to which the former Whigs were overrepresented in the councils of the post-Reconstruction Democracy is essential. Did Old Whigs actually receive a disproportionate share of the offices in the 1870s and 1880s? Again, few statistics are available, and conclusions involving prewar political affiliations of Redeemers must necessarily be tentative. Still, some criticisms of the revisionist appraisal are in order. For one thing, this "Old Whig" approach can be almost completely discounted with reference to Texas and South Carolina. Whigs had exerted relatively little influence in either of those states during the prewar years, and the same was true in the post-Reconstruction era.[19] The states that Woodward and others cite most often to illustrate the Whiggish character of the Redeemers—notably North Carolina and Tennessee—had been bastions of Whig strength before the war.[20] The election of many former Whigs in those states after Redemption is neither surprising nor conclusive proof that the remaining advocates of Whiggery exerted a disproportionate influence.

The notion of an aggressive, unrelenting, and uncompromising Whig takeover is also undermined by the rapid subsidence of traditional Whig-Democrat antagonisms after Reconstruction. Although Woodward described the Redeemer coalition as a "mésalliance" of natural enemies, a Whiggish hegemony where old-line Jacksonians could find no place,[21] the evidence suggests that cooperation between the groups was more typical than was conflict. Only in Tennessee did persisting antebellum party feuds seriously disrupt a Redeemer government, exacerbating disagreements over state finances at the start of the 1880s. And the outcome of this struggle appears to contradict the "Old Whig" thesis: Isham Harris's traditionalist Democrats soon gained the upper hand in the state, further impeding the Whig resurgence.[22]

Elsewhere, by contrast, a spirit of compromise, a willingness to subordinate old quarrels to new realities, generally prevailed, and the Redeemers (Old Whigs and Democrats alike) were willing to continue the Reconstruction-born practice of referring to themselves as "Conservatives"—thus deemphasizing their prewar party allegiances and stressing instead their common opposition to the so-called Radical Republicans.[23]

Pragmatic politics, to be sure, played a role in this reconciliation, but other more fundamental forces were at work, in particular the inexorable passage of time. More than twenty-five years separated the Redeemer period from the classic Whig-Democrat confrontations of the 1830s and 1840s, and the old antagonisms had lost much of their fervor. This rise of a new generation of southerners too young to have participated in the antebellum party battles helped to dilute the old rivalries. Professor Jack Pendleton Maddex Jr.'s 1970 study of the Virginia Redeemers analyzes prewar political affiliations of members of the Conservative Party Executive Committee and indicates that the influence of the Old Whigs and Democrats was roughly equal through the early 1870s. By 1873, however, the thirty-one-man group included some fourteen members with no discernible antebellum party ties at all—a circumstance Maddex attributes to the increasing influence of the younger generation in Virginia politics.[24] Studies of other states are necessary to determine whether similar developments occurred elsewhere, but there is little reason to doubt that such was the case. This trend further undermines the "Old Whig" thesis.

Professor Woodward's revisionist interpretation of Redeemer origins is itself in need of revision. City dwellers, parvenus, and persistent Whigs undoubtedly participated in Democratic politics in the 1870s and 1880s, but there is little evidence that they were numerically dominant in the party councils. Indeed, historical scholarship for the past three decades strongly supports the opposite conclusion. Recent state studies for the most part suggest that traditionalist, agriculturally oriented elites grasped the New South as firmly as they had the Old. William James Cooper provided the most forceful statement of this viewpoint in his analysis of Wade Hampton's South Carolina, but support for it can be found in other works as well. Allen Johnston Going and William Warren Rogers stressed the influence of Black Belt planters in Redeemer Alabama, and Roger L. Hart wrote about the return to power of a similar group in Tennessee at the start of the 1880s. C. Alwyn Barr Jr. emphasized the preeminence of cotton farmers, cattlemen, and other rural interests in post-Reconstruction Texas. William Ivy Hair and Edward Charles Williamson noted the continuing power of old-line "Bourbons" in Louisiana and Florida, respectively, and Willie D. Halsell documented the influence of agricultural representatives in Mississippi's Redeemer government, especially in the state legislature.[25] Jack P. Maddex Jr. broke with the prevailing trend by accentuating the capitalistic, entrepreneurial character of Virginia's ruling elite in the 1870s. But Allen Wesley Moger argued instead that antebellum attitudes and values permeated the Old Dominion's Conservative regime.[26]

These developments were paralleled in the other states. Indeed, only in the case of Georgia has the revisionist interpretation been fully sustained. In that state, according to Judson Clements Ward Jr., the corporate interests set the political tone and controlled the operations of the Democratic machine.[27] Elsewhere in the Redeemer South, by contrast, Whiggish innovators apparently continued to function as subordinate elements or junior partners—just as they had before the Civil War. Such findings necessarily point to the need for a reassessment of other aspects of the revisionist interpretation. If traditionalist groups dominated most of the post-Reconstruction Democratic regimes, it seems unlikely that those governments actually adopted the one-sidedly pro-urban and pro-industrial approach to the region's problems that Woodward describes. A new appraisal of Redeemer economic policies is, therefore, essential to a more accurate reinterpretation of the period.

Revisionist historians have devoted considerable attention to Redeemer economic programs, and, as noted previously, their findings have done little to enhance the image of the South's Democratic regimes. Exposés of pro-business bias fill their pages, and the evidence they advance to support their accusations is impressive. Seeking to attract capital investments, five of the post-Reconstruction state governments granted tax exemptions to new manufacturing enterprises.[28] Legislatures and state constitutional conventions granted monopolies to such companies as the infamous Louisiana State Lottery, and the convict-lease system provided cheap labor for ambitious entrepreneurs, especially for owners of railroads, mines, and lumber camps. Railroads in particular became prime beneficiaries of Redeemer largesse. Democratic regimes in North Carolina and Virginia sold state-owned railroad properties to private interests at bargain prices, and the governments of Texas and Florida encouraged the construction of new lines with massive grants of government land.[29] Further exploiting this Redeemer generosity, speculators purchased millions of additional acres of timber and mineral lands from the state and federal governments at extremely low prices.[30] Such developments, according to the revisionists, constituted nothing less than a southern-style "great barbecue," a wholesale plundering of the region's resources by avaricious capitalists.

This indictment of Redeemer economic policies is damning in tone and, for the most part, convincing in its main thrust. The Democratic regimes undoubtedly made numerous errors in their quest for economic growth. They squandered resources with little or no thought for the future and frequently confused private greed with public good. Even so, the revisionist argument is misleading in several significant respects. For one thing, the Woodward school employs this evidence of probusiness activity to support the concept of a radical break between New South and antebellum attitudes toward economic growth—a highly questionable assumption. Working essentially within the interpretive framework established by Charles A. Beard, the revisionists view the Redeemer program as marking the ascendancy of industry over agriculture in the region, the collapse of pre–Civil War agrarianism before the onslaughts of triumphant capitalism.

Analysis of the South's financial history suggests instead that the break with the antebellum values and policies was much less extensive than this approach implies. Land speculation was certainly no stranger to the region that had known the Yazoo frauds of the 1790s and the "flush times" of the burgeoning cotton kingdom, and southern states had made their initial railroad land grants during the prewar period. The Old South's state governments were not reticent about expending public funds to encourage the establishment of banks and the construction of turnpikes, canals, and railroads. Indeed, by 1860 the slave states had amassed debts of more than $100 million by supporting such projects. These activities established precedents that were followed on an even grander scale during Reconstruction; the conservative "Johnson" regimes and their Radical Republican successors funneled still more funds into internal improvements, boosting the region's public indebtedness to roughly a quarter of a billion dollars and creating bonanzas for unscrupulous financial manipulators.[31]

Viewed from the perspective of earlier activities, therefore, the Redeemers' aid to business was not a radical departure. In some respects, in fact, the Gilded Age Democrats were less generous toward the corporate interests than the antebellum or Reconstruction leaders had been. Direct state investments in business enterprises practically ceased after Redemption. Shocked by the extravagance of the Radical regimes, Democratic state constitutional conventions in the 1870s and 1880s uniformly banned future bond issues or public expenditures for internal improvements.[32] The Redeemers reinforced this trend by taking an even more drastic step: they repudiated more than half of the South's inflated governmental debt burden. All the states of the former Confederacy except Texas and Mississippi scaled down their debts during the period, alienating European and northern investors for decades to come and closing the door still further against additional bond issues.[33]

Instead, the Redeemers' help to business primarily took the form of the aforementioned land grants and tax incentives—methods that paled in comparison with the freewheeling cash outlays of previous years. The post-Reconstruction elite held a "barbecue" of sorts for the corporate interests, to be sure, but the fare was relatively meager and the hosts more frugal than in the past.

In addition to exaggerating the innovative character of the Redeemer program, the dominant Woodward interpretation of New South economic policies suffers from another significant defect: the revisionists' stress on Democratic favoritism toward business led them, for the most part, to neglect Redeemer attempts to exact concessions from the corporate interests, to tap their financial resources for the public benefit. The post-Reconstruction politicians' efforts along these lines are evident in their revenue policies. Railroad magnates and other businessmen made handsome profits from the convict-lease system, as noted previously, but they also had to pay hundreds of thousands of dollars into southern state treasuries each year in return for the privilege.[34] Louisiana derived $40,000 annually from lottery interests in compensation for gambling rights, and South Carolina reaped even greater profits from its abundant phosphate beds. Allowing private contractors to mine the rich deposits, the state siphoned off mineral royalties which amounted to over $250,000 a year by 1890.[35] Public-land sales, even at bargain prices, provided another source of funds for the Democratic regimes. Florida's Redeemer administration obtained $1 million from one such sale during the 1880s, while Texas officials employed half the state's land receipts to support the public school system.[36]

Revenues from these sources, however trifling by modern standards, constituted major windfalls at a time when a typical southern state's budget ranged from $1 million to $2 million a year. Carrying this approach still further, the Democratic leaders also demonstrated a willingness to exact license fees, sales taxes, and property taxes from the business community. Although liberal in their treatment of new factories and the railroads (many of which continued to enjoy tax exemptions under their original antebellum charters), the Redeemers showed much less consideration for the mercantile and professional classes. Southern legislatures imposed a bewildering variety of levies on storekeepers, insurance agents, traveling salesmen, liquor dealers, expressmen, money lenders, and other urban occupational groups.[37] The enactment of such measures suggests a significant conclusion: the Redeemers were less subservient to business than has generally been assumed. They granted important concessions, but they expected those interests to pay part of the cost of providing public services.

The Democrats' pragmatic attitude toward businessmen was also expressed in their penchant for retracting privileges they had previously bestowed. The opportunism of South Carolina politicians in this respect is particularly notable. After witnessing the rapid expansion of the state's textile industry at the start of the 1880s, the Redeemers in 1885 repealed the tax exemption for new factories. Tax incentives in South Carolina rapidly gave way to tax levies.[38] Southern Democrats also retreated from favoritism toward the railroads, especially after many of the lines fell under the control of Wall Street financiers during the depression of the 1870s. This northern takeover reignited old sectional antagonisms, and antirailroad sentiment surged through the former Confederacy. Responding to this unrest, Redeemer legislatures passed laws requiring the rail corporations to maintain adequate deposits, to fence their rights-of-way, and to compensate farmers for livestock killed by trains.[39] Democratic regimes in Arkansas and Florida manifested the new hostility by defeating the rail lines in the courtroom, enabling them to raise the tax assessments on railroad property early in the 1880s—in the Florida case, abolishing tax exemptions granted in 1855.[40] Most important of all, the Redeemers joined with western politicians in pioneering the practice of governmental railroad regulation. Between 1877 and 1891, all the states of the former Confederacy except Arkansas and Louisiana established regulatory commissions of one sort or another. Significant rate cuts ensued, even though the commissions were frequently hampered by corporate intransigence and judicial conservatism.[41] Not satisfied with these efforts, the region's Democrats played prominent roles in the struggle for federal railroad regulation as well. Texas senator John H. Reagan led the fight to establish the Interstate Commerce Commission, and Alabama Redeemer Walter Lawrence Bragg, another champion of the regulatory cause, served as one of the original members of the new agency.[42]

Paralleling these developments, moreover, Democratic attitudes toward the public lands underwent a similar transformation. Eager for economic growth, southerners had generally favored liberal land policies at the start of the Redeemer era. Northern lumber interests had bought timber tracts in the South in order to forestall potential competition, and other capitalists had purchased large acreages for purely speculative purposes, making no immediate effort to promote the region's prosperity. Misgivings arose about the land boom, and in 1888 southern congressmen led a successful movement to suspend cash sales of federal land, a maneuver that paved the way for reorganization of the entire public-land system along conservationist lines.[43] Two Redeemers in Grover Cleveland's cabinet also worked to improve the management of natural resources. Secretary of the Interior Lucius Q. C. Lamar of Mississippi and Attorney General Augustus Hill Garland of Arkansas took action against illegal encroachments on the federal domain, and together they expelled speculators, ranchers, and railroads from an estimated 45,000,000 acres in the South and West.[44] In land policies as well as railroad regulations, therefore, southern Democrats manifested an increasingly sophisticated attitude toward Gilded Age capitalism. Skepticism gradually supplanted gullibility; restrictions accompanied and sometimes overshadowed concessions.

Abounding in such ambiguities, the Redeemer economic program offered uncertain and tenuous encouragement for the entrepreneurial classes. Indeed, a case can be made that the Democratic elite provided more consistent and reliable support for farmers than for businessmen. Gathering most of their electoral strength from the countryside, Redeemer politicians generally reflected agrarian biases on such issues as debt scaling and railroad regulation, and their tax policies followed a similar pattern. As noted previously, they veered from one direction to another in their revenue demands on business. But they pursued a much more uniform and straightforward course with reference to property taxes—the exactions that fell most heavily on rural areas. Appalled by the high property levies of the Reconstruction years, Democratic leaders moved in the 1870s and 1880s to prevent the recurrence of such abuses. They wrote strict limits on property taxes into their state constitutions, severely curtailing the revenue-gathering authority of local as well as state governments.[45] Southern legislatures accelerated this trend with numerous tax cuts, and the results were impressive. Mississippi set the pace for the entire region by slashing its state property levy from 14 mills to 2.5 mills in 1892, a reduction of more than 80 percent. Alabama's less drastic adjustment from 7.5 mills in 1874 to 4 mills in 1889 was more typical, but substantial reductions occurred in state after state.[46] These cuts, together with the South's traditionally low assessment of property values, offered massive tax savings for the agricultural population. The impact of these reforms was readily apparent, for millions of acres that had been forfeited for delinquent taxes during Reconstruction were reclaimed by farmers in the Redeemer era.[47]

Applying political pressure through the Grange and Alliance, the rural interests derived many additional benefits from the Democratic regimes. Agricultural and mechanical colleges received increased funding, and the Redeemers established land-grant colleges in the Carolinas, Mississippi, and Virginia.[48] Government-supported agricultural experiment stations proliferated as well. North Carolina pioneered the development of experimental farms in the 1870s, setting a pattern that the rest of the South followed during the next decade.[49] Democratic legislatures provided another recognition of the farmers' importance by creating state departments of agriculture. Although hampered by inadequate budgets, these new agencies became increasingly innovative and efficient. By the 1880s, state agriculture departments were inspecting commercial fertilizers, analyzing soil samples, conducting geological surveys, encouraging immigration, providing veterinary services, dispatching speakers to farm meetings, and collecting statistics on crop yields.[50] In Alabama the Department of Agriculture eventually became the second most powerful agency in the state, enjoying an influence exceeded only by that of the governor.[51]

Southern Democrats also demonstrated their support for farmers by sponsoring agricultural societies. Legislatures appropriated thousands of dollars each year to subsidize these groups (primarily to enable them to hold state fairs).[52] Further belying the notion of the Redeemers' indifference to rural needs, the region's legislators passed hundreds of laws regarding the croplien system, the maintenance of fences and roads, and the conservation of fish and wildlife—all issues of concern to farm areas.[53] These activities reflected an essential fact: the agriculturalists still constituted the most important interest group in the South, and they received due consideration from the Democratic elite.

The Redeemers' favoritism toward farmers also influenced developments at the national level, undermining another facet of the revisionist interpretation. According to Professor Woodward, investment-hungry southern congressmen generally subordinated the needs of their section and its people to the demands of the capitalistic, conservative Northeast. If this in fact was the case, the Democratic leaders manifested their subservience in an extremely curious way—by opposing the northern business interests on almost all the great economic issues of the Gilded Age. Southern crusades for federal railroad legislation and the conservation of the public domain have been noted previously, but the Redeemers assumed anticorporate stands in other national controversies as well. The great majority of the region's political leaders denounced protective tariffs and for decades battled to reinstitute the low duties of the antebellum years. Gaining particular prominence in these struggles, newspaper editor Henry Watterson of Kentucky, together with Senator Lamar of Mississippi, formulated the famous "tariff for revenue only" pledge in the 1880 Democratic platform, and House Ways and Means Chairman Roger Quarles Mills of Texas led the unsuccessful congressional fight for tariff reform in 1888.[54]

Other aspects of the federal revenue system sparked additional Redeemer criticisms during the 1870s and 1880s. Although they clamored for the repeal of the punitive, war-inspired excises on whiskey and tobacco, most southern Democrats favored the reimposition of the federal income tax, a levy that would fall most heavily on the capitalists of the North.[55] The Redeemers displayed a similar bias in their approach to the perennially troublesome "money question." Responding to the appeals of the debt-laden agricultural and commercial classes, the South's political leaders (with a relative handful of exceptions) consistently endorsed proposals for an expanded currency supply. Two-thirds of the Redeemer congressmen flirted with the Greenback movement by voting for the controversial "Inflation Bill" in 1874, and Democratic state conventions throughout the former Confederacy endorsed the paper-money craze later in the decade. Silver coinage received even greater support. The region's Democratic senators and representatives joined with western lawmakers to pass the Bland-Allison Act in 1878 and the Sherman Silver Purchase Act in 1890. Alienated by Grover Cleveland' insistence on the gold standard, southern politicians carried their inflation campaign still further; they aligned themselves with the silverite West to back William Jennings Bryan's abortive presidential bid in 1896.[56]

The Redeemers' commitment to an increased money supply also led them to criticize the restrictive policies of the national banking system. They opposed the rechartering of many of the national banks in the 1880s, and they urged the repeal of the federal government's prohibitive tax on state banknotes.[57] Far from endorsing the Hamiltonian financial structure that had emerged during the Civil War, as revisionist historians have maintained, the southern Democrats were instead among the most persistent critics of that structure. Only with reference to federal aid to internal improvements did they find themselves in harmony with the prevailing system. Having witnessed the destruction of their ports, railroads, and levees by federal power during the war years, southerners requested federal money for rebuilding them. Even on this issue, surprisingly enough, the Redeemers' stand placed them in opposition to northern sentiment. Northeastern congressmen—Democrats and Republicans alike—had turned against government-financed internal improvements after the scandals of the Grant era, and the southerners were able to vote the funds for their projects only with the help of the West.[58] On issue after issue, therefore, the Redeemers took sides against, not with, the masters of capital.

These national developments, together with similar trends at the state level, clearly point up inadequacies in the revisionist interpretation of Redeemer origins and views. Parvenus, urbanites, and persistent Whigs made their way into the Democratic leadership during the post–Civil War years, as

Woodward and others have argued, but these potentially innovative groups proved either unable or unwilling to alter the entrenched patterns of southern government. Traditionalist forces enjoyed too much strength in both the electorate and the party hierarchy to permit any wholesale departure from established practices and policies. As a result, the southern Democrats neither abandoned the farmers nor embraced Whiggery in the aftermath of Reconstruction. Indeed, their economic programs were more congruent with the ideals of Jefferson, Jackson, or even Calhoun than with those of Clay or Webster. Although they promoted limited industrial growth, the Redeemers continued to acknowledge and reward the primacy of agriculture in their region's life. Although they accepted the defeat of secession and the collapse of the slave system, most of them also continued to regard the capitalistic North with a deep-seated antagonism. Recognizing political realities (in particular the need to win the electoral votes of New York and other key states), southern Democrats cast their presidential ballots for northeastern candidates such as Samuel Jones Tilden and Grover Cleveland in the 1870s and 1880s—just as they had voted for northerners Franklin Pierce and James Buchanan before the war. In the decisive economic clashes of the Gilded Age, however, the Redeemer South consistently joined forces with the other great agricultural section of the United States, the West. Such facts lend further support to the notion of continuity between the Old and New Souths. All things had not changed with Appomattox, much less with the Compromise of 1877.

NOTES

1. Insight into these historiographical trends is provided by Dewey W. Grantham Jr., "The Southern Bourbons Revisited," *South Atlantic Quarterly* 60 (1961): 286–95; and George Brown Tindall, *The Persistent Tradition in New South Politics* (Baton Rouge: Louisiana State University Press, 1975), 8–13.

2. These laudatory tendencies are apparent in Hilary A. Herbert et al., *Why the Solid South? Or, Reconstruction and Its Results* (Baltimore: R. H. Woodward, 1890); Claude G. Bowers, *The Tragic Era: The Revolution after Lincoln* (Cambridge: Houghton Mifflin, 1929); Philip Alexander Bruce, *The Rise of the New South* (Philadelphia: G. Barrie & Sons, 1905), 440; Holland Thompson, *The New South: A Chronicle of Social and Industrial Evolution* (New Haven: Yale University Press, 1920), 12–13, 25; William Watts Ball, *The State That Forgot: South Carolina's Surrender to Democracy* (Indianapolis: Bobbs-Merrill, 1932), 59, 150, 170, 183–84, 207; William Alexander Percy, *Lanterns on the Levee: Recollections of a Planter's Son* (New York: Knopf, 1941), 62–74.

3. Walter Lynwood Fleming, *The Sequel of Appomattox: A Chronicle of the Reunion of the States* (New Haven: Yale University Press, 1920), 280–81, 302; Albert

Burton Moore, *History of Alabama and Her People,* 3 vols. (Chicago: American Historical Society, 1927), 1:646, 656; Joseph Gregoire de Roulhac Hamilton, *North Carolina since Reconstruction* (New York: Columbia University Press, 1914), 169, 214, 218; Thompson, *New South,* 26, 46–47.

4. For examples of analogies drawn between the Redeemers and the American Revolutionaries, see Edward Laight Wells, *Hampton and Reconstruction* (Columbia, S.C.: The State Co., 1907), 108–9; David Duncan Wallace, *The History of South Carolina,* 4 vols. (Chicago: American Historical Society, 1934), 3:313; Alfred Brockenbrough Williams, *Hampton and His Red Shirts: South Carolina's Deliverance in 1876* (Charleston: Walker, Evans & Cogswell, 1935), 41; and John Gould Fletcher, *Arkansas* (Chapel Hill: University of North Carolina Press, 1947), 264.

5. Between 1917 and 1955 historians published books concerning Gilded Age agrarian unrest in Georgia, Mississippi, South Carolina, Tennessee, Texas, and Virginia; and biographies of such prominent anti-Redeemer dissidents as Thomas Edward Watson, Benjamin Ryan Tillman, William Mahone, and Leonidas La Fayette Polk appeared during the same period. These years also witnessed the publication of articles that probed the activities of Greenbackers, Republicans, and anti-Redeemer "Independents" in Alabama, Florida, Georgia, Mississippi, North Carolina, South Carolina, and Texas. For a full treatment of this historiographical trend, see Allen J. Going, "The Agrarian Revolt," in *Writing Southern History: Essays in Historiography in Honor of Fletcher M. Green,* ed. Arthur Stanley Link and Rembert W. Patrick (Baton Rouge: Louisiana State University Press, 1965), 362–82.

6. For examples of these exposés, see Fletcher M. Green, "Some Aspects of the Convict Lease System in the Southern States," in Fletcher M. Green, ed., *Essays in Southern History Presented to Joseph Gregoire de Roulhac Hamilton . . .* (Chapel Hill: University of North Carolina Press, 1949), 112–23; Allen W. Moger, "Railroad Practices and Policies in Virginia after the Civil War," *Virginia Magazine of History and Biography* 59 (1951): 423–57; Garnie William McGinty, *Louisiana Redeemed: The Overthrow of Carpet-bag Rule, 1876–1880* (New Orleans: Pelican Press, 1941), 125, 138, 142, 146, 203, 228–33, 247–48; C. Vann Woodward, *Tom Watson: Agrarian Rebel* (New York: Macmillan, 1938), 52–72; William Arthur Sheppard, *Red Shirts Remembered: Southern Brigadiers of the Reconstruction Period,* ltd. ed. (Spartanburg, S.C.: author's printing, 1940), 231, 246–47, 253–54, 291, 315–16.

7. Alex Mathews Arnett, *The Populist Movement in Georgia: A View of the "Agrarian Crusade" in the Light of Solid-South Politics,* Studies in History, Economics, and Public Law, vol. 4, no. 1 (New York: Columbia University Press, 1922), 23, 32–33; Albert Dennis Kirwan, *Revolt of the Rednecks: Mississippi Politics, 1876–1925* (Lexington: University Press of Kentucky, 1951), 3, 8–9; Woodward, *Tom Watson,* 65; William D. Sheldon, *Populism in the Old Dominion: Virginia Farm Politics, 1885–1900* (Princeton: Princeton University Press, 1935), 60; Charles C. Pearson, *The Readjuster Movement in Virginia* (New Haven: Yale University Press, 1917), 23; Benjamin B. Kendrick and Alex M. Arnett, *The South Looks at Its Past* (Chapel Hill: University of North Carolina Press, 1935), 108–12.

8. C. Vann Woodward, *Origins of the New South, 1877–1913*, vol. 9 of A History of the South, series ed. Wendell Holmes Stephenson and Ellis Merton Coulter (Baton Rouge: Louisiana State University Press, 1951), 1–22 and passim. For an assessment of the continuing impact of Woodward's synthesis of the revisionist argument, see Sheldon Hackney, "*Origins of the New South* in Retrospect," in these pages, 69–94.

9. Monroe L. Billington, *The American South: A Brief History* (New York: Scribner, 1971), 212–15; Thomas Dionysius Clark and Albert Dennis Kirwan, *The South since Appomattox: A Century of Regional Change* (New York: Oxford University Press, 1967), 53–60; William Best Hesseltine and David L. Smiley, *The South in American History*, 2d ed. (Englewood Cliffs, N.J.: Prentice-Hall, 1960), 416–25; and John Samuel Ezell, *The South since 1865*, 2d ed. (New York: Macmillan, 1975), 102–5, 111–12. A more critical view of the revisionist thesis is offered in Francis B. Simkins and Charles P. Roland, *A History of the South,* 4th ed. (New York: Knopf, 1972), 311–15, 318.

10. Allen J. Going's book *Bourbon Democracy in Alabama, 1874–1890* (University: University of Alabama Press, 1951) was published the same year as Woodward's *Origins of the New South.* Subsequent studies include: C. Alwyn Barr, *Reconstruction to Reform: Texas Politics, 1876–1906* (Austin: University of Texas Press, 1971); William J. Cooper Jr., *The Conservative Regime: South Carolina, 1877–1890* (Baltimore: Johns Hopkins Press, 1968); William Ivy Hair, *Bourbonism and Agrarian Protest: Louisiana Politics, 1877–1900* (Baton Rouge: Louisiana State University Press, 1969); Roger L. Hart, *Redeemers, Bourbons, and Populists: Tennessee, 1870–1896* (Baton Rouge: Louisiana State University Press, 1975); Jack P. Maddex Jr., *The Virginia Conservatives, 1867–1879: A Study in Reconstruction Politics* (Chapel Hill: University of North Carolina Press,1970); Allen W. Moger, *Virginia: Bourbonism to Byrd, 1870–1925* (Charlottesville: University Press of Virginia, 1968); James Tice Moore, *Two Paths to the New South: The Virginia Debt Controversy 1870–1883* (Lexington: University Press of Kentucky, 1974); William W. Rogers, *The One-Gallused Rebellion: Agrarianism in Alabama, 1865–1896* (Baton Rouge: Louisiana State University Press, 1970); Judson C. Ward Jr., "The New Departure Democrats of Georgia: An Interpretation," *Georgia Historical Quarterly* 41 (1957): 227–36; Edward C. Williamson, "The Constitutional Convention of 1885," *Florida Historical Quarterly* 41 (1962): 116–26; David M. Abshire, *The South Rejects a Prophet: The Life of Senator D. M. Key, 1824–1900,* with a foreword by Ralph McGill (New York: Praeger, 1967); Ben H. Procter, *Not without Honor: The Life of John H. Reagan* (Austin: University of Texas Press, 1962); Allen P. Tankersley, *John B. Gordon: A Study in Gallantry* (Atlanta: Whitehall Press, 1955); and Glenn Tucker, *Zeb Vance: Champion of Personal Freedom* (Indianapolis: Bobbs-Merrill, 1965).

11. Arnett, *Populist Movement in Georgia,* 31–32.

12. Arnett and those influenced by his work have shown a marked tendency to assume (without additional systematic research on Redeemer urbanism) that his Georgia findings were valid for the entire South. For examples of this approach, see Kendrick and Arnett, *The South Looks at Its Past,* 108–10; and Daniel M. Robison,

"From Tillman to Long: Some Striking Leaders of the Rural South," *Journal of Southern History* 3 (1937): 294.

13. Woodward, *Origins of the New South*, 2–22.

14. Francis Butler Simkins, *The Tillman Movement in South Carolina* (Durham: Duke University Press, 1926), 65n; and Willie D. Halsell, "The Bourbon Period in Mississippi Politics, 1875–1890," *Journal of Southern History* 11 (1945): 524, 528–31. Other statistics concerning the agriculturalists' legislative representation are less clear in their implication. North Carolina's fifty-member state senate, for example, contained seventeen farmers and five part-time farmers in 1877—an agricultural bloc composing almost half the membership; see Stuart Noblin, *Leonidas La Fayette Polk: Agrarian Crusader* (Chapel Hill: University of North Carolina Press, 1949), 106. In Alabama, farmers appear to have dominated the state legislature during the 1870s, but lawyers had gained the ascendancy by the end of the 1880s; see Going, *Bourbon Democracy in Alabama*, 47.

15. William Best Hesseltine, *Confederate Leaders in the New South* (Baton Rouge: Louisiana State University Press, 1950), 19–23.

16. Ralph Ancil Wooster, *Politicians, Planters, and Plain Folk: Courthouse and Statehouse in the Upper South, 1850–1860* (Knoxville: University of Tennessee Press, 1975), 33, 63, 66, 69, 119; of particular interest is Wooster's demonstration (63) that twenty-three of the thirty governors of the upper South in the 1850s were lawyers. In the lower South, farmers outnumbered lawyers in state legislatures by two to one in the 1850s, but many of the farmer-legislators also had interests in law or business; see idem, *The People in Power: Courthouse and Statehouse in the Lower South, 1850–1860* (Knoxville: University of Tennessee Press, 1969), 33, 35, 40.

17. Burke, who claimed for himself the title of "Major," played a shadowy role in the famous Hayes-Tilden election compromise in 1877. He subsequently became the state treasurer of Louisiana and exerted a powerful influence over the state's political life, especially through his ties with gambling and convict-labor syndicates. He absconded to Honduras late in the 1880s, leaving his state treasury accounts in arrears by almost $2 million. Joy J. Jackson, in *New Orleans in the Gilded Age: Politics and Urban Progress, 1880–1896* (Baton Rouge: Louisiana State University Press, 1969), describes Burke as a man of "humble origin" (38–39).

18. Hesseltine, *Confederate Leaders*, 16, 23, 95–96, provides the most graphic evidence of this restorationist trend. On page 16 he notes that, of 656 prominent ex-Confederate leaders who survived an appreciable length of time after the war, "only 71 failed to recover a substantial portion of the position and prestige they had enjoyed at the Confederacy's peak." The ex-Confederates' political standing in the immediate post-Reconstruction era was particularly striking. On page 23 he points out that during the heyday of Redemption (1875–1885) some 128 of the ex-Confederate leaders held office as state officials. On page 95 he observes that, of the 585 top civilian and military leaders of the Confederacy who survived the war, 418 held public office at some time during the postwar years.

19. Barr, *Reconstruction to Reform*, 22; Cooper, *Conservative Regime*, 17, 133n.

John V. Mering, in "Persistent Whiggery in the Confederate South: A Reconsideration" (*South Atlantic Quarterly* 69 [1970]: 127), offers a more striking criticism of Woodward's "Old Whig" thesis. Mering notes that of thirty-one prominent Redeemer politicians whom Woodward delineates to exemplify the Whig takeover of the post-Reconstruction Democracy in his *Reunion and Reaction: The Compromise of 1877 and the End of Reconstruction* (Boston: Little, Brown, 1951), nine had actually been Democrats in the antebellum years.

20. The Whig party in Tennessee and North Carolina had been devastated by the sectional upheavals of the 1850s, but prior to that decade the party had exerted a potent influence in both states. Between 1835 and 1853, for example, Whigs controlled the Tennessee governorship for twelve of those eighteen years. In North Carolina, Whigs monopolized the governorship from 1836 to 1850. For Woodward's emphasis on rejuvenated Whiggery in North Carolina and Tennessee, see his *Origins of the New South*, 1-4.

21. Ibid., 2, 77.

22. Hart, *Redeemers, Bourbons, and Populists*, 37, 46, 55, 58.

23. Woodward (*Origins of the New South*, 2-3) notes the popularity of the "Conservative" party label in the Redeemer South.

24. Maddex, *Virginia Conservatives*, 284-87.

25. For evidence of this concern with traditionalist and agrarian elements in the Redeemer hierarchy, see Cooper, *Conservative Regime*, 17, 39, 139; Going, *Bourbon Democracy in Alabama*, 44, 92, 110; Rogers, *One-Galloused Rebellion*, vii, 46; Hart, *Redeemers, Bourbons, and Populists*, xv, 55-57, 84, 228; Barr, *Reconstruction to Reform*, 9, 13, 22, 52; Hair, *Bourbonism and Agrarian Protest*, 21, 24, 30, 226; Williamson, "Constitutional Convention of 1885," 117; idem, "Independentism: A Challenge to the Florida Democracy of 1884," *Florida Historical Quarterly* 27 (1948): 131; and Halsell, "Bourbon Period in Mississippi Politics," 528-30.

26. Maddex, *Virginia Conservatives*, xii, 33, 121, 164-65, 276-79; Moger, *Virginia: Bourbonism to Byrd*, 4, 24-25, 44-45. See also Moore, *Two Paths to the New South*, 27-44, for additional criticisms of Maddex's assessment.

27. Ward, "New Departure Democrats of Georgia," 228, 231-33.

28. Arkansas, Florida, Louisiana, Mississippi, and South Carolina granted tax exemptions to manufacturers during the 1870s and 1880s. See Hair, *Bourbonism and Agrarian Protest*, 101; Cooper, *Conservative Regime*, 120; Dunbar Rowland, *History of Mississippi, The Heart of the South*, 2 vols. (Chicago: S. J. Clarke, 1925), 2: 224; David Y. Thomas, ed., *Arkansas and Its People: A History, 1541-1930*, 4 vols. (New York: American Historical Society, 1930) 1:166; and Woodward, *Origins of the New South*, 60.

29. The best source on the Louisiana State Lottery is Berthold C. Alwes, "The History of the Louisiana State Lottery Company," *Louisiana Historical Quarterly* 27 (1944): 112-23; Maddex, *Virginia Conservatives*, 225-27; and Mark T. Carleton, *Politics and Punishment: The History of the Louisiana State Penal System* (Baton Rouge: Louisiana State University Press, 1971). For evidence of state aid to railroads,

see Moger, *Virginia: Bourbonism to Byrd,* 13–18; Hugh Talmadge Lefler, *History of North Carolina,* 4 vols. (New York: Lewis Historical Pub. Co., 1956), 2:668; Barr, *Reconstruction to Reform,* 77, 111; and Charlton W. Tebeau, *A History of Florida* (Coral Gables: University of Miami Press, 1971), 281–82.

30. Ward, "New Departure Democrats of Georgia," 231; Going, *Bourbon Democracy in Alabama,* 24; Hart, *Redeemers, Bourbons, and Populists,* 7–8; Williamson, "Constitutional Convention of 1885," 122; Thomas, ed., *Arkansas,* 1:162; T. R. Fehrenbach, *Lone Star: A History of Texas and the Texans* (New York: Macmillan, 1968), 435–36.

31. Benjamin Ulysses Ratchford, *American State Debts* (Durham: Duke University Press, 1941), 183–229.

32. Green, "Convict Lease System," 117; Carleton, *Politics and Punishment,* 42; Going, *Bourbon Democracy in Alabama,* 86; Rowland, *History of Mississippi,* 2:236; Lawrence D. Rice, *The Negro in Texas, 1874–1900* (Baton Rouge: Louisiana State University Press, 1971), 245–46.

33. Alwes, "History of Louisiana State Lottery Company," 1001; Cooper, *Conservative Regime,* 125.

34. Tebeau, *History of Florida,* 278; Barr, *Reconstruction to Reform,* 77, 80.

35. In Virginia these levies boosted business tax revenues from 15.99 percent of state tax receipts to 36.75 percent of the total during the 1870s; see Maddex, *Virginia Conservatives,* 147, 171. See also Thomas, ed., *Arkansas,* 1:206; Going, *Bourbon Democracy in Alabama,* 86, 112; and Rogers, *One-Gallused Rebellion,* 92.

36. Cooper, *Conservative Regime,* 120–21.

37. Moger, *Virginia: Bourbonism to Byrd,* 56; Going, *Bourbon Democracy in Alabama,* 132–35; Rowland, *History of Mississippi,* 2:229; Barr, *Reconstruction to Reform,* 113–21.

38. Cooper, *Conservative Regime,* 120–21.

39. Moger, *Bourbonism to Byrd,* 56; Going, *Bourbon Democracy in Alabama,* 132–35; Rowland, *History of Mississippi,* 2:229; Barr, *Reconstruction to Reform,* 113–21.

40. Thomas, ed., *Arkansas,* 1:193–94; Tebeau, *History of Florida,* 277.

41. Arthur Stanley Link ("The Progressive Movement in the South, 1870–1914," *North Carolina Historical Review* 23 [1946]: 183–88) provides a good survey of southern efforts at railroad regulation. For insight into the achievements and problems of one of these state railroad commissions—Alabama's, in this case—see James F. Doster, *Railroads in Alabama Politics, 1875–1914* (University: University of Alabama Press, 1957), 9–36.

42. Procter, *Not without Honor,* 217, 231, 239, 258–60, 270; Going, *Bourbon Democracy in Alabama,* 137–39.

43. Paul Wallace Gates, "Federal Land Policy in the South, 1866–1888," *Journal of Southern History* 6 (1940): 327–30.

44. Wirt A. Cate, *Lucius Q. C. Lamar: Secession and Reunion* (Chapel Hill: University of North Carolina Press, 1935), 427, 444–48, 457; see also Carl V. Harris,

"Right Fork or Left Fork? The Section-Party Alignment of Southern Democrats in Congress, 1873–1897," *Journal of Southern History* 42 (1976): 499–501.

45. Hair, *Bourbonism and Agrarian Protest,* 100–101; Thomas, ed., *Arkansas,* 1: 162; Fehrenbach, *Lone Star,* 435; Going, *Bourbon Democracy in Alabama,* 24.

46. Rowland, *History of Mississippi,* 2:213, 224; Going, *Bourbon Democracy in Alabama,* 83, 86. Thomas (ed., *Arkansas,* 1:198–99) indicates that by 1885 Arkansas's state property levy amounted to only 4 mills, half of which was earmarked for support of public schools. In Florida the millage was reduced from 12.5 in 1877 to 4 in 1884; see Tebeau, *History of Florida,* 276–77. North Carolinians demonstrated their attitude toward the property tax in 1881. Receiving $600,000 from the sale of state-owned railroad properties, the North Carolina legislature used the money for current state expenses and abolished the property tax for that year; see Lefler, *History of North Carolina,* 2:648. Georgia, the state that most closely conformed to the Woodward model of Redeemer behavior, broke from the prevailing pattern by raising its property tax millage from 2.5 in 1883 to 4 in 1890 and to 6.2 in 1898, as noted in Arnett, *Populist Movement in Georgia.*

47. Woodward, in one of his few positive comments on Redeemer policies, acknowledged this trend in *Origins of the New South,* 59–60.

48. For evidence of Redeemer support for agricultural education, see Cooper, *Conservative Regime,* 166; Maddex, *Virginia Conservatives,* 214–15; Rowland, *History of Mississippi,* 2:213; Going, *Bourbon Democracy in Alabama,* 165–67; Lefler, *History of North Carolina,* 2:655; and Theodore Saloutos, *Farmer Movements in the South, 1865–1933* (Berkeley: University of California Press, 1960), 41.

49. Samuel A'Court Ashe, *History of North Carolina,* 2 vols. (Raleigh: Edwards & Broughton, 1925), 2:1182; Moger, *Virginia: Bourbonism to Byrd,* 85; Wallace, *History of South Carolina,* 3:340; Going, *Bourbon Democracy in Alabama,* 166–67.

50. These activities are noted in Sheldon, *Populism in the Old Dominion,* 62; Cooper, *Conservative Regime,* 122–23, 139–40; Ward, "New Departure Democrats of Georgia," 232; Rogers, *One-Gallused Rebellion,* 110–11, 120; Going, *Bourbon Democracy in Alabama,* 104–5; Noblin, *Polk,* 106–12; and Tebeau, *History of Florida,* 292.

51. Rogers, *One-Gallused Rebellion,* 110.

52. Cooper, *Conservative Regime,* 140–41; Going, *Bourbon Democracy in Alabama,* 105.

53. For evidence of such legislation, see Maddex, *Virginia Conservatives,* 176–78; Noblin, *Polk,* 112–14; Rogers, *One-Gallused Rebellion,* 15–20; Wallace, *History of South Carolina,* 3:328; Cooper, *Conservative Regime,* 136–39; Going, *Bourbon Democracy in Alabama,* 97–99; and Barr, *Reconstruction to Reform.*

54. Isaac F. Marcosson, *"Marse Henry": A Biography of Henry Watterson,* foreword by Arthur Krock (New York: Dodd, Mead, 1951), 139–40; Barr, *Reconstruction to Reform,* 105. See also Procter, *Not without Honor,* 270–71; May S. Ringold, "Senator James Zachariah George of Mississippi: Bourbon or Liberal?" *Journal of Mississippi History* 16 (1954): 170; Cate, *Lamar,* 395–96; and Harris, "Right Fork or Left Fork?" 488–89.

55. Harris, "Right Fork or Left Fork?" 489–93.

56. Ibid., 478–86. Harris analyzes southern congressional support for inflation. The "hard money" anti-inflation cause attracted support from such prominent Redeemers as Wade Hampton, Lucius Q. C. Lamar, and Benjamin H. Hill, but they failed to rally the bulk of the Redeemer leadership to their side. See Cate, *Lamar*, 309–10; Halsell, "Bourbon Period in Mississippi Politics," 526; and Manly Wade Wellman, *Giant in Gray: A Biography of Wade Hampton of South Carolina* (New York: Scribner, 1949), 309.

57. Harris, "Right Fork or Left Fork?" 486–88. See also James W. Garner, "Senatorial Career of Gen. J. Z. George," Mississippi Historical Society, *Publications* 7 (1903): 254, 257.

58. Harris, "Right Fork or Left Fork?" 495–99.

Place over Time: The Persistence of Southern Distinctiveness

CARL N. DEGLER

*

Of his many critics, none has been so formidable an opponent—or so much like Woodward in strengths and strategies—as Carl Degler. Also a polymath, Degler taught with distinction at Smith College and then at Stanford University. Coming relatively late in his career to a major graduate-training center, Degler thus has not influenced the profession with his students in the way that Woodward has; but the sheer force of Degler's intellect and the power of his ideas have won converts and, in some sense, "students" in many places. Like Woodward, a broad-ranging humanist, Degler enjoys comparative studies and often crosses boundaries of disciplines, regions, eras, and subjects of study. He has made major contributions in women's studies, in studies of comparative race relations, and, with the following essay, in the issue of southern identity over time. In responding to Degler's discussion in this Walter Lynwood Fleming Lecture of 1976, Woodward created the term *continuatarian,* and sardonically described Degler as a member of a sect determined to believe that things stay the same. However, as Woodward also conceded elsewhere, it takes much more than clever rhetorical devices to counter the essay that follows, and Woodward's thesis about discontinuity was never in the same shape after this assault.

* * *

Undoubtedly, the most persuasive single piece of evidence that antebellum southerners had developed a worldview different from that of other Americans is the secession of eleven southern states and the formation of the Confederacy. Certainly no other region of the nation ever felt so alienated as to take such a radical step, though New England at one time came close. Yet, as many historians have pointed out, what is striking about the Confederacy is how congruent its institutions and political values were with those of the United States. One searches in vain through the Confederate Constitution, for example, for those innovations and changes that would signal the arrival on the world stage of a slaveholders' republic, which repudiated the bourgeois elements characterizing the United States. All the protections of private property, business enterprise, and the rights of individuals contained in the United States Constitution were retained in the Confederate Constitution. Only in limiting the president to a single term of six years and its prescription that the Post Office pay its own way does the Confederate Constitution deviate from the United States Constitution in a mildly innovative way. There are protections for slavery, to be sure, but they are not nearly as strong as one might anticipate. For example, free states were not to be excluded from the new Confederacy. Even the right of secession is left unstated. It is true that "Almighty God" is invoked in the preamble, whereas the deity never appears in the United States Constitution. But that addition is not as significant as it might seem when we recollect how often Abraham Lincoln, that epitome of the bourgeois North, made references to God in state papers. The Confederate Constitution, in short, makes evident how conservative southerners were, but only in the conventional sense of minimizing or containing change, rather than in the Burkean or Hartzian sense of abandoning American liberal tradition.

Nowhere is this point more clearly recognized than in the frequently heard argument by southerners that secession was justified by the experience of Americans in 1776. On both occasions—in 1776 and 1860—southerners emphasized, the resort to radical measures was dictated by the violations of ancient rights by those in power. As one Georgian wrote, southerners should "do as Washington, Hancock, and other conservative Americans did, when coercive measures were adopted by the King and Parliament to collect three pence tax on tea imported into Boston—join the resisting party and aid in achieving perfect independence."[1] Those southerners who justified secession frequently saw themselves and their region following in the footsteps of their Revolutionary forefathers. Southerners, wrote one Georgia woman, just wanted to be "let alone. . . . The idea is preposterous," she went on, that northerners, "a people like ourselves whose republican independence was won by a rebellion, whose liberty [was] achieved by secession . . . should attempt to coerce us."[2] One southern newspaper, apparently to underscore the comparison between 1776 and 1861, reprinted in full Patrick Henry's "Give Me Liberty or Give Me Death" speech. Even those southerners who were ready to abandon the Union were still drawing upon those bourgeois political principles that all Americans adhered to, among which was the liberal principle of the right of revolution.

The comparison between the South's course in 1861 and the secession of the American colonies from the British Empire some ninety years earlier has a significance beyond the historical justification to which southerners put it. It also provides us with a fresh historical example of how two peoples might be sufficiently different for one to seek political independence from the other and yet not hold different worldviews. For as Bernard Bailyn, Gordon Wood, and other historians of the American Revolutionary era have shown, the origins of the rhetoric and political philosophy of 1776 were clearly British. And even Eugene Genovese, I think, would see America and Britain as having the same worldview in 1776. Yet, if the British and Americans shared a common worldview at the time of the Revolution, their respective societies certainly differed, just as the social character of North and South differed in 1860.

Indeed, the very defeat of the Confederacy is a succinct and striking measure of how different northern and southern societies had become as a result of slavery. Running through the conventional explanations for the South's defeat, one is always struck by the fact that each of the reasons can be traced back to the kind of society the South had become as a result of slavery. If, for example, the defeat is blamed on the South's lack of manufacturing capability, on its failure to develop an industrial base for modern war, then the commitment to agriculture that slavery fostered certainly is an important part of the explanation for defeat. Moreover, the South's emphasis upon cotton fostered just the kind of economy that could only lose in a war in which the enemy controlled the sea on which arrived the internal needs of the region's unbalanced economy. The North's diversified or balanced economy may have received some setbacks from the war, as recent economic historians have shown, but these were little more than interruptive slowdowns, not the absolute declines that the South sustained.

If, as Frank Owsley contended years ago, the South's lack of unity and the successful invoking of states' rights by leaders like Zebulon Vance, Alexander Stephens, and Joseph E. Brown were at the root of its defeat, then the elaborate defense of states' rights worked out during the antebellum years must bear a large share of the blame for the defeat. The principal reason southern political leaders and thinkers had pressed hard their defense of states' rights was to erect a barrier against a federal power that seemed to threaten slavery. Men and women trained through a lifetime of resisting centralized power in Washington in defense of slavery could not easily forget those lessons just because the central authority shifted 150 miles south to Richmond. Even a southern nationalist like Jefferson Davis found himself inhibited in using his full powers as president of the Confederacy because a lifetime of legalistic politics in defense of the South and slavery could not easily be sloughed off. Yet concern with legalities was clearly the wrong tactic when seeking to win a revolution. And if Robert E. Lee's weakness as a military commander lay in his unwillingness to look beyond Virginia, as T. Harry Williams and others have argued, then that historic, if quite understandable, emphasis upon states' rights must be recognized as another way in which the Confederacy's defeat grew out of the antebellum defense of slavery.

Slavery had always been more than a molder of peculiarly southern attitudes and social development; it had also been a source of political and social division within the South. Many nonslaveholders fought for the Confederacy, to be sure. Indeed, since only a small minority of southerners owned slaves, the bulk of the armies of the South must have been made up of nonslaveholders. Yet the division of the South into slaveholding and nonslaveholding areas was an important source of discontent and defection within the Confederacy. Northern Alabama, east Tennessee, western North Carolina, north Georgia, and northwestern Arkansas were only the largest and most familiar strongholds of southern resistance to the Confederacy. All of those I have listed, of course, were areas in which slavery was only weakly established. From these areas, too, came most of the 54,000 southern whites who joined the Union Army to help suppress the slaveholders' republic.

If one of the reasons the South was defeated was that it was unable to gain foreign recognition, then slavery played a part there, too. Although the presence of slavery in the South was not the prime reason the British failed to recognize the Confederacy, the persistence of slavery in the South after Lincoln made the Emancipation Proclamation ensured that Britain would not thereafter recognize the Confederacy. Southern leaders themselves acknowledged the burden slavery placed upon their cause when, at the very end of the war, they offered emancipation in return for British recognition of the Confederacy.

If, as Eric McKitrick has suggested, the defeat of the Confederacy was in large part a consequence of the new country's lack of a strong, competitive, two-party system, that explanation, too, can be traced to the Old South's defense of slavery. For almost twenty years, from the early 1830s on, the southern states had enjoyed a vigorous two-party system, with Whigs and Democrats contending. No state was safely Whiggish or Democratic, and between 1832 and 1852 neither party could be sure of winning the region as a whole. But that healthy political rivalry ended in the 1850s as the political defense of slavery, both nationally and regionally, intensified. As a result, the Confederacy emerged with only a single party, the Democratic. The Whig party, we now know, was underground—a strong memory in the minds of many voters but without either visibility or organization. The North, on the other hand, profited from the rivalry between Democrats and Republicans, as McKitrick has imaginatively shown.[3] Lincoln, for example, could always count upon support for his policies and for the war effort from his fellow Republicans. Jefferson Davis, who had no party organization and no rival to the Democratic party to keep it alert, lacked that advantage.

If the defeat of the Confederacy stemmed from what David Donald has called an "excess of democracy," then a South molded by slavery contributed in another way to the downfall of the Confederacy. For what Donald means by an "excess of democracy" is not so much political democracy as individualism and lack of social discipline. And these aspects of life surely can be traced in a large degree to the agricultural nature of the antebellum South, with its enduring frontier, its widespread violence, its lack of urbanization. All of these we have traced back to slavery.

Finally, the very defeat of the Confederacy, whatever reasons one might assign it, enhanced the distinctiveness of the South. As C. Vann Woodward has emphasized, no other Americans have experienced defeat in war so completely and so devastatingly. No other Americans have experienced directly an army of occupation. No other Americans, as they think about the Civil War, have that visceral reaction that William Faulkner so powerfully described in *Intruder in the Dust*:

> For every Southern boy fourteen years old, not once but whenever he wants it, there is the instant when it's still not yet two o'clock on that July afternoon in 1863, the brigades are in position behind the rail fence, the guns are laid and ready in the woods . . . and Pickett himself with . . . his hat in one hand . . . and his sword in the other looking up the hill waiting for Longstreet to give the word and it's all in the balance, it hasn't happened yet, it hasn't even begun yet but there is still time for it not to begin against that position and those circumstances which made more men than Garnett and Kemper and Armstead and Wilcox look grave yet it's going to begin, we all know that, we have come too far with too much at stake and that moment doesn't need even a fourteen-year-old boy to think *This time. Maybe this time* with all this much to lose and all this much to gain: Pennsylvania, Maryland, the world, the golden dome of Washington itself to crown with desperate and unbelievable victory the desperate gamble, the cast made two years ago.[4]

Insofar as southerners lack some of that belief in progress or that optimistic outlook upon the future which is so characteristic of Americans, that lack is surely to be related to the remembrance that the South lost a war. Certainly the modern southern interest in the Confederacy, the war, its heroes, and its legend amply testify to the persistence of that memory. Indeed, the late David

Potter traced a "deeply felt southern nationalism" to "the shared sacrifices, the shared efforts, and the shared defeat (which is often more unifying than victory) of the Civil War. The Civil War," he adds, "did far more to produce a southern nationalism which flourished in the cult of the Lost Cause than southern nationalism did to produce the war."[5]

Yet if the defeat of the Confederacy has left a long legacy of emotion and rhetoric, the ending of slavery left few regrets upon the southern mind. Although historians are in almost total agreement today about the centrality of slavery to the coming of secession and the creation of the Confederacy, the abolition of slavery in 1865 brought almost no resistance from southerners and remarkably few regrets thereafter. Even a former slaveholder and Confederate like Alabama's Henry Hilliard could assure Brazilian abolitionists in 1880 that "fortunately for us in the United States, even the humane system of slavery which prevailed there has passed away forever. The shadow upon the dial of human conscience," he went on, "must go back many degrees before any considerable number of men in the Southern States of the Union would consent to see slavery restored."[6]

For our purposes here, this clean ending of slavery has an important implication. It is true that some southerners found a slave society so congenial or indispensable that they could not contemplate a world in which the slave population was no more. Some of these people emigrated to Mexico, Cuba, and Brazil. But the great majority of southern slaveholders, including the great proportion of the leaders of the South, never seriously contemplated such a course. Even George Fitzhugh, Eugene Genovese's premier proslavery ideologue, became an agent of the Freedmen's Bureau in Virginia. Some of those who did leave the South right after Appomattox, like Jubal Early and Matthew F. Maury, changed their minds when they found out how American they were. As noted earlier, Kenneth Stampp has been so impressed by the ready acceptance of emancipation in the South as to argue that southerners really did not want to win the war secession brought, that subconsciously they almost hoped to lose because slavery made them feel so guilty about holding fellow human beings in bondage, but we do not need to go as far as Stampp does in linking these doubts to a lack of commitment to winning the war. After all, no people of modern times, except perhaps those of the Soviet Union in the Second World War, have made proportionately such heavy sacrifices of life as the people of the Confederacy. Those sacrifices alone ought to convince us that the War for Southern Independence was not halfheartedly fought. But that conclusion still leaves us with the anomaly of a war to protect slavery that ended with almost a sigh of relief when the peculiar institution was ended.

That anomaly, however, suggests that, important as slavery undoubtedly was in shaping the economy and thought of the antebellum South, its presence had not resulted in a novel worldview. Southerners relinquished the source of that allegedly different worldview much too quickly for slavery to have been firmly integrated into their value structure. Southerners were simply too much a part of the bourgeois world to accept slavery wholeheartedly, as someone like Fitzhugh—or Eugene Genovese—thought they ought to.

I do not want to push my interpretation of a smooth transition from a slave society to one without slavery too far or too hard. One must admit that abolition of slavery marked a significant change in the lives of southerners, white as well as black. Certainly it was a discontinuity in southern history. All questions of continuity are necessarily relative, however; for all history is a combination of varying degrees of continuity and change. The Civil War was certainly a discontinuity in the life of the United States; yet C. Vann Woodward, who emphasizes the deep discontinuities in southern history, contrasts the regional experience with what he calls the smooth flow of American history. To him the Civil War was a minor discontinuity for the North. It is my contention that the end of the Old South did not mark a significant break in the flow of southern history; it was only a minor disruption, with limited effects. This is not to say that the death of slavery went completely unnoticed or even unlamented. Yet it is worth observing that emancipation was not accompanied by the kind of emotional resistance that a challenge to deeply held values can be expected to call forth. The reason I can say this with some confidence is that when deeply held values *were challenged,* southerners did resist with strong emotion and tenacious determination.

What I refer to, of course, is the reaction of white southerners to the impact of Reconstruction after the war. Some years ago, in response to Kenneth Stampp's observation that the end of slavery was abrupt and did not entail what today we would call a "resistance" movement, David Potter pointed out that the Civil War was a war without a resistance, whereas Reconstruction was a resistance without a war. What Potter was telling us was that Reconstruction ought to be recognized as a true people's war on the part of the southern whites against the imposition of Negro political equality by northern political and military power. Local control of government and Negro inequality had long been values of southern life, as they were of American life nationally. Slavery had always been not only a system of labor but a means of controlling blacks as well. One of the South's prime reasons for resisting the end of slavery during four years of war, aside from the pecuniary loss emancipation would bring, was the conviction of most white southerners that blacks would not work without compulsion. This argument runs all through the public and private writings of planters before and during the war, as James L. Roark's recent researches have abundantly shown. But once slavery was destroyed by the sword, southerners soon found that they could still use free-black labor in much the same way and that free blacks could still be socially subordinated to whites. When the northern conquerors began to interfere with the whites' control over blacks, the South reacted violently. For that reason Reconstruction might well be considered a prolonged period of guerrilla warfare on the part of the white South to resist the attempt to interfere with the region's traditional attitudes toward and relationships with black people. To many white southerners—and not without reason—Reconstruction was an attempt to make the South over in the image of the North and, above all, to impose upon the South what the North itself had come to adopt only lately, namely the introduction of black men into political life as voters and officeholders. For it is a fact that, until the Fifteenth Amendment was ratified in 1870, more southern than northern states, thanks to the Reconstruction acts, extended the ballot to black men. (Of the twenty states that permitted blacks to vote at that time, only seven had done so voluntarily through the ballot box or by popular, democratic means.)

From this perspective, Reconstruction reveals much about the priorities of southern thinking and southern identity. Slavery had won the allegiance of many white southerners, but it was soon discovered that slavery was not indispensable for growing cotton or controlling blacks. What white southerners—even working-class whites—could not abide, so Reconstruction tells us, was the prospect of bringing blacks to the social and political level of whites. Southerners, in short, could accept the end of slavery, but they could not accept the end of white supremacy, especially when it was imposed by a North whose own hands in this regard were far from clean.

Today we no longer portray Reconstruction as the blackout of good government or as the domination of whites by Negroes, in the way that older historians of the South did. But our modern view of Reconstruction, however accurate it may be, does not diminish the way in which popular southern memories and myths of Reconstruction reinforced the differences between the sections and further enhanced the distinctiveness of the South. For years after 1877, southerners would recall those days that followed the war, when the white South had successfully resisted the North and turned back the attempt to impose black power upon a defeated South. Not even in the early years of secession, so the myth would go, had the southern people been so united as when they stood in solid phalanx, regardless of class, against the blacks and their carpetbag allies from the North. Those white southerners who failed to recognize the enduring value of white supremacy at its moment of danger were cast into the outer darkness, to be regarded forever as scala-wags, traitors to the South. In time, too, the southern version of Reconstruction became the national version, thus making nationwide the perception of the South as a region distinct in this respect as well as in others.

But the undoubted contribution of Reconstruction to southern distinctiveness should not cause us to overlook the continuity between the antebellum years and those after Appomattox. Thomas Alexander has documented what he has called "persistent Whiggery" in the Reconstruction years as one measure of the continuance of the old political and partisan rivalries and outlooks across the chasm of Civil War and emancipation. The Whig party was the victim of the drive during the 1850s to create a one-party South in order to defend slavery. But the antagonism between Whig and Democrat did not die, even though old Whigs and old Democrats after the war often called themselves Democrats. For many years after the war ended, the only way Democrats could get touchy former Whigs to join them was to drop the official and traditional name of their party in favor of the more nonpartisan "Conservative." Clement Eaton, in his *Waning of the Old South Civilization,* has shown how the practices and values of the Old South continued into Reconstruction and beyond. He compares the South with the late Middle Ages in Jan Huizinga's book from which his title is taken. Just as France and the Netherlands of the fourteenth and fifteenth centuries "remained medieval at heart," Eaton observes, "so did the South in 1880 remain strongly attached to the values and philosophy of the Old South, with the one important exception that relatively few regretted the passing of slavery. Despite the trauma of defeat and the political upheaval of Reconstruction, much of the Old South survived, waning very gradually. The old continued to co-exist with the new until the twentieth century."[7]

The continuity of the Old South into the New has been shown in another way in William Hesseltine's study of the activities of some 600 former-Confederate leaders in the years after 1865. Of the 656 leaders who lived long enough to make records, only 71 failed to regain a substantial portion of the prestige and wealth they had enjoyed under the Confederacy and before. More than a third of them became active in politics in one fashion or another; many became lawyers, editors, and farmers, as in the antebellum years. But the occupations that attracted many more in the years after 1865 were banking and industrial management. Only 13 of these leaders had been in banking before the war, but 23 of them entered that field after the end of hostilities. Before the war, 16 had been in railroading; after the war, 73 were. Mining and industry claimed the attention of 14 of these leaders before 1860, but in the years after Appomattox, the figure was up to 34. In large part, of course, this shift in occupational interest was a reflection of the expansion of industry and railroading in the postwar years. At the same time, however, it suggests that the value structure of the Old South did not preclude a rather quick adjustment to the ending of a slavery society. Hesseltine concludes that, although many of the Confederate leaders he studied ended the war penniless and often in debt and with families to support, few of them died in poverty. Indeed, many of them became wealthy. The implication is clear: the antebellum South, rather than being a society with a prebourgeois, anti-industrial outlook, was sufficiently like the North to have its leaders move quickly from the old into the new order of things. These leaders of the Confederacy did not exemplify the stereotype of the old planter, disheartened and demoralized by his loss of familiar slaves and plantation, sinking into an early and welcome grave on his run-down and depleted acres. Jefferson Davis, as Hesseltine observes, may have found difficulty in adjusting to the postwar order, but Robert E. Lee showed that there was little in the old order that precluded adjustment to, or success in, the new. Lee did not become a railroad executive or an industrialist, but as president of Washington College he showed himself ready to adapt collegiate education to the demands of a commercial and industrial world. He wrote to a friend who wanted to know in 1866 what he thought about emigrating to Brazil or Mexico: "I made up my mind on the subject at the first cessation of hostilities, I considered that the South required the presence of her sons more than that [sic] at any former part of her history, to sustain and restore her." [8] At no time was Lee's intense southernism a handicap in the world after Appomattox.

For some years now, historians have been writing about what they refer to as "the New South," so impressed have they been with the efforts of southern leaders after Reconstruction to "bring the mills to the cotton." The determined effort to develop the South's industrial resources captured the imagination of southern boosters long before the historians took it up. Richard Edmonds and Henry Grady were only the best-known ideologues of the New South. The very phrase suggests a sharp rupture in the continuity of southern history. Yet, when we analyze critically the gospel of the New South, continuity seems more evident than disjunction. As Clement Eaton and others have noticed, none of the advocates of the so-called New South repudiated the Old except for the antebellum South's reliance upon slavery. Daniel Tompkins, one leading proponent of a New South, went so far as to conjure up a false history of the Old South, in which the beginnings of southern manufacturing in the first two decades of the nineteenth century were said to have been killed off by the proponents of slavery and cotton growing. In Tompkins's version of history, the development of cotton manufacturing in the South was not even a new development but simply a return to an earlier and sounder South. Richard Edmonds made the same point when he said in 1903, "The South of today, the South of industrial and railroad activity, is not a new South, but a revival of the Old South, whose broad commercial spirit, crushed by the war, is again seen in the development of every line of industry in which this section was bending its energies prior to 1860."[9]

The failure of the New South's Creed to repudiate the antebellum society is not the only sign of continuity. It can also be seen in the persistence of southern patterns of life across the abyss of Civil War, emancipation, and Reconstruction. I say this even though some historians, notably Emory Thomas and Frank Vandiver, contend that the experience of the Confederacy made the South more like the rest of the country. They argue that the very act of fighting the War for Southern Independence, whatever its cause, had the unforeseen and certainly unintended result of making the South into the image of the North, economically and socially. Seeing the Confederacy as a "revolutionary experience," to use Thomas's striking phrase, is a nice exercise in irony, but it does not square with the facts. It is true that the war imposed many changes upon the South, not the least of which was a shift of capital and labor from cotton growing to industrial development, as Eugene Lerner has shown.[10] But these and other changes that Thomas and Vandiver refer to are really temporary consequences of war, not fundamental changes that alter the contours of society for the future. And the proof of that is the return of the South to the old ways, once hostilities had ceased.

The whole economic record of the so-called New South is testimony to the small amount of economic and social change wrought by the Confederate experience. Despite the hopes and propaganda of Henry Watterson, Daniel Tompkins, Richard Edmonds, Henry Grady, and countless lesser-known exponents of a New South, by the end of the nineteenth century the South was still an agricultural region with only the rudiments of a diversified and developing economy. Its proportion of manufacturing production in 1900 was smaller than in 1860; the per capita income of the region was lower in comparison with the North than it had been in 1860. Its proportion of urban population was still the lowest in the nation. In 1850 the South counted one-third of the nation's cities of 25,000 population or more; in 1900 that proportion was down to one-quarter, though its total population was more than one-third of the nation's. J. L. M. Curry wrote to his son in 1889: "In choosing the West rather than the South you did wisely, and subsequent history has confirmed the wisdom of the choice—Roseate pictures of the New South are drawn largely by speculators and so far as based on the semblance of truth are applicable to mines and towns—wealth and population seem alike to tend town-ward while agriculture and country languish."[11]

One of the aims of the advocates of the New South had been to attract immigrants to the region, partly to make up for the feared loss of black labor and partly to increase the South's share of skilled workers. Virtually all of the southern states after Appomattox organized commissions or other agencies to foster European immigration, sometimes even sending agents to Europe to entice emigrants to settle in the South. Despite the effort, few immigrants came to the South. In 1910 foreign-born whites constituted 14.5 percent of the population of the United States, but they made up only 2.4 percent of the population of the South Atlantic states and 4 percent of the population in the region comprised of Texas, Oklahoma, Louisiana, and Arkansas. Texas, thanks to its border with Mexico, counted the highest proportion of foreign-born in the South: 6.2 percent. At the same time, states far from the Atlantic and Pacific oceans, like Colorado, Idaho, and Wyoming, counted proportions of foreign-born in excess of 12 percent, that is, twice Texas's proportion.

Part of the reason that immigrants did not go to the South after slavery was abolished is that, despite the South's stated wish to attract immigrants, the qualifications it set for immigrants were scarcely encouraging. *Southern States,* the principal periodical devoted to attracting immigrants to the South, made the point clearly enough in 1895, noting that "indiscriminate foreign immigration would be a curse to the South. . . . The South wants and expects to receive a heavy immigration with the next few years; but it must be of the right sort, and she will be found heartily seconding any efforts which may be made to place governmental restrictions on the character of foreign immigrants who seek a foothold on American shores." The journal went on to say that, "of the foreigners now living in this country, there are many hundred of thousands whom the South cannot afford to encourage to settle within her borders." [12] If such was the sentiment of the foremost public advocate of immigration, one can easily imagine the image the South as a whole projected toward Europeans and Asians who contemplated settling in the region.

Philosophical and social objections to certain kinds of immigrants were not the prime reason for the South's failure to attract large numbers of foreign workers. Its relative lack of cities and manufacturing was still at the root of the matter. This is shown quite clearly when one studies the proportion of immigrants in the states with large cities and manufacturing. New York's foreign-born population in 1910 constituted almost 30 percent of the whole, and in Illinois the figure reached 44.3 percent. The economic opportunities that were the underlying attractive force for the massive immigration into the United States in the late nineteenth and early twentieth centuries simply did not exist in the predominantly agricultural, rural South. This persistently low proportion of foreign-born, even after the end of slavery, makes plain that it was the lack of economic opportunity in the South—not the immigrants' alleged aversion to slavery—that was principally responsible in the antebellum years for deflecting European immigrants away from the South.

Another measure of the relative lack of economic opportunity in the South is that growth of personal income in the South lagged behind that of the rest of the nation. During the antebellum years, as we have seen, the white South's per capita income was substantial—not as high as the Northeast's, but better than the Old Northwest's. It was this optimistic prospect that secession and the war presumably interrupted. Or did it? The question arises because, when the growth rates for the years 1840 to 1860 are studied, it becomes evident that even if the Civil War had not intervened, the South would still have fallen behind the rest of the country economically. According to Stanley Engerman's reworking of Richard Easterlin's basic data, the antebellum growth rates of Mississippi, Alabama, Tennessee, and Kentucky were lower than those of the comparably new states of the Middle West. Even without a Civil War to devastate and disrupt the South, these rate differentials—if they had continued—could explain almost alone the South's falling behind the Middle West after 1860. Moreover, as Morton Rothstein has argued, "[t]he records of other plantation areas in modern times must leave many of us unconvinced that, apart from the question of slavery, the commitment to staple commodity production for export could lead anywhere but to disaster." [13] The disaster to which Rothstein refers is not the Civil War, but the widening gap after 1865 between per capita income in the South and that of the rest of the nation. The point is that, even if one accepts the notion of a prosperous and growing southern economy on the eve of secession, as I do, underneath that immediate success lay the sources for the poverty of the South in the last third of the nineteenth century and after. Thus, even if slavery had not been abruptly ended as a result of a devastating war, it is possible to see the origins, if not the fact, of the poverty of the postbellum years in the developments of the prewar decades. Even the South's poverty has a continuity across the divide of war and emancipation.

The physical devastation, the disorganization of production, and the dislocation of labor that war and emancipation brought, certainly hastened and deepened the South's economic decline in the years after 1860. By 1880 the per capita income of southerners was only 51 percent of the national average, though in 1860 it had been 72 percent even when the slaves were counted as income receivers. By 1880 the South lagged far behind the Old Northwest as well, for, by then, the Middle West had become an industrial as well as an agricultural section of the country. But even the Great Plains area, the prime agricultural sector of the North in 1880 and 1900, according to the figures compiled by Richard Easterlin, was far ahead of the South. [14]

The continuity of the South's economy across the gulf of war and emancipation can be observed in more than the continuing dominance of agriculture and the relative poverty of the region. Many years ago Roger Shugg and C. Vann Woodward pointed out that, though the census seemed to suggest that the plantations had been broken up by emancipation, in fact they often survived, in substance, if not in the old form. The census takers counted farms, irrespective of owners, and so the average size of farms in 1880 and after fell sharply from what it had been in 1860. But when a special investigation was made by the Bureau of the Census in 1910, of 325 Black Belt counties in the eleven states of the former Confederacy, a different picture emerged. One-third of the landholdings turned out to be organized in "tenant plantations," that is, several tenant farms with a single owner. The average size of these estates held by a single owner with many tenants was 724 acres or, as Woodward writes, "more than six times the average size of holdings reported in 1900 for all holdings." [15] In order to bring the labor of the former slave to the land of the frequently impoverished, though land-rich white owner, southerners developed sharecropping in the years immediately after the war. Under the new regime, the gang labor of slavery and the communal slave quarters may have been replaced by individual family-tenant homesteads, but the plantation clearly survived in the form of the single white owner of the land directing his many black tenants.

The persistence of the old ways is shown in more detail in two important recent studies of Alabama by Jonathan Wiener. In a close examination of a single Black Belt county, Wiener tested the prevailing view that war and Reconstruction destroyed the old planter class. Using census figures, he shows that not only did the prewar planters hold onto their lands after the war, they actually increased their acreage. Moreover, they successfully resisted the efforts of a new class of merchants to contest their authority over black labor. In fact, the planters assumed the role of merchant as well as of landowner. In a second study of five Alabama counties, Wiener compares the persistent rates of antebellum planters in the postwar years with the persistent rates of other social groups elsewhere in the country. He finds that "the Alabama planter elite is . . . the most persistent rural group known to social science." [16]

The continuity in the organization of agriculture comes through, too, in some of the new studies by economic historians of sharecropping during the late nineteenth century. The central question in these studies is whether cropping was as uneconomical and as exploitative of the farmer as historians have usually believed. Richard Sutch and Roger Ransom, for example, contend that racism distorted the operation of the market system, thus putting the black tenants at an economic, as well as a social, disadvantage. Sutch and

Ransom perceive a high degree of continuity between the slave society of the antebellum years and the so-called free labor society of the postwar decades. The racism inherited from the days before the war continued into subsequent years, thus restricting black expectations and opportunities. White landowners, Sutch and Ransom argue, used race as a "signal" of potential productivity on the part of workers and thus did not deal with black sharecroppers as they would have with white croppers. They simply did not assess black behavior objectively. Ransom and Sutch, by comparing the amount of untilled land on farms among white and black owners and white and black tenants, show that Negroes consistently held less untilled land, a measure that they take as a surrogate of capital. Thus they conclude that blacks received less pay and enjoyed less easy access to the capital market than did whites.[17]

The Sutch-Ransom conclusions support the view of most historians of the South, who see racial discrimination and hostility shaping the economic situation of black agricultural workers in the South. Not all modern economic historians, however, go along with that view. Stephen DeCanio and Robert Higgs, working separately, contend that the assertion of an irrational, racist response to economic conditions by white landowners has yet to be proved.[18] Operating on the assumption that economic concerns are central in a market economy, they doubt that a white landowner would deprive himself of income simply because of prejudice against blacks. For, as economist Gary Becker has shown, discrimination based on noneconomic criteria exacts a cost from the discriminator as well as from those who are the victims of the discrimination. Higgs's and DeCanio's works do not deny the existence of racism; they merely seek to account for southern agricultural poverty in the postbellum years in ways other than by reliance on racial prejudice.

In pursuit of this objective, Higgs tries to measure the extent of racial discrimination involved in determining the size of black, as compared with white, farms in 1910. Using the census figures of that year, he finds that the difference in the average size of black and white farms in the cotton districts was fifty-nine acres. That is, Negroes' farms were fifty-nine acres smaller, on average, than were whites' farms. But if the comparison is made with kind of tenure and improvement on farms held constant, then the disparity drops to ten acres. The underlying explanation for this drop is that it was the superior wealth of the white farmers that accounted for two-thirds of the difference in size of black and white farms, not racial discrimination. The superior wealth of the whites Higgs attributes to the disadvantages of slavery for blacks; as slaves they could not accumulate capital or buy land. The argument, however, is not compelling, since racial prejudice might account as much as slavery for the lack of capital among blacks. Moreover, Higgs finds that at least one-third of the difference in size of farms between whites and blacks is probably the result of racial prejudice.

DeCanio's effort to show that racial discrimination was not at the bottom of southern agriculture's low per capita income is less vulnerable than Higgs's. But DeCanio's case is no less indicative of the continuity between the antebellum and postbellum years. DeCanio divides farmers into black and white cotton farmers and black and white noncotton farmers. He then works out the productivity of each of the four groups. His conclusion is that the productivity of white cotton farmers was highest, that of black cotton farmers next, that of black noncotton farmers third, and at the bottom, that of white noncotton farmers. On the face of it, DeCanio's evidence would deny racial discrimination, since white noncotton farmers fare less well than black cotton farmers and black noncotton farmers. DeCanio is particularly interested in this conclusion, for it seems to disprove the widely held view that the inheritance from slavery was a burden upon blacks, that blacks earned less in the postwar South because they carried with them the poor habits, the lack of skills, and the economically inhibiting values imposed by slavery.

From my standpoint, DeCanio's evidence would seem to deny continuity between the antebellum and postbellum South. It appears to show that the inheritance from slavery did not affect appreciably the life of blacks or the situation of the South in the years after Appomattox, because some whites did less well than some Negroes in agriculture. If slavery had been as devastating for blacks as is often said, one would not find that some whites were actually, on the average, less productive than blacks.

Yet, when DeCanio offers his explanation for this finding, the continuity between antebellum and postbellum South reappears. His explanation is what he calls the location and ownership hypothesis. It asserts that, where a group stood on the scale of productivity depended on where that group was located geographically on the soil patterns of the South and whether the group was historically high in land ownership. Thus the whites come out on top of the productivity scale when they held their land from antebellum years; and since it is known that the cotton planters had the best land, these whites kept their superior land after emancipation, when it was apportioned among farmers. Cotton-growing black farmers came next on the productivity scale, because, as former slaves, their farms were located on the next-best land of their former masters, who were now probably their landlords. Black noncotton farmers stood next because they were few in number in the noncotton-growing regions and so, in comparison with the many whites, tended to occupy better land because they, too, worked the land of their former masters. The land that was left was that occupied by the noncotton-growing whites—the land of least productivity. Obviously there are broad historical and economic assumptions in this explanation, but what is germane to our concern here is that even in this instance, where the intention is to play down the long-range effects of slavery, the continuity between the antebellum and postbellum South is relied upon. For DeCanio's explanation once again shows how the patterns of the antebellum years shaped the patterns of the postbellum years, despite the momentous events that intervened.

The continuity of the southern experience, as exemplified by the persistence of the South's commitment to agriculture after the end of slavery, was reinforced by the New South's insistence that the dominance of the white man must also continue in the postslavery era. For, as even Henry Grady had to acknowledge, not everything in the New South was novel. "The supremacy of the white race in the South," Grady insisted, "must be maintained forever, and the domination of the negro race resisted at all points and at all hazards—because the white race is the superior race. This is the declaration of no new truth," he maintained. "It has abided forever in the marrow of our bones—and shall run forever with the blood that feeds Anglo-Saxon hearts." [19]

In truth, the North was no more willing than the South to accord equality to blacks in the years after the Civil War. All regions of the nation after the war, as before, insisted upon the subordination of Negroes, though blacks now voted in the South as well as in the North. The essential measure of southern distinctiveness in these years, and therefore the continuity in southern history, was not the mere persistence of white supremacy, which was, after all, a national, not merely a southern, attitude. The fundamental difference between the sections in regard to race was the institutionalization of white supremacy in the South through legal segregation and disfranchisement.

The adoption of these social and political innovations in the 1890s and the opening years of the twentieth century derived from a complex concatenation of events and circumstances, among which the Populist revolt was notable. But certainly more than merely contributory was the fact that the South was the home of 90 percent of the nation's blacks and that southerners still felt what Hodding Carter has aptly called "the angry scar" of Reconstruction. In the North the small number of blacks raised no comparable threat to social and political control and stirred no memories of black men in political office. The South, like the North, had never been without some form of racial segregation in public places. But after the 1890s, separation of the races became the hallmark of the South, being insisted upon in even minor public places like telephone booths and tax assessors' windows. The systematic disfranchisement of blacks—and many whites along with them—also departed from northern as well as southern practices since the war. Even the overthrow in 1877 of the last Reconstruction governments in the southern states had not entailed the removal of most blacks from the voting rolls. In the 1890s the massive disfranchisement of blacks and the pervasive legal separation of the races in the public life of the South set the region apart from the rest of the nation. Just as the antebellum South had been known as the region of Negro slavery, so the postwar South became known as the region of segregation and disfranchisement of blacks. The South after the war, like the antebellum South, was the region in which legal institutions, as well as social and political practices, were extraordinarily hostile toward black people.

Not until well into the twentieth century were the social and economic sources and character of the South's distinctiveness seriously altered. At the time of the First World War the exodus of blacks out of the South began in earnest, creating whole new black ghettos in the major cities of the North. Yet today, half a century after the black exodus entered upon its full tide, most blacks still live in the South. According to the census of 1970, in no state of the former Confederacy, except Texas, is the proportion of black population less than 15 percent; in no state outside the South was the figure that high. Indeed, only three northern states counted more than 11.1 percent, the proportion that blacks make up in the national population.

Since 1945 the cities of the South have been the fastest growing in the nation, suggesting that by the end of this century or soon thereafter the South may have closed the gap between its proportion of urban folk and that of the remainder of the country. But as we have seen, that gap still exists, still sets the South apart from the rest of America. In 1973, George Tindall's presidential address before the Southern Historical Association stressed the continuing divergence between southerners and other Americans by referring to southerners as an ethnic minority. And a recent collection of essays by him bears the title *The Ethnic Southerners*.[20] In short, neither in the realm of social fact nor in the realm of psychological identity has the South ceased to be distinctive, despite the changes of the twentieth century.

This long persistence of a distinctive South, with its promise of enduring for many decades to come, is a challenge to those of us who seek to interpret the American experience. Too often in generalizing about Americans, whether under the rubric of national character or simply under the heading of seeing Americans as a people different from Europeans or Asians, the South as a part of America is somehow ignored. The South usually upsets all our glib generalizations about what America has been and what it is. How can one talk about the immigrant experience as fundamental to nineteenth- and twentieth-century America when so few immigrants settled in the South in those years? Or how can one generalize about the rise of industry and the spread of urbanization in the last century without recognizing that these social developments were not, for the South, nineteenth-century phenomena? For the South they are only mid-twentieth-century developments. The South's distinctiveness presents a problem to those who would talk about national character, for southerners indubitably live in America; but, equally indubitably, they are not like other Americans. They are more conservative, more nationalistic, more self-identified, more defensive, and more romantic than other Americans—or so the polls and subjective studies tell us. Their differences can be measured rather objectively and precisely, too. Southerners are less rich, less urban, less diverse demographically and religiously, and more likely to be black than the rest of Americans.

These differences have such obvious consequences for the people of the South that no one born in the region—or outside it—can afford to ignore them. Almost seventy-five years ago W. E. B. Du Bois reminded American Negroes of their two-ness, of their being both Negroes and Americans. No southerner, so far as I know, has yet seen fit to write about the two-ness of southerners, though I think someone ought to; certainly the duality is there. Lewis Killian, in his *White Southerners,* has suggested it, and Willie Morris has alluded to it. Lyndon Johnson, for one, was certainly oppressed by the disadvantages of it. In his autobiography he tells why he considered not running for the presidency in 1964:

> I did not believe, any more than I ever had, that the nation would unite indefinitely behind any Southerner. One reason the country could not rally behind a Southern president, I was convinced, was that the metropolitan press of the Eastern Seaboard would never permit it. My experience in office had confirmed this reaction. I was not thinking just of the derisive articles about my style, my clothes, my manner, my accent, and my family—although I admit I received enough of that kind of treatment in my first few months as President to last a lifetime. I was also thinking of a more deep-seated and far-reaching attitude—a disdain for the South that seems to be woven into the fabric of Northern experience. This is a subject that deserves a more profound exploration than I can give it here—a subject that has never been sufficiently examined. Perhaps it all stems from the deep-rooted bitterness engendered by civil strife over a hundred years ago, for emotional clichés outlast all others and the Southern cliché is perhaps the most emotional of all. Perhaps some day new understanding will cause this bias to disappear from our national life. I hope so, but it is with us still.[21]

Many other southerners undoubtedly have been hurt by it, too. In his memoirs Harry Truman wrote that if Senator Richard Russell had not been a Georgian he would have been president. One does not have to accept Harry Truman's particular candidate to recognize in a flash the validity of his point. Without the accident of John F. Kennedy's assassination, it seems highly unlikely that Lyndon Johnson would ever have become president. Yet, until the election of Jimmy Carter in 1976, Johnson was the only president elected from the South since Zachary Taylor in 1848.

C. Vann Woodward has been so impressed by the special experience of the South that at one time he thought southerners had gained from their past a view of the world that other Americans lacked. In his famous essay "The Irony of Southern History," which appeared in 1953, Woodward contrasted the South's experience with that of the nation. He pointed out that "the South had undergone an experience that it could share with no other part of America—though it is shared by nearly all the peoples of Europe and Asia—the experience of military defeat, occupation, and reconstruction." Because of the fact that, as he said, quoting Arnold Toynbee, "history had happened" to southerners, their history had something to teach the rest of Americans. When that history is understood, Woodward continued, we "should at least have a special awareness of the ironic incongruities between moral purpose and pragmatic result, of the way in which laudable aims of idealists can be perverted to sordid purposes, and of the readiness with which high-minded ideals can be forgotten." [22] That innocence, despite the national myth, is not a fact of our national life.

Yet one has only to read Woodward's essay "A Second Look at the Theme of Irony," published fifteen years later, to recognize the danger of reading too much into the differences between southerners and other Americans. For by then Woodward recognized that growing up in the South did not necessarily have the same effect upon all southerners that contemplating the history of the South had had upon him personally. Being engulfed in the southern past had not automatically invested southerners with that sense of limits and of life's complexities that the knowledge of the South's history had provided Woodward. The war in Vietnam and the unfinished Negro revolution, Woodward observed in 1968, brought home to Americans that, whatever they may once have thought, success is not automatic. Then comes his own shock of recognition. "If there were ever a time when Americans might profit from the un-American heritage of the South, it would seem to be the present," he candidly writes.

But if history had caught up with the Americans, it would seem that the irony of history had caught up with the ironist—or gone him one better.

For in this fateful hour of opportunity history had ironically placed men of presumably authentic Southern heritage in the supreme seats of national power—a gentleman from Texas in the White House and a gentleman from Georgia in the State Department. And yet from those quarters came few challenges and little appreciable restraint to the pursuit of the national myths of invincibility and innocence. . . . So far as the war and the pursuit of victory were concerned, the people of the South seemed to be as uncompromising as those of any part of the country and more so than many.[23]

F. Garvin Davenport Jr., in his penetrating book *The Myth of Southern History,* put the matter even more sharply. He pointedly observed that those who thought the South offered an alternative to innocence and self-righteousness were sounding "hollow by the time of the presidential campaign of 1968 when the two most important Southerners were [George] Wallace and Strom Thurmond."[24]

The South has been an alternative to the rest of the nation, for that is one of the unavoidable consequences of its distinctiveness. But, as we have seen, there are limits to that distinctiveness. Perhaps, as Woodward has argued, southern history ought to have made southerners more aware of the limits of human action and more tolerant of the need for compromise and adjustment. The trouble is that southerners exhibit these traits no more than other Americans.

Limited though the differences between southerners and other Americans may be, they are worth celebrating as well as recognizing. Too many modern southerners, it seems to me as an outlander, are prone to minimize or even deny those differences between the South and the nation. Not all of the traits that distinguish the South are admirable, to be sure. Yet what region or society is without its social blemishes? Moreover, the transformation within the South on race relations over the last decade goes a long way toward making up for the region's most glaring deficiency. Today, government reports tell us, there is less public school segregation in the South than in the North, and the election of Jimmy Carter to the presidency by the votes of southern whites and blacks tells a story of change in the South that is only beginning to be appreciated. In a profound sense, the great goal of nineteenth-century southern dissenters and Populists—cooperation between blacks and whites—has finally been achieved. Here, too, the South may well be offering an alternative to the nation. In any event, the South's powerful appeal to its own people—black and white alike—as well as to other Americans, has surely been the alternative it embodies and offers: in its landscape of wooded mountains, red clay hills, harsh sand barrens, lush forest, and watery wastes; in the humid feel of its hot climate; in the sweet, exotic tastes of its foods, in the soft, liquid sound and careless elisions of its speech; in its rurally rooted conservatism and provincialism; in the violence and conformity of its social order; in the human warmth and security of its commitment to family and kin; and, above all, in its enduring sense of personal and regional identity born from a history no other American shares.

These and other traits that help us to begin to define the South's elusive distinctiveness have an additional meaning. Many of those differences, as we have seen, can be traced back into the history of the region. In the apt metaphor of W. J. Cash, "The South . . . is a tree with many age rings, with its limbs and trunks bent and twisted by all the winds of the years, but with its tap root in the Old South" of slavery and the plantation. In the persistence for more than 150 years of those characteristics that have made the South distinctive lies the reality of the continuity of southern history.

NOTES

1. Quoted in Michael P. Johnson, *Toward a Patriarchal Republic: The Secession of Georgia* (Baton Rouge: Louisiana State University Press, 1977).

2. Quoted in James L. Roark, *Masters without Slaves: Southern Planters in the Civil War and Reconstruction* (New York: Norton, 1977).

3. Eric L. McKitrick, "Party Politics and the Urban and Confederate War Efforts," in *The American Party System: Stages of Political Development,* ed. William Nisbet Chambers and Walter Dean Burnham (New York: Oxford University Press, 1967).

4. William Faulkner, *Intruder in the Dust* (New York: Random House, 1948), 194–95.

5. David Morris Potter, *The Impending Crisis, 1848–1861* (New York: Harper & Row, 1976), 469.

6. Henry W. Hilliard, *Politics and Pen Pictures at Home and Abroad* (New York: G. P. Putnam's Sons, 1892), 421.

7. Clement Eaton, *The Waning of the Old South Civilization, 1860–1880s* (Athens: University of Georgia Press, 1968), 171.

8. "A Robert E. Lee Letter on Abandoning the South after The War," ed. William Tate, *Georgia Historical Quarterly* 37 (1953): 255–56.

9. Richard H. Edmonds, *The Old South and the New* (N.p., n.d., but ascribed to 1903), 5.

10. Eugene M. Lerner, "Southern Output and Agricultural Income, 1860–1880," in *The Economic Impact of the American Civil War,* ed. Ralph Andreano (Cambridge: Schenkman, 1967).

11. J. L. M. Curry to Manly Curry, 16 Sept. 1889, Curry Papers, Manuscript Division, Duke University Library.

12. *Southern States* 3 (1895): 401.

13. Stanley L. Engerman, "The Effects of Slavery upon the Southern Economy: A Review of the Recent Debate," *Explorations in Entrepreneurial History,* 2d ser., 4 (1967): 87; Morton Rothstein, "The Cotton Frontier of the American South: A Methodological Battleground," in *The Structure of the Cotton Economy of the Antebellum South,* ed. William Nelson Parker (Washington: Agricultural History Society, 1970), 162.

14. Richard A. Easterlin, "Regional Income Trends, 1840–1950," in *American Economic History,* ed. Seymour Harris (New York: McGraw-Hill, 1961), 528.

15. C. Vann Woodward, *Origins of the New South, 1877–1913,* vol. 9 of A History of the South, series ed. Wendell Holmes Stephenson and Ellis Merton Coulter (Baton Rouge: Louisiana State University Press, 1951), 179.

16. Jonathan M. Wiener, "Planter-Merchant Conflict in Reconstruction Alabama," *Past and Present,* no. 68 (1975): 73–94; idem, "Planter Persistence and Social Change: Alabama, 1850–1870," *Journal of Interdisciplinary History* 7 (1976): 254.

17. Roger Ransom and Richard Sutch, "Debt Peonage in the Cotton South after the Civil War," *Journal of Economic History* 32 (1972): 641–69. See also their forthcoming book, which will expand the documentation, application, and analysis in several important ways, idem, *One Kind of Freedom; the Economic Consequences of Emancipation* (Cambridge: Cambridge University Press, 1977). [Ransom and Sutch in the published book ringingly reaffirm most of Woodward's themes, and in their essay on sources direct readers to *Origins of the New South* for an overall historical view of changes after the Civil War. *Ed.*]

18. Robert Higgs, "Race, Tenure, and Resource Allocation in Southern Agriculture, 1910," *Journal of Economic History* 33 (1973): 149–70; idem, *Competition and Coercion: Blacks in the American Economy, 1865–1914* (Cambridge: Cambridge University Press, 1977); Stephen J. DeCanio, *Agriculture in the Postbellum South: The Economics of Production and Supply* (Cambridge: M.I.T. Press, 1974).

19. Quoted in Paul M. Gaston, *The New South Creed: A Study in Southern Mythmaking* (New York: Knopf, 1970), 118.

20. George Brown Tindall, *The Ethnic Southerners* (Baton Rouge: Louisiana State University Press, 1976).

21. Lyndon Baines Johnson, *The Vantage Point: Perspectives of the Presidency, 1963–1969* (New York: Holt, Rinehart & Winston, 1971), 95.

22. C. Vann Woodward, *The Burden of Southern History* (Baton Rouge: Louisiana State University Press, 1960), 169–70, 189.

23. Ibid., rev. ed. (1968), 230.

24. F. Garvin Davenport Jr., *The Myth of Southern History: Historical Consciousness in Twentieth-Century Southern Literature* (Nashville: Vanderbilt University Press, 1970), 170.

III

Building and Rebuilding:
Economic Reconstruction and
Political Compromise

✳

An Epitaph for the Writing of Reconstruction History?

AUGUST MEIER

✳

August Meier has been one of the sturdiest of scholars committed to the reformist mission in the profession of history. Raised in the Newark, New Jer-
sey, of the 1920s, Meier absorbed radical and dissident traditions but also
a certain hard-edged practicality from his Eastern European Jewish mother
and his German father, who met in socialist political campaigns. Studying at
Oberlin and then receiving his Ph.D. from Columbia University, Meier subsequently worked for two decades in predominantly black colleges of the
border South and the Deep South. From the mid-1960s to 1986, he produced, with his friend the sociologist Elliott Rudwick, some major studies:
From Plantation to Ghetto and *CORE*. At the same time and continuing into
the final decade of the twentieth century, he served the University of Illinois
Press as editor of his own superb series, *Blacks in the New World*. Sometimes likening himself to professional football's tough coach Vince Lom-
bardi, Meier often adopted a combative style in debates and discussions, but
his supple mind has been as often marked by sympathy and compassion. In
this book-review essay, he wrote an epitaph for the Beardian, and therefore
Woodwardian, historiography of Reconstruction, but he did so as much with
sadness of recognition as with any other expression of emotion, since there
have been few historians whom he has admired more than the Arkansan. He
has also noted here what is lost when the new generation abandons Woodward's class analysis and economic determinism in this Reconstruction historiography. Left unsaid is the regret that Woodward did not himself write
the grand interpretive study of Reconstruction that his many suggestive essays once promised.

✳　✳　✳

William Gillette. *Retreat from Reconstruction, 1869–1879*. Baton Rouge: Louisiana
State University Press, 1979. xv + 463 pp. Tables, notes, bibliographical essay, acknowledgments, and index. $27.50.

Otto H. Olsen, ed. *Reconstruction and Redemption in the South*. Baton Rouge: Louisiana State University Press, 1980. v + 250 pp. Notes on contributors and index. $17.50.

Two generations have passed since the appearance of the monographs associated with the Dunning school of Reconstruction history. Yet today historians of Reconstruction still tend to write with these works as their point of departure, which implies that Reconstruction historiography is still in the business of refuting this early school of historians. In actual fact, however, the point of departure that modern scholars are really using, and the interpretation that they are really refuting, is the economic interpretation of Reconstruction history so brilliantly argued by a group of influential historians from Charles A. Beard to C. Vann Woodward. When looked at closely, the bulk of writing in the past two decades has involved an attempt to undermine the approach employed by men like Beard, Howard K. Beale, and Woodward. In fact, in a curious way, as the two books under review here illustrate, the most recent scholarship has stood Dunning on his head. For, although modern students of Reconstruction do not share Dunning's animus against blacks and radical Republicans or his bias in favor of the white South, they have minimized the significance of economic motivations and of economic interest groups and have instead returned to Dunning's emphasis on politics and race.

This undermining of the economic interpretation that once enjoyed such wide popularity has come from several directions. An important ingredient of Woodward's own outlook is his serious concern with the contradiction between American ideals and American practice inherent in the oppression of American blacks. Economic interpretation of history is in and of itself ethically neutral. In the hands of the Beardians of the 1930s it was largely used to discredit the motives of the abolitionists and the Radical Republicans; in fact, I suspect that one reason scholars find it necessary to make their ritualistic obeisance to the Dunning school is just because, in the hands of the Beardians, crass economic motives seemed to justify a negative assessment of Radical and Black Reconstruction. Yet at the same time, in the hands of a masterful humanist and careful researcher, as Woodward is, such an interpretation becomes an indictment of the way in which white Americans treated blacks during Reconstruction. But Woodward, an heir of New Deal reformism as well as Beardian economic interpretation, himself did much to promote the serious and sympathetic treatment of the black people's role in the post–Civil War years.

There were, of course, the older studies by A. A. Taylor of blacks in the Reconstruction of South Carolina and Virginia (1924 and 1926), and Vernon Lane Wharton's on Mississippi (1947), but it was a Woodward student, Willie Lee Rose, who signaled the way in which the black experience has become a major concern of Reconstruction historians.[1]

Rose's work, *Rehearsal for Reconstruction* (1964), was thus more aptly named than even she divined, for it not only pinpointed the Civil War years as a rehearsal for what followed but was also a rehearsal for the new treatment of blacks that developed in mainstream writing on Reconstruction. Her line of inquiry merged in turn with another independent stream of historical writing, the new paradigm that emerged by the 1970s of what black history was all about—or the importance of studying the persistence and development of black community and a distinctive black subculture. Informed also by the attention to the ambiguities and complexities of human behavior on the part of both blacks and whites that appears in the works of Rose and especially of Eugene D. Genovese (particularly his *Roll, Jordan, Roll* [1974]), this line of inquiry achieved its mature expression in Leon Litwack's *Been in the Storm So Long* (1979). More a striking synthesis of approaches pioneered by others than an original contribution in its methodology, this is a wonderfully researched, beautifully detailed, and convincingly written volume; devoted to the period of presidential Reconstruction, it is a model that will influence works on the black experience during Reconstruction for years to come.[2]

Meanwhile, another fascinating new direction in Reconstruction historiography that served to undermine the economic interpretation was the utilization of questions and techniques derived from political science and political sociology, first expressed in Eric L. McKitrick's seminal *Andrew Johnson and Reconstruction* (1960; reprint, 1988) and brought to maturity in such thoughtful and highly sophisticated volumes as Michael Les Benedict's study of congressional Republicans during the early Reconstruction years, *A Compromise of Principle* (1974) and Thomas Holt's model state of black participation in South Carolina Reconstruction politics, *Black over White* (1977).[3]

A third source undermining the Beardian approach was, of course, the direct assault on economic determinism and motivation and the significance for southern and racial policy of economic interest groups first enunciated by Stanley Coben's pathbreaking article in the *Mississippi Valley Historical Review*, "Northeastern Business and Radical Reconstruction: A Reexamination" (1959).[4] Demonstrating in a highly convincing fashion that correlations could not be established between political alignment and economic issues, the essay paved the way for the virtual abandonment of serious efforts to ascertain the economic motives in the politics of actors on the stage of Reconstruction.

The two books under consideration here in many ways reflect the current state of affairs in Reconstruction history very well. At first glance one would think that they would be complementary volumes that would hopefully supply us with some good generalizations about the decline of Reconstruction and the victory of the Redemptionists. William Gillette's book approaches this question from the perspective of Washington, while the Otto Olsen anthology approaches this problem from the perspective of several individual southern states. Yet the two volumes offer us no basis for adequate generalization; instead they amply demonstrate the dissolution of an older synthesis.

Both volumes have admirable qualities. Most of the essays in Olsen's anthology are well-crafted summaries and analyses by experts in the individual states covered. Gillette's ambitious study, involving monumental research in newspaper and manuscript collections, is also characterized by carefully constructed arguments. It is unfortunate that he did not use quantitative techniques and that he still sticks to his original interpretation about the Fifteenth Amendment, even though it has been effectively undermined by the Coxes and Benedict.[5] Gillette's volume is a learned political narrative, analyzing the activities of Congress and the executive branch that, combined with unstable northern public opinion, led to the collapse of Reconstruction. (It would have lent more sophistication to Gillette's analysis if he had elected to pay greater attention to the role of the Supreme Court, integrating his analysis with Stanley Kutler's revisionist interpretation in *Judicial Power and Reconstruction Politics* [1968],[6] but this was admittedly beyond the parameters he had set for himself.) Although Benedict's volume argues that 1867 was, to paraphrase Trevelyan's remark about the revolutions of 1848, a kind of turning point in Reconstruction on which Reconstruction failed to turn, Gillette makes a fairly good case for his thesis that, with the election of Grant, Republicans were in a position to carry out in earnest their Reconstruction policies. That they failed to do so is the burden of this book.

The analyses of Grant's reactions to the varying situations in the different southern states is a masterful account that explains his inconsistency and why, given the situation in the different states and the volatility of northern public opinion, no consistent policy was possible for the president. Then, Gillette, turning to an analysis of the voters' behavior and the actions of congressmen, examines the tergiversations of senators and representatives, giving considerable attention to the fate of what became the Civil Rights Law of 1875 (and in the end offering an explanation of its passage no more satisfying, I think, than the explanation he earlier presented for the passage of the Fifteenth Amendment). In the final analysis, despite the fact that in his introduction Gillette asserts that the failure of Reconstruction cannot be explained by the existence of unmitigated racism, the thrust of his argument is to place the blame exactly on that source. What we are left with is a species of political and psychological reductionism—the lack of Grant's firmness in the face of complex political realities, the ambitions of northern Democratic and Republican politicians, and the deeply embedded racism of white Americans both North and South—as the explanation of the failure of Reconstruction.

Gillette is very much in the new mode of Reconstruction historiography in his obviously deliberate decision not to deal with economic motivations. The same is true for most of the essays in Olsen's anthology, although at least two of them do give fairly considerable attention to class distinction and economic factors. But Olsen's volume reveals another problem arising from modern research in Reconstruction. Clearly, the well-researched, thoughtfully interpreted case study is essential if we are to build broader generalizations about the crucial periods in American history. Yet, because each state has such a different history, and undoubtedly because each of the authors approaches his subject with different perspectives and assumptions, what emerges is confusion. We do know at the abstract level that in each ex-Confederate state Reconstruction was undermined and Redemption occurred; yet no generalizations seem to emerge as to just why this came about. Unlike the anthology of essays edited by James C. Mohr on *Radical Republicans in the North* (1976),[7] Olsen's introduction does not attempt to draw meaningful generalizations about political behavior in the various southern states and the way it fed into the process by which Reconstruction was dismantled. Undoubtedly, this is because—the excellent factual data on individual states presented in this volume notwithstanding—no such generalizations seem viable.

With the final dissolution of Woodward's synthesis, we are at loose ends. There has been excellent recent economic history (Roger L. Ransom and Richard Sutch, *One Kind of Freedom* [1977]) about the changing status of the freedmen, and there has been a sophisticated analysis of the interplay between politics and economic interest groups that later led to passage of the southern disfranchisement laws (J. Morgan Kousser, *The Shaping of Southern Politics* [1974]).[8] Yet, with all our new research techniques, and with all the data that modern technology enables the historian to accumulate and digest, the historical reality of Reconstruction seems so complex that an understanding of its dynamics continues to elude our grasp. There is also, of course, the matter of preconceptions and the kinds of queries and the modes of analysis that are employed.

Historical fashion tends to move from one thing to another, without effective synthesis of the insights of one generation of historians with those that follow. Thus, just because economic motivation, and its relationship to political action, has been shown to be so complex, there is no reason to discard it entirely. It calls instead for even more refined and complex analyses. Economic, moral, and political motivations are inexplicably interwoven in the actions and thinking of politicians and interest groups. Thus, among Republicans as among Democrats, the specific constellation of motivations varies from person to person and from group to group. The task, it seems to me, is not to try to find some easy overall generalization about the motivation of Republicans in general, or Radical Republicans as a whole, but to study how the different factors varied from person to person, becoming intricately interwoven with each other in many different ways, and how these many individual cases in turn interacted with each other to produce the constellation of forces that produced the historical results we know. (No matter how much racial attitudes and personal political ambition or party concerns influenced congressmen and presidents, to ignore—or minimize—the economic motivations of politicians and their constituencies simply means discarding the obvious insights of Aristotle and Madison about the underlying dynamics of what happens in a republican polity.)

It may be, of course, that adequate data simply do not survive to enable us to ascertain with any degree of certainty the motives of more than a handful of the major actors on the political scene. Benedict's essay in the November 1980 issue of the *Journal of Southern History* on "The Compromise of 1877" brings out this problem in a very sobering fashion. For his striking analysis of the particular set of correspondence on which Vann Woodward leaned so heavily for his interpretation of the Compromise of 1877 seems to reveal how limited can be the sources on which historians of necessity must base their important conclusions.[9]

Seldom, if ever, have competent and careful volumes such as these served simultaneously to disappoint me and yet stimulate my thinking so much. In short, the discrediting of economic analyses and interpretations in connection with political history and the return instead to a Dunning focus on politics and race provide no final answer to the questions that modern scholarship on Reconstruction is raising; or if they do, we face an epistemological crisis of the most serious proportions.

NOTES

1. Alrutheus Ambush Taylor, *The Negro in South Carolina during the Reconstruction* (Washington: Association for the Study of Negro Life and History, 1924); idem, *The Negro in the Reconstruction of Virginia* (Washington: Association for the Study of Negro Life and History, 1926); Vernon Lane Wharton, *The Negro in Mississippi, 1865–1890* (Chapel Hill: University of North Carolina Press, 1947); Willie

Lee Rose, *Rehearsal for Reconstruction: The Port Royal Experiment* (Indianapolis: Bobbs-Merrill, 1964).

2. Eugene Dominick Genovese, *Roll, Jordan, Roll: The World the Slaves Made* (New York: Knopf, 1974); Leon Litwack, *Been in the Storm So Long: The Aftermath of Slavery* (New York: Random House, 1980).

3. Eric L. McKitrick, *Andrew Johnson and Reconstruction* (1960; reprint, New York: Oxford University Press, 1988); Michael Les Benedict, *A Compromise of Principle: Congressional Republicans and Reconstruction, 1863–1869* (New York: Norton, 1974); and Thomas Holt, *Black over White: Negro Political Leaders in South Carolina during Reconstruction* (Urbana: University of Illinois Press, 1977).

4. Stanley Coben, "Northeastern Business and Radical Reconstruction: A Reexamination," *Mississippi Valley Historical Review* 46 (1959): 67–90.

5. LaWanda and John H. Cox, "Negro Suffrage and Republican Politics: The Problem of Motivation in Reconstruction Historiography," *Journal of Southern History* 33 (1967): 303–30; Benedict, *A Compromise of Principle*, chap. 17.

6. Stanley I. Kutler, *Judicial Power and Reconstruction Politics* (Chicago: University of Chicago Press, 1968).

7. James C. Mohr, ed., *Radical Republicans in the North; State Politics during Reconstruction* (Baltimore: Johns Hopkins University Press, 1976).

8. Roger L. Ransom and Richard Sutch, *One Kind of Freedom; the Economic Consequences of Emancipation* (Cambridge: Cambridge University Press, 1977); J. Morgan Kousser, *The Shaping of Southern Politics: Suffrage Restriction and the Establishment of the One-Party South, 1880–1910* (New Haven: Yale University Press, 1974).

9. Michael Les Benedict, "Southern Democrats in the Crisis of 1876–1877: A Reconsideration of *Reunion and Reaction*," *Journal of Southern History* 46 (1980): 489–524.

Was There a Compromise of 1877?

ALLAN PESKIN

✳

After the initial enthusiasm for Woodward's detective work in his 1951 description of the end of Reconstruction, critics began to question some of his conclusions about the nature of the political maneuvering that ended Republican rule in the states of South Carolina, Louisiana, and Florida but also negated Democrat Samuel J. Tilden's apparent electoral victory as president. It was Allan Peskin of Cleveland State University who asked the ultimate question, *was there actually a Compromise in 1877?* Careful search work in the personal and family papers of presidents James Abram Garfield and Rutherford Birchard Hayes, together with close reading of the secondary sources, convinced Peskin that there was no compromise after all. Although Peskin initially convinced only a few historians with this carefully investigated paper, he did provoke Woodward into a reply in the same 1973 issue of the *Journal of American History,* at the time an unusual reaction for the Arkansan (although later he did respond often and directly to critics, not only in the periodicals, but at conferences, in correspondence, and in his memoirs). In time others were inspired by Peskin, including Michael Les Benedict—who said that the Democrats and Republicans bargained purely out of fear of violence, not for the sake of economic horse-trading—and Keith Ian Polakoff, who said conversely that there really was no violence to fear and that the northern Democrats acceded to unfolding events because Tilden himself was hors de combat after a stroke and because of the inertia in their own misguided campaign.

✳   ✳   ✳

There was a time, not too long ago, when the disputed election of 1876 could be treated as a relatively uncomplicated story. The Democratic candidate, Samuel J. Tilden, had won the popular vote and undisputed title to 184 electoral votes, only one short of victory. The campaign managers of Rutherford B. Hayes claimed victory for their side on the basis of disputed returns from the three southern states still under Republican control—Louisiana, Florida, and South Carolina. The ensuing deadlock proved unresolvable by traditional means, and, in "one of the wisest pieces of statecraft ever evolved by an American Congress,"[1] an extraordinary electoral commission was created, composed of members of the Senate, House, and Supreme Court. The decision of this commission in favor of Hayes, by a strictly partisan eight-to-seven vote, so angered Democrats that many of them openly threatened revolution, while others in the House of Representatives began a filibuster to prevent Hayes's inauguration. Fortunately for the nation, reasonable men in both parties struck a bargain at Wormley's House, a hotel in Washington. There, in the traditional smoke-filled room, emissaries of Hayes agreed to abandon the Republican state governments in Louisiana and South Carolina while southern Democrats agreed to abandon the filibuster and thus trade off the presidency in exchange for the end of Reconstruction.

This familiar account was challenged in 1951 with the publication of C. Vann Woodward's *Reunion and Reaction: The Compromise of 1877 and the End of Reconstruction*.[2] Generally well received by reviewers in the major historical journals,[3] Woodward's new interpretation soon won "almost universal acceptance."[4] The thesis was widely reprinted and was incorporated, virtually unchanged, in almost every major textbook of American history,[5] achieving the status of the most influential monograph in its field.

Ignoring the electoral commission and dismissing the Wormley's House bargain as inconsequential, Woodward probed beneath the surface to discover the tangled bargain of 1877, finding in a semisecret set of negotiations between Republicans and southern Democrats the long-hidden key to the resolution of the crisis. These southerners, many of them former Whigs, represented the emerging business and industry of the New South. Many Republicans, including Hayes—himself a former Whig—had more in common with these respectable conservative southerners than they had with the Radicals, carpetbaggers, and Negroes who constituted the Republican party in the South. Drawn together by common economic interest, they hammered out a compromise that allowed Hayes to enter the White House and that, not incidentally, marked the end of an era.

Southern cooperation was not bought cheaply. The bulk of Woodward's book is devoted to computing the price tag of the agreement. It is a sophisticated, complex analysis, difficult to summarize. Subsequent historians, however, lacking Woodward's caution, have simplified his thesis to read like this: "the South settled the issue by trading the Presidency for: (1) final withdrawal of Federal troops from the three disputed sites; (2) a promise of financial aid in the construction of the Texas and Pacific Railroad; (3) the appointment of a southerner as Postmaster General; (4) the assurance of Federal subsidies to aid southern rehabilitation; and (5) a tacit admission that the South alone should resolve its racial problem."[6] In addition, some southerners promised to help the Republicans organize the next House of Representatives; and Hayes, in turn, hoped to build up a respectable, white Republican party in the South.

The result of all this bargaining, Woodward argued, was more than a political deal: "When political agreements involve the destinies of millions of people and areas of continental expanse, they ordinarily achieve a dignity above the bargain level and become diplomacy."[7] It was, in fact, a vast sectional compromise worthy to be placed alongside those of 1787, 1820, and 1850.

Yet if one tabulates the results of this famous compromise they seem surprisingly meager—no subsidy was granted to the Texas & Pacific Railroad; no southerners broke party ranks to help the Republicans control the House of Representatives; and the Republican party would have to wait for almost another century to win a foothold in the South. It appears that the road to reunion was paved with broken promises.

A deal whose major terms are never carried out appears suspiciously like no deal at all. A review of each of the components of this bargain seems called for in order to determine just what effect each had on the making of a president in 1877.

First, there was the promise of home rule. Until Woodward's work historians had placed their major emphasis on this aspect of the bargain and treated the so-called withdrawal of federal troops from the South[8] as the *quid* for which the inauguration of Hayes was the *quo*. But if southerners wanted above all else to ensure the collapse of the remaining carpetbag governments, then there was no need to trade off the presidency to achieve their goal. Why should they desert their party to obtain from Hayes what they were certain to get from Tilden? So long as the choice was between Hayes and Tilden, the promise of home rule could play no part in settling the election crisis. Once Tilden had been eliminated from consideration, especially after the decision of the electoral commission, and the choice was no longer between two candidates but between Hayes and chaos, then and only then could southern Democrats negotiate for home rule. This part of the bargain, therefore, did not determine the outcome of the election. In fact, the raising of the issue merely confirmed the hopelessness of Tilden's cause.

The same point may be made regarding some of the economic aspects of the alleged compromise—the levees, canals, harbors, and other federally sponsored internal improvements that were to compensate the South for coming late to "the Great Barbecue."[9] Certainly, southerners hungered for these benefits. And they were certainly aware that they stood a better chance

Hayes to the strategy of detaching southern conservatives from their northern Democratic colleagues,[16] was also the ranking Republican on the House
Pacific Railroad Committee. This put him in a strategic position to aid Scott,
if he were so inclined. Although sympathetic to the general idea of a railroad
linking the South to the Pacific Coast,[17] Garfield was by no means convinced
of the merits of Scott's plan. Early in 1876, he had declared that he would
oppose it even if every man in his district should favor it. At the same time,
however, he had hinted to Lucius Q. C. Lamar, the committee chairman and
Scott's friend, that he could be persuaded to change his mind.[18] If so, the most
opportune time would certainly have been during the crisis winter of 1876–
77. Garfield and Lamar were in constant communication during those hectic
months, and they understood each other well. Had the Texas & Pacific subsidy been Lamar's price for the support of Hayes, Garfield was in a position
to give a clear and explicit signal that the Republican party was willing to
pay that price. Instead, he signed the minority report, which harshly condemned Scott's plan as unwarranted, expensive, and potentially fraudulent.[19]
Privately, he was sorry that he had to disappoint Scott, for, as he told an
emissary from Hayes, he suspected that a timely subsidy to the Texas & Pacific might well win Republican support in the South and could even turn
Texas into a Republican state.[20] Yet such speculation remained a wistful regret and nothing more.

Next to Hayes himself, no one stood to gain more from a working arrangement with southern Democrats than did Garfield. Such an alliance, it was
hinted, could make him Speaker of the House, a position he openly coveted.
Yet, despite this temptation, he refused to make a gesture for the sake of the
Texas & Pacific Railroad. His reluctance was based on a suspicion of southern
good faith. When the compromise was first broached he had expressed reservations. "I am not sure that these men can be trusted,"[21] he warily recorded,
and further acquaintance with them did nothing to relieve his skepticism.

Certainly, the picture of Scott that emerges from the pages of *Reunion
and Reaction* does not seem designed to inspire anyone's confidence. He fan-
cied himself an intriguer, constantly hinting at bribed congressmen, boasting
of packed committees, and "wheeling and dealing" with manic energy. Yet,
time after time, his schemes exploded in his face. And in the end, he was
thwarted by Collis P. Huntington, who employed the straightforward, almost simple-minded tactic of building a rival railroad with his own money
while Scott was waiting for a federal subsidy. Scott and his friends may have
talked as if the backstage role of Texas & Pacific was decisive in settling the
election crisis, but lobbyists are always anxious to magnify their own influence. It can hardly be denied that Scott was engaged in furious bargaining,

but could he make good on his end of the bargain? Many men claimed to be kingmakers during the election crisis, but, as Garfield later asked with not altogether feigned innocence, "What man here had a Presidency for sale or was in the market to buy a Presidency? Let the man who claims to have had such wares to sell show his title to them." [22]

Scott boasted of controlling vast forces, but in a showdown he was not able to deliver them. The behavior of former Texas governor James W. Throckmorton is highly instructive. Throckmorton, whom Woodward classifies as "a long-term employee of Scott's and an inveterate subsidy man," [23] was regarded by a Texas & Pacific agent as "more valuable to us than any man we have here. . . . He appears to be devoted to our interests. . . ." [24] Yet when Republicans sounded out Throckmorton for support he responded with a resounding refusal. "There is no consideration that would induce me to vote for Gen. Garfield [for Speaker of the House], or any member of his party," he insisted. "As much as I am wedded to the success of the Texas & Pacific R Road, I would not do it to secure it success. To take off the yoke of military tyranny from Louisiana and North [sic] Carolina, I would not do it. There is nothing—no office in the gift of President or people or Congress that would induce me to do so. If the South cannot have full justice without such a sacrifice (as such act on my part)," he concluded, "then the South must wait." [25] If Scott could not command the vote of someone on his own payroll, whose vote could he command?

Garfield's correspondence during this period was filled with letters from men who guaranteed that their influence could make him Speaker. One, who wanted a government job, claimed that he could control the Know-Nothing vote, insisting that "the Knownothing party was still in existence in full blast, lying back like a couchant lion waiting to spring when the time comes." [26] Another, who seemed more plausible because of his position as president of the Republican Southern Association, offered to use his influence with southern congressmen, especially those close to the Texas & Pacific. Garfield encouraged his activity until he discovered that he had also approached Charles Foster with an offer to make Foster Speaker in return for $500. [27] It might seem unfair to lump Scott with a crank and a petty swindler, but, in view of the result, such a comparison is not altogether unfitting. Despite frequent assurances that Scott was "all right on your nomination for speaker," [28] Garfield found that Scott's promised legions vanished when they were needed. Scott was no power broker, only a hustler working both sides of the street and hoping to win the gratitude of whoever might wind up in a position to help him.

There remains to be considered the purely political aspect of the compromise—the agreement that southerners would support Hayes in return for federal patronage. This was the most thoroughly developed part of whatever bargain was made in 1877. Hayes kept his promise to appoint a southerner, David M. Key of Tennessee, to his cabinet as postmaster general, and under this dispensation one-third of all southern appointments went to Democrats.[29] Yet this agreement could hardly have determined the outcome of the disputed election, for if Tilden had been allowed to sit in the White House, southern Democrats could have expected three-thirds of all this patronage. Hayes could not outbid the Democrats on this score.

The rapprochement between Republicans and southern conservatives looked beyond the immediate electoral crisis to a future realignment of national party politics. The appointment of Key was originally suggested not so much as a means of settling the election crisis, but rather as a step toward that realignment.[30] If this alliance could be cemented, it was believed, the Republican party would no longer be sectional, no longer tied to the fortunes of the Negro or the leftover issues of the Civil War. Instead, it was hoped that in both the North and the South men could choose their party associates "on the great commercial and industrial questions rather than on questions of race and color." To these hopes, Hayes gave his blessing.[31]

This projected new departure was no spur-of-the-moment improvisation. It had been contemplated even before the election dispute erupted and might very well have been attempted even if Hayes had won a clear-cut victory. According to Thomas B. Alexander, southern conservatives of a Whiggish bent had been toying with the idea of a rapprochement with northern Republicans for some time, and a recent study has concluded that Hayes had also been receptive to such a move "long before anyone could know that there was going to be a disputed election and a so-called 'bargain.'"[32] The electoral crisis gave both the president and his new-found southern friends an opportunity to put into effect their long-matured plans.

Yet, in the end, this experiment proved as barren of lasting results as all the other parts of the great compromise. Neither side to the agreement was able to carry his party along the path of reconciliation. Hayes aroused the suspicion of those Republicans who saw the spoils of office slip out of their hands and fall to the enemy. One disgruntled southern Republican complained that "[t]he President is more than Christian; he seems to love his enemies more than he does his friends,"[33] while Jonathan DeFrees observed that southerners calmly accepted Hayes's patronage offers "as a matter of right and have no gratitude toward the administration." James G. Blaine, who knew well the uses of patronage, also understood its limitations and was convinced that the differences between North and South were "too deep to be bridged over by the proposed methods."[34]

Hayes, however, remained hopeful that the South would reciprocate his generosity. The test of southern intentions, all agreed, would come when the House voted for Speaker. Hayes had received positive assurance that nine southern congressmen were pledged to bolt the Democratic caucus.[35] It was also believed on good authority that Governor Wade Hampton of South Carolina would lend his influence to the movement, and other highly placed southern Democrats were expected to do the same.[36] Yet when the House was finally organized every Democrat, North and South, toed the party line and voted for Randall. A switch of nine votes would have made Garfield Speaker—exactly the number who had promised to bolt earlier that year. They were not forthcoming.

Patronage was not enough—unity of economic interests was not enough—to overcome the bitter legacy of the Civil War and its aftermath. "If Gen. Garfield . . . is counting upon the votes of Southern Democrats to elect him Speaker of the next House," a southern newspaper prophetically warned, "he is likely to come to grief. We should like to see the Southern Democrat base enough to betray not only his constituents, but manhood and common decency, by voting for that red-mouthed, false-hearted, narrow-minded, unprincipled jobber, hypocrite and persecutor of the South." [37] In the face of this sort of bitter partisanship, hopes for sectional harmony flickered and died.

If, then, none of the elements of the alleged bargain of 1877 can explain the outcome of the election crisis, how *was* Hayes able to defeat Tilden? Could it not be that, as Ellis Paxson Oberholtzer suggested, the Republicans simply "outwitted and honeyfuggled" the opposition at every step of the way? [38] They held all the high cards. One disgruntled Democrat later complained, "The republican party held four kings and a knave and a bowie knife, [and] whispered in our ears, 'If you had the cards would you not play them?'" [39] They held the Senate, the Supreme Court, the army, the legal (or at least the recognized) governments in the disputed states. Most important of all, they held an aura of legitimacy after having saved the Union and then occupied the White House for sixteen consecutive years. The Democrats faced a stacked deck. They could not appeal to the Constitution, because the president of the Senate, who had the constitutional function of counting presidential votes, was a Republican. They could not appeal to the law, because the Republicans dominated the Supreme Court. They could not appeal to force so long as a Republican president, Ulysses S. Grant, controlled the army. Nor could they appeal to public opinion because of the moral ambiguity of their claim. Of the three disputed southern states for which they cried "Fraud!" the Republicans could, with equal justice, cry "Foul!" Democratic violence and Republican chicanery in these states so nearly cancelled each other out that historians have not yet been able to determine who really won the election of 1876. The general, though by no means unanimous, consensus seems to concede Louisiana and South Carolina to Hayes, while giving Tilden a slim thirty to fifty-vote margin in Florida.[40] Considering their past record of secession and the widespread distrust of their loyalty, which had been carefully cultivated by a generation of Republican orators, could the Democrats afford to ride back into power on the basis of a handful of disputed votes cast by the same people who had earlier led the South into revolt?

Furthermore, the Democrats were paralyzed by indecision. They were, as Garfield gloated, "without a policy or a leader . . . full of passion and want to do something desperate but hardly know how to get at it."[41] While Tilden sat in his study, drafting interminable nit-picking constitutional briefs, the Republicans seized the initiative and held it. As a final indignity, they even preempted the orthodox Democratic dogma of states' rights and used it to justify their own claims.

The Democrats held only two low cards: the threat of revolution and the House of Representatives. Neither of them could take a trick. The threat of revolution was simply not credible. Woodward takes at face value Henry Watterson's threat to assemble 100,000 armed men to ensure Tilden's inauguration, but at the time Watterson's rodomontade was roundly ridiculed.[42]

Some nervous Republicans may have trembled at reports of another 110,000 angry Democrats in the West who could be mobilized and "set in motion for Washington in forty-eight hours,"[43] but these phantom armies never materialized. No one ever saw them drill; no one ever identified their commanders. Their discipline was so remarkable that, aside from an anonymous shot through Hayes's parlor window, no violence was displayed throughout the entire crisis. The House of Representatives was a somewhat more tangible asset than these mythical legions, but it was not much more effective. The House could not select a president; it could only delay a choice through a filibuster—a negative, defensive tactic that could be disastrous to the party's reputation if pushed too far.

Considering all these handicaps, it was a major triumph for the Democrats to have obtained a new set of ground rules in the form of the electoral commission. When even that failed them, they had no choice but to try to salvage some concessions in exchange for accepting defeat. But at the time the Electoral Commission was passed it was regarded as a Democratic coup. This temporary triumph was made possible by a curious coalition of northern Democrats working together with certain Republicans. Some of these Republicans were what one angry party regular characterized as "fair minded asses," the sort who seemed to think "that the truth is always halfway between God and the Devil, and that not to split the difference would be partisanship."[44] More serious was the defection of the stalwart wing of the party, led in the Senate by Hayes's friendly overtures to southern Democrats. Conkling's motives were harder to explain. Whitelaw Reid suspected that Conkling was being blackmailed, but others thought that the New York senator's massive ego was piqued at the prospect of losing control of his party.[45] Whatever his reasons, Conkling very nearly succeeded in turning a prospective Republican triumph into disaster. At the same time, his actions exposed the weakness of the compromise efforts. If one senator, who was not a party to the negotiations, could turn the crisis into such unforeseen channels, then perhaps the negotiators were not as influential as they seemed to believe.

Woodward concentrates his attention on splits within the Democratic party, entitling a key chapter "The Rift in the Democratic Ranks," but by the creation of the electoral commission Democrats demonstrated that they could exploit Republican rifts just as effectively. Had Davis not withdrawn from the commission, historians of today might well be discoursing on the Compromise of 1877 as a deal between Republican spoilsmen and Democrats, designed to give the presidency to Tilden. But it was not to be. As Garfield piously put it, "The Lord came in" and removed Davis from the commission,[46] and with him went the last hope for Tilden's success. Whether it was due to divine intervention or some lesser agency, this, rather than the compromise, was the key turning point of the election crisis. The compromise negotiations may have significance insofar as they illuminate the internal dynamics of both southern politics and the Republican party, but in the immediate context of the Hayes-Tilden dispute their impact was less than decisive.

As far as the Republicans were concerned, the flirtation with southern conservatives was just a passing incident. By 1879, when it was apparent that nothing further could be expected from the southern alliance, the ever-optimistic president considered making an alliance with the Greenbackers, who, he was somehow convinced, might join with Republicans to organize the House. Wiser heads prevailed upon Hayes to abandon this naive scheme, but the fact that he would even consider it showed how little ideological significance he had attached to his earlier plan.[47] If southern conservatives could not be won, he was perfectly willing to woo northern radicals instead. In either case, his interest was primarily short range and practical.

The election of 1880 and its aftermath would further underscore the fragile basis of that temporary understanding that had been attempted in 1877. Although Republican strategists hoped for support in the South, they did next to nothing to secure it. Instead they waged their campaign on two issues—the tariff and the bloody shirt—which could only drive southerners away. Garfield's victory was slim, but it was achieved without a single southern vote, demonstrating that the Republican party could, if need be, ignore the South and still win.

The Senate, however, was a different matter. It was evenly divided between the two parties, and in order to break the deadlock Republicans had to find one more senator who could be attracted to their cause. Although veterans of the earlier compromise, such as Benjamin Hill of Georgia, were still singing the same siren song of sectional reconciliation that had been heard four years before,[48] Republicans were no longer listening. In their efforts to gain control of the Senate they turned, not to those southern conservatives who had demonstrated their unreliability in 1877, but to William Mahone, the Virginia Readjuster. Even though Garfield regarded Mahone's election as "a serious if not fatal wound upon the honor and prosperity of Virginia," and even though his cabinet had advised the new president to "go very slow" in consummating such an unnatural alliance, expediency won out.[49] Mahone was induced to join the Republican caucus and, ultimately, the Republican party, but few southerners followed his lead.

Within the span of four years, then, Republicans had considered or concluded alliances with southern conservatives, northern Democrats (to quash the filibuster), Greenbackers, and Readjusters. None of these proposed coalitions had any lasting significance other than to illustrate how unstable political groupings could be in a period when the issues of the Civil War had spent their force and no comparable ones had arisen to take their place. To single out one of these proposed alliances as holding the key to an era is to do an injustice to what was, in truth, an extremely fluid political situation.

Reunion and Reaction was published in 1951, at a time when the so-called Dixiecrat-Republican coalition had dominated American politics for a generation. It was, perhaps, natural to seek out the historical antecedents of this coalition, but such an attempt ran the risk of reading a twentieth-century phenomenon back into the nineteenth century, where its validity might be questionable. The compromise attempted in 1877 did not give rise to the politics of the 1950s; at best it was but an isolated, abortive precursor of later developments.

NOTES

1. Paul Leland Haworth, *The Hayes-Tilden Disputed Presidential Election of 1876* (Cleveland: A. H. Clark, 1906), 333.

2. The C. Vann Woodward thesis can be found in at least three different forms. The first and most extensive version is Woodward, *Reunion and Reaction: The Compromise of 1877 and the End of Reconstruction* (Boston: Little, Brown, 1951). In

1956 a revised edition was issued that omitted the footnotes but added an introduction and a concluding chapter. A condensed version of the thesis appears in idem, *Origins of the New South, 1877–1913*, vol. 9, A History of the South, series ed. Wendell Holmes Stephenson and Ellis Merton Coulter (Baton Rouge: Louisiana State University Press, 1951), 23–50. This chapter is anthologized under the title, "The Forked Road to Reunion." Simplified and abridged for textbook purposes, the thesis appears as part of Woodward's contribution to John Blum, Bruce Catton, et al., *The National Experience: A History of the United States*, 8th rev. ed. (New York: Harcourt Brace Jovanovich, 1993). The present essay refers to the 1951 edition, hereinafter cited as *Reunion and Reaction*.

3. See Jeter A. Isely's review in *American Historical Review* 57 (1951): 178–79; and Arthur R. Kooker's review in *Mississippi Valley Historical Review* 38 (1952): 717–19. Cf. Dan M. Robison's review, *Journal of Southern History* 18 (1952): 93–95, which expresses some reservations.

4. James Garfield Randall and David Herbert Donald, *The Civil War and Reconstruction* (Lexington, Mass.: Heath, 1969), 834. Cf. Rembert W. Patrick, *The Reconstruction of the Nation* (New York: Oxford University Press, 1967), 265–66; John A. Garraty, *Interpreting American History*, 2 vols. (New York: Macmillan, 1970), 1: 363–65.

5. This author's cursory survey of leading college textbooks in 1973 showed the following to be influenced by Woodward's work: Harry J. Carman, Harold C. Syrett, and Bernard W. Wishy, *A History of the American People*, 2 vols., 3d ed. (New York: Knopf, 1967), 2: 50–53; John W. Caughey and Ernest R. May, *A History of the United States* (Chicago: Rand McNally, 1964), 274–75; Avery Odelle Craven and Walter Johnson, *The United States: Experiment in Democracy* (Boston: Ginn, 1962), 343; John Arthur Garraty, *The American Nation: A History of the United States* (New York: Penguin, 1966), 446–47; Norman A. Graebner, Gilbert C. Fite, and Philip L. White, *A History of the American People* (New York: McGraw-Hill, 1970), 634–36; Richard Hofstadter, William Miller, and Daniel Aaron, *The United States: The History of a Republic* (Englewood Cliffs, N.J.: Prentice-Hall, 1967), 478–79; Dexter Perkins and Glyndon G. Van Deusen, *The American Democracy: Its Rise to Power* (New York: Macmillan, 1964), 318–19; Thomas Harry Williams, Richard N. Current, and Frank Freidel, *A History of the United States*, 2 vols., 2d rev. ed. (New York: Knopf, 1964), 2: 58–59.

6. James P. Shenton, ed., *The Reconstruction: A Documentary History of the South after the War: 1865–1877* (New York: Putnam, 1963), 7.

7. Woodward, *Reunion and Reaction*, 209.

8. Clarence C. Clendenen argues that this traditional phrase is meaningless. He demonstrates that none of the small detachment of troops stationed in the South in 1877 was withdrawn for political reasons, though some were ordered back to their barracks for a time. Such troop removals as did take place were merely temporary transfers intended to reinforce units engaged in putting down Indian and labor troubles elsewhere in the nation. Clarence C. Clendenen, "President Hayes' 'With-

drawal' of the Troops—An Enduring Myth," *South Carolina Historical Magazine* 70 (1969): 240–50.

9. Woodward, *Reunion and Reaction*, 60.

10. James Abram Garfield to Rutherford Birchard Hayes, 13 Dec. 1876, James Abram Garfield Papers, Library of Congress Manuscript Division; hereinafter cited as Garfield Papers.

11. Woodward calculates that the filibuster could count on about fifty-seven "irreconcilables." Woodward, *Reunion and Reaction*, 201. This would have been more than enough to tie the House into procedural knots, had the speaker been inclined to allow it.

12. James Abram Garfield Diary, 1 Mar. 1877, Garfield Papers.

13. Allan Nevins, *Abram S. Hewitt: With Some Account of Peter Cooper* (New York: Harper, 1935), 386.

14. Woodward, *Reunion and Reaction*, 201, 204–7.

15. Don E. Fehrenbacher, "Disunion and Reunion," in *The Reconstruction of American History*, ed. John Higham (New York: Harper Torchbook, 1962), 115.

16. Garfield to Hayes, 13 Dec. 1876, Garfield Papers.

17. *Congressional Globe*, 41st Cong., 3d sess., 1470 (21 Feb. 1871).

18. Garfield to Harmon Austin, 9 Feb. 1876, James Abram Garfield Family Papers, Library of Congress Manuscript Division. (This collection consists of a group of Garfield papers, mainly of a personal nature, that was, for a time, retained by the Garfield family. The author wishes to thank the Garfield family, and Harry Brown and Frederick De Forest Williams of Michigan State University, for allowing him to examine the collection before it was sent to the Library of Congress.) James Abram Garfield Diary, 12 Feb. 1876, Garfield Papers.

19. *House of Representative Reports*, 44th Cong., 2d sess., 1877, H. Rept. 139, pt. 2, 1–8.

20. J. M. Cromly to Hayes, 8 Jan. 1877, typescript copy, Rutherford Birchard Hayes Papers, Rutherford Birchard Hayes Memorial Library; hereinafter cited as Hayes Papers.

21. James Abram Garfield Diary, 18 Dec. 1876, Garfield Papers.

22. *Cong. Rec.*, 45th Cong., 2d sess., 1010 (13 Feb. 1878).

23. Woodward, *Reunion and Reaction*, 231.

24. Ibid., 74.

25. J. W. Throckmorton to Jonathan DeFrees, enclosure; DeFrees to Garfield, 17 Apr. 1877, Garfield Papers.

26. James Abram Garfield Diary, 28 Mar. 1877, Garfield Papers.

27. F. N. Hill to Garfield, 25 May 1877; Charles Foster to Garfield, 18 July 1877, Garfield Papers.

28. J. B. Bowman to Garfield, 9 May 1877, Garfield Papers.

29. Woodward, *Reunion and Reaction*, 226.

30. William Henry Smith to Hayes, 17 Feb. 1877, typescript copy, Hayes Papers.

31. Garfield to Hayes, 13 Dec. 1876, Garfield Papers.

32. Thomas B. Alexander, "Persistent Whiggery in the Confederate South, 1860–1877," *Journal of Southern History* 27 (1961): 305–29; George Sinkler, "Race: Principles and Policy of Rutherford B. Hayes," *Ohio History* 77 (1968): 158.

33. John Shackelford to Garfield, 12 Feb. 1878, Garfield Papers.

34. Jonathan DeFrees to Garfield, 17 Apr. 1877; James Abram Garfield Diary, 11 Mar. 1877, Garfield Papers.

35. William Henry Smith to Hayes, 17 Feb. 1877, typescript copy, Hayes Papers.

36. James Abram Garfield Diary, 4 Apr. 1877; Jonathan DeFrees to Garfield, 28 Mar. 1877, Garfield Papers.

37. *New Orleans Democrat,* 22 Apr. 1877.

38. Ellis Paxson Oberholtzer, *A History of the United States since the Civil War,* 5 vols. (New York: Macmillan, 1917–1937), 3:307.

39. *Cong. Rec.,* 45th Cong., 1st sess., 136 (24 Oct. 1877).

40. Woodward, *Reunion and Reaction,* 19.

41. James Abram Garfield Diary, 8 Dec. 1876, Garfield Papers.

42. Woodward, *Reunion and Reaction,* 110–11; Oberholtzer, *History of the United States,* 3:291n.

43. Drake DeKay to Garfield, 27 Dec. 1876, Garfield Papers.

44. Garfield to W. C. Howells, 18 Dec. 1876, Garfield Papers; Garfield to Hayes, 19 Jan. 1877; Hayes, *Diary and Letters of Rutherford Birchard Hayes, Nineteenth President of the United States, 1865–1881,* 5 vols., ed. Charles Richard Williams (Columbus: Ohio State Archaeological and Historical Society, 1922–1926), 3:408–9.

45. Whitelaw Reid to James Gillespie Blaine, 10 Jan. 1877, Whitelaw Reid Papers, Library of Congress Manuscript Division; Garfield to Hayes, 9 Dec. 1876, typescript copy, Hayes Papers.

46. Biographical notes, Garfield Papers.

47. James Abram Garfield Diary, 23 Feb. 1879 and 6 Mar. 1879, Garfield Papers.

48. Benjamin Harvey Hill to Garfield, 7 Nov. 1881, Garfield Papers.

49. Garfield to Burke Aaron Hinsdale, 20 Dec. 1879, *Garfield-Hinsdale Letters: Correspondence between James Abram Garfield and Burke Aaron Hinsdale,* ed. Mary Louise Hinsdale (Ann Arbor: University of Michigan Press, 1949), 431; James Abram Garfield Diary, 29 Apr. 1881, Garfield Papers.

IV

That Jim Crow

Strange Careers Indeed!

JOHN HERBERT ROPER

✳

One of the distinguishing characteristics of C. Vann Woodward's career and scholarship could be called the *deep reciprocities* between the history that he has written and the history that he has lived. The term, originated by David Minter to describe Woodward's hero, William Faulkner,[1] is at least as apt to describe the admiring historian as the admired novelist. Obviously, there has been significant dialogue between Woodward and his critics, as seen in the historian's memoirs, in the representative pieces in this book, and in the bibliography—or at any given scholarly conference. But there has also been a unique dialogue between Woodward's ideas and his own experiences. In these deep reciprocities, Woodward has seen and has written, has heard and has written, and, for all his far-flung travels, the sound of the Ouachita River and the feel of the rolling Ouachita hills are always there in his works. Many of his renowned themes of analysis—certainly the southern economic "colonialism," the radical changes wrought by civil war, the irony of southern uniqueness—are things that he not only has seen and heard but also has lived.

Such a dialogue between experience and ideas is nowhere more evident than in the Jim Crow—perhaps even plural, *Jim Crows*—that he lived and that he studied. As the meticulous scholar Howard N. Rabinowitz has reminded everyone, Jim Crow has different meanings to different people, and the failures to define the term in context have certainly caused scholars to talk past each other. Borrowing from John W. Cell, *Jim Crow* in this essay is taken to mean "an interlocking system of economic institutions, social practices and customs, political power, law, and ideology, all of which function both as means and ends in one group's efforts to keep another (or others) in their place."[2] In that sense, Jim Crow is the set of phenomena most deeply reciprocal between the life of C. Vann Woodward and the history that he has written for us.

I

A number of national political controversies were joined on the campus of the Johns Hopkins University (JHU) between 1947 and 1952, when Woodward first began teaching there. Especially problematical were efforts by right-wing scholars and their political associates to limit academic prerogative and otherwise threaten academic rights. Woodward was active in the struggle to protect such academic freedoms, and he emerged vindicated on campus when JHU president Milton Eisenhower (brother of President Dwight David Eisenhower and originally somewhat "suspect" on these issues, at least as Woodward viewed him) vigorously upheld the principles of academic freedom of expression and inquiry. Since many of the extreme Right were militantly opposed to the civil rights movement, these episodes at JHU also morally empowered Woodward to take a much more active part in the unfolding story of the campaign for racial equity.[3]

By 1952 Woodward was acting on behalf of The Movement on at least three levels: first, as an investigator providing specific historical data and perspective for the research team of the legal staff of the National Association for the Advancement of Colored People (NAACP) headed by chief counsel the late Thurgood Marshall; second, as an officer in professional history associations, using his power and influence to open up opportunities in those national groups; and, third, as an inspirational writer—albeit one still locked in his lifetime struggle to find the balance between the demands of scholarship and the demands of activism—whose research and prose aspired to awaken the national conscience to its rightful mission.[4]

The work for the NAACP paid dividends all around: It let Woodward see in action the energetic and insightful Thurgood Marshall, in that era, virtually unbeatable in a courtroom contest and behind the scenes thoroughgoing in preparation and a rigorous taskmaster for his historian and political scientist research assistants; it reunited Woodward with his old friends Manning J. Dauer and William G. Carleton, with whom he had once formed the "Gainesville Musketeers" when all three taught at the University of Florida (1937–39) and campaigned together for civil rights there; it brought him into spirited partnership with scholars and activists of both races from all over the country, thereby giving him a better sense of the size and strength of The Movement; and above all else, it immersed him in the legal questions of civil rights, both in the documents from the 1890s and in the ongoing campaigns of the present. Research conducted by Woodward, Dauer, Carleton, and black historian John Hope Franklin was employed with telling effect by

Marshall in the most famous case of the era, *Brown v. Board of Education of Topeka, Kansas,* in 1954. On no other issue than the NAACP's drive for racial integration did Woodward so completely involve himself in moral and material, as well as scholarly, commitments.[5]

The research, the writing, and the campaigning flowed with no perceptible break into Woodward's activities in the professional historical organizations, especially the Southern Historical Association (SHA), which was founded in 1934, the year Woodward entered graduate school at Carolina. As his tenure among historians of the South became secure, he found himself on various program committees and even on the inside track to the eventual presidency of the SHA. He became increasingly aware of what he could do in an even more direct and personal way to provide opportunities for black scholars. Entire sessions at association meetings could be dedicated to the study of civil rights, and the meetings themselves could become scenes of less formal but equally valuable chances for interested scholars to share their findings and to encourage each other. Furthermore, these meetings were the occasion for the apprentice scholars to demonstrate their wares before the pastmasters by reading papers and participating in discussions; and they were the places where the first vital professional contacts were made for the young historians. Those, such as Woodward himself, who harbored aspirations for high office in the profession could also demonstrate competence in the administrative work of the organizations and thereby begin the climb to prominence.

Woodward, like most good historians, consciously used the organizations to help his students, introducing them to senior scholars with related research interests, to editors looking for worthy and salable manuscripts, and to university and college administrators who anticipated staff openings on their campuses. Perhaps more important, he showed his graduate students by quiet example how they could begin to make these kinds of opportunities for themselves.[6] But it was obvious that a great deal of the conference life, with its myriad opportunities, was, in actuality, closed off to such promising black scholars as John Hope Franklin, Alonzo Theodore Stephens, Elsie (Lewis) Mitchell, Charles Wesley, and Clarence Bacote, all of whom were stymied in their work by the various restrictions of the racist laws imposed at the sites of most of the historians' meetings. Although these African Americans were dues-paying subscribers to the national organizations, their exclusion from the speaker's dais, from the banquet tables, from the hotel lobbies, and from the restaurants near the host hotels—and sometimes even from the very meeting rooms of the program sessions—kept them from being full-fledged de facto members.[7]

A number of reform-minded activists, of whom the then relatively unknown Howard Zinn and August Meier were especially outspoken, had
determined by 1949 that the SHA must be genuinely integrated; and Woodward came to cooperate with these men in several actions that would greatly
improve conditions of professional life for the African American historians,
although only the passage of the Civil Rights Act of 1964 would meaningfully integrate the SHA. They chose the SHA, though for many the name
itself must have seemed ominous, because it was in many ways more important to black historians than was the American Historical Association (AHA)
or the Mississippi Valley Historical Association (predecessor to today's Organization of American Historians, or OAH). For three centuries, black history had occurred within a context that was primarily southern, and the
manuscript sources as well as the preponderance of African American scholars were in the South. To open this door, Woodward and liberal Tennessean
Bell Irvin Wiley (himself a student at Yale under the great conservative historian Ulrich Bonnell Phillips) selected John Hope Franklin for the exposure
of reading a paper at the SHA, for they agreed that Franklin was the man
with the right combination of talent, spirit, and character to establish this
precedent of black participation.[8]

They began to plot, Woodward and Franklin and Wiley. Wiley, who was
in charge of a panel for the 1949 convention, said he wanted to offer a program so attractive that scholars would attend regardless of the color of the
participants. Moreover, there was good luck in the sites already selected for
the meetings: the Williamsburg Inn and the campus of the College of William
and Mary. While the Commonwealth of Virginia seemed fully committed to
the practices of segregation, there was less reason for Franklin to fear bodily
harm; as Woodward put it to Franklin, "The insults . . . would not be too
crude." The team went into action, with a then obscure Professor Franklin
scheduled to read a paper at the 1949 convention.[9]

Those who looked through the program prospectus with care noted that
the little-known scholar taught at Howard University, the distinguished African American school in Washington, D.C. Although some white people
served on that faculty, the likelihood was that a historian there would be
black. Too, if one knew much regional racial history, Franklin's name, *John
Hope,* conjured memories of the identity of the genius who had organized
black schools in Atlanta into the successfully cooperative Atlanta University
System and who was otherwise a leader in civil rights: *John Hope* was decidedly *not* a name a white southerner would give his son.[10] A sharp-eyed reader
of programs who had a memory could see that integration was about to happen at the SHA.

In time, attention focused on Woodward, the acknowledged perpetrator of the deed. By the peculiar workings of southern racial manners, those who objected to an integrated program blamed Woodward more than they blamed Franklin. Thus the mesh of details—"Where am I gonna eat? Where am I gonna sleep?" as Franklin recalled—fell over the larger convention plans, at least in some minds. There was less talk about the subject matter of the panels and more talk about the mundane affairs of eating, sleeping, and traveling. Even if southern historians accepted a black scholar on the speaker's dais, would the convention not become a scene of confrontation between the black man and segregated hotels, restaurants, cars? Under the questioning, Woodward was cool and dispassionate, the son of the old gentry refusing to show nerves in front of those in another class. He was no less the son of academics, who knew the scholar's manners. Only occasionally stirred to gentle sardonicism, Woodward resolutely refused to demonstrate visible anger. When asked where Franklin would sleep, Woodward answered, "In a pup tent"; when asked where Franklin would eat, Woodward answered, "Oh, he's very resourceful, he'll probably bring K-rations." The whimsical replies masked his knowledge that there would be no confrontation with the town itself: Franklin would stay with the family of historian Douglas Adair, sleeping and taking his meals in seclusion from the other conference delegates.[11]

Woodward's old dissertation director, Howard Kennedy Beale, involved himself, for he was certainly one who never lost his own taste for controversy, and he sensed in this case a breakthrough. Beale drove Franklin down to Williamsburg in the family car, typically a grand vehicle that the scholar drove enthusiastically but not very carefully. The short trip from Washington to Williamsburg was a beautiful one, for the Virginia countryside sparkled with autumnal grace. After an evening with the Adairs, Franklin made his appearance at the sessions. A tall and very dignified man, the lone African American was imposing as he walked to the dais to be introduced by Henry Steele Commager, a famed liberal who had eagerly sought this task. Tension ran through the hall and even outside—many historians, students, and the curious from town peered through windows, probably hearing little but watching with keen eyes. The speech, a distillation of his forthcoming book, *The Militant South*,[12] went well, being received with an encouraging combination of personal approbation and intellectual respect.

When it was done, there was considerable relief for all concerned. Professional historians had proven themselves capable of attending a racially integrated session in a quiet college town. Later, Franklin was permitted to dine at the Williamsburg Inn with his fellow historians, although it was in obvious defiance of city laws and community practice; and this, too, was accepted.

All things, after all, start small.[13] In retrospect, the excitement of anticipation seemed a wonder, since the act itself went smoothly, even went without excitement. It was another in a series of confrontations with the monster Jim Crow in which the monster had proved to be a reluctant dragon.

II

One thing about this dragon, however, was its caprice: In a twinkling, Jim Crow could transform itself from a state of reluctance to a state of militance. Only a few years after the success at Williamsburg, Woodward and Franklin found themselves simply unable to share a Saturday meal together in the nation's capital. The two men were doing research at the Library of Congress and regularly dined together at the Supreme Court Restaurant. On Saturdays, however, government business shut down and there were no official facilities available. Then Washington reverted to the norms of the largely segregated Virginia and Maryland communities that surrounded the district. The whole experience educated Woodward about another side of the life of the black scholar.[14]

As Franklin remembered it, Woodward came around and asked worriedly, "What will you do?" His friend replied, "I eat a big breakfast, I come late [to the archives], I bring a piece of candy, and, when I can't stand it, I go home." It was this kind of mundane thing that continued to bear in on the handful of black scholars in the republic: Things concomitant with daily life for the white historian were privileges denied African Americans. Mulling it over that day, Woodward, the onetime football center, told Franklin, "I don't think I could *be* a historian if I couldn't eat dinner!"[15]

Then both men laughed, but they and others soon swung back into action. In 1952 the *Thompson* decision ended mandatory segregation in the cafeterias, hotels, and other accommodations in Washington. Things were loosening up across the border states and the upper South; but the very loosening across the northern fringe made the bonds on the former Confederacy comparatively tighter. That fall, Woodward again confronted Jim Crow inside the profession of history. Honored as president of the SHA, he was to deliver his executive address to the organization at the Knoxville meeting that session. For the occasion he had prepared an intricate examination of the peculiar relationship of the South to the rest of the republic, an examination that emphasized the special perspectives that the South could bring to bear on national history because of its being the only part of the United States that had experienced military defeat and occupation and had openly participated in an obvious evil by creating and developing the institution of slavery. The point was that the South thus had solid historical reasons for avoiding the dangers of national presumptions of innocence and invincibility. But as Woodward readied his address, the program chairman, LeRoy Graf, learned that the host hotel, the Farragut, would segregate the keynote dinner address: In other words, black historians Franklin, Bacote, Mitchell, Wesley, and Sherman Savage could not hear Woodward's speech. Graf, an Ohioan newly arrived at the University of Tennessee, was outraged, since the hotel had earlier promised an integrated session.[16]

The whole incident perfectly illustrated the convolutions that Jim Crow could take in a given instant. The association was integrated, for Franklin had established that fact by delivering a paper three years earlier. Moreover, the association purported to welcome its black members to participate in the annual meetings. Nevertheless, the Farragut exercised its legal right to segregate the dining facilities inside its walls. And as usually happened in such cases, the hotel management was unctuous in its insistence that it was not prejudiced but was only responding to the economic realities reflected by the cultural norms of upper east Tennessee, namely, the hotel feared it would lose customers if it integrated its dining room. Otherwise, the managers pointed out, African Americans were perfectly free to attend sessions in the hotel. Of course, this was the kind of specious reasoning that had kept the history profession essentially white. The dinner, which the hotel management insisted was a private affair, was in fact the forum for the presidential address; not attending dinner deprived black historians of full membership in the SHA by keeping them from the main attraction of the weekend. Beyond the professional issues—which were troubling enough—there were the continuing realities of the layered insults of persisting segregation, the accumulated weight of little insults and minor deprivations being almost unbearable. Here was still more proof that a black scholar was not really a normal professional with access to the full range of the historian's perquisites.[17]

By this time, Woodward and Franklin found that there were many others who were unwilling to put up with this kind of segregation. Graf, who had unexpectedly come onto the scene as program chairman when a senior colleague won sabbatical to study abroad, decided to take a poke at Jim Crow. He received immediate support from the young secretary of the SHA, none other than Woodward's loquacious graduate-student friend, Bennett Harrison Wall, whom Graf thankfully called "one of the beautiful young men of the South." Graf and Wall set in motion the plan, which Woodward readily approved: The entire SHA would abandon the Farragut for an outlying clubhouse-restaurant, the Whittle Springs, which was integrated. The racial, cultural, and economic rationale that the Farragut had employed would be turned back on itself. Let the management suffer the embarrassment of an entire professional organization of scholars leaving its facilities en masse. Bad manners to a few black guests would cost dearly: All the guests would seek hospitality elsewhere.[18]

Later, it seemed an amusing spectacle. Graf and Wall put most of the historians on a bus that drove them to the suburbs, while Graf had to use his own car to shuttle a late-arriving historian, Elsie (Lewis) Mitchell, when he learned that the local taxi drivers refused to give her a ride. It went off all right, although Woodward delivered the speech in his ineffective, halting style that belied its actual eloquence. The excitement of the long day overwhelmed the moment of the evening address, since few men and women had either the remaining psychic energy or the hypersensitive hearing necessary to follow what the president was saying. Ben Wall, in his almost self-caricaturing bass voice, has recalled dyspeptically: "He always was a lousy damned speaker, a lousy reader of a paper—at least he's gotten better since. A lot of people got up and left, some fell asleep, [one woman] fiddled with her [dress] during the whole speech. . . . Terrible! Later we realized [the address] was brilliant; those who read the paper saw that it was great!"[19]

Woodward was fully aware of how people responded to his style of speaking, because he had been hearing the same things since the late 1920s. As Ellen Boulware Martin Ohls (Bola), his debate coach back in Arkadelphia, Arkansas, recalled her star student's attitudes about such presentations: "He wasn't a teacher of elocution! . . . Now Vann got up and said what he had to say, and if you got it okay. . . . Those debates were graded and judged on several things. . . . Some was on delivery, where [young Woodward did very poorly]; but most was on points of argument, and there" the young debater and the mature historian both did well. More to the point, a vital principle had been established, and to some degree people's opinions of his speech were almost irrelevant in the broader context of integrating the SHA. If southern white members harbored any grudges against the black members for the relocation of the session, said Woodward later, "they didn't tell me that."[20]

III

Following these episodes, Woodward became less active in the continuing administrative processes of fully integrating the SHA and less active in research work for the NAACP legal staff, because he was turning his attention to the other level of his campaign, the inspirational scholarship of the kind that became his hallmark. By 1954 he and those who had worked to help

Thurgood Marshall prepare for the appeal of the Brown case were highly optimistic about the outcome of that hearing; and when the Earl Warren Supreme Court went beyond Woodward's hopes with a sweeping indictment of segregation, he was pleased as a researcher whose homework had been rewarded and was moved deeply as a committed reformist who sought a better life for his black friends and coworkers. But he also understood that the decision itself represented a scholar's unique opportunity, especially after he received an invitation from the University of Virginia to deliver the Richard Lecture on campus in that eventful year.[21] The problem of integration was on southern minds as never before, and now, Woodward realized, was the time to encapsulate the very mood and tone of racial reform in the country through a work of supremely usable history within the context of his ironic discussion of continuity and discontinuity.

At Charlottesville, in that most southern of environs, Woodward told a biracial (but separated) audience that one could be distinctly southern without being a segregationist. He tried to demonstrate a fair amount of legal integration and a more generous amount of practical and de facto integration that he could find among three kinds of white southerners: Conservatives such as South Carolina's Wade Hampton; Radicals such as Georgia's Populist Thomas E. Watson; and the much smaller group of Liberals such as Virginia's Louis Harvie Blair and Louisiana's expatriate George Washington Cable. He tried to show his audience that the rigid legal segregation called Jim Crow had a very brief career, begun no sooner than the era 1898–1908, and that its provenance had less to do with cultural traditions than with the aftermath of political disasters in the context of economic decline at the turn of the century.

Immediate response was hard to gauge, since the Virginia way was politic and mannerly and in any case understated. Of course, the halting, uninflected, occasionally mumbling delivery may have left unheard certain crucial elements of his complex argument. There were, of course, some signs that Woodward himself picked up as he was reading: "Oh, it was favorable. I do remember a friend, a lawyer with an awfully old Virginia name. I knew him to be interested professionally in segregation. During the speech I caught his eye—and I saw him afterward—he was awfully quiet, which was probably a negative reaction."[22]

More remarkable was the uncavalier reaction of the reading public to the book, which he released in 1955. Most were overwhelmed, buying it and talking about it. It caught the attention of the literate public outside the field of history, just as Frederick Jackson Turner drew people to the frontier thesis or Charles Austin Beard drew them to the economic interpretation of the U.S.

Constitution. It seemed to catch up Woodward's personal experiences but also those of John Hope Franklin and those of the region and such pieces of historical research for the period of the 1880s and 1890s as had been accomplished by 1954. Above all, it served a deep psychic need in The Movement, caught best by no less than the Reverend Martin Luther King Jr. when he proclaimed to a crowd of marchers that the little book was "the Bible of the civil rights movement."

In thus reaching so far beyond professional historians, Woodward did create a problem for himself, a phenomenon that Joel Randolph Williamson has labeled the "two *Strange Careers of Jim Crow;* for there was the book he wrote and there was the book people read."[23] For many, the book they read became a tract, a polemic that made the 1880s into a golden era of race relations, which made the South perpetually liberal and tolerant, which ignored racism by studying only legal formalism, and which created a morality play out of historical events.

The nature of the offering left it open to such readings; and that nature troubled Woodward's friends. As the book left the presses, crusty Bill Carleton, one of the Gainesville Musketeers, scolded his old colleague in a letter that anticipated later scholarly criticisms: It was excessively legalistic and thus overlooked less formal, de facto, arrangements to accomplish the same ends; the analogy with South Africa and its apartheid system was weakly developed and inaccurate; and the whole thing was overly popularized. Of a broader philosophical nature was David Morris Potter's question: "What has the historian to do with hope?" by which Woodward understood his old Georgia friend to be saying that historians must understand the past by its own light instead of using it to rearrange the future. This notation by Potter described the perpetual dilemma in all of Woodward's "committed" scholarship, for it was this quality of presentism that made his earlier work most tellingly relevant for a particular era, but it was this same quality that would also make the work most obviously dated in later years. In the 1950s, however, Potter's observation was not even a recognized debating point for Woodward, who then continued to give full credence to New Deal era injunctions from friends, teachers, and allies that scholars owed the public "usable" research and writing.[24]

IV

As less friendly critics entered the discussions in the 1960s, new data, far more detailed than what Woodward had found available in 1954, came to the front. Some fashioned careers out of Woodward's thesis, either by defending it or by attacking it, and Woodward was himself caught up in the second *Strange Career*, the one people were reading as opposed to the one that he had written. At times, he too seemed to be reading some other book in his efforts to defend his thesis; and in general, as Edward L. Ayers has noted in his discussion of theory and history in this book, Woodward, like most of the intellectuals of that self-styled modernist era, was unprepared to consider the interpretive power of readers in dialogue with an "open" narrative. He had tried to write a nuanced and complex accounting, and it could only be read one way. Thus, Woodward brought out revised editions, and he sometimes became defensive, in the 1960s claiming that it was his greatest work but in the 1970s discounting it as historical contribution and emphasizing the limited nature of what he had sought to prove in 1954.[25]

Briefly, in the middle 1970s, Woodward was at his least attractive, narrowing the vision of the original thesis to answer criticism, while simultaneously denying the significance of the work. Yet, as Howard N. Rabinowitz has demonstrated in fruitful detail, the debate certainly went on, ultimately to everyone's benefit, both because of and in spite of Woodward, for there was another side of this man, a warmly encouraging side; and the nature of scholarly debate—that is, the way that young historians are urged to "take on" their elders—in combination with Woodward's efforts of encouragement eventually produced some of the recent era's most interesting social history.[26] For all that, one could still legitimately ask what actually remains of *The Strange Career*, since historians in different ways have rejected large portions of it.

V

The optimism and intensity that suffuse *The Strange Career*, especially in its first three editions, cannot be gainsayed, however much such a tone came to embarrass Woodward after 1968, when he entered a more conservative political and less experimental academic phase of his career. For some years in the 1970s, he lost, for a time, any controlling sense of commitment to a social program, and he expressed a distance, almost an estrangement, from the energies that surged through *The Strange Career* and that made it the bible of The Movement. But Woodward would not remain for long in this phase, which his friend and former student William Samuel McFeely calls ruefully "his Tory period"; and besides, an author's subsequent judgment on his or her work is seldom the point. Rather, considering the question of influence in cultural and political life, Martin Luther King Jr. seems to have been right: Woodward's thesis, like the *Brown* decision itself, gave integrationists "heart to fight" because the little book's mythic qualities of inspiration were indispensably a part of The Movement. Without *The Strange Career,* some who worked for reform might have hung back from the fray in the indecisiveness of immobilized ambivalence.[27]

Shifting to another kind of question, Woodward's inspiration was also indisputably a part of the ongoing study of social history, for without *The Strange Career* as an "impertinent first question," other scholars might never have moved toward the "pertinent" answers.[28] The genius in Woodward was orchestration: His sense of timing and of arrangement, of colorature and of range. Perhaps others were on their own ways to the same thesis, but no other expressed it with the symphonic brilliance of Woodward's very first edition. By writing it as he did, when he did, he created a new debate and thus has shared in every amendment that any scholar has made to the first work, and even in the refutations. Had he not produced the first bold statement of thesis out of fragmentary evidence from a relatively unstudied period, the more mature clarifying monographs would have been postponed for decades—if written at all.

Moreover, there is a special characteristic of this work that will endure as an insight into the very nature of race relations and the institutions of Jim Crow, although it is the kind of insight that can never be effectively proved or disproved by scholars' research. This is the insistence that segregation will ultimately be defeated by the human identity itself: that basic impulses, both positive and negative, in soul and flesh, will simply overwhelm the strictures of racial separation. After all, the antebellum plantation, where the vast majority of African Americans lived their experiences, was certainly a place of cultural integration, as has been demonstrated redundantly in the superb scholarship of historians with such differing perspectives and approaches as Eugene D. Genovese, Peter H. Wood, Leon Litwack, and Charles W. Joyner. In Ralph Waldo Ellison's perfect phrase, the syncretic nature of the black experience in slavery and afterward has made it "a culture of cultures." The physical integration was there too—often in brutal form—but there unmistakably in the miscegenation and in the growing mulatto population. And the palpable physicality of the mixing was caught by William Faulkner, describing the moment when an embittered old white woman brushes against her exiled black counterpart: "There is something in the touch of flesh with flesh which abrogates, cuts sharp and straight across the devious intricate channels of decorous ordering, which makes enemies as well as lovers know because it makes them both—touch and touch of that which is the central I-Am's private own: not spirit, soul; the liquorish and ungirdled mind is anyone's to take in any darkened hallway of this earthly tenement. But let flesh touch with flesh, and watch the fall of all the egg shell shibboleths of caste and color too."[29]

In other words, Jim Crow expressed racism, a force Woodward underestimated in other places. But it also expressed a kind of separation known to the South only briefly: The syncretic qualities of the southern subculture would not have developed if the Old South had really kept apart white from black as Jim Crow in theory demanded they be kept apart. Free blacks were segregated, but the ninety and nine, the slaves, had whiteness pressed on them even as they pressed blackness on their masters and on the free whites with whom they worked. This insight of Woodward's has been seized on with telling effect by Albert Murray, who made it one of the themes of his intellectual and emotional excursion, *South to a Very Old Place.*[30] What Jim Crow marked, then, was properly called an aberration, not in extreme racism (which really came as early as 1889 before the institutions were set in legal place), but in cultural patterns: Only in the few decades starting this century have white and black moved along truly separate wavelengths.

Finally, there is a reasonable answer to the skeptical question of Woodward's friend Potter: The hope that Jim Crow would die without killing the South infuses the book; and that hope has been subsequently realized. In the years since 1954, the South has rid itself of Jim Crow, albeit without ridding itself of racism, and it has remained the distinctive section of the country. Blame for those things that have changed for the worse in the South is as well laid on the head of grasping materialism as on the death of Jim Crow. And those things that have changed for the better about the South are often directly traceable to the Supreme Court decision and its implementation.

In reflecting on this individual piece of work, one can see much the same embroidery as in all of Woodward's scholarship. All of the embroidery is fascinating, most of it is good, but *The Strange Career of Jim Crow* is his best artistry. Here he has succeeded in weaving class studies with race studies without losing sight of either; and here he has managed to express most meaningfully his love for the South without crafting for it an apologia. Furthermore, the cry for racial justice was the very definition of Woodward's contemporary liberalism; after the civil rights movement was fragmented by the myriad events culminating in 1968, Woodward could no longer define either liberalism or his own ideological stance. This work of 1955 is both self-definition for an era's liberals and a prescription for societal change; it is so charged with moral energy that, once Woodward began to doubt its significance, he lost, for a time, his moorings. But when he recovered his ironic reformism—in part by responding again to the profound challenges of racism—he was able to present the nation's thinkers with a gift of very special value.

NOTES

1. David Minter, *William Faulkner: His Life and Work* (Baltimore: Johns Hopkins University Press, 1980), ix.

2. Howard N. Rabinowitz, "More Than the Woodward Thesis: Assessing *The Strange Career of Jim Crow*," revised and reprinted in this volume; John W. Cell, *The Highest Stage of White Supremacy: The Origins of Segregation in South Africa and the American South* (Cambridge: Cambridge University Press, 1982), p. 14.

3. See John Herbert Roper, *C. Vann Woodward, Southerner* (Athens: University of Georgia Press, 1987), 160–65; interviews with Woodward, 18 and 19 July 1978, John Herbert Roper Papers of the Southern Historical Collection of the Library of the University of North Carolina, Chapel Hill; hereinafter cited as Roper Papers. See correspondence, 1947–52, between Woodward and Glenn Weddington Rainey, especially Woodward to Rainey, 26 Sept. 1951, Glenn Weddington Rainey Papers, Manuscript Division, Library of Emory University, Atlanta; hereinafter cited as Rainey Papers.

4. Interviews: Manning J. Dauer, 21 July 1979; Bennett Harrison Wall, 12 Apr. 1979; LeRoy P. Graf, 12 Apr. 1979; John Hope Franklin, 10 Nov. 1978, Roper Papers.

5. Note not only that Dauer and Carleton were on the NAACP team working for Thurgood Marshall as he prepared the brief for *Brown v. Board of Education of Topeka, Kansas,* but that the two Gainesville Musketeers were also active in drafting what ultimately became the basic plan for school integration in Florida. Interview with Dauer, 21 July 1979; Woodward to Roper, 25 June 1981, Roper Papers. See also Woodward, "Monograph on the History of Reconstruction in the South to Brief for *Oliver Brown, et al. v. Board of Education of Topeka, et al,*" filed in U.S. Supreme Court, 16 Nov. 1953; and see Bernard Schwartz, ed., *The Unpublished Opinions of the Warren Court* (New York: Oxford University Press, 1985), 485–90 and passim.

6. Interview with William Samuel McFeely, 4 Dec. 1984, Roper Papers.

7. Interviews: Woodward, 18 and 19 July 1978; John Hope Franklin and Aurelia Franklin, 10 Nov. 1978; and August Meier, 20 Apr. 1985. Meier to Roper, 17 June 1985 (amended typescript of interview, with eighteen pages of additional information); and Meier to Roper, 24 June 1985, Roper Papers.

8. Interview with Bell Irvin Wiley, 13 Sept. 1974; Wiley to Roper, 27 Nov. 1978; Meier to Roper, 24 June 1985, Roper Papers.

9. Interview with Bell Irvin Wiley, 13 Sept. 1974; Wiley to Roper, 27 Nov. 1978; Meier to Roper, 24 June 1985, Roper Papers; interview with John Hope Franklin and Aurelia Franklin, 10 Nov. 1978; Meier to Roper, 17 June 1985, Roper Papers.

10. On John Hope, see John Dittmer, *Black Georgia in the Progressive Era, 1900–1920*, Blacks in the New World, series ed. August Meier (Urbana: University of Illinois Press, 1977), 158–59, 160, 170, 175, 179–80.

11. Wiley to Roper, 27 Nov. 1978; interview with John Hope Franklin and Aurelia Franklin, 10 Nov. 1978; Meier to Roper, 17 June 1985, Roper Papers.

12. John Hope Franklin, *The Militant South, 1800–1861* (Cambridge: Belknap Press, Harvard University Press, 1956).

13. Cf. interview with John Hope Franklin, 10 Nov. 1978, who at that interview did not recall dining with white people on this occasion. Meier and LeRoy Graf, however, specifically recall dining at the inn with Franklin in the company of other white historians. After checking records of his own correspondence—noting, "If LeRoy Graf said it, it's right"—Franklin has found that he was permitted to dine at the inn with the white scholars (Meier to Roper, 17 June 1985, Roper Papers).

14. Interview with John Hope Franklin and Aurelia Franklin, 10 Nov. 1978, Roper Papers.

15. Ibid.

16. Interviews: Wall, 12 Apr. 1979, speaking after review of notes he had taken as longtime secretary of the SHA; Graf, 12 Apr. 1979, Roper Papers. This address in slightly modified form became "The Irony of Southern History," centerpiece of the collection of Woodward's essays *The Burden of Southern History* (Baton Rouge: Louisiana State University Press, 1960).

17. Interviews: John Hope Franklin and Aurelia Franklin, 10 Nov. 1978; Woodward, 18 July 1978, Roper Papers.

18. Interview with Graf, 12 Apr. 1979, Roper Papers.

19. Interview with Wall, 12 Apr. 1979, Roper Papers.

20. Interviews: Ellen Boulware Martin Ohls, 18 Mar. 1984; Woodward, 18 July 1978, Roper Papers.

21. Interviews: Ohls, 18 Mar. 1984 and Woodward, 18 July 1978. Meier has pointed out that much work remained to be done before the SHA offered real service to the African American historians; that Franklin at one point became so frustrated with lack of progress after his 1949 Williamsburg speech and after Woodward's Whittle Springs address that he declined to attend one conference (this recollection was independently corroborated by Bell Wiley in a note to Roper, 27 Nov. 1978); and that the leadership of the SHA campaign passed to Meier, Zinn, and others partly because Woodward and Franklin became engaged with other issues. After 1952 these integrationists, none of whom was then prominent, often came from black colleges, and several of them evidently considered that they had little to lose professionally by publicity about such activities. (Interview with Meier, 20 Apr. 1985, Roper Papers.) Meier has collected some of these thoughts and remembrances in his *A White Scholar and the Black Community, 1945–1965; Essays and Reflections,* afterword by John H. Bracey Jr. (Amherst: University of Massachusetts Press, 1992); and in Meier and Elliot Rudwick, *Black History and the Historical Profession, 1915–1980,* Blacks in the New World, series ed. idem (Urbana: University of Illinois Press, 1986).

22. Interview with Woodward, 19 July 1978, Roper Papers.

23. Interview with Joel Randolph Williamson, 12 Apr. 1977, Roper Papers.

24. Carleton to Woodward, n.d. [1955], carbon copy in possession of Manning J. Dauer and used here with his permission; interview with Woodward, 19 July 1978; on youthful influences for "usable past," see Roper, *C. Vann Woodward, Southerner,* passim, but esp. 20–59, 76–86.

25. See Edward L. Ayers in this volume. Cf. C. Vann Woodward, *The Strange Career of Jim Crow,* 3d rev. ed. (1974); while the 1957 and 1968 editions are essentially unchanged from the 1955 edition, this 1974 revision includes as a new concluding chapter a brilliant and very useful summary of the modern civil rights movement since the Voting Rights Act of 1965 (189–220).

26. Cf. Rabinowitz in this volume.

27. Interview with John Hope and Aurelia Franklin, 10 Nov. 1978. John Hope Franklin tells an especially charming story of taking the then graduate student Howard N. Rabinowitz to the manuscript collections at Duke University and at the University of North Carolina, in the process instructing him at several levels about the meaning and the methods of Woodward's thesis. On Woodward's attitudes since 1968 and for the King quotation, see Roper, *C. Vann Woodward, Southerner,* 233–39. Interviews: William Samuel McFeely, 4 Dec. 1984 (McFeely was glad to see the "Tory Period" end); Jack R. Pole, 10 Nov. 1983 (Pole, by contrast, was concerned about the quality of Woodward's works "of political enthusiasm," such as the Tom Watson biography or *The Strange Career of Jim Crow*), Roper Papers.

28. On pertinence and impertinence in intellectual developments, see Mortimer J. Adler, *The Paideia Proposal: An Educational Manifesto* (New York: Macmillan, 1982).

29. Ralph Waldo Ellison, *Going to the Territory* (New York: Random House, 1986); Eugene Dominick Genovese, *Roll, Jordan, Roll: The World the Slaves Made* (New York: Knopf, 1974); Leon F. Litwack, *Been in the Storm So Long: The Aftermath of Slavery* (New York: Random House, 1980); Peter Herbert Wood, *Black Majority: Negroes in Colonial South Carolina from 1670 through the Stono Rebellion* (New York: Knopf, 1974); Charles W. Joyner, *Down by the Riverside: A South Carolina Slave Community* (Urbana: University of Illinois Press, 1984); William Faulkner, *Absalom, Absalom!* (New York: Random House, 1936), 139.

30. Albert Murray, *South to a Very Old Place* (New York: McGraw-Hill, 1971), 16–26; see reprint (New York: Vintage, 1991), chapter 15. See reprint in this volume.

More Than the Woodward Thesis: Assessing *The Strange Career of Jim Crow*

HOWARD N. RABINOWITZ

✳

Howard N. Rabinowitz, professor of history at the University of New Mexico, has been among the most astute and vigorous of the critics who pursue what Woodward has called "the subject," that is, southern history. In addition to the insights gained from his own careful scholarship, Rabinowitz was in a unique position to join the debates about the nature, origins, shape, and development of the different forms of segregation and racial discrimination. Rabinowitz earned the Ph.D. at the University of Chicago under John Hope Franklin, himself an activist scholar, alongside Woodward, in the events leading up to the *Brown v. Board of Education* case of 1954 and in processes that eventually integrated the Southern Historical Association. In particular, Rabinowitz has insisted on precision in language and logic and on attention to nuance in looking at forms of racial discrimination. Most valuable has been his insight that de jure segregation in the early twentieth century was in some cases an advance, and was often so recognized and demanded as such by African Americans themselves. Sometimes segregated facilities represented the first chance *to do* something or *to have* something, especially schools and public transportation, formerly reserved for white people. Segregated access was still access, and was better than being excluded altogether. In this essay, Rabinowitz discusses the impact that the different versions of Woodward's *Strange Career of Jim Crow* have made on historians of race relations in the region of "the subject."

✳   ✳   ✳

Since its publication in 1955, C. Vann Woodward's *The Strange Career of Jim Crow* has had a fundamental impact on the study of American race relations. Although best known for its so-called Woodward thesis, that is only part of the book as it emerged through four editions over twenty years, and no one has assessed the work in its entirety since the final edition appeared in 1974.

What I want to do, then, is to consider three of the contributions of *Strange Career*. The first, of course, is the Woodward thesis concerning the origins, timing, and nature of segregation or, as Woodward sometimes calls it, Jim Crow. The second is the concept of the Second Reconstruction as a way of gaining perspective on Reconstruction or, in Woodward's term, the "First Reconstruction." The third is the masterful but neglected concluding chapter to the 1974 edition, whose strengths ironically point up some of the limitations of the earlier sections and editions of *Strange Career*.

I suspect that I have read *Strange Career* in its various forms more often than I have read any other book, except, perhaps, Woodward's *Origins of the New South*. Nevertheless, as I began to prepare this essay, I was surprised to discover not only that the book was even more subtle and substantive than I had remembered but also that there was a need to get the different editions straight. In fact, the *Strange Career* has had several careers, and I think it important to review briefly the structure of the four editions before we consider the contributions. What we really need is something comparable to Woodward's edition of the Mary Chesnut diaries.[1]

Everything began with the James W. Richard Lectures, which Woodward wrote during the summer months immediately following the *Brown v. Board of Education* decision and presented before a biracial audience of about one hundred at the University of Virginia in 1954. The manuscript for the lectures became the copy for the first edition of *Strange Career*, published in 1955. A brief preface and an introduction entitled "Of Reconstructions and the South" argued for the use of history to help understand the present and asserted the essential discontinuity of southern history. Woodward then turned in chapter 1 to the "Forgotten Alternatives" of fluid race relations in the post-Reconstruction South; in chapter 2 to the "Capitulation to Racism" at the turn of the century; and in chapter 3, "The Man on the Cliff," to the course of race relations from World War I to the *Brown* decision.[2]

Two years later in a paperback edition, Woodward added a chapter 4, "'Deliberate Speed' vs. 'Majestic Instancy,'" which brought events up to 1957. He sought not only to explain the worsening of race relations in the South since 1954 but also to provide renewed grounds for optimism by noting that the prospects for change were more promising than during the First Reconstruction. The 1957 edition remains a strangely forgotten one. It was the only one in which the subtitle, *A Brief Account of Segregation*, appeared on the cover; its foreword, which modified some of Woodward's original argument, was not reprinted with the other prefaces in successive editions; and much of its final chapter was later eliminated, including an extended comparison of the two reconstructions.[3]

The 1966 revision proved longer lasting. The preface said the new version sought to take advantage of the new perspective provided by the years since the 1955 edition, as well as to bring the account up to date and to consider new scholarly contributions to the field. The original introduction remains intact, though without a title; the original three chapters appear as chapters 2 through 4 with sections slightly altered, especially to include more information on northern race relations. A new chapter 1, "Of Old Regimes and Reconstructions," incorporates some of the modifications expressed in the 1957 foreword, adds some new ones, and considers the most serious challenges to Woodward's view of segregation as a product of the turn-of-the-century South. There is also a new concluding chapter (chapter 5), "The Declining Years of Jim Crow," which incorporates part of the final chapter of the 1957 edition and carries the story to the climactic week in August 1965 that witnessed both the signing of the Voting Rights Act and the outbreak of the Watts riot. The 1966 edition also marks the coming of age of *Strange Career* as a textbook with the addition of an index and an updated list of suggested reading.[4]

The process of "textbookization" was completed in the 1974 edition. Following a brief but important preface, this version is identical to the previous one until page 181; except for the deletion of some material on northern race relations, the rest of the book differs significantly from the 1966 version only in the addition of a sixth chapter, "The Career Becomes Stranger." The new chapter begins with Watts and closes with a typically ironic assessment of the seeming high tide (in the early 1970s) of black separatist rejection of Jim Crow's end.[5]

During the process of revision, *Strange Career* evolved from a lecture series meant for a local, predominantly southern audience and which aimed to provide a historical foundation for hopes that desegregation would be peaceful and successful, into the most widely used survey text on the nature of American race relations since the Civil War. Along the way, Woodward drew attention to his initial qualifiers and provided further modifications; he said in the original edition, "Since I am . . . dealing with a period of the past that has not been adequately investigated, and also with events of the present that have come too rapidly and recently to have been properly digested and understood, it is rather inevitable that I shall make some mistakes. I shall expect and hope to be corrected."[6] In that spirit, and with the benefit of additional years of scholarship and perspective, it is time to turn to three of the contributions of the *Strange Career*.

The heart of the book remains the Woodward thesis. In his 1986 memoirs, Woodward confirms the definition of the thesis he gave in a 1971 essay, "The Strange Career of a Historical Controversy." It was, he wrote, "first, that racial segregation in the South in the rigid and universal form it had taken by 1954 did not appear with the end of slavery, but toward the end of the century and later; and second, that before it appeared in this form there occurred an era of experiment and variety in race relations of the South in which segregation was not the invariable rule."[7] As Woodward put it in the original and subsequent editions of *Strange Career,* it was not until the post-1890 period that a rigid segregation code "lent the sanction of law to a racial ostracism that extended to churches and schools, to housing and jobs, to eating and drinking. Whether by law or by custom, that ostracism eventually extended to virtually all forms of public transportation, to sports and recreations, to hospitals, orphanages, prisons, and asylums, and ultimately to funeral homes, morgues, and cemeteries."[8] The reference to custom is misleading, however, since for Woodward, despite his partial disclaimers, the existence of a law enforcing segregation has always been the key variable in evaluating the nature of race relations. And in all editions of the book, most of the examples of flexibility before the 1890s have come from the moderate South Atlantic states.

Woodward easily weathered and even incorporated the first wave of criticism that appeared. In the new first chapter of the 1966 edition, he accepted Richard C. Wade's depiction of segregation in antebellum southern cities but discounted its importance because an all-pervasive, legally enforced system was absent and the region's urbanization limited. Leon F. Litwack's revelations about the extent of segregation in the pre–Civil War North impressed Woodward more, and he broadened his treatment of the North as a result, but he reminded readers that his concern had been primarily with the roots of segregation in the South. Joel Williamson's argument for the existence of a "duo-chromatic order" by the end of Reconstruction in South Carolina, like Wade's, was found lacking, because South Carolina "may have been exceptional in some respects," but, more important, because there, as elsewhere in the South, race relations had not yet crystallized. Having dealt firmly but graciously with his critics and even having included some additional examples of early segregation, Woodward then added a new section to the beginning of chapter 2 ("Forgotten Alternatives") that spotlighted Charles E. Wynes's support for the Woodward thesis in Virginia.[9]

Woodward did not consider further historiographical developments in his 1974 edition, instead referring readers to "The Strange Career of a Historical Controversy." Since Woodward's 1971 essay, other studies that aimed to document the prevalence and early appearance of segregation or argue for its later crystallization had appeared, and more would follow after 1974. Woodward was correct to think that those subsequent works did not significantly alter the debate, and they do not merit detailed consideration here.[10]

Increasingly, however, some historians sought to go beyond the narrow question of what segregation did the South have, and when did the South have it, a debate that often seemed to come down to whether the bourbon glass was half full or half empty. For example, although I had entered the fray in 1967 geared to write parasitic history and was therefore delighted to discover widespread legally enforced cemetery segregation that existed prior to 1890, I asked what it had replaced. I discovered that it was normally exclusion of blacks, rather than integration; ironically, segregation often therefore marked an improvement in the status of blacks, rather than a setback. That view has been widely accepted, most notably and generously by Woodward himself.[11] John Cell embraced my view and then shed further light on the issue by comparing the origins of segregation in the American South and South Africa, in a book that Woodward considers more supportive of the Woodward thesis than I do. It is worth noting, however, that Cell's experiment in comparative history and George Fredrickson's before it owed much to the pioneering comparisons with South Africa found in *Strange Career*, whose title for the "Man on the Cliff" chapter is taken from an essay by Alan Paton.[12]

The debate over the Woodward thesis has been fruitful. Yet it has often been frustrating for Woodward's critics, since the master continues to absorb what they see as knockout blows and even to incorporate adversaries' weapons into his own arsenal. A careful reading of *Strange Career* helps explain why this could happen. For, despite all that has been written about it, the contours of the Woodward thesis are not at all clear. Rather than being a firmly etched thesis, Woodward's argument is hedged, as he recalled in his memoirs, by "the carefully noted exception, the guarded qualification, the unstated assumption, the cautionary warning [which] was often overlooked or brushed aside."[13] Indeed, Woodward went to great lengths in the various editions to avoid misinterpretation. Despite his emphasis on the importance of laws, he wrote in the first edition, "Laws are not an adequate index to the extent and prevalence of segregation and discriminatory practice in the South." The same phrase appears in all subsequent editions, but beginning in 1966, Woodward italicized it to make sure no one missed the point.[14] He also sought to be even more precise in his use of evidence. In all editions, Woodward uses Negro journalist T. McCants Stewart's recollections of his 1885 trip along the South Atlantic seaboard to illustrate the absence of rigid segregation. The treatments are identical, except that the 1955/1957 account is introduced by the sentence, "More pertinent and persuasive is the testimony of the Negro himself"; the 1966/1974 account begins, "More pertinent, whether typical or not, is the experience of the Negro."[15]

Yet the fault for missing Woodward's point does not always rest with the careless reader, for in matters besides the importance of law, *Strange Career* is often contradictory. Often that is to the good, making the book more comprehensive. Woodward regularly claims that he is looking simply at segregation, defined as the physical distance between the races, but there is a wealth of valuable information about political participation, jury service, and other matters that go well beyond mere segregation. At other times the contradictions are less fortunate. Despite Woodward's reference to the progressive extension of segregation, the original edition makes clear that the claims about the fluidity of race relations did not include churches, militia companies, schools, state and private welfare institutions, and a wide range of activities. In the 1966 and 1974 versions of the book, an addition to the original paragraph on state and private welfare institutions, for example, makes Woodward's point more explicit by noting, "Both types had usually made it [segregation] a practice all along."[16] Not only was segregation the norm in many areas from at least 1865 on, but it was often, as in the case of schools, admittedly enforced by law. The Woodward thesis is therefore much narrower than commonly believed and ironically had little relevance for the cause that most concerned Woodward at the time he conceived the book, that is, school desegregation. In essence, the thesis covered the situation in public conveyances and in hotels, theaters, restaurants, and other places of public accommodation. Woodward wrote out whole aspects of southern life from the bounds of his argument, thus at the very beginning, depending on your point of view, either loading the dice or conceding much of the game to his critics.

Woodward has obviously fared best within the strict ground rules he had established. The thesis is particularly true of public conveyances, where segregation laws were generally of post-1890 origin and where a degree of integration certainly existed, though rarely on first-class railroad cars. Yet the evidence about various forms of public accommodation, most notably the limited impact of the 1875 Civil Rights Act, suggests that segregation by custom was almost certainly more common than integration.[17] On Woodward's terms, that conclusion might be a victory for the thesis, but a somewhat hollow one.

The weight of the evidence seems to be on the side of those who find segregation deeply ingrained in southern life in the immediate postwar years, if not before. More important, it is not clear that the system of segregation became as rigid after the turn of the century as Woodward suggests, or that it did so when he averred. Recent studies of early twentieth-century Georgia and Tennessee blacks, for example, note that while segregation was pervasive, integrated activities continued to exist. I suspect further probing will reveal many instances of interracial mixing through at least the 1930s and even later, particularly among the lower classes.[18] Similarly, despite Woodward's surprising assertion that after 1900 "blacks ceased to vote," only indirectly corrected in a later chapter, scattered blacks continued to vote throughout the South and sometimes, in cities such as Atlanta and Memphis, even played a pivotal role in local politics.[19] By juxtaposing the American South and South Africa, Cell and Fredrickson remind us that the twentieth-century social, political, and, especially, economic barriers between the races in the South were never as great or as rigid as Woodward posits. Indeed, I think we have probably been spending too much time on the wrong end of the Woodward thesis. We need to know as much about the fluidity during the allegedly rigid period of segregation as we know about the rigidity during the allegedly fluid years.[20] It would also help to know if supposedly new forms of segregation such as those involving phone booths, elevators, and water fountains merely coincided with the appearance of new inventions.

What, then, has been the significance of the Woodward thesis? Woodward seems to have been wrong about the extent of nonsegregated behavior and the prospects for forgotten alternatives in that realm during the Reconstruction and post-Reconstruction periods, but he did inject the issue of segregation into the study of nineteenth-century southern history. Woodward stated that previous observers had assumed the prevalence of segregation in the postwar period, but he does not give any names. In fact, segregation, while certainly taken for granted, was not a major issue in the study of the postbellum South prior to *Strange Career*. Even George Tindall's penetrating, though more limited, anticipation of the Woodward thesis for South Carolina had aroused little attention.

It can be as difficult to explain "great leaps" in the writing of history as in the unfolding of history itself. Perhaps even Woodward cannot fully account for the timing and shape of his argument. He certainly was able to draw on the work of Tindall and of social scientists, especially social psychologists interested in the uses of scapegoats and the nature of prejudice, such as Konrad Lorenz and Gordon Allport. Nor should we forget Woodward's own primary research for *Origins of the New South* and a supporting brief in the *Brown v. Board of Education* case. But more was involved than the "facts" of history or the theories of others. Critical to opening a whole new field for study and infusing it with a startling perspective was Woodward's desire to provide southerners with a more hopeful, diverse, and discontinuous "usable past" with which to confront the challenges of desegregation.[21]

And in the controversy that followed in its wake, the Woodward thesis led to new findings that transcended the narrower issue of the origin and extent of segregation.

Even more important than the injection of the segregation issue into southern historiography has been Woodward's profound insight into the importance of discontinuity in the study of southern race relations and especially the watershed nature of the 1890s. It is now clear that something highly significant happened in southern race relations during the 1890s. Though many segregation laws were already on the books, Woodward is right about the importance of post-1890 legislation. Those later laws, however, even when coming in new areas, did not create a new system of segregation. Rather, they added the force of additional laws to a system already widespread in practice. Cell reached a similar conclusion, noting that the shift during the 1890s came, not in the reality of racial contact, but in political rhetoric and law. In his recent tour de force, *The Crucible of Race,* Joel Williamson agrees but adds to the equation the sharp increase in racial violence.[22]

The question remains: Why did things change in the 1890s? Woodward attributed the altered racial climate to the erosion of northern liberalism and the weakened commitment of southern conservatives and agrarian radicals to defending black political rights. Yet recent scholarship has demonstrated that most Populists were, at best, always ambivalent about having a biracial coalition and that conservatives, rather than following, actually led in the fight for disfranchisement legislation.[23] Besides, both those groups had already long expected to be segregated from blacks in schools, churches, and places of public accommodation.

The withdrawal of northern support for blacks alone remains a convincing reason for the changes of the 1890s. But there were other forces, treated only indirectly by Woodward. As Williamson notes, the economic hard times of the late 1880s and early 1890s and the threat of renewed northern Republican interference in southern affairs encouraged a shift in racial attitudes. Cell, drawing inspiration from Woodward's *Origins of the New South,* also emphasizes the altered economic situation in the South during the 1890s.[24] Although I would agree with Cell and Williamson, I think they both ignore a possible source encouraging the creation of a more de jure pattern of racial segregation. As I have argued elsewhere, segregation emerged during Reconstruction due, in part, to the efforts of white Republicans and their black allies, two groups Woodward largely ignores. Because segregation replaced exclusion, they could see it as an improvement in the status of blacks, especially when it was presented as providing separate but equal treatment. By the 1890s white Republicans were, except in a few parts of the South, no longer a major factor in the racial equation. Blacks were, however, and their resistance to de facto segregation may have helped move white southerners in the direction of additional laws. No one, to my knowledge, has sought to systematically follow up that line of inquiry since I presented it in the mid-1970s, but I think it worth pursuing, particularly given Cell's conclusion about the role of South African blacks' "growing uppityness" in forcing whites to resort to apartheid in an effort to control them.[25] And strange as it might seem, during the entire debate over the Woodward thesis, there has been remarkably little interest in the Jim Crow statutes themselves, and no one has satisfactorily followed the life of a statute from its origins through passage and the effects of implementation.[26] I might add that in the process of sorting out the reasons for change in the 1890s it would help to be more precise in the use of "Jim Crow" and to avoid the linkage of segregation, proscription, and disfranchisement that clouds the thinking of both the supporters and critics of the Woodward thesis. For long before the de jure disfranchisement of blacks or the frightening increase in lynching, segregation had become the norm in much of southern society.[27]

A second contribution of *Strange Career* has been less controversial. Just as Woodward felt that the recent origins of segregation might make it easier to overcome, he believed that the forces of reform were better positioned in the 1950s than they had been during Reconstruction. In his view, the nation in 1955 was in the midst of a "New Reconstruction," a term later used interchangeably with "Second Reconstruction," until the latter unaccountably completely replaced "New Reconstruction" in the 1966 edition.[28] For Woodward, the New or Second Reconstruction had far better prospects for success than the First Reconstruction. In the 1955, 1966, and 1974 editions, he kept comparisons to a minimum, stressing the impact of World War II and the Cold War, the greater power of the federal government, and the commitment of both political parties to desegregation in the twentieth century. In the 1957 edition, however, during a time of renewed southern resistance to desegregation, Woodward devoted five pages of his concluding chapter to show why conditions favoring change were more encouraging in the mid-1950s than they were in the 1860s and 1870s. Unlike the earlier Reconstruction, the new one was not so strongly tied to the fortunes of a single party, blacks were in a stronger position, there was more support in the South, churches were unified in their support, the border states and mid-South were on the right side, and there were already tangible results, as in the desegregation of higher education. This time Reconstruction was national, rather than sectional, in scope and support.[29]

By 1966, Woodward evidently no longer felt the need to be so defensive about the prospects for change, and he eliminated the extended comparison while incorporating most of the chapter's remaining material in the new edition. The rest of his treatment was essentially the same except for the expanded account of the new period of reconstruction and the name change. Unfortunately, the persistence of language from the earlier editions resulted in some confusion as to periodization. Woodward continued to date the origins of the Second Reconstruction from the late 1930s; he argued that it reached full momentum in the first decade after the war and was divided into two eras by the *Brown* decision. But although he retained in the 1974 edition the earlier statement that "the Second Reconstruction shows no signs of having yet run its course or even of having slackened its pace," in his new concluding chapter he observed: "The foundations of the Second Reconstruction had, in fact, begun to crumble during the Johnson Administration." [30]

Most other scholars and politicians still use the term to describe the situation today; though, given the policies initiated by the Reagan administration and continuing even under Clinton, the number is understandably shrinking. Disregarding the questions about duration for the moment, the concept of the Second Reconstruction seems to have great value as a means of enlarging our understanding of the limitations of the First Reconstruction. For Woodward, of course, the contrast was especially useful because it suggested that the new effort had a better chance for success than the first. Yet, as Woodward realized, it is best to use the term as a shorthand way of noting that after World War II federal policy once again became vitally concerned with the status of blacks in America. Obviously, there were the differences between the two reconstructions with regard to prospects for success, as already noted, but in a passage found in all editions, which has been overlooked by those who glibly use the term, Woodward observed that the Second Reconstruction "addressed itself to all the aspects of racial relations that the first attacked and even some that the First Reconstruction avoided or neglected." He then mentions as examples the attacks on segregation in the armed services and in the public schools. [31]

And here, I think, is the key point. Unless extreme caution is employed when using the term *Second Reconstruction,* the effect will be to distort the meaning of the First Reconstruction. It seems to me that the First and Second Reconstructions not only differed in their chances for success; they were about very different things. For that reason Woodward might have been better advised to stick to the term *New Reconstruction,* which has a stronger connotation of difference. The only policy aim that really links together the two reconstructions is the desire to increase the political power of blacks, though in its enforcement provisions the Voting Rights Act is much stronger than anything earlier. For, if I am correct about the First Reconstruction's emphasis on equal access and acceptance of segregation, even for those areas in which Woodward does not acknowledge its existence, then there is no comparison with the integrationist thrust of the Second Reconstruction. Similarly, it is clear that the emphasis on jobs, housing, and other economic conditions had no counterpart in the First Reconstruction, other than perhaps the largely abortive efforts at land redistribution and tax reform. And certainly there is a world of difference between the call for equal opportunity that dominated the First Reconstruction and the demand for equality of condition that, at least after 1965, threatened to control the Second Reconstruction. But I don't think we should be surprised by those differences. Nor should we succumb, as some have, to the temptation to damn the proponents of the First Reconstruction for not going far enough in their reform efforts, a temptation Woodward staunchly resists.[32] After all, it would be ahistorical and unjust to expect mid-nineteenth-century Americans to believe and act like their late-twentieth-century descendants or to create comparable institutions to promote change.

Woodward's treatment of the Second Reconstruction led him naturally into the penetrating concluding chapter of the 1974 edition. Its contribution does not stand out like the Woodward thesis or the concept of the Second Reconstruction. Many of the ideas are derivative, and the events have been increasingly covered in more detail by others. Its greatness lies in the way Woodward has brought together an impressive amount of material in a brief space, presented it in the elegant and eloquent style that characterizes the rest of the book, and made sound judgments that continue to fly in the face of much liberal and radical cant, as they did when written in 1974.

Woodward began with the obvious question: Why, after the great successes in desegregation and voting rights, did black urban America explode? His answer was that the issues being settled did not affect poor blacks and that the emphasis on integration ignored the growing nationalist thrust of many black leaders. The fight for the end of legal Jim Crow that seemed so critical in 1954 now paled next to a rash of socioeconomic problems that neither integration nor the ballot could solve. Woodward writes with compassion of the frustration and deprivation that produced the northern riots and the shift to new leaders who espoused "liberation and separation," rather than "integration and assimilation."[33] Yet, in the midst of both black and white liberal support for such a shift, Woodward remained committed to the hopes of 1954, that is, to an integrated America.

John Roper, Woodward's biographer, interprets the 1974 concluding chapter as a product of Woodward's allegedly conservative drift during the years between the mid-1960s and 1974, a period characterized by William McFeely as Woodward's "Tory Period" and by Woodward as his "times of trouble." Another scholar, who is probably not alone, has discerned a "hostile tone" in that chapter.[34] That period was a depressing one for Woodward, both in his personal life and in the life of the country, but it would be wrong to see the chapter as part of some psychologically induced move to the right or as an example of hostility toward or deviation from the struggle for equal rights. If anything had changed, it was the times, not the man. There was, however, some overreaction on his part and even some patronizing. Though he attempted to be fair-minded, his language often gave him away—"the separatist impulse infected" civil rights organizations; Stokely Carmichael moved more and more "toward a license to hate, to violence and to rage." Yet at times Woodward seemed disturbed by his own pessimism—the 1974 chapter reminds us that, despite all the attention they received (and in the face of his own overemphasis), the separatists captured only a small segment of black America. His heroes remained the National Association for the Advancement of Colored People (NAACP), Bayard Rustin, and others committed to integration, and he was equally harsh toward black separatists and toward the guilt-ridden white liberals who gave in to their demands. About the latter, he said "at times it was a question whether it was guilt or cowardice that prevailed." Nevertheless, he provided thoughtful, if largely negative, portraits of the new black leaders like Malcolm X (his favorite), Carmichael, Huey Newton, Eldridge Cleaver, and the groups they led. Throughout the chapter, Woodward kept in mind the difference between race and class interests, as when noting that the benefits of "Black Power" accrued to the black bourgeoisie, a process hidden by the "myth of black unity." He presents an equally compelling analysis of the white backlash.[35]

In short, this is perceptive and strong stuff. No one is spared. In addition to the divisions among blacks, there were many reasons for the end of the Second Reconstruction, including sheer exhaustion, the political and judicial undercutting of federal agencies' integration efforts, and the defection of white allies, especially Jews who became concerned about rising black anti-Semitism and liberals and students who became preoccupied with the Vietnam War. Woodward concludes with an essentially positive assessment of the Second Reconstruction, but he raises a number of penetrating questions about the prospects for integration in a society where "the brute facts of demography," among other forces, were moving in the opposite direction. One could therefore expect, he concluded sadly rather than bitterly, both "demand for integration and a demand for separation. Both demands would likely heard for a long time, for the means of satisfying neither seemed yet at hand."[36]

It has been almost a generation since the appearance of that chapter. Like many Americans who had hoped that the end of legalized Jim Crow would lead to even greater progress, Woodward had been sobered by the experience of the preceding twenty years. It is not surprising that there has been no fifth edition of *Strange Career*. Fortunately, Woodward has left us with a chapter that is the best single place to go in order to understand what happened to the dream of Martin Luther King Jr. Yet it is also a chapter ironically out of place in the book as it was conceived in 1954 and nominally existed in 1974. Although Woodward had continued to add material on the North to the earlier editions, because of developments at the time, the new 1974 chapter devoted unprecedented space to northern race relations. Similarly, for a book devoted to the origins and demise of legal segregation, the chapter gave a surprising degree of attention to matters unrelated to segregation and to the effects of de facto, rather than de jure, discrimination. The most important reason for those changes was a new emphasis in a book that had admittedly been concerned with white attitudes and behavior toward blacks. Now blacks moved to center stage, and the focus was on black attitudes and behavior.

Woodward's shift to viewing blacks as subjects, rather than objects, of history was part of a general trend in black and ethnic history then under way, but he was among the pacesetters, as had been indicated by his 1969 presidential address to the Organization of American Historians.[37] In more subtle ways he had moved in that direction in the previous edition of *Strange Career*. In the 1955 and 1957 editions, for example, in discussing the origins of the Second Reconstruction, he had said, "The chief agent for the advance against Southern peculiarities of racial discrimination and segregation has been the federal government in its several branches and departments, both civil and military." In 1966, in a change kept in 1974, he substituted, "Among the chief agents," thus at least implicitly increasing the importance of other elements, including blacks, who were subsequently discussed.[38] There is nothing, however, to compare with the emphasis in 1974's new chapter.

It is worth noting the greater attention to blacks in 1974, not only because it would be impossible to understand the preceding years and Woodward's reaction to them without doing so, but also because by largely ignoring blacks' attitudes and behavior for the earlier years, Woodward missed an opportunity to provide a more compelling treatment of the origins and development of segregation. Early generations of blacks are viewed as "not aggressive in pressing their rights," "confused and politically apathetic"; Booker T. Washington is described as favoring a "submissive philosophy."[39] Only in the preface to the final edition did Woodward seek "to recall a certain ambivalence that black people have felt all along toward integration in white America," but he still incorrectly asserted that it had "been buried and put aside during the long struggle against segregation and discrimination." Unfortunately, it was too late to rewrite the early sections of the book to incorporate the new approach found in the final chapter. Had he written, for example, about the call of Atlanta blacks in 1875 for the hiring of black teachers in their segregated schools, readers would have appreciated even more the irony of the Atlanta NAACP chapter doing the same thing a hundred years later. And, in general, Woodward would not be so surprised or think it quite as "strange" to find that "black champions of separatism joined hands with white champions of segregation."[40] The 1960s and 1970s were not, after all, the first time that some blacks had opted for "separate but equal treatment."

By 1974, then, and certainly today, *The Strange Career of Jim Crow* no longer held together as well as it had in 1955. New research and further reflection had reinforced the qualifications and modifications already present in the initial edition, thus further lessening the purity of the Woodward thesis. Segregation itself no longer seemed so important an issue, whether in its de facto or de jure form. The guarded optimism of 1955 had given way to a guarded pessimism. The inattention to the actions and attitudes of blacks in the initiation of segregation after the Civil War had been revealed as a crippling shortcoming, not only by the work of others, but by a powerful new concluding chapter. An unquestioning commitment to integration and blindness to voluntary aspects of ethnic cohesion had obscured the realities of the nation's cultural pluralism. As Woodward himself had feared but expected, the passage of time and fruits of new research had exposed the risks of writing presentist and "committed history."

But does this mean that *The Strange Career of Jim Crow* must simply be consigned to the ranks of misguided classics that include *The Age of Jackson, An Economic Interpretation of the Constitution,* and *The Frontier in American History,* to be read as a period piece or the progenitor of a historiographical controversy? Woodward himself seems to take this view in his memoirs, as does his biographer.[41] Had *The Strange Career of Jim Crow* remained the series of lectures it was intended to be, that probably would have been the case. But, in the process of turning the lectures into a textbook, Woodward so broadened and modified his initial effort as to make it the best available brief account of American race relations. Historians will continue to explore the well-trod ground of nineteenth-century segregation, but Woodward has already anticipated and undercut much of what they will find, and no one has yet found fault with the essence of Woodward's twentieth-century account of the subject. As typified by its new concluding chapter, *The Strange Career of Jim Crow* remains a pathbreaking, perceptive, highly readable, judicious, and surprisingly fact-filled effort to understand far more than the roots and nature of segregation, more, even, than the strange career of Jim Crow.

NOTES

1. C. Vann Woodward, ed., *Mary Chesnut's Civil War,* by Mary Chesnut (New Haven: Yale University Press, 1981). Woodward's biographer devoted a thoughtful chapter to *The Strange Career of Jim Crow,* but concentrated on the origins of the segregation issue. There are merely scattered references to other parts of the book, and he misses the significant differences among the various editions. John Herbert Roper, *C. Vann Woodward, Southerner* (Athens: University of Georgia Press, 1987), 171–200, 247, 338.

2. C. Vann Woodward, *Thinking Back: The Perils of Writing History* (Baton Rouge: Louisiana State University Press, 1986), 82–83; Roper, *C. Vann Woodward,* 194; C. Vann Woodward, *The Strange Career of Jim Crow* (New York: Oxford University Press, 1955).

3. Woodward, *The Strange Career of Jim Crow,* rev. ed. (New York: Oxford University Press, 1957).

4. Woodward, *The Strange Career of Jim Crow,* 2d rev. ed. (New York: Oxford University Press, 1966). For the addition of material on postbellum northern race relations, see esp. 71–72.

5. Woodward, *The Strange Career of Jim Crow,* 3d rev. ed. (New York: Oxford University Press, 1974).

6. Ibid. (1955), ix.

7. Woodward, *Thinking Back,* 82–83. For the original quote in the earlier essay, see Woodward, *American Counterpoint: Slavery and Racism in the North-South Dialogue* (Boston: Little, Brown, 1971), 237.

8. Woodward, *Strange Career* (1955), 8; ibid. (1957), 8; ibid. (1966), 7; ibid. (1974), 7.

9. Ibid. (1966), 13–29, 33–34. Richard C. Wade, *Slavery in the Cities: The South, 1820–1860* (New York: Oxford University Press, 1964); Leon F. Litwack, *North of Slavery: The Negro in the Free States, 1790–1860* (Chicago: University of Chicago Press, 1961); Joel Williamson, *After Slavery: The Negro in South Carolina during Reconstruction, 1861–1877* (Chapel Hill: University of North Carolina Press, 1965); Charles E. Wynes, *Race Relations in Virginia, 1870–1902* (Charlottesville: University Press of Virginia, 1961).

10. Woodward, *Strange Career* (1974), viii. In addition to Wynes, *Race Relations in Virginia,* and George Brown Tindall, *South Carolina Negroes, 1877–1900* (Columbia: University of South Carolina Press, 1952), which anticipated the basic thrust of *Strange Career,* the following works explicitly or implicitly support the Woodward thesis: Frenise A. Logan, *The Negro in North Carolina, 1876–1894* (Chapel Hill: University of North Carolina Press, 1964); Henry C. Dethloff and Robert P. Jones,

"Race Relations in Louisiana, 1877–1898," *Louisiana History* 9 (1968): 301–23; John W. Blassingame, *Black New Orleans, 1860–1880* (Chicago: University of Chicago Press, 1973); Dale A. Somers, "Black and White in New Orleans: A Study in Urban Race Relations, 1865–1900," *Journal of Southern History* 40 (1974): 19–42; John William Graves, "Town and Country: Race Relations and Urban Development in Arkansas, 1865–1905" (Ph.D. diss., University of Virginia, 1978). In addition to Williamson, *After Slavery;* Wade, *Slavery in the Cities;* and Vernon Lane Wharton; *The Negro in Mississippi, 1865–1890* (Chapel Hill: University of North Carolina Press, 1947), which can be used to challenge the thesis, the following works provided contrary evidence for the South: Roger A. Fischer, *The Segregation Struggle in Louisiana, 1862–77* (Urbana: University of Illinois Press, 1974); Ira Berlin, *Slaves without Masters: The Free Negro in the Antebellum South* (New York: Pantheon, 1974); and Joseph H. Cartwright, *The Triumph of Jim Crow: Tennessee Race Relations in the 1880s* (Knoxville: University of Tennessee Press, 1976). For a discussion of additional titles, see Woodward, *American Counterpoint*, 234–60. For a convenient summary of the initial stages of the debate, see Joel Williamson, ed., *The Origins of Segregation* (Lexington, Mass.: Heath, 1968). I have dealt more thoroughly with the debate, including its most recent developments, in Howard N. Rabinowitz, "Segregation and Reconstruction," in Rabinowitz, *Race, Ethnicity, and Urbanization* (Columbia: University of Missouri Press, 1994), 42–58.

11. Howard N. Rabinowitz, "From Exclusion to Segregation: Southern Race Relations, 1865–1890," *Journal of American History* 63 (1976): 325–50; idem, *Race Relations in the Urban South, 1865–1900* (New York: Oxford University Press, 1978). For Woodward's reaction, see C. Vann Woodward, "Foreword," in Rabinowitz, *Race Relations in the Urban South* (rev. ed.; Urbana: University of Illinois Press, 1980), ix–x; Woodward, review of *Race Relations in the Urban South, Journal of Southern History* 44 (1978): 476–78; and Woodward, *Thinking Back,* 96–97. For the response of others, see, for example, Eric Anderson, *Race and Politics in North Carolina, 1872–1901: The Black Second* (Baton Rouge: Louisiana State University Press, 1981), ix; Lawrence O. Christensen, "Race Relations in St. Louis, 1865–1916," *Missouri Historical Review* 78 (1984): 123–36; John Cell, *The Highest Stage of White Supremacy: The Origins of Segregation in South Africa and the American South* (New York: Cambridge University Press, 1982), 133–34, 175–76, 180; George Fredrickson, *White Supremacy: A Comparative Study in American and South African History* (New York: Oxford University Press, 1981), 262–63.

12. Cell, *Highest Stage of White Supremacy,* 133–34, 175–76, 180; Fredrickson, *White Supremacy.* For his assessment of Cell's book, see Woodward, "The Edifice of Domination," *New Republic,* 27 Dec. 1982, 33–35; and Woodward, *Thinking Back,* 97. In addition, Joel Williamson, who had been largely responsible for opening the original debate, sought to "move to one side, and begin again," though in fact he is still using Woodward's work as a jumping-off point. See Joel Williamson, *The Crucible of Race: Black-White Relations in the American South since Emancipation* (New York: Oxford University Press, 1984), viii–ix, 491–93. Woodward himself

sought to go beyond the debate by applying "competitive" and "paternalistic" models of race relations to the late-nineteenth-century southern experience (Woodward, *American Counterpoint,* 243–60). For two other efforts to save the Woodward thesis by approaching it from a different perspective than had Woodward, see the cyclical explanation in August Meier and Elliott Rudwick, "A Strange Chapter in the Career of 'Jim Crow,'" in *The Making of Black America: Essays in Negro Life and History,* ed. August Meier and Elliott Rudwick, 2 vols. (New York: Atheneum, 1969), 2:14–19; and J. Morgan Kousser and James M. McPherson, eds., *Region, Race, and Reconstruction: Essays in Honor of C. Vann Woodward* (New York: Oxford University Press, 1982), xxv–xxvii.

13. Woodward, *Thinking Back,* 93.

14. Woodward, *Strange Career* (1955), 87; ibid. (1966), 102; ibid. (1974), 102. Woodward struggles with the relative importance of laws in many places. The best examples in addition to the pages already cited are the prefaces to the last three editions: ibid. (1957), xi–xvii; ibid. (1966), v–ix; ibid. (1974), v–viii. See also ibid. (1966), 24–25, 29, 31, and ibid. (1974), 24–25, 29, 31.

15. Ibid. (1955), 19; ibid. (1957), 19; ibid. (1966), 38; ibid. (1974), 38. Although Woodward does not mention T. McCants Stewart's color, he was a very light-skinned Negro, and that may help explain the ease with which he traveled through the South.

16. See ibid. (1955), 15–16, 83–84; ibid. (1957), 15–16, 83–84; ibid. (1966); ibid. (1974), 99. Exclusion from welfare institutions had been the initial policy. See Rabinowitz, "From Exclusion to Segregation: Health and Welfare Services for Southern Blacks, 1865–1890," *Social Science Review* 48 (1974): 327–54.

17. John Hope Franklin, "The Enforcement of the Civil Rights Act of 1875," *Prologue* 6 (1974): 225–35; Charles A. Lofgren, *The Plessy Case: A Legal-Historical Interpretation* (New York: Oxford University Press, 1987), 132–37; Rabinowitz, *Race Relations in the Urban South,* 186–89, 195–96.

18. John Dittmer, *Black Georgia in the Progressive Era, 1900–1920,* Blacks in the New World, series ed. August Meier (Urbana: University of Illinois Press, 1977); Lester C. Lamon, *Black Tennesseans, 1900–1930* (Knoxville: University of Tennessee Press, 1977). Woodward notes that a 1940 park segregation ordinance in Atlanta provided an exception for the Grant Park zoo, idem, *Strange Career* (1955), 104; ibid. (1957), 104; ibid. (1966), 117; ibid. (1974), 117. Yet there might be some confusion here between exclusion and segregation, since the zoo had been segregated at its opening in 1890. See Rabinowitz, *Race Relations in the Urban South,* 190. For the passage of new laws during the 1930s and even the 1940s, see Woodward, *Strange Career* (1955), 102–4; ibid. (1957), 102–4; ibid. (1966), 116–18; ibid. (1974), 116–18.

19. Woodward, *Strange Career* (1955), 91; ibid. (1957), 91; ibid. (1966), 106, ibid. (1974), 106. For reference to the "virtual exclusion for nearly half a century" of Negro voters, see ibid. (1955), 124; ibid. (1957), 124. For reference to the exclusion of "all but a tiny percentage of the Negroes from the polls in the Southern states for nearly half a century," see ibid. (1966), 141; ibid. (1974), 141. On the political role of blacks in Atlanta, see Dittmer, *Black Georgia,* 147–48; on Memphis, see Lamon,

Black Tennesseans, 42–47, 55–58, 222–23. For a broader discussion of black voting before the 1950s, see Valdimer Orlando Key Jr., *Southern Politics in State and Nation* (New York: Knopf, 1949).

20. Cell, *Highest Stage of White Supremacy,* 192–275; Fredrickson, *White Supremacy,* 199–282. For a largely unsuccessful attempt to minimize the differences between the South African and southern experiences, see Robert J. Norrell, "Caste in Steel: Jim Crow Careers in Birmingham, Alabama," *Journal of American History* 73 (1986): 669–94, esp. 671, 694. Although in *Strange Career* Woodward frequently admitted exceptions even at the peak of legalized Jim Crow, in *Thinking Back* he argues that "the new laws were of profound significance. They rigidified practice, eliminated exceptions, and applied to all on the basis of race alone" (96).

21. Tindall, *South Carolina Negroes.* In the original edition, Woodward cited several books concerned with the legal status of blacks but did not single out the most important, Gilbert Thomas Stephenson's *Race Distinctions in American Law* (London: D. Appleton, 1910), which he may have had in mind, since Stephenson had argued that Jim Crow laws often simply gave the force of law to customary practices. For influences on Woodward's new approach to the subject, including work on a brief for *Brown v. Board of Education,* 347 U.S. 483 (1954), see Roper, *C. Vann Woodward,* 171–200; and Woodward, *Thinking Back,* 81–90.

22. Rabinowitz, *Race Relations in the Urban South,* 330–33; Cell, *The Highest Stage of White Supremacy,* 81–102; Williamson, *The Crucible of Race,* 180–223.

23. For Woodward's explanation, see *Strange Career* (1955), 51–64, which is reproduced in ibid. (1957), 51–65; ibid. (1966), 69–82; ibid. (1974), 69–82. For challenges to Woodward's interpretation of Populist racial attitudes and behavior, see Gerald H. Gaither, *Blacks and the Populist Revolt: Ballots and Bigotry in the "New South"* (University: University of Alabama Press, 1977); and Barton C. Shaw, *The Wool-Hat Boys* (Baton Rouge: Louisiana State University Press, 1984). For conservative responsibility for disfranchisement, see J. Morgan Kousser, *The Shaping of Southern Politics: Suffrage Restrictions and the Establishment of the One-Party South, 1880–1910* (New Haven: Yale University Press, 1974). Woodward has only partly accepted the views of his critics on Populism but finds Kousser's argument more compelling. Woodward, *Thinking Back,* 39–40, 69, 97.

24. Williamson, *Crucible of Race,* 112–14; Cell, *Highest Stage of White Supremacy,* 82–170. Although he acknowledged the role of political and economic forces, Williamson emphasized, misguidedly in my view, psychosexual reasons for the rise of "Radicalism" after 1889. See Williamson, *Crucible of Race,* 111–79. See also Howard N. Rabinowitz, "Psychological Disorders, Socio-Economic Forces, and American Race Relations," *Slavery & Abolition* 7 (1986): 188–94.

25. Rabinowitz, *Race Relations in the Urban South,* 333–39, and "From Exclusion to Segregation: Southern Race Relations," 350; Cell, *Highest Stage of White Supremacy,* 192–229, esp. 212. For an endorsement of my position, but without new evidence, see Lofgren, *Plessy Case,* 25–26. For a mention of white fears of the "new Negro" that does not give enough credence to the justification for such fears,

see Linda M. Matthews, "Keeping down Jim Crow: The Railroads and the Separate Coach Bills in South Carolina," *South Atlantic Quarterly* 73 (1974): 117–29.

26. Two attempts would have benefited from greater attention to roll-call analysis and to the effects of the laws: Matthews, "Keeping down Jim Crow"; and John William Graves, "The Arkansas Separate Coach Law of 1891," *Journal of the West* 7 (1968), 531–41. On white Republican commitment to separate but equal train accommodations in Tennessee in 1881, see Stanley J. Folmsbee, "The Origin of the First 'Jim Crow' Law," *Journal of Southern History* 15 (1949): 243–47. For a suggestive, but only partially convincing, economic interpretation, see Walter E. Campbell, "Profit, Prejudice, and Protest: Utility Competition and the Generation of Jim Crow Streetcars in Savannah, 1905–1907," *Georgia Historical Quarterly* 70 (1986): 197–231. For an economic interpretation marred by misleading claims of originality and an inadequate grasp of the secondary literature, see Jennifer Roback, "The Political Economy of Segregation: The Case of Segregated Streetcars," *Journal of Economic History* 46 (1986): 893–917.

27. Woodward expressed this view in its classic form in a passage retained in subsequent editions: "The policies of proscription, segregation, and disfranchisement that are often described as the immutable 'folkways' of the South, impervious alike to legislative reform and armed intervention, are of more recent origin [than the immediate post-Reconstruction period]" (Woodward, *Strange Career* [1955], 47). John Cell's definition of segregation is comparable to Woodward's "Jim Crow" (which Woodward often used interchangeably with "segregation" but sometimes more broadly): "An interlocking system of economic institutions, social practices and customs, political power, law, and ideology, all of which function both as means and ends in one group's efforts to keep another (or others) in their place" (Cell, *Highest Stage of White Supremacy,* 14). On Cell's approach, see Rabinowitz, "The Not-So Strange Career of Jim Crow," *Reviews in American History* 12 (1984): 58–64.

28. Woodward, *Strange Career* (1955), 9–10, 124; ibid. (1957), 9–10, 124, 155, 175, 179; ibid. (1966), 9–10, 135, 139; ibid. (1974), 9–10, 135, 139, 209.

29. Ibid. (1957), 174–78.

30. Ibid. (1974), 8, 209.

31. Ibid. (1955), 10–11; ibid. (1957), 10–11; ibid. (1966), 9–10; ibid. (1974), 9–10.

32. See, for example, Lawrence J. Friedman, *The White Savage: Racial Fantasies in the Postbellum South* (Englewood Cliffs, N.J.: Prentice-Hall, 1970); Forrest G. Wood, *Black Scare: The Racist Response to Emancipation and Reconstruction* (Berkeley: University of California Press, 1970); and Forrest G. Wood, *The Era of Reconstruction, 1863–1877* (New York: Crowell, 1975). Woodward was even more sympathetic to the aims, legacy, and problems of the First Reconstruction in an article that also marked his full commitment to the term *Second Reconstruction.* See Woodward, "The Political Legacy of the First Reconstruction," *Journal of Negro Education* 26 (1957): 231–40.

33. Woodward, *Strange Career* (1974), 195.

34. Roper, *C. Vann Woodward*, 198, 232–67, esp. 246–47; remarks of an anonymous reader of a previous version of this essay (in Rabinowitz's possession). Roper tends to treat Woodward's views of society and history that he agrees with as "liberal" or "radical"; when he disagrees with the assessments, Woodward is wrong and "conservative." Much of Roper's evidence, including Woodward's vote for George McGovern in 1972, undercuts claims for a Tory Woodward.

35. Woodward, *Strange Career* (1974), 196, 197–98, 205, 206–7.

36. Ibid., 219, 220.

37. Rabinowitz, "Race, Ethnicity, and Cultural Pluralism in American History," in *Ordinary People and Everyday Life: Perspectives on the New Social History*, ed. James B. Gardner and George Rollie Adams (Nashville: The American Association for State and Local History, 1983), 23–49; Woodward, "Clio with Soul," *Journal of American History* 46 (1969): 5–20.

38. Woodward, *Strange Career* (1955), 123; ibid. (1957), 123; ibid. (1966), 134; ibid. (1974), 134. At times the new emphasis produced puzzling results. In his discussion of the 1965 disturbances in Selma in the 1966 edition, Woodward mentioned the murders of "Jimmie Lee Jackson, a Negro," "one of the clergymen, James Reeb," and "a woman on the highway to Selma" (187). In the 1974 edition, he repeats the reference to Jackson, but now notes "one of the clergymen died" and "a woman demonstrator" was murdered on the highway. Neither the race nor the name of the two whites is given. The woman was, of course, Viola Liuzzo, whose death received more national attention than Jackson's (184–85). The new approach also gave less emphasis to the contributions of white southerners. For the omission of Judge J. Waites Waring of South Carolina, who presided over a key white primary case, see ibid. (1955), 125–27; ibid. (1957), 125–27; ibid. (1966), 140–42; ibid. (1974), 140–42. Note especially the deletion of "As so frequently happens in this New Reconstruction, a Southern man played one of the key roles," indicating that by 1966 Woodward was less concerned about providing the South with white role models. Compare ibid. (1955), 125; ibid. (1957), 125; ibid. (1966), 141; and ibid. (1974), 141.

39. Ibid. (1966), 28, 59, 82; ibid. (1974), 28, 59, 82. For the latter two quotations, see ibid. (1955), 41, 65; ibid. (1957), 41, 65; ibid. (1966), 59, 82; ibid. (1974), 59, 82. Despite the claim that blacks were "confused," in the same paragraph Woodward shows they were not, by saying that they were beginning to think in economic terms and had seen through Democratic appeals for their votes.

40. Ibid. (1974), vi, 218. Rabinowitz, "Half a Loaf: The Shift from White to Black Teachers in the Negro Schools of the Urban South, 1865–1890," *Journal of Southern History* 40 (1974): 565–94.

41. Woodward, *Thinking Back*, 98–99; Roper, *C. Vann Woodward*, 198–200.

C. Vann Woodward and the Origins of a New Wisdom

JOEL R. WILLIAMSON

✳

It was books and documents and research in "the subject" that began the friendship, sometimes adversarial, sometimes cooperative, but always gentlemanly in the most classic southern forms, between critic Williamson and Woodward. In the essay below, the critic has described how he read everything by Woodward and how excited he was to meet Woodward on the research trail in 1965. For his part, Woodward that year in the *New York Times Book Review* took special note of Williamson's *After Slavery,* a study of Reconstruction in the critic's native state of South Carolina. Judging it to be one of the significant releases in history, Woodward admiringly called it "a down-to-the core study of the freedmen." From that engagement, the two moved on to develop the scholarly and personal relationship described below. In the historiography of Reconstruction and of segregation, Williamson was especially responsible for raising questions about the origins and the continuity of Jim Crow, not only for practices but even for the laws whose newness and discontinuity Woodward marked. Williamson's research seemed to show that even statutory laws were older than Woodward thought; and these laws, whether actually enacted before or after Reconstruction, made much less of a break with the antebellum South than Woodward thought. Too, Williamson was convinced that the psychic sources of racism were both more profound and far more intractable than Woodward realized.

✳   ✳   ✳

I first met C. Vann Woodward in Columbia during the summer of 1960 on the portico of the South Caroliniana Library on the campus of the University of South Carolina. I had just come east from Berkeley to do research on my dissertation, which became *After Slavery,* a study very much a product of the liberal integrationism and the political optimism of the late 1950s and early 1960s.

This research trip was a homecoming, too. I was born and reared in the state and had gone off to the University of South Carolina in the fall of 1946 as a freshman. I went through the college at an accelerated pace, having fallen in easily with the veterans from World War II who filled the school to over-flowing. For me, the veterans were an education in themselves and totally en-joyable. I stayed on with them to do graduate work after having taken a bach-elor's degree. The next war—the Korean War—ended all that. It was my turn. Three and a half years in the U.S. Navy, then five and a half years more at the University of California at Berkeley, and now on this warm, pleasant, sunshiny day I was home again.

My first professional job as a historian, so to speak, had been at the South Caroliniana Library, which was the university's repository for special mate-rials such as manuscripts and rare books. I must have been eighteen or nine-teen, it was a summer job, and it was a once-in-a-lifetime position because it would be done only once . . . ever. I "collated," as the archivists say, the papers of Martin Witherspoon Gary.[1] This meant that I took these papers—hundreds of manuscript letters, documents, and miscellaneous writings—out of the boxes in which they had arrived, put them in chronological order, and made a note about each item. Gary was another of those "boy" generals of the Confederacy who was lucky enough not to get killed in four years among bullets and missiles, and sufficiently gifted with martial talent to rise in rank. It was said that this fierce "Bald Eagle of Edgefield" had not stopped to sur-render with the rest of Lee's army at Appomattox, but rather had ridden away with his battle flag secreted in his clothes. He was a headstrong, self-centered, very violent man who stood out in those qualities as a leader of the Redshirts, the paramilitary groups that did the strongarm work in the Re-demption campaign in 1876 and 1877 that ended Reconstruction in South Carolina. As I recall, I was paid sixty dollars for that job and considered myself fortunate. It was heartening to see that one could make at least some money working as a historian. I think I have sometimes worked harder as a historian for less money (in "real," or inflation-adjusted terms) and certainly with less joyful excitement.

So, a dozen summers later, I was in that marvelous old building again, the South Caroliniana Library. Antebellum-built, ivy-covered, rough red bricks and cream cement, cool to the touch on the hottest days. It stands at the end of one leg of the Horseshoe that patterned the university from its first days. In front, there is the portico with large columns; behind, the garden with cement benches and goldfish in a small pool. Inside, the most striking space is the main reading-room. It has a ten-yard ceiling, a wraparound balcony, with stacks and reading spaces tucked in alcoves here and there. It is always a bit musty from the old books and papers, some of which were once held in the still-fleshed fingers of those myriad ghosts of the Carolina past—the Pinckneys, the Calhouns, the Hamptons. I could hold in my hand a piece of paper that John C. Calhoun or Wade Hampton ("The Giant in Gray") had held—smell it, too. Footsteps and voices sounded and re-sounded comfortably, as in a cathedral.

I had arrived in Columbia that day and worked all morning in the manuscripts division of the Library. About noon I headed out for lunch. Stepping onto the portico, I encountered Les Inabinet, director of the library. He was sitting on one of the cement benches by the door talking to an attractive lady of middle years. She was dressed for the weather, thin-fabric short-sleeve dress, lightly colored, narrowly belted, slightly starched against the humidity. Les had been briefly another of my roommates from the World War. He was from Charleston. He introduced me. She was Mrs. C. Vann Woodward. She was waiting for Vann, and would I not join them for lunch? Les had to remain on duty. I was shy and a little fearful of meeting so eminent a scholar. We never saw the famous eastern historians at Berkeley; we just read them, studied them, and stepped back in awe. I was failing at the effort of declining politely when Professor Woodward himself emerged from the building. At fifty, he was a man of imposing size and bearing. He was something over six feet tall when few men were, and he was solidly built—a tennis player. He was formally dressed with tie and jacket, as were all of us academic types in those times. His clothes might have been seersucker. Anyway, they looked comfortable—casually, almost carelessly, chosen—but yet they observed the proprieties. He was a handsome man, almost classically so. He was simultaneously relaxed and alert. He might have been the captain of one of the navy's battleships, but in civilian dress. He was slightly florid in complexion, with straight hair already suggesting silver and rather long but combed neatly back from the temples. He looked at people then as he still does—with a level gaze, courteous, friendly, honestly interested in you and what you have to say. Of course I would come to lunch with them—the gentle insistence—no other thought was possible.

His book *The Strange Career of Jim Crow*, being issued that very year in its third paperback edition, had sold by the hundreds of thousands, and it was, more than anything else, responsible for the currently accepted liberal scholarly perspective on the history of race relations in the South. It declared that racial attitudes had not always been the same and not the same among all whites in certain times. There had been several different ways of thinking about black people, and these ways changed over time. In brief, racism was not so monolithic and immutable as we had thought a dozen years before. In essence, Professor Woodward, who then held an appointment in Johns

Hopkins University, asked southerners to remember their traditions and thus know that they could accept desegregation and civil equality for blacks without becoming less southern. If one's family tradition was Conservative, one ought to be a protective, promotive paternalist—a helper rather than an obstructionist in the crisis of integration. If one came out of the Radical tradition, such as the Populists in the South at large or the "Readjusters" in Virginia represented, then one could assume a cooperationist stance—one that treated all of the oppressed, black and white, as "down in the ditch together" and willing to work together to get out. The thesis argued that black people in the South after emancipation were not always and everywhere oppressed by whites, but in the 1890s, coincidental with the worst worldwide industrial depression until then, a social psychology operated that caused whites to forget the alternatives offered by Conservatism and Radicalism. The inability of both Radicals and Conservatives to cope with the economic and political crisis of the 1890s caused them to become frustrated; frustration led to aggression; aggression required a scapegoat—and blacks were it. In the crisis white leaders panicked and moved to segregate, disfranchise, and proscribe black people in a legal, total, and concerted way. Thus the *close-out* came only in the 1890s and not during Reconstruction or at its end, as we had previously assumed.[2]

We went to lunch at the new faculty club, joined by an economics professor previously invited. We drove over in the Woodwards' car. All four of us got into the car through the driver's doorway. Mrs Woodward got in first, then two of us in the back and finally the driver, Vann, in his seat. It was an arcane proceeding for which Vann apologized with wry amusement. Shortly before they were to drive south, the car had sustained a hit from another car on the right side just at the center post, so that the door would not easily open, and would not close securely if opened. They had driven down anyway, rather than delay the trip. It was a modest car, perhaps a Ford, in a middle size and not new. The car was like his clothes: it got there, it did not offend the eye, and it really didn't matter.

We had lunch, the four of us. But most of all we had conversation. With total grace Vann asked what I was doing. I told him. Then, still gracefully, he told us what he had been doing. He had just spent the morning reading original material on the Hamburg "riot" or "massacre." The last word depended on which side you were on. The event happened in 1876 during the Redemption campaign. Hundreds of Redshirts surrounded several score black militiamen in a building in the village of Hamburg, just across the Savannah River from Augusta, Georgia. This was in Martin Gary's Edgefield County, notorious for violence and famous for militant political leadership, especially in the U.S. Senate. It was the home of James Henry Hammond, the U.S. senator who dared the North to make war on the South, of "Pitchfork" Ben Tillman, the U.S. senator who threatened to take that instrument to the rear parts of slow-moving and very conservative President Grover Cleveland, and latterly of J. Strom Thurmond, the long-lived U.S. senator who established world records for "filibustering" speeches that delayed civil rights legislation in that era of ferment. In the Hamburg affair, after a pitched battle in which the whites brought up a cannon and blasted away at the building, the surviving blacks surrendered, only to be marched off a short distance where many of them were shot to death. Vann Woodward was smoldering with anger. Eventually, with some relief, we turned from that subject to talk about Otis Singletary's recent book, *The Negro Militia,* a study that legitimated the actions and attitudes of such black militia forces not only in South Carolina but throughout the Reconstruction South.[3] Otis later came to be highly placed in the Kennedy administration, and then for many years he served as president of the University of Kentucky and also became a moving spirit in the national organization of Phi Beta Kappa. For me, a journeyman scholar, my first meeting with Professor Woodward was an exhilarating experience.

Since 1951, when he published two superb books in the same year, Vann Woodward had been virtually undisputed as the premier historian of the South. In 1938, when he was twenty-eight, he had published his dissertation as *Tom Watson, Agrarian Rebel.*[4] It was pro-Populist, it was passionate, and from the first it was recognized as a masterpiece of research and writing. In 1955, he had published the first version of *Strange Career,* which Martin Luther King Jr. reputedly called "the Bible of the Civil Rights Movement." When we met in 1960, Professor Woodward held a chair at the Johns Hopkins University. Soon he would move on to Yale University. In both places he attracted a flow of truly marvelous graduate students, whose dissertations became very important books, as seen in this volume's appendix.

After working a few days in South Carolina, I went on to Chapel Hill to survey the manuscript holdings in the Southern Historical Collection that might relate to my dissertation. Also, I called on Professor George Tindall, at his home. George had published a pioneering book in black history, *South Carolina Negroes, 1877–1900* (1951).[5] That book had become one of the prime sources of factual material for Professor Woodward when he built his segregation thesis. George noticed a phenomenon and gave it a name, *fluidity,* which was his term for race relations in postbellum South Carolina before 1898. *Fluidity,* for George, described a period of experimentation, including serious consideration of race relations more varied and more complex than the literally black and white separatism of Jim Crow. Among other things, my dissertation was deliberately designed to fill the space where slavery ended and George Tindall's book began.

George was very genial and helpful. He showed me sheafs of long pages of writing that would become *The Emergence of the New South, 1913–1945* (1967),[6] the sequel in a series to Woodward's monumental *The Origins of the New South, 1877–1913* (1951).[7] George's wife, Blossom, was out for the morning, but she left cornbread muffins to go with our talk. We also had Tindall's infant daughter, Blair, with us. I held the diapered Blair in my lap for a time while we talked sources, history, and historians. I knew how to hold a baby. I was the father of two, and about to make it three, including two daughters. It happened that Anne Firor Scott, later to publish *The Southern Lady* (1970),[8] had just vacated a position in the History Department in Chapel Hill—in which she taught Modern Civilization to freshmen—to take an appointment across New Hope Creek at Duke University. George urged me to talk to the chairman at UNC. I did and so stumbled onto the job that I have held for more than thirty-five academic years.

There is a great amount of South Carolina material in the Southern Historical Collection because the original organizer was J. G. de Roulhac ("Ransack") Hamilton, who was mostly from South Carolina. Hamilton became notorious for "raiding" South Carolina and other southern states when archivists in those states usually did not go out and aggressively recruit gifts of manuscripts, but rather waited for them to flow into their repositories as if by some form of archival gravity. The result was that he built a collection of southern manuscripts unmatched anywhere. I worked extensively in that collection. Indeed, it was my home away from home, in part because then-director James W. Patton befriended me and gave me space in which to work. In addition, of course, I took such trips to other archives as were necessary. Incidentally, for many years this was but another example of the path followed to Chapel Hill's collection by southern historians from California. My mentor at Berkeley, Kenneth Stampp, lived in the Chapel Hill area for a year in the mid-1950s, sortieing out as needed to collect the material that went into his masterpiece, *The Peculiar Institution* (1957).[9] Stampp's beautifully crafted book did carry the unfortunate phrase in the preface: "I have assumed that the slaves were merely ordinary human beings, that innately Negroes *are*, after all only white men with black skins, nothing more, nothing less."[10] It was a classic proclamation from the liberal integrationism of the middle and late 1950s, and of course today it is dated in a rather painful way. In any event, Stampp's book became *the* book that marked the history of slavery for the civil rights movement, much as Woodward's *The Strange Career of Jim*

Crow was its history for the era after slavery. Two other students of my mentor Stampp did the same for me, their books bracketing my own research interests in terms of class and economic activities: Robert Starobin for *Industrial Slavery* (1970)[11] and James Oakes for *The Ruling Race* (1982).[12] Another of his students, contemporary with me, William Freehling, spent months in the Chapel Hill area researching his award-winning book, *Prelude to Civil War* (1965),[13] which described the Nullification crisis in South Carolina.

As I researched *After Slavery,* I took a note every time I found a reference to *Negro, black,* or *colored.* After some months, I could look at a page of print or manuscript and know in seconds if one of the operative words was there. After researching for a couple of years and looking forward to the writing, I began to sort my notes into piles according to subject matter—economics, politics, religion, etc. Soon I found that I needed to start a pile having to do with segregation. It was a subject to which Reconstruction contemporaries, black and white, gave considerable attention. Then I found I needed to divide the pile according to whether the note indicated segregation or the lack thereof. These notes came only from original sources—letters, diaries, newspapers, and journals—and they dealt with observations made by contemporaries concerning churches, farms, trains, streetcars, restaurants, hotels, theaters, parks, and so on. The picture I got was that segregation far outran integration—though, of course, there were intriguing and highly significant instances of integration. This was contrary to what I had learned at Berkeley, contrary to Woodward as taught there. We were taught that widespread and rigid segregation should come only with the 1890s and the legislation of that era, not during Reconstruction.

In the end, I wrote a chapter on "The Separation of the Races," as people called the phenomenon during Reconstruction.[14] It described a widespread and fairly rigid pattern of de facto physical segregation of blacks and whites already in place—not immediately after slavery—by 1868. The pattern was sometimes breached. Blacks and whites came together in a revolutionary way in Republican party conventions. Now and again, blacks pressed into spaces where only whites had been before. But my notes indicated that South Carolina was substantially segregated during Reconstruction, probably more so, physically, than in slavery. I did not know what happened in the 1880s and 1890s. New laws certainly came during the turn-of-the-century years, but *why* was a mystery to me. I had not then researched the era. I assumed, perhaps too quickly, that with blacks firmly disfranchised by then and the North unwilling to act, it became safe to codify what was already the practice.

This chapter, of course, flew squarely in the face of accepted interpretations—the several Woodward theses as written, read, and taught. There had always been at least two groups of such theses, the thesis that Woodward *wrote* and the ones that historians and activists *read*. Some of those readings and certainly some of the subsequent teachings would be unrecognizable to the author, who had taken pains to condition and qualify everything that he had written. However, certain research findings made great problems even for the carefully qualified and superbly nuanced thesis that Woodward wrote. At least in South Carolina, widespread segregation followed early after the abolition of slavery. It was not instantaneous, it was not "immediate," as some readers understood me to say. Indeed, it involved a period of transition and experimentation. But it was also a spontaneous, unregulated, popular movement, almost a folk movement, and one that ran rather quickly from one pattern to another and then drifted. After 1868, when the Radical Reconstruction government was in power in South Carolina, supported by a black majority of some 57 percent, segregation of a high order persisted even in a hostile legal environment.

That chapter had dire implications for the civil rights movement. It indicated that segregation had begun and flourished without the benefit of favorable laws and that the prejudice in white minds that had justified slavery turned quickly to actuate and justify the separation of the races and discrimination generally. Further, the crucial element in the affair was not physical separation; rather it was a matter of minds. "The real color line lived in the minds of individuals of each race, and it had achieved full growth even before freedom for the Negro was born," ran a concluding line in the chapter. "Physical separation merely symbolized and reinforced mental separation." Mixing the bodies did not necessarily reduce or remove prejudice. It did not do so in slavery, where bodies were perforce mixed, and it did not do so in freedom. Thinking—psychology—was vital to the process.[15]

Historians generally liked the portion of *After Slavery* that argued that blacks could melt rapidly into the national norm, but they did not like the part that argued that segregation had come early in a major way and that implied that segregation, disfranchisement, and proscription were essentially the result of mental processes and largely beyond immediate, effective control by government. *After Slavery* suggested that segregation and the racism behind it were both older and more intractable than most historians believed. Certainly, my findings did not comport with the popular readings and misreadings of the Woodward thesis.

A very popular offering of the Woodward thesis in academic circles—one taught by professors to masses of undergraduates in colleges and universities—dramatically contrasted a happy time of race relations in the South in the 1880s with what followed. Along with this rather sanguine view of the

1880s ran a subtheme that Reconstruction was much more successful in the area of race relations than we have ever dreamed—that it abounded in instances of integration and evidences that racism among whites, particularly whites of the lower orders, was less strong than we had thought.

In its most naive but still plausible variant, the *taught* version insisted that southern whites in the 1890s had simply mistaken the Negro for the evils of industrial capitalism. The enemy was really a selfish, soulless, runaway materialism that should have been countered by democratic political and economic devices. Instead reform efforts were frustrated by reactionary, upper-class elements, the Negro was made a scapegoat to mislead the masses and thwart the reformers, legislation was enacted, and a regime of rigid discrimination was put in place. Later generations were said to accept uncritically the situation created in the 1890s and the very early years of the twentieth century, and thus people forgot that things had been quite different and substantially better before the 1890s. Southerners imagined, finally, that race relations had always been the same. Thus, in the 1950s we discovered that southerners had made a tragic error in the turn-of-the-century decades. They had built a legal system that oppressed black people when they should have engaged in political and economic reform instead. Summing up, it was a case of mistaken identity, and they really didn't mean to do it. Today, the extended argument ran, we could use legal devices—government, laws, courts, the *Brown* decision—to set things right, just as they had used them back then to set things wrong. Moreover, now that we understood the history, we could do so without undue or prolonged difficulty. White racism in the South was actually a thin, hard shell; if cracked with a strong hand and a sharp tool, it would crumble.

One of the most dedicated reformists among the observers and participants, Professor Howard Zinn, posed the issue in a simple metaphor that today seems incredibly naive.[16] If a white southerner were at a bus stop in a southern city and his bus arrived with blacks riding in the front, he would board the bus and ride among black people rather than walk. Thus integration would be achieved. Physical relations could be so arranged that white people would do the right thing, the moral thing, rather than be inconvenienced. Indeed, perhaps they would. Certainly, physical proximity between whites and blacks was and is important—that is, it is important that they actually share spaces. But the metaphor omitted what the civil rights movement omitted, specifically, a substantial concern for what white people were thinking in physically integrated situations. In short, it failed to address effectively *mental* segregation. At the national level scant attention was given—or has yet been given—to that issue. One assumption, which showed up to varying degrees in the civil rights movement, seemed to be that if we simply mix white bodies and black bodies together in all public places and turn heads away for, say, a generation, when we look back everything will be fine. There was a faith that blacks and whites, pressed into proximity to one another, would come to know and appreciate their mutual humanity. Consequently, we need not be overly concerned with what the white man at Zinn's bus stop is thinking and "feeling" in these new circumstances. What we want from him is a certain behavior, and we need not get into the tedious business of what he thinks and why. Furthermore, there is no reason to be concerned with what the black people on the bus are thinking. Indeed, so myopic, so egocentric were whites at large, including me, in the period 1959–65, that it did not even occur to us that black people could be anything but ecstatic and exceedingly grateful to be alongside those white bodies. There was only one life worth living, and it was white.

After Slavery was by no means the only and certainly not the most important book or article published in that time that cast doubts on the viability of the Woodward theses, both on the naive *taught* versions and on his own more nuanced and sophisticated version of the origins and nature of segregation. Other scholars, perhaps a dozen or so, were seeing in their own spheres of research much of what I was seeing in mine, and most were probably reacting with similar amazement. One fine book, *Jim Crow's Defense* (1965) by Idus A. Newby,[17] actually dared to render the ideology behind segregation between 1900 and 1930. Some of these other works dealt with other southern states during Reconstruction, some went beyond Reconstruction and into the early twentieth century, and some dealt with special topics. In regard to the Woodward thesis as written, some, such as Roger A. Fischer's history of black/white relations in Louisiana from 1850 to 1890,[18] were outrightly challenging and received devastating fire from the opposition. Some, such as Charles E. Wynes's 1961 study of race relations in Virginia from 1870 to 1902,[19] accepted the basic thesis but qualified it in very significant ways. Others accepted the Woodward thesis as sound but produced substantial factual evidence that could be used to argue the contrary.

I was present at the scene when one important challenge surfaced. It was at a meeting of the Southern Historical Association in Asheville in 1963. Professor Woodward had appeared on a panel at one of the sessions. I went up afterward to pay my respects. He and I were talking when Professor Richard C. Wade, at that time perhaps the leading urban historian in the United States, came up and said rather urgently that he had something he had to tell Professor Woodward. I withdrew, but I heard enough even as I left to conclude later that he was telling Woodward about his forthcoming book, *Slavery in the Cities, 1820–1860* (1964).[20] Professor Wade thought that he had discovered the real origins of segregation in the five southern cities he had studied for that work. If those five cities were representative, the origins of segregation were not in the 1890s, or even in the decade after the Civil War. Segregation had actually begun in urban life in the South in the 1850s.

After Slavery was issued in 1965, and later in that same year Vann Woodward came to Chapel Hill to give a talk. Afterward, there was a reception at the home of the late J. Carlyle Sitterson, then chancellor of the university and in the late 1930s a graduate-school associate and friend of Woodward's. Courteous as always, Woodward said good things to me about my first book. Late that night, he called and invited me to lunch with him the next day. We went to what was then *the* village restaurant in Chapel Hill, the Rathskellar. Good company, good conversation again. We talked about our experiences in the navy. He talked about his life as a graduate student in Chapel Hill. He had worked with Howard K. Beale, a Reconstruction historian who had interpreted that era through the glass of economics. As I recall, we ranged comfortably about in our conversation. We also talked about Jim Crow. After all, it was 1965 and segregation had just collapsed in a giant way. I made the case that mixing bodies did not necessarily make integration, that *minds* had to be integrated in some way too. I indicated slavery, the obvious and easy example when bodies were mixed, but minds were by no means integrated.

In our discussions, I eventually evoked our common experience in the navy. I was for two years on a ship nine hundred feet long and ninety feet wide with about five hundred other men, I said, and yet there was a thorough segregation in spite of our being physically extremely close. I used the word *propinquity* as a better term than *proximity,* because it suggests the idea of conscious, interested *nearness.* Even the kind of propinquity that we had aboard the ship did not preclude the thorough segregation of officers and men, I argued. It was done in a thousand ways beyond the symbols and rituals prescribed in navy regulations. It was done essentially by mind-sets. It was not a good analogy—perhaps it was even a bad one—because the separation was legally and officially mandated. But I was trying to make the point that in 1965 the battle was not over as so many people assumed. Indeed, it had really just begun. I worried that we were not then addressing the consequences of mental segregation even as we were succeeding in effecting a physical integration of blacks and whites. In brief, that mixing of black bodies and white bodies did not make integration. Vann Woodward did not respond directly to my argument, but he remarked on my use of the word *propinquity.* As always, he was so interested in, so very keen on language.

In the summer of 1966, I put together a reader on *The Origins of Segregation,*[21] designed for undergraduates, in which I arranged the arguments of various scholars on the issue. By the time it was issued in 1968, I had already done three years of intensive research on that subject in archives all over the South and in selected archives elsewhere. By then, I had concluded that I had to begin again, that one could not do a satisfying history for segregation alone, or for disfranchisement alone, or for proscription alone. In fact, I saw no way to do a satisfying history, even taking all of these together, without some much larger context of reference. There was no point in attempting to qualify, to refine the Woodward thesis, and there never had been any point in attempting simply to turn it upside down. However valid they might have been in the beginning, for me the three years of research rendered the existing categories ineffective. I never revised the *Origins of Segregation* reader, even though relevant literature, including even more pointed moves against the Woodward thesis, continued to appear.

The whole thing needed to be, deserved to be, refocused and rethought. Chronologically, it needed to begin with the last generation of slavery and run through "The Progressive Era" in politics well into the Woodrow Wilson administration. It had to be woven into the whole broad fabric of Western Civilization reeling, as it was in this time, under the impact of the Industrial Revolution. Black/white relations needed to be studied as contact between two large, complex, and ongoing world cultures, interrelated, even akin, but each in vital ways independent of the other. One might begin the story as economics, or politics, or class conflict, or the physical separation of the races, or any number of things, but in the end the student would need to fathom the thinking of the masses—popular *thinking,* not *thought* and distinctly not *intellectual history,* though that was in it, too. It had to be, finally, *cultural history.* I chose to emphasize white thinking—what southern whites thought and why—because clearly whites had the power, and their thinking was crucial to the process. Further, thinking—as manifested in language, literature, and art—deserved some, if not equal, time. We scholars had not previously offered that history in any large and systematic way. My faith was that, if we could understand the thinking concerning race relations, then we could understand the behavior.

Altogether, I researched very intensely for about five years. I worked in archives in Oklahoma and Texas and in Cambridge, Massachusetts, and all points in between. In 1970, I received a Guggenheim grant and wrote out a rather full manuscript, in a year of leave from teaching. In the fall of 1971, using what I had found, I began to teach a course on race relations that soon became very popular and was offered every semester. In teaching the material it worked very well, and it evolved gradually from semester to semester. But I stopped the writing. The manuscript was not good enough, true enough, to make a book, and I could not make it so. There were several years in which I taught and thought and accepted easily the idea that I would never publish the book. It would never be ready. Then, in 1977, I began again when I went for a year of writing at The Center for Advanced Study in the Behavioral Sciences at Stanford. In the spring of 1982, I finished the manuscript for what became *The Crucible of Race* (1984).[22]

C. Vann Woodward first discovered the truth that there had been a complex history of black/white relations in America—that things had not always been the same. He opened the ground, and it was a superb effort. In his 1955 preface he declared that, because of inadequate investigation in this area and rapid recent changes, it was "inevitable" that he should "make some mistakes." Consequently, he said: "I shall expect and hope to be corrected." Meanwhile, he concluded: "I feel the need of the times for whatever light the historian has to shed upon a perplexing and urgent problem justifies this somewhat premature effort."[23]

Corrections were conceived within a few years and began to appear in print in the 1960s. With Wynes in 1961, Wade in 1964, and my work in 1965, challenges to the Woodward thesis appeared, all somewhat indirect.[24] In 1966, he answered us, individually and collectively, in a revised edition.[25] The heart of his work—the interplay of Conservatives, Radicals, and the North, the written thesis itself—was not altered at all. He met critics head on. Professor Woodward preferred the adversarial manner, and he dealt with his challengers with the skill of a champion debater.[26] He yielded peripheral points with a flourish, claimed misrepresentation of his essential position, and attacked the factual basis, the interpretations, and the conclusions of studies offered by his critics. Wade and I drew hot fire. Wade did only five cities, cities were not very important anyway in the plantation South, and further the facts actually educed by Wade himself indicated fully as much integration as segregation in the cities he studied. Indeed, when Wade saw a concerted effort on the part of whites to segregate blacks, it actually meant that there was a substantial amount of mixing to be opposed. Beware, Professor Wade, the more you struggle, the tighter the noose about your neck. As for me, my Reconstruction South Carolina might have been "exceptional in some respects," but actually it was not, and the evidence is such that one could not say that race relations there or in the South generally "crystallized or stabilized" and became "what they later became." There was simply too much meeting of blacks and whites in both the old style of slavery and the new one of Reconstruction.[27] I leapt too far and too fast, he said. The portion of Wynes's book that supported the Woodward thesis was appropriated, and another book, Leon Litwack's *North of Slavery* (1961)[28] was evoked to show that, in fact, Jim Crow had existed in full development in the North before the War. Litwack's book was described as "authoritative" and Wynes's as "thorough," while mine was "full and interesting," and Wade had "produced evidence of a rudimentary pattern of segregation in some of the larger cities of the slave states."[29] Always in the end, Professor Woodward claimed the high ground, that things had not always been what they became. It was a very defensible position.

Audiences could be persuaded, but the debate on the origins of segregation could never be won, because there was always a degree of separation of blacks and whites and always a degree of mixing. In the preface to his second edition, Professor Woodward had said explicitly that by the word *segregation* he meant only "physical distance," not "social distance" between blacks and whites.[30] There is no way to measure the physical distance involved, to quantify these things and declare that one absolutely outweighs the other. One might talk about "rigid segregation," as we did. But "rigid" is a term that might be defined in various ways. When segregation became relatively comprehensive and relatively rigid is a judgment to be made impressionistically after diligent research. Scholars will disagree. In the interest of gaining perspective on the problem, it is perhaps useful to consider the idea—and, I trust, reject it—that physical segregation was never rigid in the South, either in slavery, in Reconstruction, or in the "Era of Segregation."

After 1965 the challenges continued to the Woodward thesis, some of them more directly confrontational than any before but unsustained, even sporadic, like sniper fire. In 1974, Professor Woodward published the third revised edition. Again the core was not changed. Neither was the answer given in 1966 to earlier challengers. Most curiously, there was no answer made to challengers who came into print after 1966. What was new and very interesting was a description and interpretation of race relations in America in years after 1965. These were marked by northern riots, Black Power, the Soul Movement, and Separatism. He described these things succinctly and beautifully, and concluded, accurately and a little puzzled, that black people still wanted in but were simultaneously unwilling to surrender their identity as black.

The Woodward thesis, of course, had been a plea for integration addressed to white folks. It said you could be a good white southerner and let them in. The assumption was that blacks were eager to enter that white world. How could a white man in 1974 offer an argument to black folks in the midst of a highly emotional but very substantial movement toward self-segregation? How could one tell black people engaged in Black Power, the Soul Movement, and Separatism—as they then surely were—that they should integrate? It was as if all of those black students who had integrated white schools in the South during the early 1960s had risen from their seats and walked purposefully out of the building shortly after they had marched in and sat down; in fact, two youths had done exactly that in Atlanta in an action that became symbolic of a developing mood that subsequently exploded into Separatism. Was there a forgotten alternative in the black tradition that might be turned into the case for integration, one that said you could be integrated and no less black?

Professor Woodward did not produce a fourth revised edition. It was as if the two sides were in a scholarly cold war in which the armies never met directly but rather maneuvered as the spirit moved them on perpetually different fields, increasingly as the years passed losing touch with and focus on what the war was about. Over time, the conflict melted, the whole was reduced, and sharp edges rounded. At the popular level, by 1975, the history that was in the Woodward theses, whether written, read, or taught, was simply a history that was not "useful" or "usable" any more. Nor was there an interest in a counterthesis. In fact, interest in race relations among white Americans at large entered a steep decline. The civil rights movement passed, the Soul Movement passed, and in the 1980s in America we moved into a reaction in which the nation at large definitely did not want to hear that there was a race problem. By the later 1990s, we have come to insist that the playing field is level, that it is, if anything, tilted somewhat in favor of black people and should be righted.

At the scholarly level it was a war that nobody won, a war that everyone abandoned. Even so, true to the nature of scholarship as produced and consumed by scholars, the Woodward thesis has survived in major ways in writing and reading because it was there first and strongest. In extracted form, the thesis is intriguing, a fascinating story, and a very appealing argument. It still dominates in textbooks; it is still taught in schools, colleges, and universities. Race relations is a standard topic in the curriculum, and teachers and professors are duty-bound to tell a story that explains it. Further, the thesis continues a strong and often subtle influence in the thinking, research, and writing of historians of the South. It manifests itself in a tendency to favor the study of community behavior over community thinking in race relations, sometimes to the virtual exclusion of studies about thinking. It influences the study of subjects beyond race relations. Intrinsically, dealing with what people do is easier than dealing with what they think. Economics and politics (revealed, for an extreme and perhaps unfair example, in the recent fascination with fence laws)[31] remain the dominant themes. We ask who produced what for whom to consume; who voted for whom; and we can fill our scholarly lives to the brim in responding to these questions.

Even in the behavioral history of race relations, however, there have been vital omissions. One neglected history would answer the question: Who burned whom, when, where, and how?—omitting for the present the very complex question of why. Who skinned whom alive? Who cut away the private parts of whom? In the 1890s in the South, a black man was lynched about every third day.[32] Lynchings were not secret. On the contrary, they were very public. They were widely advertised in advance and widely reported. Often, thousands attended as railroad companies ran special trains into the vicinity. The interpretive power of themes of segregation, disfranchisement, and proscription, when compared to lynching, seems weak indeed.

Professor Woodward in *The Strange Career of Jim Crow* acknowledged that lynching existed and let it go. Understandably. It hardly fit into a plea that southern tradition, truly understood, urged racial moderation. But further, none of his several dozen doctoral students wrote a book about lynching. Neither, for that matter, did one of my own two dozen students, nor had anyone else even begun such a study before recent times. It is a remarkable, a striking, omission in the historiography. But it is a gruesome subject, awesome in emotional power, difficult to deal with within the accepted canons of the historian's profession. It is, at one level, a sort of American Auschwitz. Describing this behavior is hard labor; explaining it is virtually impossible.

And yet this is the most striking behavior in race relations in the South in the turn-of-the-century years, the era with which *The Strange Career of Jim Crow* centrally deals. There were whipping and murder in slavery, there were whipping and murder in Reconstruction. An example of the latter was the Hamburg Massacre that so outraged Vann Woodward. Lynching, coming on strongly in and after the spring of 1889, was a new phenomenon, clearly beyond the whipping and murder of preceding centuries. It was also worse than anything that came later. It was undeniably, dramatically, *the thing* in black/white relations that was not always the same. It establishes beyond a doubt that race relations in the South in the 1890s were not what they had become in Reconstruction, nor were they what they later became. Professor Woodward was right about the *hot* time, the *deep-change* time in black/white relations in the South. It was during the turn-of-the-century decades.

One can no longer tell the story of race relations in the South without including lynching. And any explanation of lynching—and the mass rioting that filled the years from 1898 to 1907 in which any black person took the place of the alleged criminal in lynching—requires a fresh inquiry into the minds of the masses, and that inquiry will take us far beyond the grisly phenomenon.

In retrospect, it seems that we had all been wrong and we had all been right. Professor Woodward was most right in focusing closely on the turn-of-the-century years. It was indeed the *turn time* in race relations, a revolution in the quality of violence. Behind that was a mutation in white thinking about black people. It molded and cast the regime into which we were all born in the early to mid-twentieth century and with which we still contend. But it was an even more complex play than Professor Woodward or any of us had imagined; actors were on the stage whom we did not pay attention to.

I had been wrong in thinking that the kinds of things that whites thought about blacks were so firm, so fixed and unchanging. For instance, I failed to grasp before I was well into the research and writing of *The Crucible* that there was a story of evolving interracial sex and mulattoes that commenced in 1850 and evolved over two or three generations to end about 1915. In 1976 I found only one book on that subject, published in 1918 by an anthropologist arguing that good things in black culture spring from white blood in black people. Thus, during my first seven months at Stanford I wrote *New People; Miscegenation and Mulattoes in the United States* (1980)[33] because I felt that it was a book that had to be written. Then I began to write *Crucible* again.

The Crucible of Race is a book about thought and action at the popular level. In researching for that book in original sources, I learned about lynching and rioting in the turn-of-the-century years. The participants told me about it, even though at least one relevant book, William Hair's superb *Carnival of Fury*,[34] and several articles had appeared before my manuscript found print. There is a chapter in *Crucible* on these phenomena, called "In Violence Veritas." It stands with other parts of the book that attempt to get at the minds of the people, the southern people, who did these things. We are, of course, not responsible for what our ancestors did, but they are responsible for us and much of what we do. Historians do need an answer to the question of how people in a culture could do these things, how could white southerners ritualistically, with thousands present and watching and millions witnessing through the press, burn these people alive and rake the still-smoldering embers for relics of teeth and bones? Among other things, *Crucible* offers an elaborate history and explanation of that extravagant behavior, perhaps in form more lengthy than a reader wants or needs.

In 1966 in editing and producing the *Origins of Segregation* reader, I had attempted a brief array of the Woodward thesis as written and its critics. I was trying to focus the debate, to say that there was a problem here for scholars. There were other similar efforts, but never a concert of opposition. The debate waned, but not before the Woodward thesis, often in extracted form, became a part of traditional literature and thinking. There could be no factory recall.

As noted, *Origins of Segregation* appeared in 1968; meanwhile, my own historiography had changed. I had gone back and started again. By the time I finished *Crucible*, I felt that I had taken from the Woodward thesis the really substantial amount that could be taken and had blended this into my own work. This time I wanted to get that offering to a persuadable audience. I took a year of writing time to carefully cut the book to half its original size. The abridgment was printed under the title *A Rage for Order* (1986).[35] This time, obviously, I was striving to get audience from students, from young scholars rather than old, and from intelligent nonscholarly readers wherever I could find them. It was not a factory recall; it was a new model—but very hard to sell. It was a hard fight in America in the late 1980s to get audience anywhere for a book on race relations. It has been no easier deep into the decade of the 1990s. But it is a necessary effort because next time we must not be so naive again. There will be a next time, and when it comes some of us, black and white, must know the history.

My historiography has changed, and so has my thinking about race. I no longer believe that black people are simply white people with black skins, that black culture is the "mark of oppression." There is a separate culture that is constructive, beautiful, and ongoing. There is much in that culture that is virtually independent of whiteness. It is not innate, any more than white culture and white characteristics are innate, but it is exceedingly unwise to think about either culture or cultural practices as if such things are temporary.

I still do believe that the great quantity—not the quality—of physical segregation, the physical distance between the races, came early after slavery and persisted. I never did use and never would have used the word *immediate* in describing the process. There was a period of transition, of intense and heated experimentation. I did use the word *early,* and I chose that word carefully, deliberately. The new pattern was indeed revolutionary compared to the pattern of physical relationships that had obtained in slavery. I was always much more interested in "social distance" than in physical distance. Indeed, I felt that a large concern for the latter carried a danger of being more distracting than useful. On the other hand, I always thought that segregation laws were important; at the very least they were tokens pointing in a direction reversed from the recent mode of token integration. But in 1965 I had not researched the 1890s, in which a flood of these laws came, and I knew that I had not. Certainly, in *After Slavery* my interpretations of events in the 1880s and 1890s are briefly offered and admittedly ad hoc.

Most of all, I still do believe physical segregation is only one place to start the story, and that it is not the best place to commence. There are other forms of discrimination. The most important element of all is not even racism. It is the thinking that lies behind racial prejudice, a "worldview" that is whole, that includes but is not confined to matters of race. In particular, I still believe that the underdone part of the history of race relations is the history of popular thinking. White thinking, as distinguished from black, is vital.

White people in the South do rule there, and they make of race relations very much what they want to make of them and deal with the consequences later. This is clear, and historians do well to follow closely behind the white person who does get on the bus with blacks. In effect, that is what has happened. Everybody is on the bus now. *After Slavery* was right, if I may say so, in emphasizing the persistence of racial prejudice, whatever its form, in the white mind. It said that an ostensible revolution, a legal revolution, a rhetorical revolution, even a seemingly visible revolution in the mixing of black bodies with white and a change in ostensible behavior might not be a real revolution. *After Slavery* was wrong in not understanding the evolutionary potential in the white mind as it thought about black people. The character of white racism has changed and does change. The evolution can be for worse as well as for better. When race relations in the South have changed for the better, it is because people shifted in the cast of their thinking and deliberately made things better. When they have changed for the worse, it is also because people *made* them so. Better race relations do not just happen, they have to be made to happen.

Much of the work that any of us has done in this field reflects a dialogue begun by C. Vann Woodward; much of it reflects lessons learned in discussions with him, both in person and within our minds. Above all, to study Jim Crow and race relations in the South, historians have not only to read what Woodward has written, but we also *have to do* what Woodward has done. He has engaged humanism, committed scholarship, and personal responsibility to *do* his regional history. He has led in the struggle, and in all these processes, intellectual and political, leadership has always been key. He has led us to the next level of responsibility, and subsequently we may have to go places that he never went and never thought of going. But when we do, we will still be following his lead in a sense.

In our relatively open, free, democratic society, better race relations have to be effected by unceasing, sensitive, informed effort, and some of that effort has to be in the highly intangible area of teaching and learning—of education, of persuasion. And it takes time, even generations. It is not like schoolboys doing sums on the blackboard. Others must now lead where once Woodward led. If I have learned anything about race relations in the South and in America over four decades of concentrated researching, thinking, and writing, it is that we carry our destiny in our hands, our hearts, and our minds—in thoughts, feelings, and actions.

NOTES

1. Martin Witherspoon Gary Papers, Manuscript Collection of the South Caroliniana Library, Columbia, South Carolina.

2. C. Vann Woodward, *The Strange Career of Jim Crow*, rev. ed. (New York: Oxford University Press, 1960).

3. Otis A. Singletary, *The Negro Militia and Reconstruction* (Austin: University of Texas Press, 1961).

4. C. Vann Woodward, *Tom Watson, Agrarian Rebel* (New York: Macmillan, 1938). Note that the biography received not only favorable but front-page treatment in the Sunday *New York Times Book Review,* and from the nation's premier historian of that day, Allan Nevins ("Tom Watson and the New South," *New York Times Book Review,* 3 Apr. 1938, 1, 26).

5. George Brown Tindall, *South Carolina Negroes, 1877–1900* (Columbia: University of South Carolina Press, 1952).

6. George Brown Tindall, *The Emergence of the New South, 1913–1945,* vol. 10 of A History of the South, series ed. Wendell Holmes Stephenson and Ellis Merton Coulter (Baton Rouge: Louisiana State University Press, 1967).

7. C. Vann Woodward, *Origins of the New South,* vol. 9 of A History of the South, series ed. Wendell Holmes Stephenson and Ellis Merton Coulter (Baton Rouge: Louisiana State University Press, 1951).

8. Anne Firor Scott, *The Southern Lady: From the Pedestal to Politics, 1830–1930* (Chicago: University of Chicago Press, 1970).

9. Kenneth Milton Stampp, *The Peculiar Institution; Slavery in the Ante-Bellum South* (New York: Knopf, 1955).

10. Ibid.; cf. Stampp, ibid. (1955; New York: Random House paperback, 1956), p. ix. In the paperback issue, Stampp placed an asterisk at the end of the much discussed prefatory phrase, and the asterisk directed the reader to this amended 1956 statement: "I did not, of course, assume that there have been, or are today, no cultural differences between white and black Americans. Nor do I regard it as flattery to call Negroes white men with black skins. It would serve my purpose as well to call Caucasians black men with white skins. I have simply found no convincing evidence that there are significant differences between the innate emotional traits and intellectual capacities of Negroes and whites."

11. Robert Starobin, *Industrial Slavery in the Old South* (New York: Oxford University Press, 1970).

12. James Oakes, *The Ruling Race: A History of American Slaveholders* (New York: Knopf, 1982).

13. William Freehling, *Prelude to Civil War: The Nullification Crisis in South Carolina, 1816–1836* (New York: Harper & Row, 1965).

14. Joel Randolph Williamson, *After Slavery: The Negro in South Carolina during Reconstruction, 1865–1877* (Chapel Hill: University of North Carolina Press, 1965), 274–99.

15. Ibid., 298–99.

16. Howard Zinn, *The Southern Mystique* (New York: Knopf, 1964). Williamson was correct to call Zinn a dedicated reformist, for the latter was particularly important in the processes that fully integrated the professional historical associations; too, Zinn took special pains to make African American scholars *welcome* in the professional associations, and he took considerable professional and personal risks on behalf of The Movement. See August Meier and Elliott Rudwick, *Black History and the Historical Profession, 1915–1980*, Blacks in the New World, series ed. Meier (Urbana: University of Illinois Press, 1986).

17. Idus A. Newby, *Jim Crow's Defense: Anti-Negro Thought in America, 1900–1930* (Baton Rouge: Louisiana State University Press, 1965); see also, idem, comp. and ed., *The Development of Segregationist Thought* (Homewood, Ill.: Dorsey Press, 1968); note book review, Williamson, "*Jim Crow's Defense,*" *Journal of Southern History* 32 (1966): 261–63.

18. Roger A. Fischer, *The Segregation Struggle in Louisiana, 1850–1890* (Urbana: University of Illinois Press, 1974).

19. Charles E. Wynes, *Race Relations in Virginia, 1870–1902* (Charlottesville: University Press of Virginia, 1961); see also idem, comp., *The Negro in the South since 1865; Selected Essays in American Negro History* (University: University of Alabama Press, 1965).

20. Richard C. Wade, *Slavery in the Cities: The South 1820–1860* (New York: Oxford University Press, 1964).

21. Joel Randolph Williamson, comp. and ed., *The Origins of Segregation* (Lexington, Mass.: Heath, 1968).

22. Joel Randolph Williamson, *The Crucible of Race* (New York: Oxford University Press, 1984).

23. Woodward, *Strange Career* (1955), preface; cf. ibid. (1974), xvii.

24. Wynes, *Race Relations in Virginia;* Wade, *Slavery in the Cities;* Williamson, *After Slavery.*

25. Woodward, *Strange Career* (1966). See also idem, "The Strange Career of a Historical Controversy," in Woodward, *American Counterpoint: Slavery and Racism in the North-South Dialogue,* 2d rev. ed. (Boston: Little, Brown, 1982).

26. Woodward had been a champion debater as an undergraduate, winning a state championship in Arkansas in 1928 (Roper, *C. Vann Woodward,* 23–30).

27. Ibid. (1966); quotations, 25–26.

28. Leon F. Litwack, *North of Slavery; the Negro in the Free States 1790–1860* (Chicago: University of Chicago Press, 1961).

29. Ibid. (1966), passim, but esp. 13.

30. Ibid. (1957), xi; ibid. (1966), xi.

31. See especially Steven Hahn, *The Roots of Southern Populism; Yeoman Farmers and the Transformation of the Georgia Upcountry, 1850–1880* (New York: Oxford University Press, 1983), esp. 239–68. Cf. debate over fencing laws spawned by Hahn's book in *Journal of Southern History* 59 (1993): Shawn Everett Kantor and J. Morgan Kousser, "Common Sense or Commonwealth? The Fence Law and Institutional Change in the Postbellum South," 201–42; Steven Hahn, "A Response: Common Cents or Historical Sense," 243–58; and Kantor and Kousser, "A Rejoinder: Two Visions of History," 259–66. Note that Hahn and Kousser are Woodward students.

32. Statistics compiled by the National Association for the Advancement of Colored People (NAACP) indicate 123 lynchings or more in each of the years 1893 and 1894, the worst years of the worst decade (NAACP, *Thirty Years of Lynching in the U.S., 1889–1918* [New York: NAACP, 1919]); the same table, updated to include the next decade of lynchings, is in appendix to the extended, and very poignant, essay by NAACP activist Walter Francis White, an eyewitness to at least one lynching and an investigator of many others (White, *Rope and Faggot: A Biography of Judge Lynch* [New York: Knopf, 1929]).

33. Joel Randolph Williamson, *New People; Miscegenation, and Mulattoes in the United States* (New York: Free Press of Macmillan, 1980).

34. William Ivy Hair, *The Carnival of Fury* (Baton Rouge: Louisiana State University Press, 1976) tells the story of a New Orleans riot and massacre of black people by white people *after* a black suspect, Robert Charles, had been captured and put in jail. A similar story for Wilmington, North Carolina, has been told by H. Leon Prather Jr., *"We Have Taken a City": Wilmington Racial Massacre and Coup of 1898* (Cranbury, N.J.: Fairleigh Dickinson Press, 1984). The latter riot is distinguished by the prominence of the families whose men were involved in the violence, and by the likely unprecedented way that the violence removed African American officeholders, hence the *coup* in Prather's title. A full eyewitness account by George Rountree, a participant in the Wilmington riot, is available in manuscript, George Rountree Papers, 1898, Southern Historical Collection of Library of the University of North Carolina, Chapel Hill.

35. Joel Randolph Williamson, *A Rage for Order: Black/White Relations in the American South since Emancipation* (New York: Oxford University Press, 1986).

V

Taking His Measure:
The Gift and the Critics

"New Voices in the Land and New Forces Astir": C. Vann Woodward, Southern Historian

PAUL M. GASTON

✳

Paul M. Gaston, professor of history at the University of Virginia, came from a very Woodwardian place, being born and raised in a utopianist community in southern Alabama, where the inhabitants not only study economic justice and racial equity but practice the same. From such beginnings, he went naturally enough to the study of New South history and has done so with the irony of one who sees dissidence from the inside of the protestors' and prophets' communities, even as his friend Woodward has seen dissidence from a vantage point inside the aristocracy. After taking the Ph.D. from the University of North Carolina, Gaston has served effectively at the University of Virginia during four different decades. In 1970, he produced *The New South Creed,* an elegant study that cuts a Gordian knot that Woodward discovered—or perhaps it is that Woodward himself originally tied this knot. Woodward, with his idea of a radically different postbellum South, must still explain *why* the bourgeois elite so consistently appealed to agrarian traditions to defend their actions. Gaston, rather than write them off as Catoists, has described a *creed,* hardly one that he likes any better than does Woodward, but no less real for all that; and this creed is a sincere statement of long-running beliefs in cavalier charm and in racism, both of which are used to legitimate the actions taken by the new elite. As critic Sheldon Hackney shows, Gaston's tour de force still reinforces the Woodward thesis about discontinuity, for the elite *needs this creed* to defend the changes that they are making. Having solved a problem for the master, Gaston is in a special position to evaluate the life's work of Woodward, especially as that life's work is revealed in and by his superb graduate students from The Johns Hopkins University and from Yale University (see appendices A and B for complete lists). The occasion of the publication of a festschrift in honor of Woodward produced this review essay by Gaston.

＊　＊　＊

Region, Race, and Reconstruction: Essays in Honor of C. Vann Woodward. Edited by J. Morgan Kousser and James M. McPherson. New York: Oxford University Press. $25.00.

Most of us recall with special clarity the formative intellectual experiences of our youth and the ways in which those experiences helped us to come to terms with our heritage. The urge to look back on those days may come at any time, but it often asserts itself when we reach the middle years. C. Vann Woodward was into that era of his own life in 1956 when he published an essay on southern letters in the *Virginia Quarterly Review*. He began with a personal memory: "The Southerner who graduated from college about 1930 was soon aware of new voices in the land and new forces astir." These "voices" and "forces" would help to reshape his land so that Woodward found "the early thirties were stirring years to be discovering the South and its history and spending the years of one's youth." Drawn to history as a career, he was buoyed by an "awakening of historical scholarship," which he saw as part of "a wider intellectual awakening in the South."

For southerners who graduated from college in the early 1950s, there also were new voices in the land and new forces astir. By the mid-1950s the young southerners who had decided on history as a career found swirling about them the beginning of what Woodward would name the Second Reconstruction of the South. There was drama and excitement in the fact that the crisis seemed to turn so heavily on historical questions. Could the South change? Could it be made to change? What was the relationship between past and present? Was segregation an immutable folkway, something that had always been there and could not therefore be rooted out without destroying the region itself? Or was southern history more complex, less well understood than most people thought? Answers to these questions were freely and heatedly offered in those days and were the staple of public debate as well as cocktail-party chatter. Everyone had the historian's answer.

For the southern historian who chose Virginia as the theater in which to find one's own answers to these questions, the contrasts were sharp. On the one hand, the suave and well-mannered men of money and authority fell in line behind Senator Byrd, their tribal guru it seemed, to declare that they would resist—and resist massively—all attempts to change what they called their way of life. An ambitious Oklahoma-born journalist on the Richmond afternoon paper draped the mantle of Jefferson and Madison over the defiance, to give the Virginians an air of decorum that set them apart from their uncouth allies in the Mississippi and Alabama Citizens' Councils and Klan Klaverns. On the other hand, for all the vituperation and moral pressure, there was no real threat to intellectual freedom at the university founded by Jefferson. The resident faculty debated serious questions, and, when they brought outsiders in to lecture, they sometimes chose uncommonly well.

When C. Vann Woodward came down from Baltimore to give the James W. Richard Lectures at the University of Virginia in the autumn of 1954, he was impressed by his reception. He wrote later that the lectures "were given before unsegregated audiences and they were received in that spirit of tolerance and open-mindedness that one has a right to expect at a university with such a tradition and such a founder." Those lectures, published the next year as *The Strange Career of Jim Crow,* were to become the most widely read of all Woodward's works—works that in all have sold perhaps a million copies. Journalists carried copies of the small book with them across the South, covering one racial confrontation after another; civil rights workers distributed them at their workshops; students in college classes found the book showing up on their lists of assigned reading. For many people, then, to discover the South and its history in the 1950s was to discover the writings of C. Vann Woodward.

The Jim Crow book was the culmination of a series of books that made southern history alive and intelligible, rescuing it from pedants and apologists alike. Starting with *Tom Watson, Agrarian Rebel* (1938), Woodward studied the ways in which class and racial loyalties and fears forged the destinies of southern whites and blacks. Watson, the hero of Populism, turned out to be a symbol of hope in the first half of the book, as he penetrated the shibboleths that had divided the downtrodden and, in the last half, an example of the tragedy of southern history as disillusionment turned him into a fierce demagogue. In *Reunion and Reaction* (1951), Woodward ingeniously constructed an account of how the material interests of southern and northern conservatives had merged to force the abandonment of the defense of freedmen's rights and lay the basis for the rise of southern conservatives at the expense of the southern masses, whites and blacks alike. The themes of these works were joined and expanded in *Origins of the New South, 1877–1913* (1951). Richly textured, informed by irony and compassion, Woodward's masterpiece traced the rise of the new ruling class, the heavy toll it exacted from the southern people, and the emergence and crushing defeat of a popular and humane protest movement. To a friend who had written admiringly of the book, he wrote, "My sympathies were obviously not with the people who ran things, and about whom I wrote most, but with the people who were run, who were managed and maneuvered and pushed around."

In the crisis of the 1950s, Woodward's historical scholarship and personal example were an inspiration to southerners who, like him, put their sympathies with those who were run, who were managed and maneuvered and pushed around. They admired him when he consulted with Thurgood Marshall on how to present the case against segregation to the Supreme Court and when he turned his scholarly talents to the history of segregation, declaring that things had not always been the same. Admiration of his moral courage was made easier by the fact of his craftsmanship—no one wrote better, had a more thorough command of the sources, or had a keener sense of irony and the complexity of southern history. No one who cared about the course of events in the past was more scrupulous in writing history addressed to the present. He was also admired because his interpretive essays—especially "The Irony of Southern History" and "The Search for Southern Identity"— elevated southern studies to the level of national, even international, importance, providing the kind of reach and resonance for historical studies that Faulkner's novels had given to southern fiction.

The late David Potter once said that Woodward's "greatest significance to historical studies may lie in the fact that he has made himself the foremost practitioner of a concept of history which holds that the experience of the past can find its highest relevance in the guidance which it offers in living with the problems of the present."[1] The wonder is that Potter should have found among his fellow historians so few "practitioners" of this "concept of history," for without some sense of responsibility, some concern for the consequences of what one writes, history is depleted of its vitality and becomes simply an intellectual game played by clever people, usually at the expense of other clever people. In any case, Potter thought it took special qualities to succeed if one had the present very much in mind. Woodward, he believed, was a remarkable success. He showed that "history can retain its basic scholarly validity even in a context of active presentism." It is unlikely that Woodward has ever used a term such as "active presentism," but he was fond of quoting Faulkner, especially his character Gavin Stevens who says, "The past is never dead. It's not even past." With this kind of sensibility informing his writing, Woodward has of course found it impossible to write history that does not speak to the present.

Because of his scholarship, his southern ancestry, and his concern for the fate of his region in a time of crisis, Woodward attracted to his seminars, first at Johns Hopkins and then at Yale, a remarkable group of students. More than forty of them—white and black, male and female—completed the doctorate. Many of the forty gathered in Philadelphia in 1982 to present to their teacher a book that seventeen of them had written to honor him. According to reports from some who were there, Woodward wanted to make no speech but felt under some obligation to comment on what it was he thought he and they had been up to as historians. He did this by reciting for them a passage from *Absalom, Absalom!* The Mississippian Quentin Compson is addressed by his Harvard roommate, a Canadian: *Tell about the South. What's it like there. What do they do there. Why do they live there. Why do they live at all.*

The essays in the book his students gave him that evening help us to understand the answer to the question Quentin was asked. Editors James McPherson and J. Morgan Kousser aimed to produce a volume that was in some sense coherent. In the end they decided to organize it around three major themes of Woodward's writings—region, race, and reconstruction. What makes the South distinctive as a region? How has race—the fact of race and concerns about race—shaped and misshaped southern history? How has the South been reconstructed and by whom and with what consequences? These broad questions come close to casting a net wide enough to cover the question Quentin was asked, to let the Woodward students, in their own voices, "tell about the South."

In the opening section on the South as a region, Daniel T. Rogers writes brilliantly about the Chapel Hill Regionalists who dominated the agenda for southern reform in the 1930s. Rogers not only succeeds in dissecting their agenda but also constructs (one wonders whether intentionally) a portrait of the intellectual world in which Woodward did his graduate work. Rogers is particularly good in uncovering some of the shortcomings of Regionalism (its skittishness about racial and class confrontations, especially) that must have troubled the young Woodward. Bertram Wyatt-Brown's reconsideration of the proslavery doctrine ingeniously makes a strong case for the antebellum South's tendency toward industrial apartheid, suggesting yet another dimension to the discussion of Woodward's Jim Crow thesis. Steven Hahn revisits Woodward's abiding concern with Populism by way of a compelling analysis of the Georgia controversy over fencing cattle in the post-Reconstruction era. Robert Dean Pope writes a tantalizing essay about biographical studies of southern political figures in the Age of Segregation and laments what he takes to be the present low status of the art. He urges historians to renew their interest and reminds us that Woodward found his study of Watson to be a revealing window through which he came to see the larger history of the period. The section on region concludes with an elegant Willie Lee Rose piece, a portrait of the South and its race problem in popular culture, specifically in the books (and the plays or films inspired by them) *Uncle Tom's Cabin, The Clansman, Gone with the Wind,* and *Roots.* These "reading-viewing" events serve "as vehicles for celebration of shared convictions," Mrs. Rose reminds us, "the public vehicle of new agreements on what to believe, at the growing point of American myth."

To "tell about the South" in such neat divisions as the editors have imposed upon their book is not easy. In the middle section, on race, for example, Tilden Edelstein's survey of American productions of *Othello* echoes themes from Mrs. Rose's piece. It appears in the right section, however, because the underlying theme is the uncertainty Americans have betrayed over what really constitutes race. This is a theme explored in imaginative and arresting detail by Barbara Fields, who argues that race is not a physical fact at all, but an ideological construct. These pieces are followed and complemented by Charles Dew's reconstruction of the life of the slave Sam Williams, Louis Harlan's account of Booker T. Washington's relationship with American Jews, and Robert F. Engs's penetrating but sad account of how American Indians assigned to Hampton Institute were victims of racism. Each essay opens up unsuspected dimensions of the history and concept of race.

None of the five chapters in the concluding section on Reconstruction offers us an interpretive key to the period, perhaps because old consensuses have been broken down and new ones have yet to emerge. When they do, Woodward's students will be in the forefront. One dimension surely to be emphasized is the comparative study of emancipation experiences, a subject Woodward urged on historians years ago. Thomas C. Holt writes about such comparisons in the histories of the United States and the British West Indies, making us anxious for his larger study of the subject. Lawrence N. Powell gives new meaning to old facts in writing of the quarrels among carpet-baggers and helps us better understand the factionalism that undid the Republican party in the South. William S. McFeely tells us of a Republican who was both carpetbagger and scalawag and makes clearer the problems of conscience and politics during Reconstruction. J. Mills Thornton III declares that one of the reasons historians have botched their Reconstruction studies is that most of the specialists in that subject know little about the antebellum period. To illustrate his point, he explains how Republicans unwittingly adopted tax policies that drove the white, small farmers into the camp of the opposition. The last essay, appropriately enough, is a reexamination by Vincent P. De Santis of the end of Reconstruction and a defense of Woodward's thirty-year-old interpretation of that episode.

The essays so briefly summarized here will be required reading for historians of the South. Happily, they are accessible to others as well. All of Woodward's students agree that their teacher never imposed on them a point of view or a methodology, but instead helped them to find their own way and their own voices. One sees proof of this in the rich variety of talents evident in their book. But if Woodward made no explicit demands on his students, he inevitably presented to them, in his own person and work, a model which inspired and molded them all. Such influences, of course, are difficult to trace precisely. Yet they can be clearly seen—in the mastery of the sources and the experimentation with appropriate methods of exploiting sources, in the taste for irony and the striving for literary grace, and, perhaps most important of all, in the underlying awareness that history is not a game intellectuals play but a real voice of the South never to be severed from forces astir in the region.

NOTES

1. David Morris Potter, "C. Vann Woodward: Pastmaster," in this volume, 266–98.

From a Chase to a View:
The Arkansan

MICHAEL O'BRIEN

✳

Michael O'Brien, quiet but fervent Englishman, is an intellectual's intellectual, who has made much greater impact on practicing historians than on the laity. He is thus quite different from Woodward but also is in just the right position to offer an evaluation of the master: Few can speak so authoritatively about how Woodward's many seminal ideas continue to affect intellectuals of the region. The original version of this essay O'Brien produced while still a graduate student, and some years of maturing and still more of his own research and the opportunity to talk at length with Woodward have combined to make a much better product in this revision. O'Brien himself has been no amateur in the uses of irony, and indeed even his endnotes in this piece offer witticisms and criticisms in the most deftly managed tones. Of particular note in this essay is the enveloping, almost strangling irony that the critic, O'Brien, judges much of Woodward's work to remain dominant, yet finds overwhelming, even fatal, flaws in the best of that work.

✳   ✳   ✳

C. Vann Woodward is not easy to catch. He knows that there are taxidermists who would nab him for the display cases of historiography, and so he has taken to hovering near his critics, close enough to encourage the chase, far enough to avoid capture. He has often said that it is better to be criticized than to be forgotten. There is a cunning in the quarry who courteously offers the chase, runs on, doubles back, feints, leaves a half-concealed trail, yet manages to be back in his lair at night, safe in the knowledge that the woods echo with blundering hunters, who exclaim to one another that the old fox is here somewhere, if only they knew where. The elusive quarry makes the hunter his accomplice in sport, though they play a different game. The quarry plays for survival; the hunter, for blood. The term Woodward has coined for this sport is *gerontophagy*, the eating of elders.[1]

But this is Woodward in old age. The young C. Vann Woodward was very different and played a game that had higher stakes, not mere personal survival but no less than improvement for his society. The old Woodward has given us some insight into the young, though through the selective sensibility of memory, and should be given due weight as the best witness we have but one scarcely detached and decidedly reserved.

He was born in Arkansas in 1908, the son of a Latin teacher and school principal, in the flat delta whose landscape was then crowded with black and white sharecroppers, mules, tumbled shacks, cotton, and poverty, and is now almost devoid of people, being instead the empty domain of soya and the occasional Japanese company. Vanndale stands on the Arkansas side of Memphis, as Faulkner's Oxford stands on its Mississippi side, and the juxtaposition is worth bearing in mind. Woodward's own family was scarcely indigent, nor utterly obscure. His birthplace bore his maternal family name, his forebears had owned slaves, an uncle was a sociologist at Southern Methodist University, and governors of Arkansas might come to call. The family was Methodist, and seriously so, enough that one of Woodward's dissents was a reticent agnosticism. Religion is conspicuously absent from his vision of southern history.[2]

His family moved on to Morrilton, a small market town in the Arkansas River valley, a far different landscape, wooded, gentler, a town with more decided amenities, such as a railroad and a Carnegie Free Library, where the inquiring adolescent son of a schoolmaster might extend his learning. The town was mostly beyond the state's black population, fading into that limbo between South and West that marks the indeterminate culture of western Arkansas. But it had the Ku Klux Klan, whose leader, in full regalia, might drop in to church to make a welcome donation and whose members Woodward once saw gathering to commence a lynching.[3] Woodward was a junior member of the modest and small southern bourgeoisie, and his father was moving up, not down, from crossroads to small town, from teacher to college dean. Implicitly, Woodward's own youthful act of gerontophagy was a repudiation of the class that had bred him and a conscious reaching out in sympathy for those with whom he had little in common, the dirt farmers and blacks who were far from his own parents' front parlor. This moral education seems to have been accidental in a young man whose career drifted into a vocation. Certainly, his formal education seems to have been unrewarding. Little was to be expected from two years at Henderson College in Arkadelphia, and little more, on his own testimony, was received from Emory. More might have been expected from Columbia University, but this northern foray was brief and unsatisfactory. He wobbled in his intellectual interests: philosophy as an undergraduate major, sociology for two days at Columbia, political science for a master of arts degree, literature as a hobby. He worked on farms, taught English at Georgia Tech, traveled to the Soviet Union, all the while observing.

Woodward has become a calm and reserved man, but there is reason to think that he was an intense and reserved youth. He took social injustice as a personal affront and, if he was not formally a socialist, adopted the passionate language of class warfare. His biography of Tom Watson freely speaks of "capitalist expansion," of the Old South as a "feudal system," of "class conflict," of "crushing oppression," of "reactionary capitalist allies," of the "southern urban proletariat" being only "an embryonic class," not yet "class conscious." A favorable comment upon Watson by Eugene Debs occurs on the final page as a sort of benediction.[4] It is no surprise to learn that Woodward later thought about writing a biography of Debs. Labor organizers felt free to use his couch in Atlanta; he was glad to lend support to the young communist Angelo Herndon, absurdly indicted on a charge of raising an insurrection against the state of Georgia. With such an education, and with less reserve, he might have made a serviceable apparatchik. Instead, and improbably, he decided to write a book, a collective biography of seven southern demagogues, portentously entitled *Seven for Demos*. He had studied little history and had been bored by that he had read, and the venture was undertaken outside the apparatus of the academy.[5]

In his memoirs Woodward has made much of the barrenness of the historical writing of his youth. There is no reason to doubt that the old American Nation series was a rigidifying experience, leading a young historian to think he was entering a vocation, not of necromancer to others, but of undertaker to himself. As for southern historians, the precedents were unencouraging. Ulrich Bonnell Phillips applied the supposed ethic of New South efficiency to the Old South, Douglas Southall Freeman wrote hagiography, the spirit of William Archibald Dunning presided over Reconstruction. The very small band who had written the history of the New South offered little but the propaganda of the middle class.[6] The reform tradition was the liberal tradition, which then meant segregation, an alliance with northern industrialism, disfranchisement for blacks and poor whites alike, many empty promises, emptier for the starkness of the Depression. Yet the liberals had their moments: some, such as Will Alexander, could fight lynching; others might rally to save Angelo Herndon; some, such as Howard Odum, might care for social justice. Rupert Vance, an old friend from Morrilton, had written eloquently and in detail about the failures of the cotton economy and would try to make sociology a humane discipline.[7] And the national liberals had moved to embrace Roosevelt's peculiar and reluctant radicalism. Woodward himself supported the second New Deal and spent the summer of 1935 surveying the backcountry of Georgia, to be moved and shocked by the rural poverty for which James Agee was later to find words. So liberalism was a tradition that had alternately to be embraced and pushed away, depending on the time, place, and issue. There were to be moments when he would not, but always it was a tradition with which he was obliged to maintain a fruitful tension.[8]

If little had been done by historians, more was being achieved by southern poets and novelists. Woodward was to become one of the great celebrators of the Southern Renaissance, doffing his cap in the direction of Faulkner, Warren, Welty. His *Origins of the New South,* though showing some sympathy for the naturalism of Theodore Dreiser and Jack London, otherwise judges the literature of the late nineteenth century by the critical standards of the 1930s.[9] His memoirs reinforce the impression of a young man eagerly devouring the fresh new books that came gleaming from the press to testify of the possibilities of achievement by a southern intelligence.[10] Unfortunately, the evidence from the 1930s does not entirely endorse this impression and suggests a refinement.

In 1938 Woodward gave a Phi Beta Kappa lecture at the University of Florida, "The South in Search of a Philosophy." Much of it expresses the Beardian analysis of the New South that his *Tom Watson* was concomitantly embodying. But there are passages about contemporary southern letters that now read oddly. He speaks dismissively of the literature of the 1920s as "in flight from realities, or in obsession with the more nauseating realities." James Branch Cabell and the Fugitives are said to have "sought sanctuary in the ivory tower and fled to the French Quarter of New Orleans, or, when they had the money, to the Left Bank in Paris." Faulkner is characterized as one "who seemed to draw most of his subjects out of abandoned wells." To which is added, "One can only speculate with misgivings upon what future literary historians will make of the earth-departing fantasies and the neurotic grotesqueries that constitute the literary output of the South from 1919 to 1929."[11] We fortunately need not speculate, since one of the future literary historians was to be C. Vann Woodward, and his verdict reads very differently.

There are passages, too, from 1938 that discuss the Agrarians. Woodward was never to find them plausible, except as they condemned the inhumanity of industrialism. But his explanation for their origin as romantic poseurs holds especial interest. He notes correctly that *I'll Take My Stand* was a product of revulsion at the materialist faith of the 1920s and less correctly that it was a product of the 1930s and their "extreme disillusionments." But this is his chronology for the Agrarian movement: "On the Boulevard de Montparnasse, Southern esthetes of the Fugitive school sat around the same sidewalk café tables with Northern esthetes of the Humanist school—both convivial in a self-imposed exile—as long as their stocks and bonds returned dividends. When dividends began to fall in 1929, the Northern expatriots returned to New York to find themselves sudden converts to communism, while the Southern expatriots returned to Louisiana and Tennessee to find themselves sudden converts to agrarianism." This is bizarre both as criticism and as history. The only person to whom it remotely applied was Allen Tate, of whose arrogance and incivility Woodward had had a sight in 1936, when Tate had grandiloquently walked out of a session of the Southern Historical Association in which the Agrarians had been criticized.[12]

What is more important, Woodward gives evidence here of an inattentiveness to and lack of sympathy for contemporary southern literature. Unusual for him, he seems to have been taking stereotypes from American history—in this case, from Malcolm Cowley's *Exile's Return*—and imposing them on the South. But his logic is clear enough from later passages where he extols the Chapel Hill Regionalists as seekers after "facts, facts, facts, dug out, tabulated, and analyzed by professional students of society." He wanted then, whatever he was to want later, stern social realism, not irresponsibility, not art for art's sake, not art for the wrong social causes, but men who might grasp "the possibility of using industry under social control for the achievement of a better society under a new type of political and economic government."[13]

So Woodward's recent version of his intellectual apprenticeship in the 1930s needs to be taken with a grain of salt. He speaks lightly of his engagement with Chapel Hill, of mixing with the wrong set, the aesthetes of Franklin Street, but such hard evidence as we have (itself, of course, selective) shows a more earnest young man, emotional, self-consciously dissident.[14] It is true that his interracial friendships, his sympathy for organized labor, his distaste for the bourgeoisie placed him well outside the mainstream of Odum's thought. But Woodward lived in a time, the 1930s of the New Deal, and a place, the Chapel Hill of Frank Graham, in which dissidence was acceptable and brought few punishments. Odum arranged a fellowship for him and helped to find a publisher for his biography of Tom Watson. Many around him, including Wilbur Cash of Charlotte, spoke confidently of the utility of critical realism, and of themselves as the useful critical realists. The University of North Carolina had fashioned a breathing space for dissidents such as Woodward, and he used the maneuvering room to seek out other dissidents in the southern past.

He turned to Populism, a step not entirely original, for there had begun to be scattered studies by such historians as Benjamin B. Kendrick, Alex Mathews Arnett, and Francis B. Simkins.[15] As Woodward himself was to remark: "It was easier in the 1930s than it is in the 1950s to understand the

1890s. For the look of things in the South in the trough of the Great Depression did a lot toward making the desperate mood and temper of the South of the nineties wholly credible." [16] But no one made Populism as central to modern southern history, welded it into a Beardian analysis that was applied in turn within southern society, or showed such respect for the bottom rail, the gesture and hope of rebellion. *Tom Watson* is a book perhaps most marked by its distaste for the powerful and rich, who usually appear as hypocrites, charlatans, a "grim and bearded lot" never to be trusted. [17] In Watson, Woodward found a man who resisted the divisiveness of racism and sought to yoke together poor white and black in a common front against economic oppression. In this, Woodward may have been lucky. Watson was not entirely typical in his sympathy for the black. [18] As Woodward himself was later to establish, poor-white democracy went hand in hand with the elimination of blacks from politics and the rise of Jim Crow. But there was a difficulty on this score even in Watson's career. The tribune of the underdog in the early 1890s, Watson became in the twentieth century the foremost vilifier in Georgia of Negro, Jew, and Catholic. Woodward faithfully chronicled both aspects of Watson's story but kept them distinct, thereby neatly avoiding a considerable difficulty for himself as a southern dissident. If the bitterness of Tom Watson was the logical and necessary consequence of his disappointed crusade, the moral was an uncomfortable one. By splitting the first part of Watson's career off from the second, Woodward neutralized the issue. He did admit that the two might be related but not that they were an organic whole. For it was crucial to Woodward to believe that Watson could have succeeded.

Woodward has consistently stressed change in the southern past, because he has wanted change. If southern history is a remorseless unity, unbroken in its social conservatism and unchallenged by a significant radicalism, the task of the southern reformer is futile. He is trying to sow on ground so stony that it is not worth buying the seed: one might as well go off to a better plot, as did many liberals of George W. Cable's day. On the other hand, if southern history is ferment and change, in which conservatism has triumphed only after a desperate struggle and holds an insecure victory, there is hope. It has been Woodward's insight to point to this volatility. Woodward has charged as the central fault of Cash that he overestimated the unbroken flow of southern history: "The history of the South . . . would seem to be characterized more by *dis*continuity, one trait that helps account for the distinctiveness of the South and its history. . . . Southerners, unlike other Americans, repeatedly felt the solid ground of continuity give way under their feet." [19] Hence he was to deplore, in 1964, the stereotype of the conservative South and point to examples of southern dissent, such as the abolitionism that existed below the

Potomac before the Civil War and to the writings of George W. Cable after it. "It would be a tragic decision to make intransigence and desperate adherence to a discredited code the test of southern loyalty."[20] Alternatives were sanctioned by the lessons of the southern past and by the thoughts and actions of southerners.

Woodward sought out those "forgotten alternatives"[21] that would have created a more liberal South if they had succeeded. *The Strange Career of Jim Crow* is perhaps the most sustained example of this search. There he examines the history of southern race relations and notes that segregation, the Jim Crow of the statute book, was not the immediate sequel of emancipation. Dating from the 1890s, it was an institution scarcely old enough to encompass the life span of a single individual: it was not the immutable system that southerners imagined in the passions of the 1950s. There was no golden age, but there was a moment of some flexibility in the relationship of black and white in the South. Now that the crisis over the dismantling of segregation has passed, and with it the need to prove the transience of Jim Crow, the book reads less compellingly. It looks the most wistful of Woodward's attempts to find a usable past, as well as the most successful in reaching a wide and active audience. As Woodward himself has been forced to recognize, segregation was only the structure of a relationship and not the heart of the matter. His glimmer of hope seems a faint light beside the fact of consistent discrimination.[22]

It is important to remember that Woodward has always sought the indigenous solution, obliged to find his glimmers within the southern tradition. Whatever his flirtations with socialism, they gave him no taste for the solidarity of the oppressed of all nations or the opportunities offered by the insights of Marx or Gramsci. His opinions of those who lingered on the boulevard Montparnasse have already been cited. His experience of Oxford is mentioned without enthusiasm in *Thinking Back,* with the commentary, "I knew that I would never be a Christ Church princeling and would never feel comfortable in a Sorbonne beret." He has been inclined to poke fun at the North, whose Emersons have condescended to the South as the "less-civilized portion of the country," and one detects a note of satisfaction in his essays of the 1960s, which observe a historiography that punctured the egalitarian myths of the abolitionist and neoabolitionist. Though he has offered his patronage to comparative history, he has written little of it himself, rather puckishly rejoicing in the title of a provincial. Maneuvering room has been constricted because he has so consistently adhered to the Chaucerian sentiment that serves as an epigraph to *Thinking Back:* "But trusteth wel, I am a southren man."[23]

If one sets aside the diversion of the Second World War, the period from *Tom Watson* to *The Strange Career of Jim Crow,* and including *Origins of the New South, 1877–1913* and *Reunion and Reaction,* may be regarded as a unity. The biography served as an introduction and apprenticeship. The commission to write the New South volume for the History of the South series obliged him to synthesis, which, being established, generated his lectures on segregation and his detective story on the Compromise of 1877. They are very much of a piece, which is partly because they were researched and written, if you eliminate the years of the war, within a relatively short span, just twelve years from 1938 to 1954. The edifice was essentially complete by the time Woodward was forty-six. *The Strange Career of Jim Crow* may, it is true, be regarded as a transitional book, in that it draws on the hard work for *Origins* but begins to ease Woodward into the role of his maturity, that of the critical essayist.

This pattern had several causes, but one is worth noting. The task of fulfilling his commission from the Littlefield Fund forced Woodward into extensive manuscript research, rather against his temperament. As he confessed in the bibliography to *Origins of the New South,* "The historian is driven to manuscripts by necessity rather than zeal."[24] The admission is candid and is borne out by the rest of his career. With the partial exception of his edition of Mary Chesnut, neither the necessity nor the zeal to penetrate archives seems to have recurred, even though the span of the New Woodward now far exceeds the chronological span of the Old Woodward.[25] The commission may even have forced him into the role of synthesizer more than may have been native to him.

The analytical standpoint of his magnum opus was partly borrowed from Charles Beard, though Woodward made intrasectional class and racial conflict more important than intersectional strife. Nonetheless, however much it marked a beginning for southern thought, *Origins of the New South* stood at the end of a national tradition. In many ways the book was the last triumph of the Progressive school, though declaring the bankruptcy of the middle class. Woodward carried the tradition to its logical conclusion, purging naïveté and methodological shortcomings, understanding the force of myth.[26] Above all, he wrote in the modern manner, with sharp irony. But his passion for synthesis has had its limits, and they are suspiciously congruent with the obligations imposed on him by that commission. He has never, for example, felt the necessity to elaborate a coherent vision of the Old South, except to declare that, whatever it was, it was different from the New South. His reviewing of recent works on the New South, while always generous, is pointedly vigilant, whereas his comments upon the historiography of the Old South have conferred his blessing upon a bewildering range of contradictory viewpoints, from Robert Fogel and Stanley Engerman to Eugene Genovese to Bertram Wyatt-Brown—strange bedfellows.[27]

Origins of the New South is a complex book. Not the least of its merits was the closing of a gap. On the eve of its publication in 1951, Woodward wrote of a new book on Mississippi politics: "Falling between the period when the historians generally leave off and the period when the sociologists take over—between the end of Reconstruction and the very recent past—the half century studied by Mr. Kirwan represents the most neglected cycle of Southern history. It is therefore a compliment of a dubious sort to say that he has written the best political history of the period covered so far available for any state of the region. The fact is he did not have a lot of competition." [28] Woodward's bibliography, itself the first of its kind, was a tale of woe: "Biographies of this period have only recently emerged from the commemorative stage and published correspondence is all but non-existent," he lamented; and then added, "A list of prominent figures of the post-Reconstruction South who have yet to find competent biographers would probably be longer than a list of those who have been so fortunate." Seldom has a subject been raised from such obscurity to such illumination at a single bound. Just as a piece of technique, an effort of research, the book was a virtuoso performance. [29]

More than that, *Origins of the New South* was the fulfillment of his new image of the southern past, the fresh moral geography at which he had hinted in the 1930s. And the vision is moral, maintained throughout the work with a tenacity whose coherence makes the book one of the few works of art that southern historical literature has produced. The vision is expressed not merely in conclusions but in the structure and style of the analysis.

Woodward used irony, that idiom most complex, phenomenological, and evasive. Irony is a mood that often occurs in his writing and needs careful discussion, for Woodward has used it in two senses, one rhetorical, the other philosophical, though the two blend imperceptibly. Irony's rhetorical purposes will become evident from an examination of Woodward's writings. Its philosophical meaning is less elusive, being used in the manner of Reinhold Niebuhr. By this usage, people are deemed free to choose their acts but not to control the consequences of action. Human nature is inescapably a compound of virtue and vice; and history, so unpredictable that virtue can generate vice and vice can generate virtue. Precision of vision is impossible, though illusions can sometimes be detected and, by commentary, mitigated. So irony denotes both the situation of those caught in history and the awareness of the historian, who sees irony and is condemned to express it. [30]

At the level of rhetoric, irony has served many purposes in conveying Woodward's voice. On one level, irony in his narrative has discriminated between heroes and villains for a mind too subtle to want to name heroes and villains. Of Robert Dabney, for example, Woodward commented: "Never, of course, was there the remotest chance of Dabney's goose quill prevailing against the chattering presses of Grady and Dawson, Tompkins and Edmonds. Anyway, the New South had no ear for pessimism—not with Georgia boasting eleven millionaires in 1892 and Kentucky twenty-four, and New Orleans alone thirty-five!" Or note his scathing characterization of the myth of the Old South, created in the 1880s: "What bittersweet tears washed Nashville's grimy cheeks over Page's *In Ole Virginia!* 'Dem wuz good ole times, marster—de bes Sam ever see! Dey wuz in fac'! Niggers didn' hed nothin' 'tall to do.' Embarrassing race conflict dissolved in liquid dialect, angry Populist farmers became merely quaint in Billy Sanders' vernacular, depression rolled aside, and for a moment, 'de ole times done come back again.'" Such passages contrast strongly with the seriousness of tone in the chapters on Populism. One can sense the satisfaction in a sentence like "Not until the New South was confronted by the Populists did it meet with a challenge that set it back on its heels for a spell." Irony thus expressed the morality of a man who elsewhere directly remarked of a Progressivism for whites only that it "no more fulfilled the political aspirations and deeper needs of the mass of the people than did the first New Deal administration." [31] This phrase, "deeper needs of the mass of the people," neatly expressed Woodward's basic moral precept.

A central tradition of American historical literature has been its moralism. As one social morality has succeeded another, interpretation has supplanted interpretation with a remarkable fidelity. Consistent with this, Woodward's writing represented a shift in the morality of southern thought. He turned its concerns from the bourgeoisie to the southern masses. He widened it to include blacks, whose social inferiority had been a central assumption of earlier generations. He raised the broad issue of social responsibility in southern politics. Woodward has had to fight his battles among a southern historical profession that has scarcely been radical, as when he desegregated the annual banquet of the Southern Historical Association in 1952, the year of his presidency. But on the whole, his views on race generated surprisingly little outcry among his southern contemporaries, however much they doubtless grumbled in private. It is hard to imagine that he would have escaped so unscathed or proceeded so laden with honors if he had written forty years earlier.

Yet the meaning of irony was more complex than just advancing the purposes of morality. [32] The mood had been present in his *Tom Watson.* Sometimes irony was just pleasure in a phrase well turned, perhaps influenced by Gibbon, who once nearly tempted Woodward into Roman history. The spirit of Lausanne may linger in a sentence like this: "He [Watson] was attracted and repelled at the same time: it was magnificent to be incorrigible, but it was practical to be conciliatory."[33] Sometimes irony expressed itself in a Menckenian joy at the absurdity of humanity. Woodward was then beginning to be, as he has remained, a comic writer of suppleness, with gifts of timing and bathos. Sometimes irony became so heavy that *sarcasm* seems the better term.

Tom Watson was a more rambling, more linear book (longer by five pages, if you exclude the paraphernalia of bibliography and index) than *Origins of the New South*. The later need to compress seems to have had the effect of making irony leaner, more businesslike. In *Origins of the New South,* irony is less in the phrasing, more in the structure of the book. More fundamentally, the will to believe had been stronger in the young dissident, writing when the second New Deal was fresh. The desire to believe was as strong in 1951, but evidence for the possibility of progress was more mixed, the intractability of history more apparent. Irony became more insistent as detachment from the hopes of dissidence grew.

There was little bleakness in this. After all, there was sometimes hope of progress. Involved in legal cases that would help to remove the legal barriers of segregation, Woodward knew matters could change. Even so, like many others, he was to be surprised at the rapidity of change once launched in the civil rights movement, enough to be lured temporarily into speaking of a national commitment to equality not only in his own times but in the first Reconstruction.[34] Thus irony became a stance of dissidence, less for society, more for the satisfaction of the ironist, a kind of quiet testimony. This transition has much to do with the special power of *Origins of the New South*. The young Woodward supplied the stamina and indignation to make research worthwhile, the older informed the voice of the book.

The 1950s were not years of encouragement. Charles Beard's vision of American history as a record of social struggle was not one to conjure with in the intellectual atmosphere of the 1950s. It was, after all, the heyday of consensus, of the attempt to find the common denominators of American culture. When Richard Hofstadter wrote of the "common climate of American opinion" and remarked that its existence "has been much obscured by the tendency to place political conflict in the foreground of history,"[35] he gave a new mandate to the historical profession in America, which Woodward ignored. Right in the middle of his foreground was the angry Populist farmer, though Woodward has always been more interested in the forces that damaged the farmer than in the farmer himself. Though his work has immensely impelled the development of southern social history, and made possible the Carlo Ginzburgs of a recent southern generation, he himself, perhaps from a desire to avoid condescension, has avoided recreating the *mentalité* of anonymous southerners.

Woodward kept up a running dialogue with the consensus perception, though muffled by his friendships with Hofstadter and David Potter, until the events of the 1960s reasserted the impression of social division. He insisted upon the validity of dissent, whether of an underclass from a business culture or of the South from the national pattern. In 1959 he published a critique of the new hostility toward Populism, partly exemplified in Hofstadter's *The Age of Reform*. Woodward conceded the existence of nativism among Populists, their hatred of the Jew and the foreigner, their provincialism. But the Arkansan in Woodward clearly rose against the New Yorker in Hofstadter. He pointed out that these were not characteristics peculiar to Populists, nor were they always true of Populists themselves. He referred to the case of Tom Watson, seeing positive value in this tradition of revolt: "One must expect and even hope that there will be future upheavals to shock the seats of power and privilege and furnish the periodic therapy that seems necessary to the health of our democracy. But one cannot expect them to be any more decorous or seemly or rational than their predecessors." Moreover, the intellectual has a role to play, as he did during the New Deal: "For the tradition to endure, for the way to remain open, however, the intellectual must not be alienated from the sources of revolt."[36] Later Woodward returned more explicitly to the consensus school, in an essay called "The North and the South of it." He asserted that "what America has lacked in the way of class tensions she has made up in the indigenous tensions of her peculiar heritage. Americans have characteristically thought in terms of regional, religious and racial or ethnic rather than class conflict." He added, "We have been somewhat hasty in sweeping under the rug of liberal consensus this ancient question."[37]

But what was the dissident to offer in reply when Populism had so dwindled? If the present was unencouraging, history might give some useful testimony. In this mood, Woodward wrote in the 1950s his most influential essays, "The Irony of Southern History" and "The Search for Southern Identity." He examined previous attempts to capture the essence of the South: Ulrich Phillips, who saw the resolution to maintain white supremacy as the cardinal test of the southerner; and the Agrarians, for whom the South was the agricultural way of life. He found both to be at fault. One can be a southerner without believing in black inferiority—on Phillips's logic, Woodward himself would not be a southerner, an obviously intolerable conclusion— and to live in a city like Atlanta does not disqualify one from that identity. What then is different about the South? Woodward pointed to its variance from the norm of American experience. As the nation has been characterized by economic abundance, success, and the legend of innocence, so the South, in counterpoint, has been a land of poverty, failure, and the bitter realism born of such experience. "In that most optimistic of centuries in the most optimistic part of the world, the South remained basically pessimistic in its social outlook and its moral philosophy."[38] In a nation without a heritage of feudalism, the South had slavery. In a country rootless with social mobility, the South and its literature are firmly tied to a place. But what is the use of this peculiarity? Scarred like Europe with war, the South has a sense of realism. It may be that the irony of the southerner's position may make him more adept in an international world where American innocence is no asset.

In a revised edition of *The Burden of Southern History*, Woodward was to return to this problem. At the end of the 1960s, he was forced to note how that decade's events had dismantled the national myth of innocence and success. His case might have been strengthened if the South had been innocent of the disorder of Vietnam and the black revolt, but "the irony of history had caught up with the ironist—or gone him one better. For in this fateful hour of opportunity history had ironically placed men of presumably authentic Southern heritage in the supreme seats of national power—a gentleman from Texas in the White House and a gentleman from Georgia in the State Department. And yet from those quarters came few challenges and little appreciable restraint to the pursuit of the national myths of invincibility and innocence. Rather there came a renewed allegiance and sustained dedication."[39]

The curious thing about Woodward's initial essays on southern identity, tacitly recognized in the revision, was his reliance on the consensus theory—the same idea he had so resisted in his own work on the South. However much the region had bred in him a pessimistic skepticism, it departed when he raised his eyes to the nation. He accepted the homogenized version of the American past contained in such books as David Potter's *People of Plenty*. His insight about the South gave him no advantage over northern historians in seeing suffering north of the Potomac. In truth, it could not. His idea needed the counterpoint of southern realism and northern innocence, southern poverty and northern wealth. Without it, the distinctiveness of the South melted away. And it was part of his task to establish that singularity.

As the 1960s dealt savage blows to the consensus school, so they undermined Woodward's definition of the South. He was left only with the conclusion that "Americans might still have something to learn, if they would, from the un-American and ironic experience of the South with history." With that phrase, "if they would," his case slipped away. Woodward could only claim that, although there are lessons in the southern past, they are there only for those who care to learn them. Thereby he lost the one point that would prove his theory: Something in the southern milieu compels southerners to learn these lessons; it is the unavoidable burden of southern identity. In *Thinking Back,* Woodward has had to concede the point, to indicate his use of the subjunctive in these essays, not to what was, but to what might be.[40]

These essays also testify to the peculiarity of Woodward's stance. Those southerners most marked by the pessimistic resistance to panacea, to which Woodward gave his approval, are southern conservatives. It is they who have felt most sharply the sting of defeat and drawn lessons from it. But they were conservative lessons. Southern liberals took the same events with comparative lightness because they were not intellectually involved in them. If one examines the genteel historians whom Woodward himself supplanted, one sees that the very things they ignored in the southern past were those episodes richest in social disappointment. Their task, after all, was the southern future and a judicious edition of the southern past, not the responsibility for Jefferson Davis's aberrations.

Their vision of that future was euphoric. Liberals such as Walter Hines Page were constantly heralding the dawn of a new age. Edwin Mims's *The Advancing South* was as far removed from social pessimism as one can imagine: "No one can have too high a hope of what may be achieved within the next quarter of a century. Freed from the limitations that have so long hampered it, and buoyant with the energy of a new life coursing through its veins, the South will press forward to a new destiny."[41] A main task of southern liberalism has been to assimilate the South to the nation. It has been an impulse toward, not away from, innocence. If the Vietnam misadventure can be seen as an exercise of American innocence, the role of Lyndon Johnson in it was entirely faithful to that southern tradition of liberalism. He was more typical of it than was Woodward himself, who, by his own testimony, has drifted in and out of that tradition.

Rather, Woodward has blended the pessimistic moral diagnosis of the conservatives of the Southern Renaissance with his own Populist variant of southern radicalism. Perhaps it is little wonder that he found it natural in 1960 to sympathize with George Fitzhugh, the intellectual sui generis.[42] The idiosyncracy of the vision needs emphasizing because it has been masked by its apparent triumph among the recent generation of southern historians.

Nonetheless, components of the synthesis command varying degrees of respect. The account of the Compromise of 1877 is more or less intact. The claim that the New South was run by new men is looking frail but is still workable. The theory of the taking of a political right fork, an alliance with the Northeast, has been badly dented. The analysis of the origins of segregation has been so qualified, its chronology so revised, that little of its original pungency remains. The account of Populism, though Woodward's version of its racial attitudes has been softened, remains definitive, as does his explanation for the origins of disfranchisement and the character of southern Progressivism. His definition of the South as a colonial economy has been powerfully reinforced.[43] The House of Woodward may have peeling paint, the odd room may be unusable, but it is still the only hotel in town worth the price.

And yet the triumph of *Origins of the New South* was always curiously illusory, since what Woodward most cared for, the centrality of the Populist vision, is what most of his readers, though they were polite, could not follow. Like Turner's frontier, celebrated because it was dying, Woodward's Populists were given their proper due, but it was posthumous. The synthesis was founded on a regret and a hope, and now the hope is gone.

This has given him the status of an outsider, the essayist carefully following the upheavals of the 1960s and still commenting on current affairs. The civil rights movement brought him fleetingly into the mainstream of southern liberalism, the moment when, in debate with a Marxist, he felt able to call himself a "liberal, even more, a southern white liberal." Martin Luther King himself read passages from *The Strange Career of Jim Crow* before the state capitol at Montgomery, as Woodward watched.[44] The historian marched at Selma.

An outsider in politics, he was the insider among historians. As the upheavals of the 1960s reverberated through scholarship, Woodward found himself a critic of new views. Once outflanked by Cold Warriors to his right, he was now bedeviled by existentialist presentists to his left. With sane irritation, he strove to represent the nature of "mixed motives, ambivalence, paradox, and complexity."[45] It was in these years that his writings began to show a sharp awareness of the conflict of intellectual generations and to develop rules by which the genteel brutality of that campaign may be conducted. He has played his role with firmness but with compassion, encouraging debate, indulging the raw and young. Power has brought responsibilities, which have been scrupulously discharged. But the role has served others better than it has served Woodward, for the reviewer has tended to supplant the historian, to the point where he has come to review himself.

The shift may even be located as far back as the 1950s. His "The South in Search of a Philosophy," the lecture of 1938, was a search for an energizing praxis. His search for southern identity twenty years later was a meditation upon the self-critical voice, a scrutiny of the nature of experiencing, a

denoting of the quality of irony. This transition from an emphasis upon action to a concern with the private voice was, for the discipline of southern
history, a fruitful step, for it promoted the historical study of southern self-
awareness. But it marked a turning inward.

The role of the essayist has existed in counterpoint with that of the teacher,
both functions of a desire to help others grow. Of his teaching one can say
little, except to note that in his time and at his behest, first Johns Hopkins,
then Yale, became the focus of advanced graduate studies in southern history.
The quality of his students has scarcely been matched; their devotion to him
is fierce.[46] They have policed and marked out the boundaries of his achievement, though they are of motley complexion, a diversity of liberals, socialists,
conservatives, all different, yet all believing that they sustain Woodward. He
has become a kind of pope, with the gift of spotting talented young parish
priests, giving them the confidence to become themselves bishops and archi-
mandrites. A few have become archbishops. One or two may be *papabile.*
But upon the evidence of *Thinking Back,* they will have to wait until a Cardinal Camerlengo taps his silver hammer in New Haven. This is no Celes-
tine V, who retired before his time.

NOTES

I have used passages from "C. Vann Woodward and the Burden of Southern Liberalism," *American Historical Review* 78 (1973): 589–604, but this essay is partly
new. On some issues, most notably the closeness with which Woodward may be understood to stand in the liberal tradition, I have changed my mind. Woodward has
gone to the trouble of telling me I was wrong, and on a matter of self-perception he
should know. Other problems, unapparent to a twenty-three-year-old living in England, now draw my eye. There has been a considerable body of writing on Woodward since 1973, some of which has made my own contribution supererogatory or
mistaken. Most important, Woodward has contributed his own *Thinking Back,* with
its distinctive combination of autobiography, memoir, and critical discourse. The
book is dedicated to his critics, "without whose devoted efforts life would have been
simpler but less interesting." I would not wish Professor Woodward's life to become
uninteresting.

   1. C. Vann Woodward, *American Counterpoint: Slavery and Racism in the North-
South Dialogue* (Boston: Little, Brown, 1971), 282; idem, *Thinking Back: The Perils
of Writing History* (Baton Rouge: Louisiana State University Press, 1986), 5, 4.

   2. John Herbert Roper, "C. Vann Woodward's Early Career—The Historian as
Dissident Youth," *Georgia Historical Quarterly* 44 (1980): 7–9. Religion occupies
five pages (448–53) of Woodward's *Origins of the New South, 1877–1913,* vol. 9 of
A History of the South, series ed. Wendell Holmes Stephenson and Ellis Merton Coulter (Baton Rouge: Louisiana State University Press, 1951).

3. Roper, "Woodward's Early Career," 7–8.

4. C. Vann Woodward, *Tom Watson: Agrarian Rebel* (New York: Macmillan, 1938), 53, 59, 165, 217, 229, 219, 486.

5. Woodward, *Thinking Back*, 86; Roper, "Woodward's Early Career," 13.

6. Woodward, *Thinking Back*, 21–27.

7. Roper, "Woodward's Early Career," 11–12; Rupert Bayless Vance, *Human Factors in Cotton Culture* (Chapel Hill: University of North Carolina Press, 1929).

8. Woodward, *Thinking Back*, 135–36.

9. Woodward, *Origins of the New South*, 429–36.

10. Woodward, "The Historical Dimension," in *The Burden of Southern History*, rev. ed. (Baton Rouge: Louisiana State University Press, 1968), 27–39; idem, "Why the Southern Renaissance?" *Virginia Quarterly Review* 51 (1975): 222–39; idem, *Thinking Back*, 23.

11. C. Vann Woodward, "The South in Search of a Philosophy," *Phi Beta Kappa Addresses at the University of Florida* 1 (1938): 15.

12. Ibid., 15–16; idem, *Thinking Back*, 18–19.

13. Woodward, "The South in Search," 17–19.

14. Woodward, *Thinking Back*, 17–20.

15. Benjamin B. Kendrick, "Agrarian Discontent in the South: 1880–1900," *Annual Report of the American Historical Association: 1920* (Washington: AHA, 1920), 267–72; Alex Mathews Arnett, *The Populist Movement in Georgia* (New York: Columbia University Press, 1922); and Francis Butler Simkins, *The Tillman Movement in South Carolina* (Durham: Duke University Press, 1926).

16. C. Vann Woodward, "Preface to the 1955 Reissue," in *Tom Watson: Agrarian Rebel* (1938; reprint, New York: Macmillan, 1955). Hereinafter, citations will be to the 1955 edition.

17. Ibid., 88.

18. See Robert Saunders, "Southern Populists and the Negro, 1893–1895," *Journal of Negro History* 54 (1969): 240–61. Saunders expresses reservations about the "Populist failure to accept the Negro as an intellectual, moral or political equal."

19. C. Vann Woodward, "The Elusive Mind of the South," *New Review of Books* 4 Dec. 1969, reprinted with revisions in idem, *American Counterpoint*, 261–83; quotation, 275–76.

20. C. Vann Woodward, "The Question of Loyalty," *American Scholar* 33 (1964): 561–67.

21. This is the chapter heading of the first lecture in Woodward's *The Strange Career of Jim Crow* (New York: Oxford University Press, 1955).

22. Howard N. Rabinowitz, "The Woodward Thesis and More: Three Contributions of *The Strange Career of Jim Crow*," address, American Historical Association, 1986. Rabinowitz is severe about the accuracy of Woodward on segregation in the late nineteenth century, while arguing that Woodward on the late twentieth century is unusually prescient. (I am obliged to Professor Rabinowitz for showing me his paper.) See also bibliography and Rabinowitz's revised essay in this volume.

23. Woodward, *Origins of the New South*, 142–43; idem, ed., *The Comparative Approach to American History* (New York: Basic Books, 1968); idem, *Thinking Back*, 104–5, 2.

24. Woodward, *Origins of the New South*, 482.

25. I say "partial exception" because Woodward (ed., *Mary Chesnut's Civil War* [New Haven: Yale University Press, 1981], xi–xii) thanks no fewer than twenty-eight people for assistance with transcription, collation, and annotation.

26. George M. Fredrickson, "The Renaissance of Southern History: Or the Life and Work of C. Vann Woodward," *Dissent* 34 (1987): 68.

27. The nearest to an extended analysis of the Old South is in the group of essays in *American Counterpoint* that deal with slavery.

28. C. Vann Woodward, review of *Revolt of the Rednecks: Mississippi Politics, 1876–1925*, by Albert Dennis Kirwan, *American Historical Review* 56 (1951): 918.

29. Woodward, *Origins of the New South*, 482, 499.

30. See Reinhold Niebuhr, *The Irony of American History* (New York: Scribner, 1952); and the useful commentary of Richard Reinitz, "Niebuhrian Irony and Historical Interpretation: The Relationship between Consensus and New Left History," in *The Writing of History: Literary Form and Historical Understanding*, ed. Robert H. Canary and Henry Kozicki (Madison: University of Wisconsin Press, 1978), 93–128.

31. Woodward, *Origins of the New South*, 174, 167, 395.

32. Robert B. Westbrook, "C. Vann Woodward: The Southerner as Liberal Realist," *South Atlantic Quarterly* 77 (1978): 54–71.

33. Woodward, *Thinking Back*, 22; idem, *Tom Watson*, 95.

34. Woodward, *Thinking Back*, 88–89; idem, *Burden of Southern History*, 69–107; idem, *American Counterpoint*, 163–83.

35. Richard Hofstadter, *The American Political Tradition and the Men Who Made It* (New York: Knopf, 1948), vii.

36. C. Vann Woodward, "The Populist Heritage and the Intellectual," *American Scholar* 28 (1959): 55–72, reprinted, idem, *The Burden of Southern History* (1968 ed.), 141–66; quoted passage, *Burden*, 166.

37. C. Vann Woodward, "The North and South of It," *American Scholar* 35 (1966): 648.

38. Woodward, *The Burden of Southern History*, 21. In fact, I am not sure the Old South was "basically pessimistic."

39. Ibid., 230.

40. Ibid., 233; Woodward, *Thinking Back*, 117.

41. Edwin Mims, *The Advancing South: Stories of Progress and Reaction* (Garden City, N.Y.: Doubleday, Page, 1926), 315.

42. "George Fitzhugh: *Sui Generis*," in George Fitzhugh, *Cannibals All! or, Slaves without Masters*, ed. C. Vann Woodward (Cambridge: Harvard University Press, 1960), vii–xxxix.

43. All of this criticism is usefully listed in Woodward, *Thinking Back*, 147–51.

44. Ibid., 92.

45. C. Vann Woodward, "Clio with Soul," *Journal of American History* 56 (1969): 20; see also idem, "The Future of the Past," *American Historical Review* 75 (1970): 711–26.

46. Both quality and devotion can be measured in J. Morgan Kousser and James M. McPherson, eds., *Region, Race, and Reconstruction: Essays in Honor of C. Vann Woodward* (New York: Oxford University Press, 1982).

The Strange Career
of C. Vann Woodward

M. E. BRADFORD

*

The late Melvin Eustace Adonis Bradford (1934–1993) ably represented the right wing of the activist-scholar traditions in southern studies. Long a distinguished teacher at the University of Dallas, Bradford was a student of the Agrarianism of his beloved professor in graduate school at Vanderbilt, Donald Davidson. A graceful stylist, as befits one overwhelmed by a vision of history as grand tragedy that is concrete, inescapable, intensely local, and marked by profound continuities, Bradford was thus a faithful proponent for Davidson's oft-expressed claim that there is a *long street* of southern traditions, that is, the folkways of the region run a long, long way back, and run deep, although the roadway itself may be narrow and is always winding and circuitous. Bradford produced much valuable literary criticism as well as studies in social criticism, *A Better Guide than Reason, A Worthy Company,* and *Essays on the Origins of the U.S. Constitution.* Most memorably, he wrote the trenchant summary statement for the neo-Agrarians in *Why the South Will Survive; by Fifteen Southerners.* He worked on a major biographical study of his mentor Davidson, but died without completing it, leaving behind some fascinating essays in the fragmentary project.

* * *

Sometimes an image can teach us more about our times than volumes of exposition. This is especially the case when it is a poet who has framed the image, finding a meaningful metaphor in the raw materials of a familiar world. When, in the spring of 1961, the southern literary critic Donald Davidson cast about for a contemporary historian whose views would chastise his "too, too Southern flesh," he turned to C. Vann Woodward. In an address delivered at Nashville's Belmont College, Davidson spoke of sitting "puritanically upright" in an "uncomfortable chair" enduring the requisite mortification of reading Woodward's *The Burden of Southern History.* Clearly, the Tennessee traditionalist knew what he was doing when he selected a representative of the "new breed" of southern scholars as a symbolic adversary, and *The Burden of Southern History* to represent that new breed.

U. B. Phillips has been the figure of reference among southern historians in the 1920s and '30s, and Frank Owsley the most important authority in the same field in the '40s and '50s. Well before Davidson poked fun at him, Comer Vann Woodward of Arkadelphia and Morrilton, Arkansas, had become the leading spokesman and role model for a group of southern historians who reached the top of their profession after World War II and who had a more difficult, problematic relation to the regional past than had their most eminent predecessors in the discipline. These historians worked to change the accepted view of the southern past, and they reshaped it to suit the preoccupations of the country at large during the era of the Warren Court, the New Frontier, and the Great Society: to mesh properly with the Second Reconstruction, which was well under way in 1961. C. Vann Woodward's career after 1947 and the publication of his nonpolitical *The Battle for Leyte Gulf* were certainly made possible by this atmosphere of progressive expectation and expansive compulsory reform. In his choice of themes and his organization of evidence, Woodward's mature work is affected by the political battles of his time.

Woodward was something beyond a rank-and-file revisionist. He was not just a representative of this new group but among its best and was involved with assorted causes, by his own description, as a "presentist," "moralist," or "active partisan." In his books and essays, and in the training of his graduate students, Woodward has been at the cutting edge in the continuing attempt to "tell about the South": in the now fashionable analysis of dissident eccentrics in the region's history, in the focus on populism and economic conflict, and in addressing the black experience, the myth of the "New South," and the value of cross-cultural comparisons. He has led the way in the kind of history written to improve the world—in the words of his biographer, John Herbert Roper, "a history he can use"—stretching the boundaries of legitimate learning in order to incorporate fashionable partisan causes. It is fair to say that no other major historian of his generation has been called upon more often to speak for the progressive side before the High Court. Woodward, by his own confession, has always had a "weakness for history with a purpose." Despite this authorial partisanship, he has also remained open to criticism and ready to learn, even at the expense of his fondest hopes and deepest convictions. His irony at his own expense, his commitment to his own discipline, his horror of reductionist social science and of the excesses of the New Left at least match his passion for political improvement and have grown with the passage of time. The breadth and penetration of his scholarship, in short, argue against the case for indictment as a mere doctrinaire, implying the need for a more inclusive view of this very divided man.

As Davidson suggested, Woodward's work is usually interesting and well written even when (to conservatives) his conclusions are disagreeable. As he has demonstrated in his memoir/apologia, *Thinking Back,* his confrontation with any subject is so rich and many-sided that we can rarely help learning from him. Woodward is sometimes myopic in his focus and often mistaken in his understanding of the record, but he never condescends to history as a mode of knowledge, never takes his subjects for granted or undervalues their importance. This quality explains why he has been one of the major American historians of this generation, a measure of what his discipline can achieve in a time when recognized authorities speak of the past as dead. Despite his internal division between academic priorities and political goals, Woodward has known better than to think it all a game. The pattern of his career, which Roper details in the 1987 biography *C. Vann Woodward, Southerner,* has been animated by a strange type of oscillation. This has been even more than what might have seemed predictable, given the strength of Woodward's personality and the public respect he now commands.

Comer Vann Woodward was born in Vanndale, Arkansas, on 13 November 1908, into a family of teachers, planters, and pious Methodists. He was educated at Henderson-Brown College and at Emory, Columbia, and the University of North Carolina, where in 1937 he completed his doctorate. Roper suggests that Woodward's youthful association with "advanced spirits" propelled him toward an academic career and a faith in the power of politics to remake a sometimes recalcitrant world. This process intensified when the Woodwards moved to Georgia, where his father served as dean of a junior college at Oxford, while his uncle Comer served as dean of men at Emory. Life inside a liberal and well-educated subculture in Atlanta put Woodward on a course from which only three years of military service diverted him. His earliest teaching assignment was as an instructor of English at Georgia Institute of Technology, an occupation interrupted by an M.A. in political science from Columbia University (1932) and by a trip to France, Germany, and the Soviet Union. His impassioned defense of a young black communist against charges of insurrection, combined with budgetary difficulties, cost Woodward his post at Georgia Tech. For a time he returned to his father's house. He worked briefly for the Works Progress Administration (WPA) and began writing a study of a local Populist hero, Tom Watson. This project sent him in the direction of Chapel Hill and a life's work as a historian. Eventually, the study of Watson—which grew out of a larger project on seven southern radicals, "Seven for Demos"—became Woodward's dissertation and later his first book, *Tom Watson, Agrarian Rebel*. The search for a liberal strain within southern history was to occupy much of Woodward's time and energy throughout the rest of his career and to animate his lifetime interest in the Populists.

Roper suggests that a professional situation outside the South was a necessary precondition for the direction Woodward's career was to follow. He may be correct. But first came marriage; teaching in Florida, Virginia, and California; a military interruption; and a series of relocations. Finally, in 1947, Woodward and his household moved to Baltimore, where he joined the faculty of The Johns Hopkins University.

A watershed in the development of Woodward's reputation came in 1951. In that year, Woodward published what were arguably his two best books, *Reunion and Reaction: The Compromise of 1877 and the End of Reconstruction* and the still authoritative *Origins of the New South, 1877–1913*. The narrative elements in both books are strong. And though they arrive at conclusions that are still in dispute, each is clearly more an attempt to explain events—the Compromise of 1877 and the southern experience after Reconstruction through the inauguration of Woodrow Wilson—than an effort to influence behavior. Both works are history *first,* and a call for reform only incidentally. Moreover, they leave open the question of what kind of reform is appropriate for the South. Finally, after more than thirty years, both books have held their place in the serious scholarly dialogue on the postbellum South. Other interpreters of the period might not have been as critical of the alliance between the old southern ruling class and the Gilded Age bankers and industrialists, of the covert bargain made by southern politicians in the election of Rutherford B. Hayes, as was Woodward. Other historians might not have focused on the class conflict in the Populist rebellions. Nor would those who recognized the humiliated South's determination not to accept total racial equality or black political domination have been so certain that the racial arrangements developed in that era were purposely malicious and designed only to perpetuate the power and wealth of southern white leadership and the misery of the freedmen. As Woodward himself has since admitted, prevention of conflict was a seriously intended rationale of Jim Crow, supported by Republicans, Negroes, preachers, aristocrats, and common folk. This was especially true of certain types of segregation affecting social relations. Whether such arguments should have been used to codify separation of the races according to some rigid schema is, of course, another question, one to which our era has made another answer. It is also doubtful that the original Reconstruction could have worked in the South had northern states rejected the same racial policies of their region. In other words, with the abandonment of Reconstruction in 1877, no betrayal of the Negro occurred, for no large promises had been made except by the Republican Radicals. And by 1877 these were in the minority, even in the North, and often viewed as compromised because of their involvement in financial scandal.

The conspiracy theory that undergirds *Reunion and Reaction* is of doubtful merit. Yet, even so, Woodward's account of how Reconstruction came to an end is generally comprehensive—leaving out only the growing conservatism of the North and its disenchantment with plans to control a troublesome Dixie through rigged elections. In *Thinking Back,* Woodward mentions two other weaknesses: a failure to consider the important part played by northern Democrats in legitimating Hayes's election and an overemphasis on the Texas and Pacific Railroad. Finally, Woodward depends too much on economics in explaining his American Thermidor, even though a return to self-government was clearly the primary concern of the southerners who had any stake in the business. But the continuity of southern history is a notion that rarely occurs to C. Vann Woodward—even when he helps us to make a case for it.

Reunion and Reaction was an offshoot of Woodward's research in preparation of *Origins of the New South.* Its argument is summed up in volume 9 of the distinguished Louisiana State University series *A History of the South.* Admirers have spoken of *Reunion and Reaction* as a virtuoso performance, and their judgment is a reasonable one. All of the elements of history had a hand in creating the New South—and the necessary illusion that there would be no impiety toward a sacred past in establishing prosperity. The War between the States—defeat and occupation, malice and exploitation, outrage and poverty—changed the South forever. Yet it was important, even necessary, for southern leaders after 1877 to pretend that it had not brought any real change of mind or heart. And, in more ways than they knew (or Woodward ever admits), they were correct. The colonial status of the southern economy, the freeing of the slaves, the loss of the most promising young men in battle, and an uneven industrial development left the region in a grim condition for almost eighty years after Appomattox. Indeed, until 1945 there was no "New South." The federal government, through discriminatory credit policies, tariffs, and even minimum-wage laws, kept the South down as long as it was feasible. The South's sense of deprivation in turn expressed itself as devotion to the "Lost Cause." On the general theme of southern development by northern money, Woodward writes the gospel truth; and he is also persuasive in depicting the South's unrelenting poverty. But he sometimes forgets that there has been a Populism of the Right as well as of the Left. George Wallace's message to the "Big Mules" in Atlanta, Dallas, or Charlotte was to put things back as they were—for the leaders of southern society to behave like kinsmen, friends, and neighbors. Populist orators from Nathaniel Bacon to Wallace have made considerable noise about betrayal from within, because their rhetorical targets have often been people who were expected to behave better, to give proof of their commitment to a corporatist life protective of lower-class southerners. Where Woodward sees primarily a debate about equality and class struggle, he has misrepresented his subject; he has applied a "foreign" overlay to explain a native phenomenon. Thus he has been unclear about the difference between the Populist Tom Watson and the radical Tom Paine. It is a large difference, too big to have been overlooked unless we have been blinded by our own preconceptions.

Despite such myopia, Woodward shapes the record of the South from 1877 until 1913 from the perspective of so many different kinds of activity—education, art, literature, politics, architecture, religion—that the result is impressively rich and generally persuasive. Still, he fails to make allowances for those who defy his ideological assumptions. Over against Woodward's progressive view of history and his contempt for the old southern ruling class, we might cite Sul Ross of Texas or P. G. T. Beauregard of Louisiana, both men of honor from the old guard. Instead of the favorite effusions of assorted hypocritical Progressives, we might recommend to Woodward a close reading of Robert L. Dabney, Basil Gildersleeve, Albert Taylor Bledsoe, and Raphael Semmes, as well as figures discussed in Richard M. Weaver's *The Southern Tradition at Bay: A History of Postbellum Thought*. Roper is clearly on target when he argues that Woodward's *Origins*, despite its temperate and measured tone and its ironic smile at the expense of hypocrisy, is a book flawed by the author's inability to give "serious consideration [to] the possibility that large numbers of intelligent and honorable people actually believed, and believed intensely, in the values . . . encompassed as the Lost Cause." This habit of not taking such people on their own terms, this "empathetic shortfall," is precisely what is wrong with Woodward's book, despite the honors conferred on it. His work goes too far in denying real cultural continuity in the southern experience. Woodward is now, perhaps, less simplistic about southern piety than he was in the 1950s and '60s—less determined to describe the old South as a rhetorical invention. However, in being willfully oblivious of the persistence of a certain set of attitudes among southern conservatives (Roper cites Carl Degler, Jay Mandle, and James Charles Cobb for recent explanations of why they survive), Woodward showed tactical sense. The more monolithic the solid South was, the less precedent there was for southern liberalism of the kind he preferred; and because precedent is so important to traditional southerners, the greater is the difficulty in engendering such liberalism where it had no established roots, no "fathers." In a southern context, the fight over the past is (and always has been) primarily a dispute about present and future choices. It is never mere antiquarianism. As Woodward himself has written, "[t]he present proceeds [always] on some theory about history." At some point, once the story has been properly told and heard, the southerner as historian asks, "What are we to do?" Even when he appears to be interested only in railroads in Texas or butchers in New Orleans, his glance is "over the hill."

THE STRANGE CAREER OF JIM CROW

Woodward's most popular work, issued in serial revisions to reach a mass audience through more than 500,000 copies, is *The Strange Career of Jim Crow* (1955). It is a monograph/essay-in-opinion that grew directly out of his practical involvement in the struggle for social reform, that is, racial integration in the nation's public schools. In 1952–53 Woodward joined several other liberal scholars in writing a history of Reconstruction in support of the NAACP brief in the case of *Brown v. Board of Education of Topeka, Kansas*. In 1954 he lectured on the South at the University of London and served as James W. Richard Lecturer at the University of Virginia, where he dealt with racial issues. Woodward's biographer (who sees no harm in the truth about these events) says that the Arkansas historian was never more partisan than at this point in his career. In such a mood he converted the Richard lectures into *The Strange Career of Jim Crow*. In this book he suggested that there had been a time of easy relations between black and white in the South before the adoption in the 1890s of the rigid systems of de jure segregation. The argument was calculated to discourage southern resistance to court-mandated desegregation by implying that, contrary to what the great southern social historian U. B. Phillips had maintained, such an innovation would not violate any deeply rooted regional values. Woodward exaggerated his case, implying some connection between old-fashioned de facto segregation, modified by paternalism, with a totally open, color-blind society. In any case, his book became a sacred text to a generation dedicated to social change. After Woodward's evidence and conclusions had been challenged by more careful study of the subject, he brought out new editions of *The Strange Career* in 1957, 1966, and 1974, along with the apologies for the book that appeared in his *American Counterpoint: Slavery and Racism in the North-South Dialogue* and *Thinking Back*. He also reviewed in various periodicals much of the research undercutting his original views on the history of Jim Crow. This indicates how problematic his most popular book has been for his own scholarly standing.

The Strange Career of Jim Crow has become a work continuously in progress, a testimony, and a tract for the times—all of these elements gathered around a small scholarly core. It is a book that Woodward has explained and, by now, almost explained away. A product of strong and generous feelings, it is now defended by reference to the motives behind its composition, not in the name of its organizing method or content. Even so, it has given Woodward a place in history, as the author of what Martin Luther King Jr. called "the bible of the civil rights movement." As Woodward acknowledges in his memoir, the book made his name famous and his theories a point of departure for most subsequent discussions of race relations in the South after emancipation. While his earlier books were biased only by focus, selection of evidence, and the nature of questions asked, his work on segregation in all its editions has been explicitly political.

The core of dependable narrative that sustains Woodward's original argument is the clear evidence that, after 1890, the separation of races did become part of a more systematic legal pattern than it had been under the Redeemers (that is, the old southern relay families that briefly came back into power at the end of Reconstruction and before the Populist ascendancy in the South during the 1880s and 1890s). Moreover, self-styled southern Progressives saw to it that such regularity flourished in the place of local or private customs. Woodward maintained that shifts toward a better-organized and codified set of racial distinctions were concessions by the Redeemers, tossed out to pacify lower-class whites while diverting their attention from economic concerns.

To the contrary, Roper notes, recent research demonstrates that the movement toward statutory Jim Crow was "initiated by the radical, white Republicans" and "supported or requested by their black allies." In other words, the beginnings of the social establishment brought to its final fruition before 1900 were, for the South after emancipation and defeat, imports from the Midwest—and related to a desire for social peace and independence for the freedman: benevolent in responding to his desire for facilities of his own. Furthermore, the schools, like the churches, were segregated from the first: by Congress (in the District of Columbia), by most of the northern states, by blacks and radicals involved in Reconstruction. Even the most perfervid friends of black rights—in the ambitious Civil Rights Act of 1875 and certainly in all earlier Reconstruction laws and amendments—declined to reach toward integrated schools. This was true of even such self-described advocates of racial justice as Thaddeus Stevens and Justice Harlan. Therefore

Woodward's discussions of other kinds of racial separation *by policy*, in steamboats or trolley cars, were not a proper introduction to considerations of more important forms of Jim Crow—and the "fluidity" in relations that Woodward emphasized was not visible in the context where his history lessons should count for something. To leap from his selective choice of evidence to a theory of integrating schools by judicial fiat was in no way justified.

Finally, as Woodward admitted after reading Joel Williamson, John W. Cell, and Howard Rabinowitz, racial feeling in the New South was often more critical than economic interest in shaping policy; and Jim Crow was sometimes a protection from even worse situations, including persistent physical danger confronting many people on both sides of the color line. There is also the matter of black separatism, which is still very much with us. The study of the Negro in American society has become a very complicated matter since Woodward first agreed to participate for the plaintiffs in preparing the *Brown* case. Also, the lessons to be extracted from the history of that question become more elusive with the passage of every new law, the promulgation of every new regulation or court decision ostensibly calculated to resolve the issue. In a healthy society, law is not a proper lever for engineering revolutionary changes. That is, it cannot reach after such a possibility unless one adopts Robespierre's view of its potential—a view that leaves us beyond the protection of constitutional morality, in the hands of a politicized justice that might, in due course, as readily threaten African Americans as assist them in realizing their potential as a free people.

In looking back at the impact of *The Strange Career of Jim Crow*, Woodward claims to have been shocked by how his words were sometimes used. He criticizes "presentists" and "instrumentalists" and declines "to be classified among them, save as an interloper." Yet he also declares of his role in the business that "on the whole" he is "quite unrepentant" and refers with such language to much more than success in calling to the nation's attention the injustice of Jim Crow laws. If, regardless of our national passion for assuming (without risk or expense) self-satisfying, moralistic postures, the truth of history is important, then we must conclude that his most famous book has done about as much harm as good. Like the old laws requiring Jim Crow arrangements in the private sector, it distorted the heritage that it pretended to explain. So much for Woodward's sense of the "adventure" in having written such a volume!

WOODWARD'S LATE WRITINGS

Little that Woodward has authored since *Strange Career* has escaped the shadow of his chief work. Yet most of the material contained in *The Burden of Southern History* (1960) and *American Counterpoint: Slavery and Racism in the North-South Dialogue* (1971) is more impressive to the knowledgeable student of American history than was his more celebrated book. The glaring exception to this generalization is the essay "Equality: The Deferred Commitment," which was first given as an address at Gettysburg College in Pennsylvania in the fall of 1958. In this work, Woodward invokes the Declaration of Independence, understood metaphysically, and declares that after 1875, having first made a commitment to someday realize the full meaning of emancipation, the United States "defaulted on its moral debt" and declared a "moratorium" on it—a delay of "more than eight decades." Here again, Woodward, following the "ticking bomb" theory of the Declaration, *used* history to sanction his own values. Within a few years he repudiated the argument he made about equal rights for freedmen as a northern war aim. Learning more history—especially of the North—he corrected himself in "Seeds of Failure in Radical Race Policy" and "The Northern Crusade against Slavery"—both reprinted in *American Counterpoint.* These later essays are ably argued. The same can be said of Woodward's work on the implacable John Brown of Pottawatomie; his "The Irony of Southern History"; his essay on Melville, Adams, and James; and his thoughtful (though mistaken) "The Search for Southern Identity." In dealing with the Southern Literary Renaissance, he is less satisfactory, depending too much on the aesthetic of alienation to understand the relationship of many southern writers to what is given in their inherited perspective upon the world. But "The Historical Dimension" is nonetheless a useful connection between the critic of southern literature and the southern historian, one that has already produced moments of insight for both disciplines.

In *American Counterpoint,* assembled out of essays written after Woodward's 1961 departure from Johns Hopkins to be Sterling Professor of History at Yale, there are other successful studies, especially "The Southern Ethic in a Puritan World" (a treatment of southern distinctiveness) and "Protestant Slavery in a Catholic World" (a discussion of the humane and paternal character of North American countries). A weak essay in this collection is the one dealing with Woodward's own *Strange Career.* Roper, in his *C. Vann Woodward, Southerner,* argues that somewhere in the 1960s his subject "lost the edge of his former commitments" only to recover his sense of purpose and passion for reform after he was once more enlisted by liberals in Congress to write history with a purpose, looking forward to a possible impeachment of President Richard Nixon in 1974. Roper admires this Woodward and also the retired senior historian who in 1981 testified before a committee of the House of Representatives, urging a readoption of the Voting Rights Act of

1965. I believe that Roper is correct about Woodward's increased fastidiousness concerning the integrity of his discipline, which appears in the 1960s, but incorrect about any renewed tendency toward presentism *after* 1974. Woodward learned a lesson from *The Strange Career of Jim Crow,* which he was not about to "unlearn," whatever his political mood. One proof for this assertion is *Thinking Back*—as artful and gracious a defense of Woodward's career as we could imagine coming from a man who summarily denies that "history need be written for ideological purposes" or that his own views of the region's past were ever "suggested for partisan uses."

What makes us almost believe Woodward's own reconstruction of his career in *Thinking Back* is his gracious absorption of criticism, and his corrections of his original opinions on various subjects. These corrections are even more temperate and thoughtful than what that criticism suggested as an alternate reading of the evidence in question. In reading *Thinking Back* there is no painful penance, even for southern conservatives. This book followed *American Counterpoint* and the professional memoir *Mary Chesnut's Civil War,* an impressive but, as Kenneth S. Lynn has suggested, anachronistic reading of the Civil War period. Even so, there is no overt flavoring of tendentious political distortion in these episodes of hypothetical feminism. Moreover, Woodward, since his retirement in 1978, has continued to write excellent academic journalism, to edit and contribute to a collection on the comparative approach to American history, and to assemble another volume from the papers of the acerbic Mrs. Chesnut of South Carolina—*The Private Mary Chesnut*—her unpublished Civil War diaries, out of which she shaped the more ambitious, imaginative narratives contained in Woodward's Pulitzer Prize–winning volume of 1981. There is evidence of new dimensions in Woodward's thought in the work of his later years and refinements of language and presentation that leave far behind the enthusiasms of his *Tom Watson, Agrarian Rebel* and early work on race; touches of qualification, irony, and understatement. But what is most unusual about Woodward's work since 1960 and about his career is the extent to which they develop out of a reaction to what had not been careful and disengaged in his earlier work—the writings that had made him an oracle and a famous man, perhaps like no other historian in his time.

Concerning Woodward's editorial memory of his partisan past, Roper, in his perceptive biography, writes that "he was unmistakably involved in scholarship which was both leftist and activist." He finds the mature Woodward's "embarrassment" at what he had attempted as a young man "inappropriate" and seems not to recognize what political preoccupation has cost Vann Woodward in the way of academic reputation. The erstwhile president of the

Southern Historical Association, the Organization of American Historians, and the American Historical Association reveals something about himself in *Thinking Back*. This statement in his eighth decade compares his work as a historian to that of the novelist who renders a world but follows "no theory about past, present, and future": like the artist, the mature historian deals in the particular and the concrete. Both men are correct about the portion of reality of which they choose to speak. When Woodward denies that ideological considerations had any influence over his choice of profession, he is clearly improving on his own personal history. But it is also true that those qualities that he now values in his earlier works would have been visible in them even if he had not been a liberal when they were written—qualities of narrative, reportage, characterization, analysis, and exposition visible in his writing from the first—would have been there because he *is* a historian. The genuine ideologue is not so careful about modest, qualified conclusions in arguing *ad verecundiam*. No dreadful division in the soul of this historian can be documented from a little ordinary topicality, since, as Woodward has always maintained, the scholar is inevitably a man or woman of a particular place; living in the present, he or she has obligations to it as well as to the past. With this doctrine any responsible conservative historian would agree. Beyond place and ordinary topicality, Woodward does not usually extend.

Roper is correct in discovering political implications in Woodward's strong commitment to the decorums of his profession. In this attitude there is something more than academic reserve. To say that such rectitude presupposes a certain conservatism is not to imply that Woodward is drifting toward reaction or that he is about to return to the Methodist Church. Rather, it is to insist that the inquiring, skeptical view of the world—the view of the trained scholar in the approach to evidence—will never trust science, dialectics, or "moral suasion" to "fix it": The reputable scholar will recognize how easily all the parts of the human order may be forfeited in the attempt to perfect them. Such a mind operates on the assumption that knowledge is more than power; it is finally a process for refining and improving the self, based on respect for "authorities" and on what appears as written in the original bill of things. It views the ameliorative process as uncertain and unpredictable, working slowly and with difficulty. To be a scholar on these terms is to be suspicious of simplification. In our time the peril of being a historian, of which Woodward speaks so often, comes not from uncritical nostalgia for the past but from too close an identification with the present. This obsession with the present leads scholars into forgetting the difference between describing the world and acting on it. The Woodward who writes in *Thinking Back*, and is explained in *C. Vann Woodward, Southerner*, is a product of the intellectual life of the South. He is both a critic and a reflection of a southern way of life, whose permanent character he denies. In light of his continuing south-ern connection, I am delighted to read his handiwork and to consider the details and the pattern of his biography, though preferably at my ease and sitting in a comfortable chair.

C. Vann Woodward: Pastmaster

DAVID MORRIS POTTER

✳

"What has a historian to do with hope?" was a question posed to Woodward by David Morris Potter, friendliest of critics, and personally closest to him despite interpretive differences. Potter (1910–71), a native of Augusta, Georgia, grew up in Atlanta, attended Emory University, and thus shared some of Woodward's undergraduate experiences and knew some of the same personalities of campus and community. He studied southern history at Yale University, initially with the great conservative Ulrich Bonnell Phillips (who died before Potter completed his Ph.D.) and also with Ralph Henry Gabriel. Like Woodward, a fine interpreter of social-science ideas, Potter was prominent in the so-styled Consensus School of American History, which emphasized a fairly narrow range of ideas, mostly a product of John Locke's constitutionalism and the lack of an aristocratic resistance to a rising bourgeoisie. He produced the Consensus classic, *People of Plenty*. Long a distinguished professor at Yale, Potter at the height of his career removed to Stanford University, but terminal cancer took him away before he could complete his ambitious and promising project, a major interpretation of the causes of the Civil War. Even so, his graceful essays, collected in *The South and the Sectional Conflict* (1968), and the posthumously published study *The Impending Crisis, 1848–1861* (1976) together show some of the direction of a major new interpretation. Irony—in fact, any literary device—was dear to Potter, who also enjoyed and participated in the flowering of the Southern Renaissance. However, he was far more conservative than Woodward (suggesting once to U. B. Phillips's daughter that the public schools are the wrong place to start integration; and the 1950s, the wrong time), and, despite the praise in this essay, he was deeply troubled by the idea of a usable past, because of his disdain for presentism.

✳   ✳   ✳

In 1938, the Macmillan Company published a biography, *Tom Watson, Agrarian Rebel,* by a twenty-nine-year-old assistant professor of social science at the University of Florida, Comer Vann Woodward. At the time the book appeared, Woodward had lived for all but one year in the South. The son of Hugh Allison and Bess (Vann) Woodward, he was born in 1908 in the tiny village of Vanndale, Arkansas, some fifty miles from the Mississippi River. Later, he attended high school at Morrilton, a town of four thousand population at that time, near the center of the state. After two years at a small college in Arkansas, he went to Emory University in Atlanta, where he took his bachelor's degree in 1930. During the next three years he taught English for a year at Georgia Tech, spent a year getting an M.A. at Columbia (1932), went back for another year of teaching at Georgia Tech, and then, in 1934, enrolled at the University of North Carolina at Chapel Hill, where he wrote his study of Watson as a doctoral dissertation. Receiving his Ph.D. in 1937, he married Glenn Boyd Macleod and went to the University of Florida.

Atlanta and Chapel Hill were lively places for a young southerner in the years between 1926 and 1937, for they were two of the strategic points where the postbellum South, running about thirty years behind the calendar, began to move into the twentieth century. For two generations after Appomattox, the compulsive memories of the Lost Cause had held the southern mind in thrall; myth had grown like ivy over the brick and mortar of southern historical experience; sentimentality and veneration had inhibited realism.

But, by the late twenties, the ancient post-Confederate monolith was breaking up. Voices from the outside were coming in. Students at Emory and North Carolina could read in the *American Mercury* H. L. Mencken's monthly excoriations of the South as a Bible Belt and a Sahara of the Bozart (Beaux Arts). Atlanta was the headquarters of the Commission on Interracial Cooperation, founded in 1919, through which Will W. Alexander was working tirelessly to make white southerners aware of the injustice with which southern Negroes were obliged to live. Emory had as a debate coach a young but influential graduate student, Glenn Rainey, whose probing questions led a good many southern youths to reflect for the first time that segregation was perhaps not a necessary part of the order of nature, like sunrise and sunset.[1] Rainey showed the tenor of his social thought by writing an M.A. thesis on the riots in Atlanta in 1906, which exposed racism at its worst. About 1930, Rainey went to an appointment in English at Georgia Tech, where he was so outspoken that at one time the Georgia legislature, which could not fire him, could at least reduce the annual appropriation of the institution where he taught, by the exact amount of his salary, with his name specified in the bill. Both Rainey and Alexander were, significantly, friends of Woodward's.

Alexander, who was very active in securing foundation support for southern schools and scholars, both white and Negro, was more or less in charge of a program of southern fellowships offered by the Social Science Research

Council, and he spotted Woodward as a suitable recipient for one of these fellowships. After holding the fellowship, Woodward was a frequent visitor at the offices of the Interracial Commission. Similarly, Rainey was responsible for the fact that Woodward was twice appointed to teach English at Georgia Tech. Woodward later warmly acknowledged his intellectual appreciation of Rainey in the introduction to his study of Watson.[2]

The changing temper of the times in Atlanta was also suggested by the fact that it was there that Angelo Herndon, a young Negro Communist who had organized demonstrations by unemployed Negroes, was arrested in 1932 and prosecuted under a statute (dating from the Civil War) that made it a capital offense to incite "insurrection."

The Herndon case was like the more famous Scottsboro case, which occurred at about the same time, in the sense that the Communist Party attempted to exploit it to propagate communism rather than to save the accused. Woodward was active in efforts to save Herndon—too active, in fact, to suit Alexander's taste. He became a temporary chairman of a local committee for Herndon's defense and was later left in an awkward position by the party's cynical takeover of the case as a propaganda device.[3]

If Atlanta offered a number of new outlooks upon the South, Chapel Hill offered still others. In fact, the University of North Carolina, in the years when Woodward was there, was experiencing a remarkable period of creative activity. Within the South, it was excelled in the field of literature by Vanderbilt, where John Crowe Ransom, Allen Tate, Robert Penn Warren, Andrew Lytle, Donald Davidson, and others were joining in an "Agrarian" protest against modern industrialism and were proclaiming, for the first time since the Civil War, that the South, as an agrarian stronghold, had a significant message to offer to the nation. But Agrarianism was nostalgic and devoid of a realistic or even recognizable program. By contrast, North Carolina was the headquarters of a pragmatic school of Regionalism, headed by two master sociologists, Rupert B. Vance and Howard W. Odum. Vance and Odum conceived of the South in terms of a regionalism that would no longer isolate Dixie from the national scene but would enable it to share in the prosperity and the constructive activities of the nation, while preserving its own distinctive qualities and values. Woodward, whose father had become head of the Emory Junior College in Oxford, Georgia, met Odum, whose family also lived in Oxford, and Odum helped arrange a General Education Board fellowship, on which Woodward went to Chapel Hill. It was in 1936, while Woodward was there, that Odum completed the work on his great milestone, *Southern Regions of the United States.*[4] Although Woodward was in history, working under the direction of Howard K. Beale, he was much influenced by

Odum and Vance. Also during these years, on a visit to Nashville, he formed a lasting friendship with Robert Penn Warren.[5]

There are certain similarities and certain differences in the point of view of Beale and in the later point of view of Woodward, and it is instructive to compare the two, for Woodward avoided a certain basic fallacy from which Beale did not escape. Though Beale was not a southerner, this was a fallacy to which scholars who combined an intellectual commitment to liberalism with a personal loyalty to the South were peculiarly liable.

Essentially, this fallacy was to regard the South as dominantly "agrarian," as opposed to the "North," which was dominantly industrial. This simple dualism had been put forward by Charles A. Beard, a notably hardheaded and "realistic" historian. It incorporated, of course, a large measure of truth, but in a falsely simplified form it provided southerners with a remarkably effective device for sweeping the awkward questions of slavery and the Negro under the rug. In a sense, this was an old piece of southern legerdemain. The southern acceptance of Jefferson and Lee (two critics of slavery) rather than Calhoun and Davis (two apologists of slavery) as patron saints of the South gave evidence of the South's psychological need for a self-image that would divert focus from the subordination of the Negro, either as a slave or as a sharecropper. The work of such southern historians as William E. Dodd and Frank L. Owsley reinforced this self-image at a more intellectual level by treating the South of Jefferson as normative and the South of Calhoun as an aberration, and by picturing the antebellum South as a yeoman society in which slaveholders were not dominant and slaves were somehow just not a central part of the picture. The curious effects that could be attained by the employment of this concept became particularly evident when it was applied to the Reconstruction period. Treated in this way, the struggles of Reconstruction could be made to appear not as a contest between defenders and opponents of Negro rights but as a battle between the landed ("agrarian") cause and the cause of industrial capitalism, defended by the Radical Republican hirelings of the new postwar robber barons. Did not the Radicals conspire to frame a Fourteenth Amendment, which, under the pretense of protecting the freedmen, would in fact protect corporations from control by the states? So strong was the psychological impulse to identify with the opponents of the robber barons that it lured more than one defender of civil rights as a twentieth-century issue into the anomalous position of defending the southern whites of the 1860s who enacted the Black Codes and resisted every measure in support of Negro citizenship, Negro enfranchisement, distribution of land to Negroes, and all other measures to improve the lot of freedmen. A supreme bit of irony lay in the fact that Andrew Johnson was rehabilitated as the protagonist who held the Radicals at bay, and thus Lloyd Paul Stryker, soon to become a dedicated civil rights zealot, published in 1936 a long and adoring biography of the president who vetoed every piece of civil rights legislation for Negro welfare between 1866 and 1869.[6]

Howard Beale, a devoted liberal and an active member of the American Civil Liberties Union and of an organization for conscientious objectors, accepted this simplified agrarian-industrial dualism, and in 1930 he set the theme for his book *The Critical Year* by picturing the situation after the defeat of the Confederacy in 1865: "an industrialized Northeast, dominated by business principles that were to create the machine-made America of today, faced an agrarian South and West contending for those time honored principles of frontier individualism and plantation aristocracy which had dominated an America that was passing."[7] Beale's sympathies were all with the South.

Woodward's sympathies were with the South also, and he too was a devoted liberal, but he was too shrewd and too realistic to accept the old dualism. Where previous students had seen only what may be called an "external" fight between victorious northern industrialists and defeated southern agrarians, Woodward, far more subtly, perceived that there had always been Whiggish forces in the South, ready to embrace industrial goals, and that the defeat of the Confederacy had set the stage for these forces to take over. Therefore the real struggle was internal—within the South—rather than external. It began at Appomattox and continued so steadily for the remainder of the century that the traditional historical emphasis upon the end of Reconstruction as a major breaking point between two eras was largely illusory. In his first published article, Woodward laid his doctrine on the line: "The class that seized power in Georgia after the overthrow of the Reconstruction regime was neither the old planter oligarchy nor the small farmer. It was the rising class of industrial capitalists."[8] For purposes of protective coloration, these industrial capitalists—notably Joseph E. Brown, John B. Gordon, and Alfred Colquitt—wrapped themselves in the Confederate flag and offered prayers at the shrine of the Old Order. But Woodward was not to be deceived. He recognized that, when the agrarian cause discovered a leader in the person of Tom Watson, that leader found all the forces of the orthodox southern establishment arrayed against him.

This point of view had been partially foreshadowed in previous works—notably in Benjamin B. Kendrick and Alex M. Arnett, *The South Looks at Its Past* (1935)[9]—but most earlier writers had blurred the point by picturing the struggle as a conflict between an Old South party of agrarianism and a New South party of industrialism. But Woodward saw that the agrarian view had not really been dominant in the Old South or the New, and that the conflict was far more than a rivalry between those who looked to the past and those who looked to the future.

Woodward's vision of the so-called Redeemer period between 1877 and the end of the century was a startling one. Previous writers had pictured it as an era of solidarity in the fullest sense. Southern whites had been portrayed as standing united in a single party to prevent the recurrence of Negro rule and the other traumas of Reconstruction. Concurrently, all worked together to fulfill the gospel of a New South, in which industry would restore the vigor of a region prostrated by military defeat. But to Woodward it was a period of profound division, with the "wool-hat boys" conducting the political equivalent of an unsuccessful guerrilla warfare against the Confederate brigadiers.

Woodward's basic recasting of postbellum southern history was accomplished primarily in three books published over a period of thirteen years. First, there was the biography of Watson (1938); second, a study of the Hayes-Tilden election contest of 1876–77, entitled *Reunion and Reaction* (1951); and later in the same year, *Origins of the New South, 1877–1913*. During these years, Woodward had moved from Florida (1937–39) to a visiting appointment at the University of Virginia (1939–40); from Virginia to an associate professorship at Scripps (1940–43); from Scripps to three years of service (1943–46) as a lieutenant in the navy (Office of Naval Intelligence and Naval Office of Public Information); and from there to The Johns Hopkins University. He was to remain at Hopkins for fourteen years and then to move once more, to a Sterling professorship at Yale in 1961.

The historiographical structure that Woodward erected in these three books has won such wide acceptance today that it will be difficult for many readers to grasp how sweepingly his revision altered the prevailing version of southern history. Before his life of Watson was published, there was no mature treatment available on the history of the South since Reconstruction. Historiographically, the whole subject remained in a relatively primitive stage. A number of good monographs existed on limited topics such as, for instance, the history of Populism in a particular state, but the subject as a whole had been only superficially treated in a literature ridden with clichés about the "New South," the "Redeemer governments," the restoration of honest politics through the elimination of the corrupt Negro between 1890 and 1908, etc. Woodward detected these banalities with unerring accuracy, demonstrated their flimsiness with trenchant evidence, and put in their place a mature and comprehensive history of the period from 1877 to 1913, based for the first time on extensive research in the primary sources.

Building upon his basic concept of the internal struggle between agrarian and industrial forces, and the defeat of the agrarians, Woodward was able to revise many important features of the then accepted version of postbellum southern history.

First, he recognized that the Civil War had not solved the problems of southern Negroes by emancipation and that the end of Reconstruction had not solved them by leaving it to southern whites to set the pattern of race relations in the South. In the New South the rigors of tenancy and of agricultural exploitation had their most brutal impact upon the Negro. Moreover, Woodward avoided the practice of using emphasis upon the agrarian tradition, as it had so often been used, to divert attention from the unlovely realities of the biracial system. Indeed, an agrarian emphasis, instead of diverting attention from the Negro, required an especial focus upon the Negro, for the people who had their roots most firmly in the soil were not the landowners, who might even be absentee, but the cultivators, who, more likely than not, were ragged Negroes, owning perhaps a mule and a plow but not owning any land whatsoever. The biography of Watson showed in full detail not only Watson's own ideals of a neo-Jeffersonian agrarian society but also the complex of legal disabilities, self-perpetuating debt, economic handicaps, and social discriminations that prevented black farmers, as well as most whites, from attaining anything like true agrarian status as independent, landowning, diversified farmers who produced for their own use rather than for market.

When this basic approach was applied to specific developments, it exposed an overlay of myth that had completely encrusted many familiar themes, and it led to a remarkable transformation in many images of the past.

To begin with, Woodward's studies demolished the traditional Reconstruction melodrama, which depicted all Republicans as spoilsmen and looters, while the Redeemers were separated from them by an impassable gulf and were the saviors of honesty and probity. Others had made this point before, but none quite so effectively as Woodward. He showed clearly that political opportunists like Joseph E. Brown moved readily back and forth across party lines and that, after the carpetbaggers had been driven out, orthodox Democrats used the "New South Gospel" as a cover for lucrative alliances with prominent robber barons. For instance, John B. Gordon was not only the most eloquent eulogist for the Confederacy but also one of the most valuable allies of Collis P. Huntington.

A second ironical feature of the post-Reconstruction South that Woodward brought into clear focus was the relationship between the "Bourbons" (though Woodward avoids this ambiguous term) and the Negro vote. Post-

Reconstruction mythmakers had created the impression that the Democratic party became the party of white supremacy during the contest with the carpet-baggers in the seventies and that it remained the inveterate foe of Negro participation in politics thereafter. But again Woodward clearly demonstrated that, in 1877, leaders of the southern whites pledged themselves to protect Negro suffrage and that, after Reconstruction, the Democrats of the Black Belt counties, who were the most rock-ribbed Democrats of all, not only countenanced a continuation of Negro voting but even controlled a captive Negro vote and employed it flagrantly to defeat the white voters of the hill counties, who were more numerous than those in the Black Belt. This practice became a characteristic phenomenon in the nineties and was used with deadly effect against the Populists. More than once, as Woodward shows, it was the black vote that "saved the party of White Supremacy."

Transcending all such points as these, however, are the skill and subtlety with which Woodward has handled the interplay of race and class in the half-century after Reconstruction. Very often the truly significant political issues involved interest groups, for instance, the desire of southern promoters to secure a vast federal grant for a railroad across Texas to California, or the desire of property interests to neutralize the power of agricultural protest organizations—both Negro and white—during the nineties. But these issues between interest groups or social classes were made to appear as race issues, partly in order to conceal the conflict of interest among whites, partly to capitalize on racial antipathies, and partly to divide the white and Negro tenant farmers from one another. For instance, the decision of southern congressmen not to obstruct the counting of the electoral vote in favor of Hayes was explained to their constituents in terms of a sacrifice made for the sake of inducing Hayes to withdraw federal troops, thus ensuring the overthrow of carpetbag governments in South Carolina, Louisiana, and Florida. But in fact the apparent willingness of Hayes to countenance the Texas and Pacific legislation, and the unwillingness of Tilden, was decisive in determining the course of many southern congressmen. Similarly, the disfranchisement of the period 1890–1908 was made to appear simply as a device to eliminate voting by Negroes, on the ground that these votes were ignorant, controllable, and corruptible, and that their elimination was necessary to achieve honest elections. But in fact, the disfranchisement of illiterate voters by a literacy test or of impoverished voters by a poll tax had the effect of eliminating many low-income whites as well as virtually all Negroes. In many southern states, the franchise was confined, for practical purposes, to less than half of the male citizenry, and to that part in which property ownership was concentrated.

Significant and revealing insights such as these were set by Woodward in a context of skillful and expert historical exposition. This is a quality not easy to explain, or to illustrate by examples, but yet it has been a vital factor in gaining for Woodward the commanding position that he occupies among American historians. The biography of Watson, although his first book, is the best and most revealing biography that has been written of any southerner living in the period since the Civil War. Moreover, it is one of the foremost psychological studies in American historical literature, even though Woodward abstains completely from offering psychological hypotheses or from applying formal psychological theory. In terms of technique, Woodward is an expert and remarkably versatile historian. For instance, in his *Reunion and Reaction* he has unraveled, from the sources, the story of a secret negotiation between southern Democrats, interested in the Texas and Pacific Railroad project, and northern Republicans, interested in the election of Hayes to the presidency. This negotiation had been hidden for more than seven decades, and the parties to it had taken care to avoid leaving any explicit record. Yet, by the kind of detective work that historians dream about but are seldom challenged to employ, Woodward reconstructed virtually every step in the cryptic process by which the participating parties, highly distrustful of one another and acutely apprehensive of disclosure, made indirect approaches to one another, arrived at a scarcely spoken understanding, and ultimately threw dust in the eyes of the spectator public, so that the real basis of cooperation was hardly suspected.[10]

In all of this work, Woodward combined a solid command of freshly mined data with a singular talent for interpretation and a capacity for perceiving the meaningful item and for construing his material in broad terms. In fact, it may be said that very few historians have combined his closeness in research with his flair for interpretation, and this combination has been a source of great strength to him. The rare quality of the combination becomes evident when one tries to think of other historians who possess the same dual strength. Often, the man who compares with him in one respect falls short in the other. Richard Hofstadter, for instance, may be his peer in interpreting the Populists, but Hofstadter's data seem sketchy and insubstantial compared with Woodward's.[11] On the other hand, John D. Hicks probably researched the Populists quite as thoroughly as Woodward has done, but the thoroughness of his investigation did not give him the insights upon society as a whole that Woodward was able to derive from delving into the southern Populist sources.[12]

From the outset, it was evident that Woodward had exceptional versatility as well as interpretive power. This versatility is perhaps best illustrated by his second book, *The Battle for Leyte Gulf,* which preceded *Reunion and Re-*

action and *Origins of the New South* by four years. As a result of his naval service, mentioned above, he had been drawn into an intensive study of the operations that took place in the Philippine seas in October 1944. Abrupt retooling was demanded of many scholars in the years between 1942 and 1945, but few such conversions were more drastic—or more effective—than this one, which required a historian who had previously dealt only with the South, the Negro, the cotton economy, and the politics of agrarian frustration and discontent, to write expertly of Japanese admirals, naval strategy, the firepower of fighting ships, and the complexities of navigation amid the islands of the Philippine archipelago. The history of naval operations is among the more technical branches of historical study, but Woodward mastered it so thoroughly that he was able to make a clear and vivid narrative of a particularly complex series of naval engagements. Not many books have come out of the Second World War possessing both the narrative and dramatic qualities that appeal to a wide public and the technical virtuosity that wins the respect of professional warriors, but *The Battle for Leyte Gulf* is one of the few that does both.[13]

The Battle for Leyte Gulf is a tour de force that showed what a wide range of things Woodward could do when he put his hand to them. But it is almost purely narrative and reveals little of his historical philosophy. This philosophy is concerned primarily with the relation of history to society's understanding of itself, and it is most clearly evident in a number of brooding, deeply reflective essays that have very far-ranging implications.

It is perhaps natural that his concern with this broader problem grew out of his preoccupation with southern history, especially since southern history, more than most branches of historical study, seems to point up the anomalous relationships between the past, or our image or legend of the past, and the present, or our image of the present. He first came to grips with this question in a presidential address to the Southern Historical Association in 1953, entitled "The Irony of Southern History." Woodward's title was doubtless suggested by Reinhold Niebuhr's *The Irony of American History* (1952),[14] and it shared Niebuhr's skepticism concerning the American idea of progress as an antidote against evil. But its especial focus was to suggest parallels between the moral dogmatisms of the 1860s and those of the 1950s. In brief, this paper began by arguing that a sense of history involves an awareness of the tragic aspects of life, which lie beyond human control. History is incomplete without the dimension of human error and disaster following from error. Human history began, as one might paraphrase it, not with the Garden of Eden and Adamic innocence but with the loss of innocence and the expulsion from the Garden. But the American experience has lacked this basic historical component, because the American record has been one of uninterrupted and invariable "success." Americans were invincible; there was nothing they could not accomplish; they assumed "that American ideals, values and principles invariably prevail in the end. . . . [T]he assumption exposes us to the temptation of believing that we are somehow immune from the forces of history."[15] Hence we have viewed our past in moralistic rather than in historical terms—that is, in terms of categorical choice between right and wrong, rather than in terms of the ambiguities and moral compromises inherent in the human condition. Hence we are especially prone to take dogmatic or absolutist positions—positions that are untempered by a sense of the magnitude of the gap between human aspiration and human attainment. In developing this theme, Woodward drew a parallel between the southern defense of slavery in the 1840s and 1850s and the American defense of capitalism in the 1940s. The South in the 1840s needed intersectional friends, especially in Western Europe. Both sought to win these friends. Yet the South made the mistake of insisting that the West accept "a system totally unadapted to the conditions and needs of the territories and often offensive to their moral sensibilities" (181). The South also "abandoned its tradition of tolerance" and imposed a rigid demand for orthodoxy on the subject of slavery. The United States might now profit from this experience, Woodward suggested, first, to avoid alienating its potential Western European friends by demanding that they embrace a species of capitalism that many of them regarded with disapproval, and second, to avoid reducing its own vigor by imposing internal controls upon the free discussion of alternatives to the sacrosanct system of capitalism.

But it was not only the South that offered a warning example. There was also a lesson to be learned from the position of the North in the Civil War crisis. For the North had been "overwhelmingly moralistic in its approach." People who subscribe to the moralistic view tend "to appeal to a higher law to justify bloody and revolting means in the name of a noble end" (186). This had happened in the Civil War, and to clinch his argument Woodward quoted Kenneth Stampp: "Yankees went to war animated by the highest ideals of the nineteenth-century middle classes. . . . But what the Yankees achieved—for their generation at least—was a triumph not of middle-class ideals but of middle-class vices. The most striking products of their crusade were the shoddy aristocracy of the North and the ragged children of the South. Among the masses of Americans, there were no victors, only the vanquished" (187).

"The Irony of Southern History" appeared at the height of the McCarthy era and an early phase of the Cold War. It was, of course, written with reference to these circumstances. In it, Woodward showed more clearly than in any of his previous writings his unusually strong conviction that history should speak to the present. With his subtlety of mind and his disciplined awareness that our image of the past is the product of historians rather than of history, he of course avoided the simplistic ideas that "history repeats itself" or that analogues are ever complete. The context of "The Irony" reminded the reader that slavery was not capitalism, the western states and territories were not the nations of Europe, and the moral validity of a crusade against slavery was not interchangeable with the moral validity of a crusade against communism. But if the lessons were not read too literally, he believed, the past had a relevance not only in shaping the present but in guiding our response to the present. In the case under discussion, the past might serve to remind us that ideological dogmatism could separate a society from its friends and could impair the realism of the society itself; that there was no direct ratio between the degree of moral purpose that went into a crusade and the degree of moral gain that came out, even when the crusade proved "successful"; and that war can have victors without necessarily having winners.

In 1958, Woodward returned to his efforts to relate the unique experience of the South in the past to the generalized experience of American society in the present. In "The Search for Southern Identity," he observed that, economically, the South, so long a distinctive region, was becoming more and more homogenous with the rest of the country; the "Bulldozer Revolution" was making it so. With the traditional doctrines of white supremacy discredited, the distinctive southern feature of segregation was also about to disappear. But when these tangible differentials were obliterated, would there be any distinctive feature left to keep the South from being "submerged under a national steamroller" and rendered "virtually indistinguishable from the other urban-industrial areas of the nation"? Yes, said Woodward, the South would still have its distinctive past experience: this experience included military defeat and subjugation and economic poverty and frustration in a nation that had known only victory and affluence; it included the psychological, subconscious awareness of the guilt of slavery and of discrimination against the Negro in a nation that has known only a complacent and two-dimensional "innocence"; it included the life of an organic society, with strong communal ties and a coherent social order, in a nation that has been structured by rational abstractions operating upon isolated individuals outside of any nexus of concrete personal ties such as one found in the kinship systems of the South. In this essay, the discourse of the past with the present was brief, but it was pungent. Why did it matter at all whether southerners preserved any distinc-tive identity? And if they did preserve it, why did it matter for them to rec-ognize it? It mattered because

> The South . . . remains more American by far than anything else, and
> has all along. After all, it fell to the lot of one Southerner from Virginia
> to define America. The definition he wrote in 1776 voiced aspirations
> that were rooted in his native region before the nation was born. The
> modern Southerner should be secure enough in his national identity to
> escape the compulsions of less secure minorities to embrace uncritically
> all the myths of nationalism. He should be secure enough also not to
> deny a regional heritage because it is at variance with national myth. It
> is a heritage that should prove of enduring worth to him as well as to his
> country.[16]

"The Search for Southern Identity," like "The Irony of Southern History," dealt with the relation of past and present, especially in terms of the South and the southerner. But in "The Age of Reinterpretation," a paper delivered at the meeting of the American Historical Association in 1959, Woodward turned in far more general terms to the problem of the role of the historian as an intermediary between the experience of men of the past and the under-standing of men of the future. In this essay, which is widely regarded as his most significant single piece of work and as one of the major contributions to the interpretation of American history, he pointed out, first, the rapidity of change in modern society, and the perspective that this change gives us upon the past. Since 1945, we have entered an age of thermonuclear weapons and intercontinental missiles, and we have seen the end of the world hegem-ony of the nations of Western Europe. As these epochal changes occur, they throw much of our past experience into a new light. To begin with, they give us a focus, for the first time, upon the fact that for a century and a half the United States enjoyed a unique condition of "free security." During this era of immunity from military or naval threats from other countries, we did not have to use our resources for the maintenance of armament or the energies of our young men for military service. In terms of economic growth alone, this freedom to direct all our strength into economically productive activities, without diverting it into military preparation, was an inestimable boon and contributed significantly to the rapid rate of American economic growth in the nineteenth century. Because of its pervasive nature, this security also had some far-reaching side effects. For instance, it got us into the careless prac-tice, in rare occasions of crisis, of going to war first and preparing for it after-ward. Another, more important, consequence was that it enabled us to get along without real concentrations of political power. Distrustful of power as we had been ever since the time of George III, we happily accepted this opportunity to dispense with it, and set up a governmental system that, through the separation of powers and through checks and balances, was subject to long intervals of governmental paralysis, deadlock, or inertia. But our free security enabled us to afford the luxury of a political system that operated only intermittently.

Second, our passage into the nuclear age now enables us to see the history of war in a new light. When war occurs today, we try to keep it a limited war, meaning a nonnuclear war, but all wars before 1945 were nonnuclear wars. As such, they had relevance to one another. The warriors of World War II might still learn from the operations of the Civil War, just as the generals who fought between the Potomac and the James might profit by studying Napoléon's maxims or the military doctrine of Jomini. But changes in the powers of destruction since 1945 have rendered most of our past military experience obsolete: "We can already see that the vast fleets that concentrated off the Normandy beaches and at Leyte Gulf, or the massed armies that grappled in the Battle of the Bulge or across the Russian Steppes, or for that matter the old-fashioned bomber squadrons that droned back and forth across the English Channel year after year dropping what the air force now contemptuously calls 'iron bombs' were more closely related to a remote past than to a foreseeable future." [17]

Here, as I read it, Woodward is saying that devotees of history frequently seek to justify their study on the ground that there is always a continuity between the past and the present. The study of the past, it is assumed, will reveal the continuity and thus will offer guidance for the present. But, he implies further, this assumption is sometimes wrong. In times of very rapid and fundamental change, the continuity between the past and the present is broken. The task of the historian is not simply to trace the continuity, even when it is tenuous, but to examine the relationship between past and present for the purpose of exposing the discontinuity as much as for emphasizing the continuity. For we could be as dangerously misled by an apparition of continuity that does not really exist as by a failure to recognize continuities that are genuine.

Much of the existing historical literature was written when "free security" was taken for granted and when wars were fought with limited weapons, and that was taken for granted also. It will be a large task to rewrite this history in a way that takes account of our new awareness that these factors were peculiar to a given place and time, and were neither universal nor immutable. But an even greater body of the existing literature was Europe-centered. This literature, also, was most pervasive. Non-Europeans as well as Europeans shared the orientation that saw Europe as the center of the world. "The . . . assumptions of Europocentric history have very largely shaped the interpretation of Asiatic, African, and other non-European history . . . for Europe successfully marketed its historiography abroad, along with its other cultural products, in remote and exotic climates" (15). The recognition, at last, of the restrictiveness of this view creates a need for the rewriting of a very substantial proportion of all of modern history from a new standpoint.

From these three new challenges to the historian, Woodward turned back, near the end of his essay, to an evocative and statesmanlike affirmation, again, of the role of the historian. The historians of this generation, he asserted, have a peculiar responsibility as intermediaries between a past that could not foresee the future and a future that may not be able to understand the past. For these historians carry with them into the new order a personal experience of the old:

> Americans among them will remember a time when security was assumed to be a natural right, free and unchallengeable. Among them also will be men of many nations who manned the ships and fought the battles of another age of warfare. And nearly all of this generation of historians will have been educated to believe that European culture was Civilization and that non-European races, if not natively inferior, were properly under perpetual tutelage. They will be the only generation of historians in history who will be able to interpret the old order to the new order with the advantage and authority derived from firsthand knowledge of the two ages and participation in both. (18)

Here Woodward again affirmed his faith that it is not enough for historians to understand the past; they must also interpret it to those who live in the present. In the final paragraph of "The Age of Reinterpretation," he made this affirmation even more explicit. The accelerated process of historical change, he said, gives a peculiar urgency to the public demand for answers to questions about the past and its relation to the present and the future:

> If historians evade such questions, people will turn elsewhere for the answers, and modern historians will qualify for the definition that Tolstoi once formulated for academic historians of his own day. He called them deaf men replying to the questions that nobody puts to them. If, on the other hand, they do address themselves seriously to the historical questions for which the new age demands answers, the period might justly come to be known in historiography as the age of reinterpretation. (19)

In this statement, renouncing a traditional concept of restrictions upon the academic historian, Woodward formally enunciated a position that, in operative terms, he had occupied from the beginning of his career. Consistently, his writing had reflected a purpose to identify the true values of the past and to make them meaningful to his contemporaries. In his quest for values, he held to two especially.

One of these was from his own birth and rearing—the value of the southern heritage. In "The Search for Southern Identity," he had said, "After Faulkner, Wolfe, Warren, and Welty, no literate Southerner could remain unaware of his heritage or doubt its enduring value." [18] This belief in the enduring values of the South is deep-seated, and when Woodward totally rejects the traditionally southern attitudes on race, he regards it not as a rejection of southernism but as a rejection of a spurious value that has discredited the true southern position. But he is still capable of resenting even attacks on biracialism when they run over into disparagement of the South as a whole. This fact was evident in his courteous but nonetheless devastating review of Dwight Dumond's indiscriminately worshipful treatment of the abolitionists in a work entitled *Antislavery*. [19] It was evident also in some pointed comments in his essay "From the First Reconstruction to the Second" (1965):

> The South has lately had its "Epitaph" written and its "Mystique" debunked. The implication would seem to be that the South's disputed "distinctiveness" and Southern identity inhere essentially in retrograde race policies and prejudices. With the gradual disappearance of these, Southerners are expected to lose their identity in a happily homogenized nation. Quite apart from the South's preferences, there are other reasons for skepticism in this matter. The South has long served the nation in ways still in great demand. It has been a moral lightning rod, a deflector of national guilt, a scapegoat for stricken conscience. It has served the country much as the Negro has served the white supremacist—as a floor under self-esteem. This historic role, if nothing else, would spare the region total homogenization, for the national demand for it is greater than ever. [20]

To say that the southern heritage had enduring value meant that it must not be defined in terms of things that lacked value—such as segregation and the doctrine of white supremacy. Hence Woodward rejected Ulrich Phillips's formulation of "The Central Theme of Southern History," which identified the South in terms of the region's conviction that the South "shall be and remain a white man's country." [21] There is, of course, copious and unedifying evidence that this conviction has been an enduring element in the quality of southernism, and people who do not like the South are quite ready to make racism a prominent factor in their analysis of southernism. But precisely because Woodward attached enduring value to some aspects of the southern tradition, he could not accept their view. The South might have, in one side of its character, a quality of racism, discrimination, and repression, but it also had, on the other side, a record of Jeffersonian liberalism. It must be saved from its worse side by an appeal to its better side. Once before, the South had made the mistake of giving "priority to the worse side by choosing to identify its whole cause with one institution [slavery] that was most vulnerable," and it had paid dearly for this folly. This must not happen again: "if Southernism is allowed to become identified with a last ditch defense of segregation, it will increasingly lose its appeal among the younger generation. Many will be tempted to reject their entire regional identification, even the name 'Southern,' in order to disassociate themselves from the one discredited aspect." [22]

As a comment on the consequences of identification with a discredited cause, this observation was, no doubt, pragmatic and sagacious, but, in terms of historical method, it possessed startling implications. For it clearly implied that the degree of the historian's emphasis upon the identification of the South with slavery and later with segregation should be determined not by the actual extent of the South's commitment to these practices, but by the effect that such an identification would have upon the loyalties of southerners to the better values of southernism. The use of history to sanction meritorious values would take a priority over the use of it to portray realistically some of the evils of the past.

To leave the statement at this point would do an injustice to Woodward by picking out one strand of his thought and separating it from the broader fabric of which this strand was a part. This broader context was one of scrupulous adherence to rigorous historical criteria. As much as almost any contemporary American historian, Woodward has approached his material with a dedicated purpose to take the whole record into account, to see all sides of a topic, to qualify and hedge his generalizations, and to avoid the ease of simplification. These traits are strikingly evident, for instance, if one compares his treatment of slavery with the treatments of William E. Dodd and Frank L. Owsley. All three of them were southerners; all were committed to a liberal's sympathy with the dirt farmer; and all were embarrassed by the southern treatment of the Negro. Dodd and Owsley expressed this embarrassment by avoiding the issue—Dodd by arguing that the South would, on its own initiative, have gotten rid of slavery but for the distorting effect of extraneous forces; Owsley by constructing an image of a South populated by "plain folk" (white) or yeomen—a land in which slaveholders were not important and slaves were, somehow, not quite visible.[23] Woodward, by contrast, faced up to the problems of racism, and the latter half of his biography of Watson is a grim record of Negrophobia, blatant discrimination, and lynch law, just as the first half is a record of Watson's effort, in the first phase of his life, to achieve an accord between Negroes and whites in the Populist movement. ("The People's Party," declared Watson, "says to these two men [the Negro farmer and the white farmer], 'You are made to hate each other because upon that hatred is rested . . . the financial despotism which enslaves you both.'")[24]

Woodward found an ideal topic in Watson, because the early part of Watson's career brought Woodward's second major value, liberalism, into conjunction with his first, the value of the southern tradition properly understood. The early Watson hated economic exploitation, hated racial antagonism, denounced lynch law, and demanded recognition of the legal rights of Negroes. Woodward, looking for such experience in the past as would be meaningful to the present, found it, almost to perfection, in the career of Watson. That career did not conceal the grim and realistic actuality that segregation and injustice to the Negro dominated the southern scene in the first two decades of this century, but it did show that *there had been an alternative*. Watson had seen the alternative, though his vision later failed and he lost sight of it. To Woodward, with his conviction that the historian must reconstruct the past accurately and at the same time make it speak to the present, the accuracy of the reconstruction lay in the recognition of Watson's failure and in the ultimate ascendancy of the worst features of his nature. But the message for the present lay in the fact that Watson had for a time seen a vision of a better way. The better way was not illusory; it had been a viable alternative. It failed, not because inevitable forces caused it to fail, but because men who might have grasped it did not do so. Other men, in the present, might do so. No deterministic force, in Woodward's belief, foredoomed their effort, for as he has declared, "I am not a determinist of any sort."[25] The first lesson of the past to the present is that people have choices and that no iron law of the operation of blind forces prevents them from exercising these choices.

This viewpoint was peculiarly pertinent to southern attitudes toward segregation, for white southerners showed a marked tendency to believe that the sharp separation of Negroes and whites was as old as the world, a reflex of basic human nature, and quite beyond the reach of any social policy. Many developments in the 1930s and 1940s led liberals to believe, with increasing conviction, that segregation must be done away with and that social attitudes toward questions of race must be changed in order that racial relations might change. This conviction was already strong when the decision of the Supreme Court in the case of *Brown v. Board of Education* was handed down in May 1954. When the Court spoke, the first reaction throughout the country was to ask, how would the South respond? Would it show the old fierce resistance to "outside" attempts to change the harsh taboos of racial separation, or would it comply with the decision of the Court? Here was a time, indeed, for the past to speak to the present in other than purely traditional terms.

During the following autumn, Woodward delivered the James W. Richard lectures at the University of Virginia. In 1955, while Woodward was Harmsworth Professor of American History at Oxford, they were published under the title of *The Strange Career of Jim Crow,* and they quickly became and have remained his most famous book. These lectures really do not compare with his *Watson* or his *Origins of the New South* as major works of history, but they will nevertheless require almost as extensive discussion here, because of the misunderstandings and controversy that they engendered and the fundamental questions that they raised.

In the first chapter of *The Strange Career,* significantly entitled "Forgotten Alternatives," Woodward sought to develop a point that he had stated clearly, in more condensed form, in *Origins of the New South* (209–12), namely, that the formal structure of legal segregation that the South believed had existed forever had, in fact, not existed in full form until some years after the end of Reconstruction. True, he recognized, separation began soon after the Civil War in the churches, and it began in the schools as soon as former slaves began to go to school. But there was, he believed, scarcely any "evidence of a movement to make segregation universal. . . . More than a decade was to pass after Redemption [the end of Reconstruction] before the first Jim Crow law was to appear upon the law books of a Southern state, and more than two decades before the older states of Virginia, North Carolina, and South Carolina were to adopt such laws." [26] In elaboration of this statement, Woodward proceeded to quote two northern travelers, one British traveler, two southern editorials, one southern white, and one Negro, all seven of whom testified that Negroes and whites in the South mingled, with very little tension and with considerable spontaneity and ease, in public saloons, dining rooms, trains, streetcars, theaters, and soda fountains. If this evidence was limited, it was explicit and seemingly quite reliable. With scrupulous care, Woodward also pointed out that there had never been a "golden age of race relations" in the South and that "the evidence of race conflict and violence, brutality and exploitation in this very period is overwhelming" (25). But the overall impression, formed by many readers, was that this was a subsidiary point.

Having made this qualification, he then moved on to say that, "before the South capitulated completely to the doctrines of the extreme racists, three alternative philosophies of race relations were put forward" (26): one a conservative or aristocratic philosophy, which accepted a responsibility for the paternal care of the Negroes and regarded all lower-class people, either Negro or white, with very much the same condescension; another, a radical philosophy, which sought to form a political combination of Negro and white dirt farmers against those who were economically exploiting them; and third, a liberal philosophy, which, on principle, advocated equal rights and protection for all citizens. He briefly traced each of these three and then again entered a disclaimer: he did not wish to exaggerate the degree of interracial harmony. There were Negrophobes and hypocrites in all of these camps. Indeed, he concluded:

> My only purpose has been to indicate that things have not always been the same in the South. In a time when the Negroes formed a much larger proportion of the population than they did later, when slavery was a live memory in the minds of both races, and when the memory of the hardships and bitterness of Reconstruction was still fresh, the race policies accepted and pursued in the South were sometimes milder than they became later. The policies of proscription, segregation, and disfranchisement that are often described as immutable "folkways" of the South, impervious alike to legislative reform and armed intervention, are of a more recent origin. The effort to justify them as a consequence of Reconstruction and a necessity of the times is embarrassed by the fact that they did not originate in those times. And the belief that they are immutable and unchangeable is not supported by history. (47)

Despite all Woodward's care to insert caveats, qualifiers, and disclaimers, *The Strange Career* ran into two difficulties. First was the problem that, when the past speaks to the present, it cannot speak to everyone alive in the present but must speak to particular groups. When Woodward delivered the Richard Lectures at Charlottesville, he was speaking to such a group—to southern whites who needed to learn that segregation had not been included among the Ten Commandments. If he had been able to limit his message to the audience for whom it was intended, there would never have been any confusion. The audience knew that segregation and discrimination had been the dominant patterns of the South, and what Woodward told them was that these patterns had not been absolute or universal or immutable. This was a useful fact for them to learn. But as soon as the lectures were published, they reached a vast audience. Ironically, Woodward's least substantial book was the one that made his public, as distinguished from his professional, reputation. More than any modest man could possibly have anticipated, he found himself addressing a vast, amorphous audience of people, many of whom had formed their impressions of the South from *Gone with the Wind* or *Tobacco Road,* who regarded the region as a never-never land, and who, unlike the people of Charlottesville, were prepared to believe anything. Many of these avid readers wishfully read into Woodward's lectures an idyllic image of a South in which race antagonism did not rear its unlovely head until the twentieth century.

To state this in another way, historians who seek to interpret the life of the past to the people of the present usually wind up by giving less attention to reconstructing what the past was "really" like than to identifying the misconceptions of people in the present and devising ways to correct these misconceptions. But since all sorts of various people entertain all sorts of various misconceptions, the labor of correcting the misconceptions impels historians to address themselves to a focus that is neither unitary nor fixed. What one writes will be relative in any case, but instead of being relative to what happened to a determinate group of people in the past, it becomes relative to what misconceptions are held, at a given moment, by indeterminate groups of people in the present. This task becomes a labor of Hercules. Perhaps the labor it most closely resembles is that of cleaning the Augean stables.

The second difficulty encountered by *The Strange Career* arose from the fact that, when a historian has a strong ideological commitment, a tension may be set up between his or her devotion to the commitment and his or her devotion to realism for its own sake. In Woodward's own terms, it is ironically conceivable that, when a deaf man gives answers to questions that no one is asking, he may be worth listening to precisely because he is more concerned with what he himself sees than with what other people, at the moment, want to know. In any case, Woodward had undertaken the arduous task of finding answers in the southern past to questions that people were asking in 1954. This undertaking never led him to the obvious fallacies of simpler minds engaged in the same task—the fallacy, for instance, of believing that the South seriously considered abolishing slavery as late as 1830. But it did lead him to an inner struggle in which his historical realism was pitted against his liberal urge to find constructive meaning in the past for the affairs of the present. His realism never lost hold, but his liberal urge constantly impelled him to emphasize viewpoints that his realism constantly impelled him to qualify and dilute.

This inner struggle was, I believe, especially evident in *The Strange Career*. It was evident in the sense that the array of evidence presented, though by no means all on one side, would lead a reader to minimize the importance of segregation in the South in the 1870s, 1880s, and 1890s, far more than the general bulk of other evidence would do.[27] This fact became apparent subsequently, from a series of intensive analyses of Negro-white relations in the late nineteenth century by a number of investigators working state by state: Charles E. Wynes for Virginia (1961), Frenise A. Logan for North Carolina (1964), and Joel Williamson for South Carolina (1965).

Of these "revisionists," only Wynes discussed Woodward by name, and Wynes was the least disposed of the three to take issue with him. The picture of segregation in Virginia between 1870 and 1900, as Wynes saw it, was mixed. Often the Negro who sought to frequent places of public resort met with rebuffs, but "[o]ccasionally the Negro met no segregation, when he entered restaurants, bars, waiting rooms, and other places of public amusement." "The Woodward thesis," he thought, "is essentially sound," but "most of the time, however, he [the Negro] did meet segregation, opposition, or eviction." For North Carolina, Logan emphasized the dominance of segregation somewhat more: "The most effective limitations . . . on the relationship between white and Negro were the unwritten agreements among the whites that any approach to 'social equality' should be resisted at all costs. The matter of social equality was most sharply focused upon when it revolved around the segregation of Negroes on public carriers, in waiting rooms, and in hotels and restaurants." But it was Williamson's conclusions that were most at variance with Woodward's. His evidence seemed to show that "the physical separation of the races was the most revolutionary change in relations between whites and Negroes in South Carolina during Reconstruction." "The pattern of separation was fixed in the minds of the whites almost simultaneously with the emancipation of the Negro. By 1868, the physical color line had, for the most part, already crystallized." But the real separation, he continued, was "mental separation. . . . The rigidity of the physical situation, set as it was like a mosaic in black and white, itself suggested the intransigence of spirit which lay behind it . . . the heartland of racial exclusiveness remained inviolate; and South Carolina had become, in reality, two communities—one white and one Negro."[28]

More telling, perhaps, than any of these analyses of the postbellum period was Richard C. Wade's study in 1964, *Slavery in the Cities*. Woodward had regarded it as almost axiomatic that "segregation would have been impractical under slavery"—that where slavery existed, the circumstances giving rise to segregation did not exist. But Wade presented evidence to show that in the towns of the South long before the Civil War, where the surveillance of the Negroes, characteristic of the slave system, could no longer be maintained, "the distinction between slave and free Negro was erased; race became more important than legal status; and a pattern of segregation emerged inside the broader framework of the peculiar institution."[29]

In later editions of *The Strange Career,* Woodward scrupulously took note of these studies, and in fact he anticipated them as early as 1957, in a foreword to the first paperback edition, in which he recognized that segregation was initially foreshadowed in the cities, even before the end of slavery, and in which he called attention to a number of early segregation laws (Mississippi and Florida, 1865; Texas, 1866; Tennessee, 1881),[30] which were inconsistent with his earlier statement that it was more than a decade after Redemption "before the first Jim Crow law was to appear upon the law books of a Southern state."

If Woodward's dislike of segregation influenced him to minimize its prevalence, some critics have also felt that his desire to demonstrate the historical possibility of close and harmonious working relationships between Negroes and whites led him to overemphasize the importance of the cooperation between Negro and white farmers' alliances in the Populist contests of 1892. Again, this is very much a matter of emphasis. But, in any case, Woodward had not failed to point out that Watson himself, the chief architect of the cooperation, had recognized that race antagonisms were extremely real and that the race issue was a great handicap to southern Populism ("Bryan had *no everlasting and overshadowing Negro question to hamper and handicap his progress.* I HAD," said Watson).[31]

But there was one other case in which his impulse to find sanction in the past for ideas that he approves in the present may have led him to take a position from which he later felt impelled to withdraw. In 1958, in the *American Scholar* he published an essay, "Equality, the Deferred Commitment." In this paper he discussed the war aims of the Civil War: first, simply the preservation of the Union; later, freedom for the slaves; and finally, near the end, equality for the freedmen. The commitment to this third aim, he recognized, was never as clear-cut as the first two commitments—there was never an equality proclamation. But though "made piece-meal . . . and with full implications not spelled out until after the war . . . it [the commitment] was made." Challenged by southern aggression against Negro rights after the war, the radical Republicans "proceeded to make equality as much the law of the land as freedom." Citing the Fourteenth and Fifteenth Amendments and the Civil Rights Acts of 1866 and 1875, Woodward concluded that:

by every device of emphasis, repetition, reenactment, and reiteration, the radical lawmakers and Constitution-amenders would seem to have nailed down all loose ends, banished all ambiguity, and left no doubt whatever about their intention to extend Federal protection to Negro equality. So far as it was humanly possible to do so by statute and constitutional amendment, America would seem to have been fully committed to the principle of equality.[32]

Here again, Woodward was seeking to make the past speak to the present. The past had made a promise to American Negroes and then defaulted on it. It was the obligation of the present to honor and fulfill the promise. But some other scholars hesitated to read the promise of the past in this way or to agree that the United States had made a firm commitment a century ago to racial equality in the full sense. For instance, W. R. Brock, in his influential study *An American Crisis* (1963) wrote that "racial equality was a hypothesis which was generally rejected. It was not accepted in the North any more than it was in the South and even abolitionists were anxious to disclaim any intention of forcing social contacts between the races and all shied away from the dread subject of racial amalgamation."[33]

Brock did not go into much detail about the enactment of the specific measures that were regarded as embodying the principle of equality, but also in 1963, in a doctoral dissertation on radical Republican policy toward the Negro, written at Yale just before Woodward went there, Selden Henry presented a full and close analysis of the many complexities, parliamentary and otherwise, attending the enactment of the principal "equalitarian" measures. Henry made a strong, detailed demonstration that none of these measures involved a clear-cut showdown between the advocates and the opponents of equality for Negroes, and his evidence indicated that opposition to full equality remained in the ascendant throughout Reconstruction.[34]

Woodward, it should be said, had always recognized, even in his "deferred commitment" essay, that there were many crosscurrents in the public attitude toward the freedmen and many mental reservations in the acceptance of equality, but as he considered the problem further, he began to stress the qualifications more than the thesis. By 1965 he was writing, "Even in [the Civil Rights acts, the Reconstruction acts, and the Fourteenth and Fifteenth Amendments]—the very legal foundation for the new order of freedom and equality—can be found the compromises, half-measures, and ambivalences that are in essence concessions to racism." In another year, he made his reversal explicit in an essay in which he cited Henry and declared, "On the issue of Negro equality, the party remained divided, hesitant, and unsure of its purpose. The historic commitment to equality it eventually made was lacking in clarity, ambivalent in purpose, and capable of numerous interpretations." A footnote adds the laconic comment: "This admittedly represents a change from views earlier expressed on the subject by the author."[35]

The urgency of Woodward's desire to find answers in the past that would aid in the quest for solutions of the problems of the present must have had some effect upon these views of the past. If it could be shown historically that legalized segregation was a relatively new phenomenon, and that promises of equality were a century old, it might be easier to induce people to abandon segregation and to accord equality to Negroes. Since Woodward himself later modified or even changed his position on both of these matters, it seems reasonable to suppose that the tension between his devotion to liberal goals and his devotion to historical realism distorted his image of the past, at least for a time and to a limited degree.

But, as has already been suggested, Woodward never ignored the complexities. He never failed to point out that he was engaged in weighing conflicting bodies of evidence and that important evidence existed that ran counter to the view he was presenting. Always committed to the historian's task of translating the past to make it intelligible to the present, he was also always scrupulous not to translate too freely. But what he did not reckon with was that many of his readers, with far less disciplined ideological commitments than his, and with painfully limited appreciation of the historical context in which he was writing, did some translating of their own of his translation. The result was that many such readers came away from his writings with the totally fallacious notion that the American people had accepted Negroes as equals a hundred years ago and that a utopia of racial harmony and goodwill had prevailed until the 1890s.

Woodward has commented unhappily on the strange career that *The Strange Career of Jim Crow* has experienced. In the preface to the second revised edition (1966), he said: "Books that deal with subjects over which current political controversy rages are prone to uses and interpretations beyond the author's intentions or control. The present work has proved no exception and the author has been embarrassed by finding it cited—and misinterpreted—for purposes with which he sympathizes as well as for purposes he deplores." More recently, in *Harper's Magazine*, speaking of himself in the third person, he wrote:

> One historian suggested that the full blown system of legally enforced segregation was not an immediate sequel of Appomattox, only to find

himself cited as authority for the doctrine that Jim Crow was superficially rooted and easily eradicated. And when he called attention to
the union of Negroes and whites in Southern Populism, he was interpreted as prophesying millennial developments in politics. It is no news
to teachers, of course, that the lessons taught are not always the lessons
learned.[36]

If Woodward has been troubled to find his words read in a way that he did
not intend, he has clearly been much more troubled to have his hopes for the
steady advancement and peaceful success of the civil rights movement frustrated. With a liberal's conviction that truth about the past can contribute
with certainty to win public backing for voluntary, broadly based social
progress, Woodward always intended for history to serve the cause of civil
rights without sacrificing its integrity, and for the civil rights cause to prevail
without destroying the vital values of the southern tradition. In the first edition of *The Strange Career*, he spoke of "the need of the times for whatever
light the historian has to shed upon a perplexing and urgent problem." He
also asserted that the changes in "the old system of disfranchisement and
segregation" were so extensive that they could be termed a "New Reconstruction." His tone, as he himself expressed it, was one of "restrained optimism," and in the 1957 edition he said, "In spite of resistance and recent
setbacks, therefore, the preponderant evidence points to the eventual doom
of segregation in American life and the triumph of the Second Reconstruction
in *the long run*." [37]

One feature that accentuated the optimistic tenor of *The Strange Career*
was that, in it, Woodward did not, in fact, attempt to treat the whole biracial
system, in all its historical, economic, and cultural complexities. Instead, he
dealt quite explicitly with only one feature, namely, the structure of formal,
institutional arrangements—mostly in the form of statutes or ordinances—
by which the separation of whites and Negroes had been enforced. Indeed it
was this structure, strictly speaking, that constituted the "Jim Crow" phenomenon. The Jim Crow structure, of course, did much to maintain the
whole system of biracialism and was so interwoven with the whole system
that some optimists mistakenly believed that biracialism could not exist
without it. Woodward did not make this error, but he did restrict his focus
to one aspect of the system, and to the most vulnerable aspect of all. Once
the *Brown* decision had been made, it was relatively easy to sweep away all
the accumulation of public regulations that had imposed legal disabilities and
de jure segregation upon Negroes. After the court decisions were reinforced
by a series of civil rights acts by Congress in 1957, 1960, and 1964, and

by a voting rights act in 1965, it was possible to say, as Woodward did in the 1966 edition of *The Strange Career,* that "Jim Crow as a legal entity was dead."[38]

But written statutes in books are far easier to change than educational differentials, employment differentials, residential differentials, and other disparities that have already molded the society and irrevocably shaped the lives of millions. Also, formal enactments are easier to get at than covert attitudes and unspoken feelings of apartness. Therefore, even at a time when Jim Crow was dying, racial tensions were becoming in some ways more acute. Because of this, readers of the 1966 edition of *The Strange Career* were brought abruptly at the end of the book to the disconcerting realization that, while their attention had been focused upon the slow demise of formal segregation, the principal issues of interracial antagonism had been shifting elsewhere as the black revolution appeared and changed the course of the civil rights movement. Only five days after Lyndon Johnson signed the Voting Rights Act, which might be regarded as the final step in the elimination of Jim Crow, the Watts Riot broke out in Los Angeles.

Just as the abolition of slavery had ended one stage of the relationship of Negroes and whites in America without solving the problem of that relationship, the abolition of Jim Crow ended another stage, but again without solving the problem of the relationship. Woodward recognized this in three final paragraphs in the 1966 edition, in which he asserted vaguely that "civil rights laws were not enough" and that "broader and more drastic remedies" were needed.[39]

Woodward's impulse to think of the handicaps of African Americans in terms of formal segregation was, of course, in line with most of the thinking on the subject during the first decade after the *Brown* decision. Most of the reform activity of that decade was directed toward destroying the barriers of legal separation in schools, buses, waiting rooms, restaurants, etc. So long as this was so, the decline of Jim Crow gave the deceptive appearance of being equivalent to the ending of racial tensions. For a long time no one asked about the cultural, occupational, economic, and other disparities that would be left when formal segregation was swept away, and about the antagonisms that might develop when discrimination and Negro disadvantages were found to remain after all legal inequality had been abolished. Woodward's view was no more restrictive than anyone else's, but his hope, as a southerner, for a new order, voluntarily instituted, and his faith, as a liberal, in rational, peaceful reform through mediated changes in public policy—these things had given him a perfect affinity for the civil rights movement, but found him far less compatible with the impulses toward black revolution. It is, of course, not yet clear how much of a revolutionary component the black movement holds, nor is it clear just how Woodward will respond to some aspects of it. His difficulty in responding showed up rather clearly in 1966 in the brief, hasty, tacked-on passages about the Watts Riot. These seemed far less thoughtful than most of his writing, which has consistently been distinguished for its contemplative quality and its interpretive power.

But in January 1967, in an essay in *Harper's Magazine* entitled "What Happened to the Civil Rights Movement?" he gave a more considered evaluation to the confused status of current black-white relationships. This statement offered some striking perspectives, if few answers, and it showed one more phase in Woodward's own quest for the use of history as a means of enabling the past to speak to the present.

From his viewpoint as a liberal,[40] he found the situation discouraging. The article was as pessimistic as any that he has published. Beginning with a foreboding reminder of the way in which the First Reconstruction (1865–77) had lost its idealistic momentum, he sketched the peak of high idealism that the Second Reconstruction (since 1954) had reached in the sit-in movement, the marches on Washington and other cities, and all the singing and the dedication. From this peak, there had been a swift descent with "the triumph of tokenism," the divisions among Negroes, the ghetto riots, and the falling away of white participants in The Movement as they shifted their attention to Vietnam, reacted negatively to black militancy, or simply became bored with long-sustained idealism, as people so often do. "If we are realists," he said, "we will no longer pretend that the movement for racial justice and Negro rights is sustained by the same foundation of moral assurance, or that it is supported today by the same political coalitions, the same inter-racial accommodations, and such harmony of purpose, commitment and dedication as recently prevailed." Noting "numerous white defections from the commitment to racial justice, the sudden silence in many quarters recently vocal with protest, the mounting appeal to bigotry and the scurry of retreat in Congress," he warned that "it would be the better part of realism to expect things to get worse before they get better." He suggested no specific measures that could make things better.[41]

But even as he discounted the social hopes that have shone implicitly through all of his writings from *Tom Watson* on, even as he recognized the fact that the present, at least at the moment, is not prepared to hear from the past the things that he has spent thirty years trying to show that the past has to say, he reaffirmed the two personal commitments, to historical realism and to liberalism, which he has sometimes had difficulty driving in tandem, but which he has used in conjunction as purposefully, as successfully, and with as evenhanded a respect for the integrity of both commitments as any American historian.

His basic historical philosophy from the outset has been that the multiplicity of elements in any situation always offers diverse potentialities, and these diverse potentialities always offer society a choice of alternatives. History can help to show these alternatives. When society sees them, it can escape determinism and exercise choice. In the situation in 1967, Woodward saw many factors reducing the force of the civil rights movement, but he also saw the presence of the largest body of independent black voters in history, and the existence of "a corps of Negro leaders that has not been surpassed in dedication, astuteness, and moral force by the leadership of any other great social movement of the century." The presence of these factors offered an alternative to the threatened deterioration of the civil rights movement. So long as such elements exist, "there is no realism in accepting the current reaction as irreversible, and no rationality in despair."[42]

This statement was not only a seasoned evaluation, at a crucial transition point in its history, of a movement with which Woodward has been concerned from the beginning. It was also an affirmation, in a new context, of his conception of history as a key that the past gives us for guidance in confronting the problems of the present. But the difficulty with this concept lies in the dilemma: Can history retain its integrity as a rigorous and disciplined form of scholarly inquiry even while partaking of public and functional uses in our encounters with current issues? The ideological assertion that it can is not a new conception and does nothing to resolve the dilemma. The resolution can be meaningful only at the operative level, and it is here that Woodward has made one of his most distinctive contributions to historiography. Despite what may have been his errors in regard to the absence of formal segregation in the generation after Reconstruction, and the nature of the commitment to equality in the decade after Appomattox, he has been remarkably successful in demonstrating that history can retain its basic scholarly validity even in a context of active presentism. It is not by theoretical logic that he has done this, but by his own treatment of the history of race relations in America.

His greatest significance to historical studies may lie in the fact that he has made himself the foremost practitioner of a concept of history that holds that the experience of the past can find its highest relevance in the guidance that it offers in living with the problems of the present. His work has shown that history can be used in this way, but only in the hands of a scholar of extraordinary maturity, humane understanding, breadth of mind, and capacity to combine tolerance with idealism. And his vicissitudes have shown that, even for a man with these qualities, this may be the most difficult as well as the most rewarding use of history.

NOTES

1. This comment is based in part on personal knowledge, for I was an undergraduate at Emory, 1928–32, knew Woodward and Rainey, was coached in debate by Rainey, and was on a debate team with Woodward against the University of Florida. [The correspondence between Woodward and Rainey in the period 1930–65 is especially rich, filled with sardonic but generally optimistic observations about their region; see Glenn Weddington Rainey Papers, Manuscript Collection of the Library of Emory University, Atlanta. See also interviews with Rainey, Roper Papers.—Ed.]

2. C. Vann Woodward, *Tom Watson, Agrarian Rebel* (New York: Macmillan, 1938), ix.

3. Wilma Dykeman and James Stokely, *Seeds of Southern Change: The Life of Will Alexander* (Chicago: University of Chicago Press, 1962), 155–56; Angelo Herndon, *Let Me Live*, rev. ed., preface by Howard N. Meyer (New York: Arno/New York Times, 1969) gives a long and full account of his imprisonment and defense but does not mention Woodward or the names of any persons who helped him, other than his lawyers. [Woodward consistently describes Communist Party actions for Herndon, and by extension for the Scottsboro Boys, in this way; see interviews, Woodward, Roper Papers. Dan T. Carter, in his magisterial study, *Scottsboro: A Tragedy of the American South* (Baton Rouge: Louisiana State University Press, 1969), also imputes purely cynical motives to the CP. His book was very favorably reviewed by Woodward in the *New York Times Book Review*, 9 Mar. 1969, 5. However, James E. Goodman in a recent reinterpretation is far more sympathetic with the CP (idem, *Stories of Scottsboro* [New York: Pantheon, 1994]); in like manner, Charles H. Martin was also sympathetic with the CP in his account of Herndon's case (idem, *The Angelo Herndon Case and Southern Justice* [Baton Rouge: Louisiana State University Press, 1976]). Ed.]

4. Howard Washington Odum, *Southern Regions of the United States* (Chapel Hill: University of North Carolina Press, 1936).

5. Woodward, *Tom Watson*, ix; Woodward to Potter, 23 June 1967, letter in possession of author.

6. Lloyd Paul Stryker, *Andrew Johnson: A Study in Courage* (New York: Macmillan, 1936).

7. Howard Kennedy Beale, *The Critical Year: A Study of Andrew Johnson and Reconstruction* (New York: Harcourt, Brace, 1930), 1.

8. Almost the only previous writer who had recognized this point even partially was Paul Lewinson, in *Race, Class, and Party: A History of Negro Suffrage and White Politics in the South* (New York: Oxford University Press, 1932), and his development of the topic was not comparable to Woodward's. Also, for further analysis of the class

factor in politics, see Woodward's essay, "The Populist Heritage and the Intellectual," *American Scholar* 28 (1959): 55–72, reprinted in Woodward, *The Burden of Southern History* (Baton Rouge: Louisiana State University Press, 1960), 141–66.

9. Benjamin B. Kendrick and Alex Mathews Arnett, *The South Looks at Its Past* (Chapel Hill: University of North Carolina Press, 1935).

10. For some comments on especial points in *Reunion and Reaction,* see Harry Barnard, *Rutherford B. Hayes and His America* (Indianapolis: Bobbs-Merrill, 1954), which argues that the factors contributing to the result were more varied than Woodward's account indicates; Joseph Frazier Wall, *Henry Watterson: Reconstructed Rebel,* introd. by Alben W. Barkley (New York: Oxford University Press, 1956), 159–67, which denies Woodward's contention that the southern Democrats were more instrumental than the northern Democrats in giving up the filibuster against counting the electoral vote; and Thomas B. Alexander, "Persistent Whiggery in the Confederate South, 1860–1877," *Journal of Southern History* 27 (1961): 324–35, which suggests that the Whiggishly inclined bloc of southern Democrats might have acted as it did even if there had been no Texas and Pacific lobby at work.

11. Richard Hofstadter, *The Age of Reform: From Bryan to F.D.R.* (New York: Knopf, 1955). Issued in paperback in 1955 by Random House Vintage Paperbacks, *The Age of Reform* won the Pulitzer Prize for History in 1956.

12. John D. Hicks, *The Populist Revolt: A History of the Farmers' Alliance and the People's Party* (Minneapolis: University of Minnesota Press, 1931), available to and cited by young Woodward. Reissued and cited here, ibid. (Lincoln: University of Nebraska Press, 1961).

13. Captain Paul F. Dugan, U.S.N., review of *Battle for Leyte Gulf* by C. Vann Woodward, in U.S. Naval Institute, *Proceedings* 73 (1947): 457–58.

14. Reinhold Niebuhr, *The Irony of American History* (New York: Scribner, 1952); see also idem, *The Children of Light and the Children of Darkness: A Vindication of Democracy and a Critique of Its Traditional Defence* (New York: Scribner, 1944).

15. C. Vann Woodward, "The Irony of Southern History," in *The Burden of Southern History* (Baton Rouge: Louisiana State University Press, 1960), 169. Parenthetical numbers in the text refer to page numbers therein.

16. C. Vann Woodward, "The Search for Southern Identity," in ibid., 6, 8, 25.

17. C. Vann Woodward, "The Age of Reinterpretation," *American Historical Review* 66 (1960): 11. Parenthetical numbers in the text refer to page numbers therein.

18. C. Vann Woodward, "The Search," reprinted in *Burden* (1960 ed.), 25.

19. Woodward, "The Antislavery Myth," *American Scholar* 31 (1962): 318–36. Cf. Dwight Lowell Dumond, *Antislavery: The Crusade for Freedom in America* (Ann Arbor: University of Michigan Press, 1961).

20. Quoted in *Harper's Magazine,* Apr. 1965, 133.

21. Ulrich Bonnell Phillips, "The Central Theme of Southern History," *American Historical Review* 34 (1928): 30–43.

22. Woodward, "The Search," reprinted in *Burden* (1960 ed.), 11, 12.

23. William Edward Dodd, *Statesmen of the Old South: Or, From Radicalism to*

Conservative Revolt (New York: Macmillan, 1929); Frank Lawrence Owsley, *Plain Folk of the Old South,* Walter Lynwood Fleming Lecture Series (Baton Rouge: Louisiana State University Press, 1949).

24. Woodward, *Tom Watson,* 220.

25. C. Vann Woodward, "What Happened to the Civil Rights Movement?" *Harper's Magazine,* Jan. 1967, 32.

26. Woodward, *Strange Career* (1955 ed.), 16.

27. Barton J. Bernstein calls my attention to the relevance of the Civil Rights Act of 1875 in connection with this question. Evidence concerning this act has been neglected by scholars, but it is very pertinent in two ways: (1) there is palpably a question of why the act's supporters deemed it necessary unless discrimination was being practiced; (2) considerable evidence of such discrimination was presented in support of the proposed measure. Of course, the discrimination may have been practiced informally and therefore may not have involved any action by southern state governments, but the issue of segregation was certainly involved, whether or not in the form of Jim Crow.

28. Charles E. Wynes, *Race Relations in Virginia, 1870–1902* (Charlottesville: University Press of Virginia, 1961), 68–110, 144–50, esp. 149–50; Frenise A. Logan, *The Negro in North Carolina, 1876–1894* (Chapel Hill: University of North Carolina Press, 1964), 174–88, 209–19, esp. 215; Joel Randolph Williamson, *After Slavery: The Negro in South Carolina during Reconstruction, 1861–1877* (Chapel Hill: University of North Carolina Press, 1965), 240–99, esp. 274, 298–99.

29. Woodward, *Strange Career* (1955 ed.), 14; Richard C. Wade, *Slavery in the Cities: The South 1820–1860* (New York: Oxford University Press, 1964), 266.

30. Woodward, *Strange Career* (1957 ed.), xv–xvi. Other works treating the degree of segregation in the postbellum South, and which Woodward took into account in the first edition of *Strange Career,* include: Vernon Lane Wharton, *The Negro in Mississippi, 1865–1890* (Chapel Hill: University of North Carolina Press, 1947) and George Brown Tindall, *South Carolina Negroes, 1877–1900* (Columbia: University of South Carolina Press, 1952). The whole question of the origins of segregation has now assumed the dimensions of a full-scale historical controversy, and Joel Randolph Williamson has edited a brief volume of selections from Woodward and twelve other writers, including all those cited from note 28 through this note: *The Origins of Segregation,* ed. Williamson, Problems in American Civilization Series (Lexington, Mass.: Heath, 1968).

31. Woodward, *Tom Watson,* 220.

32. Woodward, "Equality, the Deferred Commitment," reprinted in *The Burden of Southern History,* 75, 77, 78.

33. William Ranulf Brock, *An American Crisis: Congress and Reconstruction, 1865–1867* (New York: St. Martin's Press, 1963), 285–86.

34. G. Selden [not Seldon] Henry, "Radical Republican Policy toward the Negro during Reconstruction (1862–1872)" (Ph.D. diss., Yale University, 1963). It is noteworthy that even Woodward's own student James M. McPherson (*The Struggle for*

Equality: Abolitionists and the Negro in the Civil War and Reconstruction [Princeton: Princeton University Press, 1964]) provides copious evidence of a preponderant northern sentiment against equality for Negroes. At his conclusion, McPherson states that, when the Radical Republicans abandoned the federal enforcement of Negro rights in the South (far short of equality) "[t]he mass of Northern people had never loved the Negro, were tired of 'the everlasting Negro question' and were glad to see the end of it" (431).

35. Woodward, "Flight from History: The Heritage of the Negro," *Nation,* 20 Sept. 1965, 142–46; idem, "Seeds of Failure in Radical Race Policy," in *New Frontiers of the American Reconstruction,* ed. Harold M. Hyman (Urbana: University of Illinois Press, 1966), 130.

36. Woodward, *Strange Career* (1966 ed.), vii; idem., "What Happened to the Civil Rights Movement?" 36.

37. Quoted passages: Woodward, *Strange Career* (1955 ed.), ix, 124; ibid. (1957 ed.), 153, 178–79.

38. Ibid. (1966 ed.), 189.

39. Ibid., 190–91.

40. The attribution perhaps requires no proving, but Woodward specifically classified himself as "a liberal, even more, a Southern white liberal" in a commentary at a Socialist Scholars Conference in 1966. See *Studies on the Left* 6 (1966): 35.

41. Woodward, "What Happened to the Civil Rights Movement?" 32, 34, 37.

42. Ibid., 37.

VI

A Final Riff

The Spitting Image of the Old Life and Casualty Insurance Man: Whose Is This One?

ALBERT MURRAY

✳

Albert Murray is a New York writer who was born in Nokomis, Alabama, in 1916 and grew up in Mobile. Educated at Tuskegee Institute, he taught literature at that school and at least six other colleges, served as an officer in the United States Air Force, and has written both creative fiction and critical essays. Fascinated by the complex interplay between white and black, South and North, and male and female, Murray has emerged as an especially trenchant observer of modern culture because of his insistence that enemies are finally so like each other and allies so often unlike each other that almost nothing is really as it seems on first examination. He published *The Omni-Americans* in 1970, and then in 1971 produced *South to a Very Old Place*, an experiment in jazz-based writing. Each section of the essays has a musical structure, and he has produced "word-riffs" about the southern white literary characters that he interviewed on a trip from his home in New York to his starting-point in the Deep South. A *word-riff* he has defined as a vignette that uses the musical qualities of jazz to develop and "play-off of" a theme.

Along the way, he stopped in at New Haven when Woodward and the late poet Robert Penn Warren were both still actively teaching there. During this visit, Murray discovered again his subtheme that southerners of both races take themselves, their identities, and their shared culture wherever they go, even into an Ivy League academic cove of the industrial northeastern corridor. He calls this cultural phenomenon *going south*.

This excerpt is a word-riff on historian Woodward, from the first section, entitled "Deposition for Two at Yale."

✻　✻　✻

You can also go south from midtown Manhattan by taking another north-bound train from Forty-second Street: one going up beneath and then above

Park Avenue. Take the Yankee Clipper, for instance, or the Merchants Limited, or the Bay State Special. But this time you keep on past 125th Street. This time you roll on across the Harlem River and continue on through the Bronx and that part of suburbia to Connecticut. Then one hour and maybe fifteen, maybe twenty, maybe thirty or thirty-five minutes later you are that many statute miles farther north from Mobile than Lenox Terrace, but you are also pulling into New Haven, where Yale has some very special downhome dimensions indeed these days. Nor are all of them derived from Yankee-shrewd concessions to militant civil rights rhetoric. There is Robert Penn Warren and there is C. Vann Woodward.

Because yes as seldom as such things are ever mentioned with longing, whing-ding-doodle banjos and twang-nosed-talking-Jim-Crow-walking guitars and barnyard saw-fiddle music or any hints thereof even on a TV soundtrack can also take you back as rapidly as anything else. Even from Lenox Terrace. Because, after all, like it or not, or concede it or not, long before it became your boy-blue stamping ground the old country had already been old man whicker-bill's buckskin camping ground, back when it was still Indian territory.

So, what with somebody forever forgetting to turn the radio off, you are carried back almost as often by such ragtime rooty-toot trumpets as used to talk confederate bugle talk above the two-beat razzmatazz of knock-down drag-out Saturday night roadhouses and moss-point casinos back when the best bootleg whiskey came from the sheriff's private stock. Yes there are also Harlem airshaft reverberations of all that too. So also such slow-dragging circus-tiger vibrato trombones as not only used to but still do tailgate such magnolia sundown sadness as is fit to test the patience of even the most gracious-seeming evil-tempered cooks and waiters and bellboys who ever shucked, stuffed, and took care of business on any steamboat or in any steamboat-gothic hotel—who could and still do endure it but not without badmouthing it to hell in the process: "Man ain't no goddamn wonder so many of them people don't like nobody. Hump-the-goddamn-hump dancing like that some of these sommiches bound to start whooping and hollering for somebody's blood and balls. Man, that music ain't getting nothing together."

Anyway all of that is also part and parcel of something else to which you are always returning without even going as far back south from Lenox Terrace as 110th Street: that interior benchmark site where things are still very much the same as they once were when you used to squint one of your whicker-bill-mocking eyes and stiffen the weather-beaten whicker-billness of your neck not only as if it were red-devil tootletoddle red but also as if it were wrinkled and stringy from too much tobacco chewing and so much white *shirt-and-collar-and-tie wearing; standing with one foot forward and your whicker-bill elbows stuck out skinny, holding your back and shoulders as if you were just about to break into old man whicker-bill Charley Comesaw's bony-butt, high in-step strut as soon as the billygoat fiddles started sawing — that crackerjack gesture, however, being the whole joke, because as far as you were concerned just about the only white man who really knew how to strut his stuff walking back in those days was not anybody anywhere in and around or even near Mobile, Alabama. It was a western cowboy. It was the one and only Tom Mix walking neither pasty-faced nor red-necked but bow-legged; and then standing not like a flat-assed cracker deputy but hip-cocked and pointy-toed, with his thumbs hooked into his low-riding two-gun car-tridge belt, his silk neckerchief knotted to one side, the angle of his ten-gallon western cowboy hat as sporty as a flashy-fingered piano player's gambling-hall fedora.*

Nor did many things ever strike you as being more laughable than coming back down into the Saturday afternoon daylight of the Pritchard, Alabama, main street from the fabulous peanut-gallery darkness of King's Palace The-atre and seeing Pritchard, Alabama, white boys trying to act like Tom Mix (or Buck Jones or Fred Thompson or Ken Maynard) — and only looking more like whicker-bill peckerwoods than ever. How could Pritchard, Ala-bama, peckerwoods ever know what Tom Mix was all about?

All the same, all of them and all of that and more are no less warp and woof of what home on the outskirts of Mobile, Alabama, was also very much about. Which specifically includes all that which somebody who could easily have been one of your up-north uncles or cousins Remus was talking about when he said to Quentin Compson: "You're right, they're fine folks. But you can't live with them"; which no doubt was the same situation on which some of the old heads by the fireside were musing when they used to come to the end of some story about somebody being in trouble, and mutter: "You got to know how to handle them; you got to outthink them, you got to stay one jump ahead of them"; but which so far as any number of others, old and young, yourself included, were concerned was a very good reason to un-ass the area. Not simply in flight, escape, and hence abdication, however, but also in exploration, quest, and even conquest.

One snatch of either whing-ding or rooty-toot and even as you sit looking at the midtown Manhattan skyline from 132nd Street, looking south as you once did from the northward outskirts of Mobile, you are also back in the old spyglass place seeing all of them and that once more. But in better per-spective, in proper complexity and with proper awareness of the ambiguity and ultimate obscurity of not just black and white motives downhome but of all human motivation everywhere. Because after all that instantaneous, popeyed, no-matter-how-fleeting expression of drawing-room outrage you register at the impropriety of all that old narrow-nosed, shaggyheaded blue-eyed talk when you hear it outside the South is perhaps as much an expression of kinship as of aginship whether you can admit it or not. Because if one part of your reaction is supercilious, another is quite obviously interwoven with nothing so much as having to witness homefolks cutting a "country hog" in town, among strangers. Interwoven with something else also: a grudging admiration in spite of yourself because suddenly you also have to realize that if such talk did cut a hog, the scandal was either intentional or was likely to become defiantly so as soon as there was any hint that the hog cutting was being noted.

So, with however much ambivalence, yes them too: and besides sometimes what they represent as much as anything else is an old familiar difference and even a similar otherness, which is sometimes, especially in situations outside the South, even familiar when other: "Man goddamn where the hell these white folks come from? Man, these some of your goddamn white folks? Man, who the goddamn hell white folks these?"

And no less for all the trouble so many of them represent either. Because wherever and whenever downhome tales tall or otherwise are told, some of the very best are always about all of that too, and there is as much bragging about the extent and intensity of the obstacles, the conflicts, and the show-downs as about anything else, probably more (certainly more than either propriety or hipness will permit about any poon-tang conquest, for instance): "Man, you ain't seen no bad-assed crackers like them bad-assed crackers we had down my way. Man, I'm talking about some mean and gentlemen I mean some sure enough mean-ass peckerwoods. I'm talking about some hoojers so goddamn mean and evil they breathe like rattlesnakes. Man, hell, what you talking about is just some old pore-assed white-assed damn trash. I'm talking about some bad-assed peckerwoods, and you better believe it. You ain't never in your born days seen no bad-assed crackers like them bad-assed crackers we had where I come from. You know them crackers around Bay Minette, Alabama, and on down toward Flomaton and into that old pineywoods country down in North Florida; you know how bad them dried-up-assed rosum-chewing squint-eyed crackers looking like they always sight-ing down a gun barrel at you, used to be out around Leaksville, Missippi, and all out through in there? Sheeeet, man, them old crackers ain't nothing to these old goddamn crackers I'm talking about!"

Yes alas and alas, the also and also of all them and that all of that, plus

*much more; and furthermore, "what clashes here of wills gen wonts," which
is to say shaggyheads versus woollyheads much the same, alas, as if they were
still "ostrygods gagging fishygods" has never been any less familiar than all
the rest and best of it.*

The one that Robert Penn Warren looks and walks and talks like is not old
man Whicker-Bill Comesaw, but Red Scarborough in the old Texaco filling
station out on old Telegraph Road. As for C. Vann Woodward, whing-ding
fiddle talk and Jim-Crow walk or not, he is the spitting image of the old Life
and Casualty Insurance man (or maybe it was Tennessee Life and Casualty
or the Industrial Benefit man), whose Willys-Knight you used to snag as if
it were a gas-driven L & N switch engine. Anyway, anytime anybody from
downhome sees you with either one of them and cocks an ear, popping or
cutting his eyes (mostly without changing expression), and waits for you to
answer whose is this one and what kind and whose that one, you can say:
Filling Station Red. But from Kentucky this time, remembering the smell of
the Texaco gas pumps and the inner-tube patching, remembering the free air
hose and the old wooden grease rack with the galvanized oil tub, and also
remembering the football games on the Atwater Kent radio.

Or in the case of Woodward you can say: Tennessee Life; but from somewhere out in Arkansas this time, remembering how easy it used to be to hobo
on dirt-road switch engines, what with spare tires on the back like life pre-
servers—and how easy it was also because he mostly pretended not to see
you, and if nobody in the neighborhood spotted you he wouldn't say what
he always said until he was ready to pick up speed because he was coming to
where the macadam began. And of course you also remember how much fun
it also was mocking him in your best whicker-bill twang-nosed throat-locked
soda-cracker voice as he pulled on away and out of earshot, you and whoever
was with you that particular day saying not, "All right now ya'll scat off there
now," but: "Say now by Gyard, git the hell and skedaddle offen that durn
tyar dang bust you little possums. Dang bust you little possums. Dang bust
you little possums. Dang bust you little possums." Which was really what
old man Lee G. Heatherton from the grocery store always used to say when
you snagged the back of the delivery wagon.

You can say that's all right about whing-ding guitars and Jim Crow fiddles
this time because this one turned out to be the kind who, at a time when most
students of life in the United States seem to think that cultural assimilation
should be measured in terms of Reading Test scores, can say: "The ironic
thing about these two great hyphenate minorities, the Southern Americans

and the Negro Americans, confronting each other on their native soil for three and a half centuries, is the degree to which they have shaped each other's destiny, determined each other's isolation, shared and molded a common culture. It is in fact impossible to imagine the one without the other and quite futile"—he might, for the benefit of not a few social-science-oriented New York intellectuals, have said "perverse"—"to try"; who in the very same article had written in part: "Two thirds of all the Negroes now living in the North and West were born and raised in the South. They constitute a tremendous Southern impact on the North. Within a few years many of our largest non-Southern cities will be predominantly Negro in population. The North in fact is confronted with a Southern invasion vaster by far than the one General Lee threatened. Under the skin the new invaders are Southern too, even to the second and third generation of them . . . if they can preserve their Southern heritage of endurance, courage and grace under pressure, their country will be the better for it. . . ."

You can say: It is C. Vann Woodward, not Beard, Morrison, Commager, Nevins, or even Aptheker and certainly not Genovese (nor, alas, John Hope Franklin either, though he has other glories) who so far as I know has made a special point of saying and reiterating: "I am prepared to maintain . . . that so far as culture is concerned, all Americans are part-Negro. Some are more so than others, of course, but the essential qualification is not color or race." Not to mention also making a point to add: "When I say all Americans, unlike Crèvecoeur, I include Afro-Americans. THEY ARE PART NEGRO, BUT ONLY PART." Nor is the "only" a slur on the African part—nor is he likely to hold much brief for those who suggest that the white part of the so-called half-breed and mulatto is the part that spoils things. No, the point he makes is that "Negroes are not white people disguised beneath dark skins and Caucasians are not black people beneath white skins. . . ."

Not that there aren't other Woodward formulations that you find somewhat, well, questionable: For instance, in the very same magazine article in which he defines downhome Negroes as quintessentially southern he suddenly gets going on the so-called Negro Middle Class and turns into a social-welfare polemicist right before your scandalized eyes. Saying such completely un-southern things as, "While the small, mobile, trained middle class has been moving up, the great mass of Negro workers has been stagnating or, relative to white workers, losing ground." Jolly good Big Daddy Moynihan nonviolent war on poverty jive. But would C. Vann Woodward the historian draw the same comprehensive inference from a statement to the effect that the great mass of American colonists were not moving up at a rate equal to that of the small mobile trained class that included Thomas Jefferson, George Washington, and James Madison? Isn't that small trained elite precisely the class that keeps the historians in business? Or is Woodward going to give up biography at its age-old literary best for statistics at its politically opportunistic worst? You doubt it. As well you should, for was it not Woodward himself who called upon the historian to abandon false analogies with the natural sciences?

Nor do you feel that fellow southerner Woodward, as highly as you mostly recommend him, has given proper attention to the question of Negroes and Immigrants. Not that he has ignored the subject. He has some significant things to say about Immigration as such. But when he describes U.S. Negroes as "unneeded and unwanted" he is, to your exasperation, being as soft on the implications of white European immigration as any white supremacist you ever saw in your life. And besides, you have every reason to believe that Woodward, the very embodiment of southern memory, knows that the Civil War was fought precisely because Negroes were the most wanted laborers in the history of Western civilization, and that he also knows therefore that just as Africans had been trained and conditioned to plantation work they no doubt would have been retrained also to fulfill the requirements of late-nineteenth- and early-twentieth-century industrialization, but for the influx of white immigrants on preferential quotas. What the hell was Booker T. Washington so concerned about in that Atlanta Compromise speech if not what the immigration of hungry white Europeans would do to the black freedmen? What if not white European immigrant labor was he talking to white Americans about when he not only advised but implored them to "Let down your bucket where you are"?

When Woodward permits himself to say that Negroes were unneeded and unwanted, he is, to put it mildly, indulging in polemical abstraction. On the other hand, to point out that white Europeans were permitted to come over here and take jobs that in any other country would have gone first to native-born citizens is to state a historical fact of crucial significance to the present state of the nation's health.

For all that, however, it is C. Vann Woodward (the old life-insurance collector who used to stand in the front yard with one Stacy Adamsed foot propped on the second step scribbling in the policy book) you think about as often as any other historian when you think about new perspectives for American experience. For not only was it the old neatly dressed soft-voiced and not unkindly policyman from Emory in Atlanta, not some Ivy League liberal, who places the Reconstruction sell-out in the context of a national racism geared to imperialism, it is this same downhome white fellow who wrote: "National myths, American myths have proved far more sacrosanct and inviolate than Southern myths. Millions of European immigrants of diverse cultural backgrounds have sought and found identity in them. . . . European ethnic groups with traditions far more ancient and distinctive than those of the South have eagerly divested themselves of their cultural heritage in order to conform."

It was also this same downhome-raised historian who, with a discernment conspicuously missing in even the best northern historians and reporters, wrote: "The separatists and nationalists have had their native American leaders. But I am more impressed with the association of extremist doctrines of separatism with Caribbean and West Indian leaders and origins going back to Edward W. Blyden of St. Thomas, who swept the South in the nineties, and other worthies including Marcus Garvey of Jamaica and all their mystique of just how black you had to be to be a Negro." On the other hand, most northern reporters seem to cling to the old assumption that all Negroes are the same—or should be.

One specific reason for coming to Yale this time is to get his downhome reaction to all of the up-north cocktail-party glibness about the alleged historical differences and natural antagonisms between the descendants of the so-called field Negroes and house Negroes. Because a few misguided TV outspokesmen and consequently a number of white northern journalists are by way of propagating another one of those Elkins-type theories of black experience that, to paraphrase Woodward himself, almost make you "despair of history as a path to wisdom."

You have come to this veritable citadel of Yankeedom to see if it is possible to share with him and with Robert Penn Warren something which both he and Robert Penn Warren have claimed as an essential part of the heritage of all post-Confederate downhome folks, "black and white": that *"instinctive fear—that the massiveness of experience, the concreteness of life will be violated: the fear of abstraction."*

So you sit there in his Sterling Library office looking at him almost exactly like the old life and casualty man of your Mobile, Alabama, boyhood, looking precisely as if while you were growing up to go to Mobile County Training School and Tuskegee and so on, he had collected enough policy money to go on off to Emory in Atlanta and then to Columbia and Oxford. This time your response to the whicker-bill otherness of his Arkansas bearing and manner is to remember a scene between Joanna Burden and Joe Christmas in *Light in August,* a scene you have been playing your own changes on ever since you first read it and discussed it with Jug Hamilton at Tuskegee thirty years ago: *Kneel, you look at him thinking, I don't ask it. Kneel. Not to me. Not to God. Not to me for forgiveness. Not before God in repentance, which is what Miss Joanna, the liberal do-gooder, who was pregnant, wanted. Not for your grandfathers and the plantations. Not for your father's generation and the Klan. To the facts of life. It is not me that asks it. Remember that. All I ask is that you respect the massiveness of experience, the concreteness of Southern life. All I ask is that you remember what you really know, not what some goddamn Yankee polemicist expects all crackers to feel. Man, just consider this: Even old Ulrich B. Phillips (whom shit on) comes closer to the texture of life in bondage as described by my grandparents and yours too than all that Sambo Elkins jive you once gave such a generous blurb to.*

And his response to your question about slave categories is the one you had every reason to expect from a man who has no excuse for not knowing exactly where the old plantations were, where the big houses (some of which were not very big at all) were, where the slave quarters (which were far from always being compounds) were; a man who didn't have to go to Emory and certainly not to Columbia and Oxford to find out who worked precisely where and for how many hours a day and what the daily menu was; a man who, like William Faulkner, not only knows who owned whose grandparents but also, as little as it is mentioned outside Faulkner, whose blood brothers and sisters and cousins are whose.

"I remember *some* of them from my childhood," he says as unhurriedly as a cracker-barrel stick whittler, "and as you know this goes back some sixty years, when there were quite a few still around." He pauses, whittling. Then: "Yes, my father had dealings with them. We never thought of them like that." Then whittles his metaphorical stick on into an account of the House Slave/Field Slave Dialectic as it is currently being expounded, "by one of my colleagues, a Negro, here at Yale," treating each detail as if it had the challenging insightfulness of Max Weber or Thorstein Veblen. Then he whittles (or cleans and stuffs his metaphorical pipe some more) and adds: "He is quite literally taken with it. But I have serious doubts about its validity."

It is not a very long visit. There is not really enough stick-whittling time to get into some of the other questions you had in mind, questions, for instance, about whether slaveowners regarded the word "Negro" as being more opprobrious than the word "black," a word whose overwhelming connotations of the negative, even the terrifying (the unknown, the mysterious, and death itself—being, incidentally, a universal color of mourning), are by no means limited to references to African-derived Americans. After all, what is largely at issue in the current Afro-Negro-Black controversy over what African-derived Americans should now be called is the white master's usage. As for yourself, you grew up under the impression that white people felt that "Negro" (but not "negress," which is another story, like "jewess") was not only a far more respectable term than "black," which always smacked of cargoes, but was actually too dignified to be pronounced correctly—or to be capitalized. It took years of civil rights protest to get certain national publications to capitalize the word Negro.

Meanwhile, every comment he has made on what you do have time to talk about will stand up very well indeed in all of the best barbershops you have ever known. So *him too. Because if somebody who may be a brownskin Yale student, a brownskin Yale professor, or even a brownskin Yale waiter happens to see you standing there shaking hands and hears the barnyard fiddles in his voice, and just by looking once and a half asks if he is a pretty good one: "Whose is this one? Who's vouching this time?" you can smile back nodding without nodding with your eyes saying yes, one of mine, so to speak, me. Yes, better than pretty good, one of the very best around and getting better all the time—and without anybody really checking on him yet. But don't take my word. Check him out for yourself. Read what he writes. Nor is it necessary to begin with* The Strange Career of Jim Crow. *Either* Tom Watson, Agrarian Rebel, Origins of the New South, *or* The Burden of Southern History *will do just fine.*

Appendix A:
Ph.D. Students from Johns Hopkins
University, 1947–1960

✳

Student	Graduation Date	Dissertation
Daniel H. Calhoun	1956	The American Civil Engineer, 1792–1843
Suzanne Carson (Lowitt)	1952	Samuel Chapman Armstrong: Missionary to the South
Vincent De Santis	1952	Republican Efforts to Break up the Democratic South, 1877–1892
Charles B. Dew	1964	Southern Industry in the Civil War Era: Joseph Reid Anderson and the Tredegar Iron Works, 1859–1867
Tilden G. Edelstein	1961	Strange Enthusiasm: Thomas Wentworth Higginson, 1823–1877
Louis R. Harlan	1955	Separate and Unequal: Public School Campaigns and the Race Issue in the Southern Seaboard States, 1901–1915
Warren W. Hassler Jr.	1954	George B. McClellan in the Civil War: A Revision
Ludwell H. Johnson III	1955	War, Politics, and Cotton: The Red River Expedition of 1864
Charles F. Kellogg	1965	The Early History of the National Association for the Advancement of Colored People
James M. McPherson	1962	The Abolitionists and the Negro during the Civil War and Reconstruction
Otto H. Olsen	1959	A Carpetbagger: Albion W. Tourgee and Reconstruction in North Carolina
Willie Lee Nichols Rose	1961	Rehearsal for Reconstruction: The Port Royal Experiment

Robert P. Sharkey	1957	Money, Class, and Party: An Economic Study of Civil War and Reconstruction
Gustavus G. Williamson	1954	Cotton Manufacturing in South Carolina, 1865–1892
Bertram Wyatt-Brown	1962	Partners in Piety: Lewis and Arthur Tappan, Evangelical Abolitionists, 1828–1841

Note: List supplied by C. Vann Woodward and supplemented by *Doctoral Dissertations Accepted by American Universities*, vols. 15–22 and *Index to American Doctoral Dissertations*, 1957–65.

Appendix B:
Ph.D. Students from
Yale University, 1961–1979

✳

Student	Graduation Date	Dissertation
John Blassingame	1971	A Social and Economic Study of the Negro in New Orleans, 1860–1880
Frederick A. Bode	1969	Southern White Protestantism and the Crisis of the New South, North Carolina, 1894–1903
David L. Carlton	1977	Mill and Town: The Cotton Mill Workers and the Middle Class in South Carolina, 1880–1920
Ruth F. Claus	1975	Militancy in the English and American Woman Suffrage Movements
Daniel W. Crofts	1968	The Blair Bill and the Elections Bill: The Congressional Aftermath to Reconstruction
Robert F. Engs	1972	The Development of Black Culture and Community in the Emancipation Era: Hampton Roads, Virginia, 1861–1870
Barbara J. Fields	1978	The Maryland Way from Slavery to Freedom
James R. Green	1972	Socialism in the Southwestern Class Struggle, 1898–1918: A Study of Radical Movements in Oklahoma, Texas, Louisiana, and Arkansas
F. Sheldon Hackney	1966	From Populism to Progressivism in Alabama, 1890–1910
Steven H. Hahn	1979	The Roots of Southern Populism: Yeoman Farmers and the Transformation of Georgia's Upper Piedmont, 1850–1890

Thomas Holt	1973	The Emergence of Negro Political Leadership in South Carolina during Reconstruction
Frank J. Huffman	1974	Old South, New South: Continuity and Change in a Georgia County, 1850–1880
J. Morgan Kousser	1971	The Shaping of Southern Politics: Suffrage Restriction and the Establishment of the One-Party South, 1880–1910
Marc W. Kruman	1978	Parties and Politics in North Carolina, 1836–1865
John L. McCarthy	1970	Reconstruction Legislation and Voting Alignments in the House of Representatives, 1863–1869
Richard L. McCormick	1976	Shaping Republican Strategy: Political Change in New York State, 1893–1910
William S. McFeely	1966	The Freedmen's Bureau: A Study in Betrayal
Geraldine M. McTigue	1975	Forms of Racial Interaction in Louisiana, 1860–1880
Bruce Palmer	1972	The Rhetoric of Southern Populists: Metaphor and Imagery in the Language of Reform
Robert Dean Pope	1976	Senatorial Baron: The Long Political Career of Kenneth D. McKellar
Lawrence N. Powell	1976	New Masters: Northern Planters during the Civil War and Reconstruction
Daniel T. Rodgers	1973	The Work Ethic in Industrial America, 1865–1917
Richard Skolnik	1964	The Crystallization of Reform in New York City, 1890–1917
J. Mills Thornton III	1974	Politics and Power in a Slave Society: Alabama, 1806–1860
Bert H. Thurber	1973	The Negro at the Nation's Capital, 1913–1921
Michael S. Wayne	1979	Ante-Bellum Planters in the Post-Bellum South: The Natchez District, 1860–1880
John A. Williams	1966	Davis and Elkins of West Virginia: Businessmen in Politics

Note: List supplied by Registrar, Department of History, Yale University and supplemented by *Index to American Doctoral Dissertations*, 1960–81.

Bibliography: The Writings of C. Vann Woodward

✳

BOOKS

Ed. *After the War: A Tour of the Southern States, 1865–1866*, by Whitelaw Reid. 1866. Reprint. New York: Peter Smith, 1965.

American Attitudes toward History. Oxford: Clarendon, 1955.

American Counterpoint: Slavery and Racism in the North-South Dialogue. Boston: Little, Brown, 1971.

The Battle for Leyte Gulf. New York: Macmillan, 1947.

The Bougainville Landing and the Battle of Empress Augusta Bay, 27 October– 2 November 1943. Restricted distribution. Washington: U.S. Government Printing Office, n.d. [ca. 1947].

The Burden of Southern History. Baton Rouge: Louisiana State University Press, 1960.

Ed. *Cannibals All! or, Slaves without Masters*, by George Fitzhugh. 1857. Reprint. Cambridge: Belknap Press, Harvard University Press, 1960.

The Civil Rights Movement Re-examined: Three Essays, with Paul Feldman and Bayard Rustin. New York: A. Phillip Randolph Education Fund, n.d. [ca. 1956].

Ed. *The Comparative Approach to American History*. New York: Basic Books, 1968.

The Future of the Past. New York: Oxford University Press, 1989.

Kolombangara and Vella Lavella, 6 August–7 October 1943. Restricted distribution. Washington: U.S. Government Printing Office, n.d. [ca. 1947].

Ed. *Mary Chesnut's Civil War*, by Mary Chesnut. New Haven: Yale University Press, 1981.

The National Experience: A History of the United States, with John Morton Blum, Edmund Sears Morgan, Willie Lee Rose, Arthur Meier Schlesinger Jr., and Kenneth Milton Stampp. New York: Harcourt Brace Jovanovich, 1963.

The Old World's New World. New York: Oxford University Press, 1992.

Origins of the New South, 1877–1913. Vol. 9 of *A History of the South*, edited by Ellis Merton Coulter and Wendell Holmes Stephenson. Baton Rouge: Louisiana State University Press, 1951.

Ed. *Oxford History of the United States*. Vols. 1 and 2. New York: Oxford University Press, 1982, 1983.

Ed. *The Private Mary Chesnut: The Unpublished Civil War Diaries*, by Mary Chesnut. New York: Oxford University Press, 1984.

Ed. *Responses of the Presidents to Charges of Misconduct.* New York: Delacorte, 1974.

Reunion and Reaction: The Compromise of 1877 and the End of Reconstruction. Boston: Little, Brown, 1951.

Ed. *A Southern Prophecy: The Prosperity of the South Dependent upon the Elevation of the Negro (1889),* by Lewis Harvey Blair. Boston: Little, Brown, 1964.

The Strange Career of Jim Crow. New York: Oxford University Press, 1955. Rev. ed., 1957. 2d rev. ed., 1966, 3d rev. ed., 1974.

Thinking Back: The Perils of Writing History. Baton Rouge: Louisiana State University Press, 1986.

Tom Watson: Agrarian Rebel. New York: Macmillan, 1938.

ARTICLES AND ADDRESSES

"After Watts—Where Is the Negro Revolution Headed?" *New York Times Magazine,* 29 Aug. 1965, 24–25, 81–89.

"The Age of Reinterpretation." *American Historical Review* 66 (1960): 1–19.

"The Aging of Democracies." *Southern Humanities Review* 26 (1992): 1–8.

"American Attitudes toward History: An Inaugural Lecture Delivered before the University of Oxford." 22 Feb. 1955.

"American History (White Man's Version) Needs an Infusion of Soul." *New York Times Magazine,* 20 Apr. 1969, 32–33, 108–14.

"The Antislavery Myth." *American Scholar* 31 (1962): 312–28.

"The Black and the Red." *New Republic,* 16 Mar. 1987, 32–36.

"Bourbonism in Georgia." Address, Southern Historical Association, Durham, N.C., 1937. *North Carolina Historical Review* 16 (1939): 23–35.

"The Bubbas." *New Republic,* 1 Feb. 1993, 30.

"Can We Believe Our Own History?" *Johns Hopkins Magazine* 5 (1954): 1–6, 16.

"The Case of the Louisiana Traveler (Plessy v. Ferguson, 163 U.S. 537)." In *Quarrels That Have Shaped the Constitution,* edited by John Arthur Garraty, 135–58. New York: Harper & Row, 1964.

"Clio with Soul." *Journal of American History* 56 (1969): 5–20.

"Collapse of Activism: What Happened to the 1960s?" *New Republic,* 9 Nov. 1974, 18–25.

"Comment: What Is a Liberal—Who Is a Conservative? A Symposium." *Commentary* 62 (1976): 110–11.

"Comment on Eugene D. Genovese, 'The Legacy of Slavery and the Roots of Black Nationalism.'" *Studies on the Left* 6 (1966): 35–43.

"Comments by Writers and Scholars on Books of the Past Ten Years." *American Scholar* 34 (1965): 492.

"Communication." *Journal of Southern History* 48 (1982): 160.

"Communication: Gore Vidal's *Lincoln*?: An Exchange." *New York Review of Books,* 28 Apr. 1988, 56–58.

"Communication: *Illiberal Education:* An Exchange." *New York Review of Books,* 26 Sept. 1991, 74–76.

"Communication: Wallace Redeemed? An Exchange between Stephan Lesker and C. Vann Woodward." *New York Review of Books,* 1 Dec. 1994, 58–59.

"Communication: Yes, There Was a Compromise of 1877." *Journal of American History* 60 (1973): 215–23. Reply to Allan Peskin, "Was There a Compromise of 1877?" *Journal of American History* 60 (1973): 63–75.

"The Comparability of American History." In *The Comparative Approach to American History,* edited by Woodward, 3–17. New York: Basic Books, 1968.

"Confessions of a Rebel: 1831." *New Republic,* 7 Oct. 1967, 25–28. Reprinted in *The Nat Turner Rebellion: The Historical Event and the Modern Controversy,* edited by John B. Duff and Peter M. Mitchell, 168–73. New York: Harper & Row, 1971.

"Conversations about the South." *Atlanta Journal-Constitution,* 12 Jan. 1997, sect. R, 1, 2.

"Correspondence." *Commentary* 25 (1958): 76.

"Correspondence from Contributors." *New Republic,* 14 Apr. 1986, 4, 41.

"The Crisis of Caste." *New Republic,* 6 Nov. 1989, 38–43.

"Defending Liberalism." *Daily Tar Heel* (Chapel Hill), Feb. 193[6?]. Clipping in Glenn Weddington Rainey Papers, Manuscript Division, Emory University Library, Atlanta.

"The Disturbed Southerners." *Current History* 32 (1957): 278–82.

"The Elusive Mind of the South." *New York Review of Books,* 4 Dec. 1969. Reprinted with revisions in *American Counterpoint,* 261–83.

"Emancipations and Reconstruction: A Comparative Study." In *XIII International Congress of Historical Studies, Moscow.* 1970. Reprint. Moscow: Navka Publishing, 1970.

"Emory Landlubber Goes to Sea." *Atlanta Journal,* 8 Sept. 1929, 7.

"Equal but Separate." *New Republic,* 15 July 1991, 41–43.

"Equality: America's Deferred Commitment." *American Scholar* 27 (1958): 459–72. Reprinted in *The Burden of Southern History,* rev. ed., 69–88.

"The Erosion of Academic Privileges and Immunities." *Daedalus* 103 (1974): 33–37.

"An Expert Pick of the Pack." *New York Times Book Review,* 5 Dec. 1965, 5, 52–54.

"The Fall of the History Adam." *American Academy of Arts and Sciences Bulletin* 35 (1981): 24–33.

"Flight from History: The Heritage of the Negro." *Nation,* 20 Sept. 1965, 142–46. Reprinted in *The State of the Nation,* edited by David Boroff, 174–82. Englewood Cliffs, N.J.: Prentice-Hall, 1965.

Foreword to *France and England in North America,* vol. 1, by Francis Parkman. Edited by David Levin. New York: Library of America, 1984.

Foreword to *Mary Boykin Chesnut: A Biography,* by Elisabeth Muhlenfeld. Baton Rouge: Louisiana State University Press, 1981.

Foreword to *Southern Negroes, 1861–1865,* by Bell Irvin Wiley. 1938. Reprint. New Haven: Yale University Press, 1965.

"Fortenbaugh Lecture on the American Character." Robert Fortenbaugh Memorial Lecture, Gettysburg, Pa., 1981.

"Freedom of Speech, Not Selectivity." *New York Times,* 15 Oct. 1986, sec. A, 27.

"From the First Reconstruction to the Second." *Harper's,* Apr. 1965, 126–33. Reprinted in *The Burden of Southern History,* 127–33 (rev. ed.); reprinted in *The South Today, 100 Years after Appomattox,* ed. Willie Morris (New York: Harper & Row, 1965), 1–14.

"The Future of Southern History." In *The Future of History: Essays in the Vanderbilt University Centennial Symposium,* edited by Charles F. Delzell, 135–50. Nashville: Vanderbilt University Press, 1977.

"The Future of the Past." *American Historical Review* 75 (1970): 711–26.

"The Ghost of Populism Walks Again." *New York Times Magazine,* 4 June 1972, 16–17, 60–69.

"The Great Civil Rights Debate: The Ghost of Thaddeus Stevens in the Senate Chamber." *Commentary* 24 (1957): 283–91.

"The Greying of America: Reflections upon Our Most Enduring National Myth as We Put the Bicentennial behind Us, and Move On." *New York Times,* 29 Dec. 1976, 25.

"The Hidden Sources of Negro History." *Saturday Review,* 18 Jan. 1969, 18–22.

"Hillbilly Realism." *Southern Review* 4 (1939): 676–81.

"The Historian's Verdict on the Johnson Years." *Newsweek,* 20 Jan. 1969, 19.

"The Historical Dimension." *Virginia Quarterly Review* 32 (1956): 258–67.

"History and the Third Culture." *Journal of Contemporary History* 3 (1968): 23–35.

"History from Slave Sources." *American Historical Review* 79 (1974): 470–81.

"Homegrown Radical." *New Republic,* 4 Feb. 1991, 40–42.

Introduction to *Life and Labor in the Old South,* by Ulrich Bonnell Phillips. Boston: Little, Brown, 1963.

Introduction to *Rehearsal for Reconstruction: The Port Royal Experiment,* by Willie Lee Rose. Indianapolis: Bobbs-Merrill, 1964.

"The Irony of Southern History." *Journal of Southern History* 19 (1953): 3–19.

"Jefferson Memorial Address on the National Character." National Endowment for the Humanities Lecture, Washington, D.C., 1978.

"John Brown's Private War." In *America in Crisis,* edited by Daniel Aaron, 109–32. New York: Knopf, 1952. Reprinted in *The Burden of Southern History,* rev. ed., 41–68.

"The Jolly Institution." *New York Review of Books,* 2 May 1974, 3–6.

Letter. *New York Review of Books,* 7 Feb. 1980, 53.

"Letter: Academic Freedom: Whose Story," with Edmund Sears Morgan. *Columbia University Forum* 11 (1968): 42–43.

"Letter: Adam Clayton Powell as Symbol." *New York Times,* 18 Jan. 1967, 42.

"Letter: Comparative History." *New York Review of Books,* 2 June 1988, 41.

"Letter: Concern for Cambodia and Campus," with Felix Gilbert, Richard Hofstadter, H. Stuart Hughes, Leonard Krieger, Fritz Stern, and Gordon Wright. *New York Times,* 10 May 1970, sec. 4, 17.

"Letter: Emerson and Racism." *New York Review of Books*, 14 June 1990, 61.

"Letter: Indignity at Princeton's Institute for Advanced Study." *New York Times*, 13 Mar. 1973, 38.

"Letter: On David Donald's 'Radical Historians on the Move.'" *New York Times Book Review*, 30 Aug. 1970, 22.

"Letter: On Forestalling Watergates." *New York Times*, 26 June 1975, 38.

"Letter: Religion and American Historians." *New York Review of Books*, 16 May 1991, 65.

"Letter: Scottsboro: A Reply." *New York Times Book Review*, 22 June 1969, 34.

"Letter: Speaking Southern." *New York Review of Books*, 15 Feb. 1990, 52.

"Letter: *Time on the Cross*, A Reply." *New York Review of Books*, 13 June 1974, 41.

"Letter: Wheels." *New York Review of Books*, 21 Dec. 1989, 70.

"Look Away, Look Away." *Journal of Southern History* 59 (1993): 487–504.

"The Lowest Ebb." *American Heritage* 8 (1957): 106–9.

"Mary Chesnut in Search of Her Genre." *Yale Review* 73 (1984): 199–209.

"A Mickey Mouse Idea." *New Republic*, 20 June 1994, 15–16.

"Monograph on the History of Reconstruction in the South to Brief for *Oliver Brown, et al., v. Board of Education of Topeka, et al.* Filed in U.S. Supreme Court, 16 Nov. 1953.

"National Decision against Equality." *American Heritage* 15 (1964): 52–55.

"The New Reconstruction in the South: Desegregation in Historical Perspective." *Commentary* 21 (1956): 501–8.

"The North and the South of It." *American Scholar* 35 (1966): 647–58.

"The Northern Crusade against Slavery." *New York Review of Books*, 27 Feb. 1969. Reprinted in *American Counterpoint*, 140–62.

"The Past Is a Foreign Country." *History and Theory* 26 (1987): 346–52.

"Our Past Isn't What It Used to Be." *New York Times Book Review*, 28 July 1963, 1, 24–25.

"Plessy v. Ferguson: The Birth of Jim Crow." *American Heritage* 15 (1964): 52–55, 100–103.

"The Political Legacy of Reconstruction." *Journal of Negro Education* 26 (1957): 231–40. Reprinted in *The Burden of Southern History*, rev. ed., 89–108.

"The Populist Heritage and the Intellectual." *American Scholar* 28 (1959): 55–72. Reprinted in *The Burden of Southern History*, rev. ed., 141–66.

"The Price of Freedom." In *What Was Freedom's Price?* edited by David G. Sansing, 93–113. Jackson: University Press of Mississippi, 1978.

"Protestant Slavery in a Catholic World." In *American Counterpoint*, 46–77.

"The Question of Loyalty." *American Scholar* 33 (1964): 561–67.

"Race Prejudice Is Itself a Form of Violence." Comment for "Is America by Nature a Violent Society?" *New York Times Magazine*, 28 Apr. 1968, 114.

"Reading, Writing, and Revolution: Comments by Historians on Books in American History." *Washington Post*, 22 Feb. 1976, sec. E, 1, 4.

"Recommended Summer Reading." *American Scholar* 37 (1968): 553–54.

"Reflections on a Centennial: The American Civil War." *Yale Review* 50 (1961): 481–90.

"Reflections on the Fate of the Union: Kennedy and After." *New York Review of Books,* 26 Dec. 1963, 8–9.

Remarks, University of South Carolina Conference on *Time on the Cross,* 2 Nov. 1974, Columbia.

"Report on Current Research." *Saturday Review,* 4 Apr. 1953, 16–17, 48.

"Richard Hofstadter, 1916–1970." *New York Review of Books,* 3 Dec. 1970, 10.

"The Search for Southern Identity." *Virginia Quarterly Review* 34 (1958): 321–28.

"Seeds of Failure in Radical Race Policy." *Proceedings of the American Philosophical Society* 105 (1966): 1–9. Reprinted with substantial revisions in *American Counterpoint,* 163–83; reprinted in *New Frontiers of the American Reconstruction,* edited by Harold Hyman. Urbana: University of Illinois Press, 1966, 125–47.

"Segregation." In *Encyclopedia Americana* 24 (1978): 523–24.

"Share-the-Wealth Movements." In *Dictionary of American History,* vol. 5, edited by James Truslow Adams, 64. New York: Scribner, 1940.

"Shop from Which Tech Grew." *Atlanta Journal* [1933?]. Clipping in Glenn Weddington Rainey Papers, Manuscript Division, Emory University Library, Atlanta.

"A Short History of American History." *New York Times Book Review,* 8 Aug. 1982, 3, 14.

"The Silver Panacea." In *Populism: The Critical Issues,* edited by Sheldon Hackney. Boston: Little, Brown, 1971, 11–20.

"The Sources of Southern History." Fiftieth Anniversary Celebration of the Southern Historical Collection, Chapel Hill, N.C., 24 Oct. 1980.

"The South and the Fury." *New Republic,* 23 Aug. 1993, 41–45.

"The South and the Law of the Land: The Present Resistance and Its Prospects." *Commentary* 26 (1958): 369–74.

"The South in Search of a Philosophy." *Phi Beta Kappa Addresses at the University of Florida,* vol. 1 (1938): 1–20.

"A Southern Critique for the Gilded Age." In *The Burden of Southern History,* rev. ed., 109–40.

"The Southern Ethic in a Puritan World." *William and Mary Quarterly,* 3d ser., 25 (1968): 343–70. Reprinted in *American Counterpoint,* 13–46.

"Southern Mythology." *Commentary* 39 (1965): 60–63.

"Southern States in the World of Thomas Malthus." In *American Counterpoint,* 78–106.

"A Southerner's Answer to the Race Question." *Reporter* 30 (1964): 39–44.

"Statement in Favor of Abolishing Poll Taxes." *Congressional Digest* 20 (1941): 309–10.

"Statement in Favor of Extending the 1965 Voting Rights Act." In *Extension of the Voting Rights Act: Hearing,* 97th Cong., 1st sess., 24 June 1981, pt.3: 1999–2028.

"*Strange Career* Critics: Long May They Persevere." In *Journal of American History* 75 (1988): 857–68.

"The Strange Career of a Historical Controversy." In *American Counterpoint,* 234–66.

"The Test of Comparison." In *The Comparative Approach to American History,* edited by Woodward, 346–58. New York: Basic Books, 1968.

"That Other Impeachment." *New York Times Magazine,* 11 Aug. 1974, 9, 26–32.

"Them and Us: An American Looks at European Perceptions of the New World." *Times Literary Supplement,* 22 May 1992, 3–4.

"Thomas Edward Watson." In *Dictionary of American Biography,* 19: 549–51.

"Times of Trouble." *Pennsylvania Gazette,* Dec. 1981, 16–19.

"Tom Watson and the Negro in Agrarian Politics." *Journal of Southern History* 4 (1938): 14–33.

"Townsend Plan." In *Dictionary of American History,* vol. 5, edited by James Truslow Adams, 288. New York: Scribner, 1940.

"Toynbee and Metahistory." *American Scholar* 27 (1958): 384–92.

"The Troublemaker." *New Republic,* 27 June 1994, 34–39.

"The Unreported Crisis in Southern Colleges." *Harper's,* Oct. 1962, 82–89.

"The Uses of History in Fiction: A Discussion with Ralph Ellison, William Styron, and Robert Penn Warren." *Southern Literary Journal* 1 (1969): 57–90.

"W. J. Cash Reconsidered." *New York Review of Books,* 4 Dec. 1969, 28–34.

"Weil Lecture on European Images of America." Weil Memorial Lecture, Chapel Hill, N.C., 1983.

"What Happened to the Civil Rights Movement?" *Harper's,* Jan. 1967, 29–37.

"What Happened to the Diary of Mary Boykin Chesnut?" Address, Organization of American Historians, New Orleans, 13 Apr. 1979.

"What Is the Chesnut Diary?" In *South Carolina Women Writers: Proceedings of the Reynolds Conference,* 24–25 Oct. 1975, edited by James B. Meriwether, 193–206, 263–85. Spartanburg, S.C.: Reprint Company, 1979.

"White Racism and Black Emancipation." *New York Review of Books,* 27 Feb. 1969, 5–11.

"Why the Southern Renaissance?" *Virginia Quarterly Review* 51 (1975): 22–39.

"Young Jim Crow." *Nation,* 7 July 1956, 9–10.

BOOK REVIEWS

Aaron, Daniel, *The Unwritten War: American Writers and the Civil War. New York Review of Books,* 21 Feb. 1974, 26–29.

Adams, Henry, Library of America reprint ed. of *History of the United States of America during the Administrations of Thomas Jefferson. New York Times Book Review,* 6 July 1986.

Ashmore, Harry, *An Epitaph for Dixie. Virginia Quarterly Review* 34 (1958): 292–94.

Barnard, Harry, *Rutherford B. Hayes and His America. Nation,* 28 May 1955, 467.

Baruch, Bernard, *My Own Story. Saturday Review,* 31 Aug. 1957, 13–14.

Barzun, Jacques, *The House of Intellect. Key Reporter* 25 (1959): 6.

Bazelon, David T., *Power in America: The Politics of the New Class. Commentary* 44 (1967): 92–95.

Beale, Howard Kennedy, ed., *Charles A. Beard: An Appraisal. New York Times Book Review,* 5 Sept. 1954, 9.

———, *The Diary of Gideon Welles. Key Reporter* 26 (1960): 6.

Beard, Charles Austin, *The Republic. Virginia Quarterly Review* 20 (1944): 150–54.

Beard, Charles Austin, and Mary Ritter Beard, *America in Midpassage. Virginia Quarterly Review* 15 (1939): 632–36.

Belden, Thomas, and Marva Belden, *So Fell the Angels. New York Herald Tribune Book Review,* 29 July 1956, 3.

Beringer, Richard E., Herman Hattaway, Archer Jones, and William N. Still Jr., *Why the South Lost the Civil War. New York Review of Books,* 17 July 1986, 3–6.

Bernstein, Barton J., ed., *Towards a New Past: Dissenting Essays in American History. New York Review of Books,* 1 Aug. 1968, 8–12.

Berwanger, Eugene, *The Frontier against Slavery. New York Review of Books,* 27 Feb. 1969, 5–11.

Billington, Ray Allen, *Land of Savagery, Land of Promise: The European Image of the American Frontier in the Nineteenth Century. New York Review of Books,* 11 June 1981, 33–35.

Binkley, Wilfred, *American Political Parties: Their National History. Virginia Quarterly Review* 20 (1944): 150–54.

Black, Earl, and Merle Black, *Politics and Society in the South. New York Review of Books,* 11 June 1987, 7–9.

Bleser, Carol, ed., *The Hammonds of Redcliffe. New York Review of Books,* 22 Oct. 1981, 47–48.

Brodie, Fawn, *Thaddeus Stevens: Scourge of the South. New York Times Book Review,* 22 Nov. 1959, 66–67.

Bruckberger, R. L., *Image of America. Key Reporter* 25 (1959): 6.

Burger, Nash K., and John K. Bettersworth, *South of Appomattox. New York Times Book Review,* 29 Sept. 1959, 46.

Burton, Orville Vernon, *In My Father's House Are Many Mansions. New York Review of Books,* 10 Oct. 1985, 30–31.

Cahnman, Werner, and Alvin Boskoff, eds., *Sociology and History: Theory and Research. New York Times Book Review,* 24 Jan. 1965, 1, 44–45.

Califano, Joseph A., *The Triumph and Tragedy of Lyndon Johnson: The White House Years. New York Review of Books,* 5 Dec. 1991, 6–10.

Cappon, Lester J., ed., *The Adams-Jefferson Letters,* vols. 1–2. *Key Reporter* 25 (1960): 7.

Carter, Dan T., *Scottsboro: A Tragedy of the American South. New York Times Book Review,* 9 Mar. 1969, 5.

Carter, Hodding, *The Angry Scar: The Story of Reconstruction. New York Times Book Review,* 1 Feb. 1959, 5, 33.

Cash, Wilbur J., *The Mind of the South. Journal of Southern History* 7 (1941): 400–401.

Commager, Henry Steele, *Majority Rule and Minority Rights. Virginia Quarterly Review* 20 (1944): 150–54.

——— and Richard B. Morris, eds., *The Spirit of Seventy-Six. New York Herald Tribune Book Review,* 2 Nov. 1958, 4.

Connelly, Thomas L., *The Marble Man: Robert E. Lee and His Image in American Society. New York Times Book Review,* 3 Apr. 1977, 12.

Constantine, J. Robert, ed., *Letters of Eugene V. Debs, 1874–1926. New Republic,* 4 Feb. 1991, 40–42.

Conway, Alan, *The Reconstruction of Georgia. American Historical Review* 72 (1967): 1502–3.

Couch, William Terry, ed., *These Are Our Lives. Virginia Quarterly Review* 15 (1939): 632–36.

Cunningham, Noble E., *The Jeffersonian Republicans: The Formation of Party Organization, 1789–1801. Key Reporter* 24 (1958): 7.

Current, Richard N., *The Lincoln Nobody Knows. Key Reporter* 24 (1959): 6.

———, *Those Terrible Carpetbaggers. New Republic,* 14 Mar. 1988, 40–42.

Dabbs, James McBride, *The Southern Heritage. Nation,* 15 Nov. 1958, 365.

Dabney, Virginius, *The Jefferson Scandals: A Rebuttal. New York Times Book Review,* 5 July 1981, 1, 14.

Dallek, Robert, *Lone Star Rising: Lyndon Johnson and His Times, 1908–1960. New York Review of Books,* 5 Dec. 1991, 6–10.

———, *Ronald Reagan. New Republic,* 2 Apr. 1984, 31–35.

Daniel, Pete, *The Shadow of Slavery: Peonage in the South, 1901–1969. Journal of American History* 59 (1973): 1030–31.

Daniels, Josephus, *Editor in Politics. Mississippi Valley Historical Review* 28 (1941): 285–86.

———, *Tar Heel Editor. New Republic,* 1 Jan. 1940, 27–28.

Davidson, Chandler, *Biracial Politics: Conflict and Coalition in the Metropolitan South. New York Review of Books,* 14 Dec. 1972, 37–40.

Davidson, Elizabeth H., *Child Labor Legislation in the Southern Textile States. Journal of Southern History* 5 (1939): 407–8.

Degler, Carl N., *The Other South: Southern Dissenters in the Nineteenth Century. New York Times Book Review,* 10 Mar. 1974, 4.

De Leon, David, *The American as Anarchist: Reflections on Indigenous Radicalism. New York Review of Books,* 5 Apr. 1979, 3–5.

Donald, David Herbert, ed., *Inside Lincoln's Cabinet: The Civil War Diaries of Salmon P. Chase. Pennsylvania Magazine of History and Biography* 79 (1955): 131–32.

———, *Liberty and Union. New York Times Book Review,* 19 Nov. 1978, 13.

Donald, Henderson H., *The Negro Freedman: Life Conditions of the American Negro in the Early Years after Emancipation. Saturday Review,* 13 June 1953, 45.

Dovring, Folke, *History as a Social Science: An Essay on the Nature and Purpose of Historical Studies. American Historical Review* 66 (1961): 1079.

Draper, Theodore, *The Roots of American Communism. Key Reporter* 22 (1957): 5.

D'Souza, Dinesh, *Illiberal Education: The Politics of Race and Sex on Campus. New York Review of Books,* 18 July 1991, 32–37.

Dugan, James, *The Great Iron Ship. Saturday Review,* 6 Feb. 1954, 19.

Durden, Robert F., *Reconstruction Bonds and Twentieth-Century Politics: South Dakota v. North Carolina, 1904. American Historical Review* 68 (1963): 840.

Dykeman, Wilma, and James Stokely, *Neither Black nor White;* Harry Ashmore, *An Epitaph for Dixie. Virginia Quarterly Review* 34 (1958): 292–94.

Eaton, Clement, *Henry Clay and the Art of American Politics. New York Herald Tribune Book Review,* 14 July 1957, 9.

Evans, Eli N., *Judah P. Benjamin: The Jewish Confederate. New York Review of Books,* 14 Apr. 1988, 6–9.

Faulkner, Harold Underwood, *Politics, Reform, and Expansion: 1890–1900. Key Reporter* 25 (1959): 6.

Faust, Drew Gilpin, *The Creation of Confederate Nationalism: Ideology and Identity in the Civil War South. New York Review of Books,* 15 Mar. 1990, 39–41.

Fehrenbacher, Don E., *The Dred Scott Case: Its Significance in American Law and Politics. New York Review of Books,* 7 Dec. 1978, 30–31.

———, and Carl N. Degler, eds., *The South and the Concurrent Majority,* by David Morris Potter. *Journal of American History* 60 (1973): 123–24.

Field, James A., Jr., *The Japanese at Leyte Gulf: The Sho Operation. American Historical Review* 53 (1947): 82–84.

FitzGerald, Frances, *America Revised: History Schoolbooks in the Twentieth Century. New York Review of Books,* 20 Dec. 1979, 16–19.

Floan, Howard, *The South in Northern Eyes, 1831–1861. Key Reporter* 23 (1958): 4.

Fogel, Robert William, and Stanley Engerman, *Time on the Cross: The Economics of American Negro Slavery;* idem, *Time on the Cross: Evidence and Methods, a Supplement. New York Review of Books,* 2 May 1974, 3–6.

Foner, Eric, *Politics and Ideology in the Age of the Civil War. New Republic,* 22 Nov. 1980, 34–35.

———, *Reconstruction: America's Unfinished Revolution, 1863–1877. New York Review of Books,* 12 May 1988, 22–27.

Foote, Shelby, *The Civil War: A Narrative,* vol. 3. *New York Review of Books,* 6 Mar. 1972, 12.

Fox-Genovese, Elizabeth, *Within the Plantation Household: Black and White Women of the Old South. New York Review of Books,* 8 Dec. 1988, 3–6.

Franklin, John Hope, *The Militant South, 1800–1861. New York Times Book Review,* 23 Sept. 1956, 3.

———, *Racial Equality in America. Journal of American History* 64 (1977): 776–77.

Fraser, Hugh Russell, *Democracy in the Making. New Republic,* 4 Jan. 1939, 265.

Fredrickson, George M., *The Black Image in the White Mind: The Debate on Afro-American Character and Destiny, 1817–1914. New York Review of Books,* 12 Aug. 1971, 11–14.

———, *White Supremacy: A Comparative Study in American and South African History. New York Review of Books,* 5 Mar. 1981, 26–28.

Freidel, Frank, *Franklin D. Roosevelt: The Ordeal. New York Herald Tribune Book Review,* 31 Jan. 1954, 7.

———, *Franklin D. Roosevelt: The Triumph. New York Herald Tribune Book Review,* 9 Sept. 1956, 4.

Garrow, David J., *Bearing the Cross: Martin Luther King, Jr., and the Southern Christian Leadership Conference. New York Review of Books,* 15 Jan. 1987, 3.

Genovese, Eugene D., *In Red and Black: Marxian Explorations in Southern and Afro-American History. New York Review of Books,* 12 Aug. 1971, 11–14.

———, *Roll, Jordan, Roll: The World the Slaves Made. New York Review of Books,* 3 Oct. 1974, 19–21.

Gillette, William, *Retreat from Reconstruction, 1869–1879. New York Review of Books,* 20 Nov. 1980, 49–51.

Ginzberg, Eli, *The Negro Potential. Commentary* 20 (1956): 288–92.

Going, Allen Johnston, *Bourbon Democracy in Alabama, 1874–1890. Mississippi Valley Historical Review* 38 (1952): 719–20.

Goodwyn, Lawrence, *Democratic Promise: The Populist Moment in America. New York Review of Books,* 28 Oct. 1976, 28–29.

Gore, Albert, *Let the Glory Out: My South and Its Politics. New York Review of Books,* 14 Dec. 1972, 37–40.

Green, James R., *Grass-Roots Socialism: Radical Movements in the Southwest, 1895–1943. New York Review of Books,* 5 Apr. 1979, 3–5.

Guerin, Daniel, *Negroes on the March. Commentary* 20 (1956): 288–92.

Halsey, William F., *Admiral Halsey's Story. American Historical Review* 63 (1948): 898.

Hammond, Bray, *Banks and Politics in America from the Revolution to the Civil War. Key Reporter* 23 (1958): 4.

Harlan, Louis R., ed., *Booker T. Washington,* vol. 2. *New York Times Book Review,* 22 May 1983, 13, 36.

———, *The Booker T. Washington Papers,* vols. 1–2; idem, *Booker T. Washington: The Making of a Black Leader, 1865–1901. New Republic,* 11 Nov. 1972, 20–22.

Havard, William C., ed., *The Changing Politics of the South. New York Review of Books,* 14 Dec. 1972, 37–40.

Hesseltine, William B., *Confederate Leaders in the New South. Journal of Southern History* 17 (1951): 270–71.

Higgs, Robert, *Competition and Coercion: Blacks in the American Economy, 1865–1914. Agricultural History* 52 (1978): 194–95.

Hobson, Fred, *Mencken: A Life. New Republic,* 27 June 1994, 34–39.

Hofstadter, Richard, *The American Political Tradition and the Men Who Made It.* *Mississippi Valley Historical Review* 35 (1949): 681–82.

———, *The Paranoid Style in American Politics, and Other Essays. New York Times Book Review,* 14 Nov. 1965, 3, 84.

Horn, Stanley F., *Invisible Empire: The Story of the Ku Klux Klan, 1866–1871. New Republic,* 26 July 1939, 341–42.

Hough, Frank O., *The Island War: The United States Marine Corps in the Pacific. Pacific Historical Review* 16 (1947): 459–60.

Howe, Irving, *Socialism and America. New York Review of Books,* 30 Jan. 1986, 26–29.

Huggins, Nathan, ed., *Writings of W. E. B. Du Bois. New Republic,* 16 Mar. 1987, 32–36.

James, Marquis, *Mr. Garner of Texas. Virginia Quarterly Review* 16 (1940): 129–34.

Jocher, Katharine, Guy B. Johnson, George L. Simpson, and Rupert B. Vance, eds., *Folk, Region, and Society: Selected Papers of Howard W. Odum. New York Times Book Review,* 27 Sept. 1964, 48.

Johnson, Gerald W., *America's Silver Age: The Statecraft of Clay–Webster–Calhoun. New Republic,* 29 Nov. 1939, 176–77.

Jordan, Winthrop D., *White over Black: American Attitudes toward the Negro, 1550–1812. New York Times Book Review,* 31 Mar. 1968, 6, 43.

Kahler, Erich, *The Meaning of History. New York Times Book Review,* 26 July 1964, 5.

Key, V. O., Jr., *Southern Politics in State and Nation. Yale Review* 39 (1949): 374–76.

Kilpatrick, James Jackson, *The Sovereign States: Notes of a Citizen of Virginia. Commentary* 24 (1957): 465–66.

King, Ernest J., and Walter Muir Whitehill, *Fleet Admiral King: A Naval Record. Saturday Review,* 22 Nov. 1952, 26.

Kirwan, Albert Dennis, *Revolt of the Rednecks: Mississippi Politics, 1876–1925. American Historical Review* 56 (1951): 918–19.

Kohn, Hans, *American Nationalism: An Interpretive Essay. Key Reporter* 22 (1957): 5.

Kolchin, Peter, *Unfree Labor: American Slavery and Russian Serfdom. New York Review of Books,* 19 Nov. 1987, 38–43.

Kraditor, Aileen, *Means and Ends in American Abolitionism. New York Review of Books,* 27 Feb. 1969, 5–11.

Lambert, John R., *Arthur Pue Gorman. American Historical Review* 59 (1954): 1027–28.

Lesher, Stephan. *George Wallace: American Populist. New York Review of Books,* 20 Oct. 1994, 49–52.

Levenson, J. C., *The Mind and the Art of Henry Adams. Key Reporter* 22 (1957): 5.

Lief, Alfred, *Democracy's Norris. Virginia Quarterly Review* 16 (1940): 129–34.

Link, Arthur Stanley, *Wilson: The Road to the White House. Pennsylvania Magazine of History and Biography* 72 (1948): 97–98.

Litwack, Leon F., *Been in the Storm So Long: The Aftermath of Slavery*. New York Review of Books, 16 Aug. 1979, 8–9.

Logan, Frenise A., *The Negro in North Carolina, 1876–1894*. American Historical Review 70 (1965): 584.

Logan, Rayford W., *The Negro in American Life and Thought: The Nadir, 1877–1901*. Yale Review 43 (1954): 604–7.

Lorant, Stefan, *The Life and Times of Theodore Roosevelt*. Key Reporter 25 (1960): 7.

Lord, Russell, *The Wallaces of Iowa*. Mississippi Valley Historical Review 34 (1948): 703.

Lumpkin, Katharine Du Pre, *The Making of a Southerner*. Mississippi Valley Historical Review 34 (1947): 141–42.

Mabry, William A., *The Negro in North Carolina Politics since Reconstruction*. North Carolina Historical Review 18 (1941): 82–83.

McCullough, David G., *Truman*. New York Review of Books, 16 July 1992, 26–30.

McDonald, Forrest, *We the People: The Economic Origins of the Constitution*. Key Reporter 24 (1959): 6.

McFeely, Mary Drake, and William Samuel McFeely, eds., *Ulysses S. Grant: Memoirs and Selected Letters*. New York Review of Books, 8 Nov. 1990, 29–32.

McFeely, William Samuel, *Grant: A Biography*. New York Review of Books, 19 March 1981, 3–6.

———, *Yankee Stepfather: General O. O. Howard and the Freedmen*. New York Review of Books, 27 Feb. 1969, 5–11.

McKitrick, Eric, *Andrew Johnson and Reconstruction*. New York Times Book Review, 25 Sept. 1960, 3, 24.

McMillen, Neil R., *Dark Journey: Black Mississippians in the Age of Jim Crow*. New York Review of Books, 29 June 1989, 15–17.

McPherson, James M., *The Struggle for Equality: Abolitionists and the Negro in the Civil War and Reconstruction*. New York Times Book Review, 3 Jan. 1965, 6.

Malone, Dumas, *The Sage of Monticello*, vol. 6. New York Times Book Review, 5 July 1981, 1, 14.

Marcosson, Isaac F., *"Marse Henry": A Biography of Henry Watterson*. Journal of Southern History 18 (1952): 97.

Masur, Louis P., ed., *"The Real War Will Never Get in the Books": Selections from Writers during the Civil War*. New York Review of Books, 7 Apr. 1994, 36–37.

May, Henry F., *The End of American Innocence: A Study of the First Years of Our Own Time, 1912–1917*. American Historical Review 65 (1960): 637–38.

Mazlish, Bruce, and Edwin Diamond, *Jimmy Carter: A Character Portrait*. New York Review of Books, 3 Apr. 1980, 9–11.

Meade, Robert D., *Patrick Henry*, vol. 1 *Patriot in the Making*. Key Reporter 23 (1957): 5.

Meyers, Marvin, *The Jacksonian Persuasion*. Key Reporter 23 (1958): 4.

Michie, Allan, and Frank Ryhlick, *Dixie Demagogues. Virginia Quarterly Review* 16 (1940): 129–34.

Miers, Earl Schenck, *Robert E. Lee: A Great Life in Brief. New York Herald Tribune Book Review,* 10 June 1956, 3.

Miller, Merle, *Lyndon, an Oral Biography. New Republic,* 1 Nov. 1980, 29–31.

Miller, William D., *Memphis during the Progressive Era, 1900–1917. American Historical Review* 64 (1958): 200–201.

Mitchell, Broadus, *Alexander Hamilton: Youth to Maturity, 1755–1788. Key Reporter* 22 (1957): 5.

Mitchell, Reid. *The Vacant Chair: The Northern Soldier Leaves Home. New York Review of Books,* 7 Apr. 1944, 37–38.

Mollenhoff, Clark R., *The President Who Failed: Carter Out of Control. New York Review of Books,* 3 Apr. 1980, 9–11.

Moore, Barrington, Jr., *Social Origins of Dictatorship and Democracy: Lord and Peasant in the Making of the Modern World. Yale Review* 56 (1967): 450–53.

Moore, John Hammond, ed., *Before and After; or, The Relations of the Races at the South,* by Isaac DuBose Seabrook. *American Historical Review* 73 (1968): 1255–56.

Morgan, Edmund Sears, *The Puritan Dilemma: The Story of John Winthrop. Key Reporter* 24 (1958): 7.

Morgenstern, George, *Pearl Harbor: The Story of the Secret War. American Historical Review* 53 (1947): 188.

Morison, Samuel Eliot, *History of United States Naval Operations in World War II.* Vol. 7 *Aleutian, Gilberts, and Marshall, June 1942–April 1944. Saturday Review of Literature,* 24 Nov. 1951, 14–15, 45.

———, *History of United States Naval Operations in World War II.* Vol. 6 *Breaking the Bismarck's Barrier, 22 July 1942–1 May 1944. Saturday Review of Literature,* 24 Feb. 1951, 15, 16.

———, *History of United States Naval Operations in World War II.* Vol. 4 *Coral Sea, Midway, and Submarine Actions, May 1942–August 1942. Saturday Review of Literature,* 29 Oct. 1949, 20, 21.

———, *History of United States Naval Operations in World War II.* Vol. 12 *Leyte, June 1944–January 1945. Key Reporter* 24 (1959): 6.

———, *John Paul Jones: A Sailor's Biography. New York Times Book Review,* 13 Sept. 1959, 3.

Morris, Richard B., ed., *Encyclopedia of American History. Saturday Review,* 13 June 1953, 45.

Morrison, Joseph L., *W. J. Cash, Southern Prophet. New Republic,* 9 Dec. 1967, 28–30.

Mowry, George E., *The Era of Theodore Roosevelt, 1900–1912. Key Reporter* 24 (1958): 7.

Mudge, Eugene Tenbroek, *The Social Philosophy of John Taylor of Caroline. North Carolina Historical Review* 17 (1940): 273–75.

Nevins, Allan, *Allan Nevins on History,* compiled by Ray A. Billington. *Reviews in American History* 4 (1976): 25–26.

———, *The War for the Union,* vol. 1. *The Improvised War, 1861–1862. Key Reporter* 25 (1959): 6.

———, *The War for the Union,* vols. 2 and 4. *New York Times Book Review,* 26 Dec. 1971, 5, 17.

Nichols, Alice, *Bleeding Kansas. New York Herald Tribune Book Review,* 25 July 1954, 3.

Nichols, Lee, *Breakthrough on the Color Front. Yale Review* 43 (1954): 604–7.

Nixon, Raymond B., *Henry W. Grady: Spokesman of the New South. Journal of Southern History* 10 (1944): 114–15.

Noblin, Stuart, *Leonidas La Fayette Polk, Agrarian Crusader. American Historical Review* 55 (1950): 1002–3.

Nugent, Walter T. K., *The Tolerant Populists: Kansas Populism and Nativism. Mississippi Valley Historical Review* 50 (1963): 516–17.

Odum, Howard Washington, *American Social Problems. Virginia Quarterly Review* 15 (1939): 632–36.

Oliphant, Mary C. Simms, Alfred Taylor Odell, and T. C. Duncan Eaves, eds., *Letters of William Gilmore Simms,* vols. 1–2. *American Historical Review* 59 (1954): 466–67.

———, *Letters of William Gilmore Simms,* vols. 3–5. *American Historical Review* 63 (1958): 529–30.

Olsen, Otto H., ed., *Reconstruction and Redemption in the South, New York Review of Books,* 20 Nov. 1980, 49–51.

Palmer, R. R., *The Age of the Democratic Revolution,* vol. 1. *Key Reporter* 25 (1960): 7.

Parkman, Francis, *France and England in North America,* edited by David Levin. *New York Times Book Review,* 3 July 1983, 3, 18.

Peirce, Neal R., *The People's President: The Electoral College in American History and the Direct-Vote Alternative. New Republic,* 1 June 1968, 33–34.

Pelling, Henry, *America and the British Left. Key Reporter* 22 (1957): 8.

Perkins, Dexter, *The New Age of Franklin Roosevelt, 1932–1945. Saturday Review,* 6 July 1957, 16.

Peterson, H. C., and Gilbert C. Fite, *Opponents of War, 1917–1918. American Historical Review* 63 (1957): 155–56.

Pole, J. R., *Paths to the American Past. Times Literary Supplement,* 30 May 1980, 609.

Rabinowitz, Howard N., *Race Relations in the Urban South, 1865–1890. Journal of Southern History* 44 (1978): 476–78.

Ramsdell, Charles W., *Behind the Lines in the Southern Confederacy,* edited by Wendell Holmes Stephenson. *American Historical Review* 49 (1944): 754–55.

Ratner, Lorman, *Powder Keg: Northern Opposition to the Antislavery Movement, 1831–1840. New York Review of Books,* 27 Feb. 1969, 5–11.

Riencourt, Amaury de, *The Coming Caesars. Key Reporter* 23 (1957): 5.

Roseboom, Eugene H., *A History of Presidential Elections. Key Reporter* 23 (1957): 5.

Rowan, Carl T., *Go South to Sorrow. Commentary* 24 (1957): 271–72.

Royster, Charles, ed., *William Tecumseh Sherman: Memoirs. New York Review of Books,* 8 Nov. 1990, 29–32.

Ruchames, Louis, *Race, Jobs, and Politics: The Story of FEPC. Yale Review* 43 (1954): 604–7.

Safire, William, *Freedom. New York Review of Books,* 24 Sept. 1987, 23–26.

Samuels, Ernest, *Henry Adams, The Middle Years. Key Reporter* 23 (1957): 5.

Saveth, Edward N., ed., *American History and the Social Sciences. New York Times Book Review,* 24 Jan. 1965, 1, 44–45.

Schlesinger, Arthur Meier, Jr., *The Age of Roosevelt: The Crisis of the Old Order. Saturday Review,* 2 Mar. 1957, 11–12.

———, *The Disuniting of America: Reflections on a Multicultural Society. New Republic,* 15 July 1991, 41–43.

Sellers, Charles Grier, Jr., *James K. Polk: Jacksonian, 1795–1843. Key Reporter* 22 (1957): 5.

———, ed., *The Southerner as American. Journal of Southern History* 27 (1961): 92–94.

Silver, James W., *Mississippi: The Closed Society. New York Review of Books,* 20 Aug. 1964, 13–14.

Simkins, Francis Butler, *Pitchfork Ben Tillman: South Carolinian. North Carolina Historical Review* 23 (1945): 378–79.

Simpson, Lewis P., *Mind and the American Civil War: A Meditation on Lost Causes. New York Review of Books,* 15 Mar. 1990, 39–41.

Singletary, Otis A., *Negro Militia and Reconstruction. Key Reporter* 23 (1957): 5.

Smith, Page, *The Historian and History. New York Times Book Review,* 26 July 1964, 5.

Stampp, Kenneth Milton, *The Peculiar Institution: Slavery in the Ante-bellum South. New York Herald Tribune Book Review,* 21 Oct. 1956, 6.

Sternsher, Bernard, *Consensus, Conflict, and American Historians. American Historical Review* 81 (1976): 438–39.

Strout, Cushing, *The Pragmatic Revolt in American History. Key Reporter* 24 (1959): 6.

Styron, William, *The Confessions of Nat Turner. New Republic,* 7 Oct. 1967, 25–28.

Taft, Philip, *The A.F. of L. in the Time of Gompers. Key Reporter* 23 (1957): 5.

Takaki, Ronald, *Iron Cages: Race and Culture in Nineteenth-Century America. New York Review of Books,* 22 Nov. 1979, 14–16.

Taylor, Joe Gray, *Louisiana Reconstructed, 1863–1877. Louisiana History* 17 (1976): 97–98.

Taylor, William R., *Cavalier and Yankee: The Old South and American National Character. New York Times Book Review,* 24 Dec. 1961, 6.

Thomas, Emory M., *The Confederate Nation, 1861–1865. New Republic,* 17 Mar. 1979, 25–28.

Thomas, John, *The Liberator, William Lloyd Garrison: A Biography. New York Times Book Review*, 30 June 1963, 6.

Thorp, Willard, *A Southern Reader. American Quarterly* 8 (1956): 284–85.

Trelease, Allen W., *White Terror: The Ku Klux Klan Conspiracy and Southern Reconstruction. New York Times Book Review*, 23 May 1971, 5, 28.

Trowbridge, John T., *The Desolate South, 1865–1866. New York Herald Tribune Book Review*, 30 June 1963, 6.

Tugwell, Rexford Guy, *The Democratic Roosevelt. Key Reporter* 23 (1958): 4.

Turner, Arlin, *George W. Cable: A Biography. Journal of Southern History* 23 (1957): 133–34.

———, ed., *The Negro Question: A Selection of Writings on Civil Rights in the South*, by George Washington Cable. *New York Times Book Review*, 27 July 1958, 6.

Van Deusen, Glyndon G., *The Jacksonian Era, 1828–1848. New York Herald Tribune Book Review*, 22 Mar. 1959, 4.

Vandiver, Frank E., *Mighty Stonewall. Key Reporter* 23 (1958): 4.

Voegeli, V. Jacque, *Free but Not Equal: The Midwest and the Negro during the Civil War. New York Review of Books*, 27 Feb. 1969, 5–11.

Wall, Joseph Frazier, *Henry Watterson: Reconstructed Rebel. Mississippi Valley Historical Review* 43 (1956): 137–38.

Walters, Raymond, Jr., *Albert Gallatin: Jeffersonian Financier and Diplomat. Key Reporter* 23 (1957): 5.

Warren, Robert Penn, *Who Speaks for the Negro? New Republic*, 22 May 1965, 21–23.

White, Leonard D., *The Republican Era, 1869–1901: A Study in Administrative History. New York Times Book Review*, 30 Mar. 1958, 3, 26.

Wilkins, Thurman, *Clarence King: A Biography. Key Reporter* 24 (1958): 7.

Wilkins, J. Harvie, III, *From "Brown" to "Bakke": The Supreme Court and School Integration, 1954–1978. New Republic*, 23 June 1979, 27–29.

Williamson, Joel Randolph, *The Crucible of Race: Black/White Relations in the American South since Emancipation. New Republic*, 15 Oct. 1985, 29–32.

———, *William Faulkner and Southern History. New Republic*, 23 Aug. 1993, 41–45.

Wills, Garry, *Under God: Religion and American Politics. New York Review of Books*, 14 Feb. 1991, 11–13.

Wilson, Charles Reagan, and William Ferris, eds., *Encyclopedia of Southern Culture. New York Review of Books*, 26 Oct. 1989, 13.

Wilson, Edmund, *Patriotic Gore: Studies in the Literature of the American Civil War. American Scholar* 31 (1962): 638–42.

Wood, Forrest G., *Black Scare: The Racist Response to Emancipation and Reconstruction. New York Review of Books*, 27 Feb. 1969, 5–11.

Wyatt-Brown, Bertram, *The House of Percy: Honor, Melancholy, and Imagination in a Southern Family.* And idem, *The Literary Percys: Family History, Gender, and the Southern Imagination. New York Review of Books*, 22 June 1995, 32–36.

Index

✳